Women We Love

T0244346

Women We Love

Femininities and the Korean Wave

Edited by SooJin Lee, Kate Korroch, and Liew Kai Khiun

Hong Kong University Press
The University of Hong Kong
Pok Fu Lam Road
Hong Kong
https://hkupress.hku.hk

© 2023 Hong Kong University Press

ISBN 978-988-8754-20-5 (*Paperback*)

British Library Cataloguing-in-Publication Data
A catalogue record for this book is available from the British Library.

Digitally printed

Contents

Part III: Fans and Fan-Producers

Figures

Tables

Acknowledgments

The beginning of this book project goes back to 2012 in Chicago, when SooJin Lee and Maud Lavin began talking and writing about the complexities of femininities in contemporary South Korean popular culture. After a long hiatus, it was again Maud Lavin who encouraged SooJin Lee to develop an anthology on the theme. With the joining of Kate Korroch and Liew Kai Khiun as coeditors, this idea quickly evolved into a reality. We, the editors, express sincere and deep thanks to Maud for her continuous support and inspiration as a scholar and person.

Over the last ten years, not only the international status of Korean popular culture but also the ways in which it is produced and consumed have changed a lot. People have seen BTS, *Parasite*, and *Squid Game* literally become global phenomena and set new milestones in the history of global culture. However, femininities remain an underexplored and marginalized issue in discussions of contemporary Korean popular culture. We would like to thank the staff of Hong Kong University Press for supporting this project on such a rare but important topic. Our gratitude also goes to the labor of love, intellectual rigor, and playful prose that the contributors bring to this project.

We gratefully acknowledge the permission to republish the following articles in this volume. Maud Lavin's chapter was previously published in *Situations: Cultural Studies in the Asian Context* 8, no. 1 (2015): 45–69; Jieun Lee and Hyangsoon Yi's chapter in *Korea Journal* 60, no. 1 (Spring 2020): 17–39; and Gi Yeon Koo's chapter in *Journal of Middle East Women's Studies* 16, no. 2 (July 2020): 144–64.

Our greatest thanks are extended to our mothers who have rooted in us the courage and wisdom to care and love.

Note on Romanization

This book uses the Revised Romanization of Korean—the official romanization system in South Korea—except when commonly accepted or preferred romanizations of proper names or terms are used.

This book spells Korean names in the East Asian style, which is to put the family name before the given name, except when commonly accepted or preferred styles are used.

Introduction

Femininities and the Korean Wave

Kate Korroch, SooJin Lee, and Liew Kai Khiun

Women We Love is a playful and nuanced text that takes the offerings of Korean Wave stars, idols, and fans seriously, and grapples with what they bring to conversations about gender and sexuality. There are 89 million Korean Wave fans in 113 countries; 66 percent of these fans are under thirty years old, and roughly 90 percent are female.[1] Despite that, several of the stars and idols that receive scholarly consideration are male. *Women We Love* looks closely at the relationships that form on-screen and are projected to millions of people all around the world. Further, this collection parses how those projections take on new life as they enter the milieu of the fan. The chapters look at how the fans take up their idols' emanations to create their own versions of nonconformist femininity and sexuality.

Beginning in the 1990s, Hallyu (한류), the "Korean Wave," began permeating cultural borders regionally in Asia and across the globe. Driven by Korean popular music (K-pop) and dramas (K-drama), the faces and methods of Hallyu have not only shaped the world's perception of South Korea (Korea hereafter) but also influenced popular culture on an international scale. Hallyu's vast influence demonstrates the global interconnectedness of a local Korean cultural output. Impacting various genres and riding the "wave" of the internet, Hallyu is available in multiple media, on various platforms, and across cultural formats.

---

1. Kwak Yeon-soo, "89,000,000 'Hallyu' Fans Worldwide," *Korea Times*, January 11, 2019, http://www.koreatimes.co.kr/www/art/2021/04/732_261877.html; Kim Yunmi, "K-Pop Drives Hallyu Craze: Survey," *Korea Herald*, June 13, 2011, http://www.koreaherald.com/view.php?ud=20110613000731. Caitlin Kelley, "BTS Lead the Growth of Hallyu to Nearly 90 Million Fans Worldwide In 2018," *Forbes*, January 11, 2019, https://www.forbes.com/sites/caitlinkelley/2019/01/11/bts-lead-growth-of-hallyu-90-million-fans-2018/.

By the early 2000s, Hallyu's stars had become household names: the star of beloved K-drama *Winter Sonata* (2002), Bae Yong-joon stole hearts, and PSY's record-breaking music video "Gangnam Style" (2012) could be heard almost anywhere. Recently, BTS was featured in a star-studded Grammy performance (2020), and Bong Joon-ho's *Parasite* won Best Picture at the 92nd Academy Awards (2020). Each popular male-centered example and the fandom surrounding them contributes to a formalized male-oriented aesthetic of the Korean Wave. Such maleness becomes in turn synonymous with Ju Oak Kim's framing of the globalization of K-pop as "BTS as method," with its counter-hegemonic cultural formations and networks engendered from the peripheries in decentering Hollywood's dominance in popular culture.[2] Citing Kuan-hsing Chen's influential book, *Asia As Method* (2010), BTS as method follows and realizes the scholarly emphasis from inter-Asia cultural studies academic networks on positioning "Asia as method" in cultivating more unique regional subjectivities, methods, and references.[3]

This collection pushes aside the male centeredness of the Korean Wave and focuses on the femininities that are birthed from popular Korean cultural production.[4] In turn, such femininities should be critically integral to methodologies in understanding the Korean Wave. Hallyu may be closely identified critically with women consumer cultures. But the lived experiences, spaces, and practices of such cultures should transcend the static treatment of women in the binaries of passive consumers manipulated by neoliberal capitalism. Here, through feminist and queer critical regionalities, Audrey Yue has provided a discursive addendum to "Asia as method" within the inter-Asia subjectivity with new practices of solidarity and intimacy.[5] Access to media networks by the constantly burgeoning middle class has created new mobilities from otherwise highly embedded and immobile structures. Beyond the celebratory accounts of making inroads into the Western market, Hallyu's narratives should also be understood in terms of the more diffused, cosmopolitan, transcultural femininities that this project seeks to position.[6]

2. See Kim Ju Oak, "BTS as Method: A Counter-Hegemonic Culture in the Network Society," *Media, Culture & Society* 43, no. 6 (September 2021): 1061–77, https://doi.org/10.1177/0163443720986029.
3. Kim, "BTS as Method," 1064.
4. For more on hegemonic masculinity in South Korea, see Moon Seungsook, "The Production and Subversion of Hegemonic Masculinity: Reconfiguring Gender Hierarchy in Contemporary South Korea," in *Under Construction: The Gendering of Modernity, Class, and Consumption in the Republic of Korea*, ed. Laurel Kendall (Honolulu: University of Hawai'i Press, 2002), 79–114; Moon Seungsook, *Militarized Modernity and Gendered Citizenship in South Korea*, ed. George Steinmetz and Julia Adams (Durham, NC: Duke University Press, 2005).
5. Audrey Yue, "Critical Regionalities in Inter-Asia and the Queer Diaspora," *Feminist Media Studies* 11, no. 1 (March 2011): 131–38, https://doi.org/10.1080/14680777.2011.537042.
6. See Sun Jung, "K-Pop beyond Asia: Performing Trans-Nationality, Trans-Sexuality, and Trans-Textuality," in *Asian Popular Culture in Transition*, ed. John Lent and Lorna Fitzsimmons (London:

In this project, "women" is an inclusive term extending to all those who self-define as women. Harnessing the genderqueer potentialities, we use the plural of *femininity* to communicate dynamic intersectionality; femininities allow us to deconstruct representations that have been used as a foil to masculinity and have become spaces for gender experimentation. In line with Amelia Jones and Erin Silver's framing of queer feminist art history, rather than a singular definition, *Women We Love* presents a constellation of possibilities of what plural femininities can be.[7] Makiko Iseri posits femininities as flexible in her analysis of popular Japanese star Kyary Pamyu Pamyu.[8] Iseri argues that Kyary's costumes and performances exaggerate femininity into a grotesque domain that pushes that which is sanctioned to be feminine out of the realm of heteronormative desire. Namely, these constellations and flexibilities intersect via their relationship to hegemonic gender construction in Korea, in Asia, and around the world. The chapters in this volume present fresh understandings of femininity and seek new frameworks for existing femininities circulating among Korean Wave stars and their fans.

The Absence of Analysis of Femininities and the Korean Wave

Women We Love sits at the scholarly intersection of texts about the Korean Wave, gender studies, media studies, and fandom studies. Although femininities in the Korean Wave have not been addressed thoroughly in current scholarship, we draw inspiration from texts that have approached gender and sexuality within popular media and fan studies. Kim Gooyong's astute analysis in *From Factory Girls to K-Pop Idol Girls: Cultural Politics of Developmentalism, Patriarchy, and Neoliberalism in South Korea's Popular Music Industry* (2019) addresses Korean cultural and socioeconomic contexts of the Korean Wave alongside a discussion of binary female gender within the music industry.[9] *Women We Love* broadens this scope of analysis to the global market of the Korean Wave, extends the potential of femininity beyond binary gender, and addresses the multimedia scope of the phenomenon. Broadening the reach of analysis to music, dramas, and their global reception, Sun Jung's book *Korean Masculinities and Transcultural Consumption: Yonsama, Rain, Oldboy, K-Pop Idols* (2011) examines distinctive

---

Routledge, 2013), 108–31; Vincenzo Cicchelli and Sylvie Octobre, *The Sociology of Hallyu Pop Culture: Surfing the Korean Wave* (Cham, Switzerland: Palgrave Macmillan, 2021), 309–18.

7.   Amelia Jones and Erin Silver, eds., *Otherwise: Imagining Queer Feminist Art Histories*, Rethinking Art's Histories (Manchester, UK: Manchester University Press, 2015).

8.   Makiko Iseri, "Flexible Femininities? Queering *Kawaii* in Japanese Girls' Culture," in *Twenty-First Century Feminism: Forming and Performing Femininity*, ed. Claire Nally and Angela Smith (London: Palgrave Macmillan, 2015).

9.   Kim Gooyong, *From Factory Girls to K-Pop Idol Girls: Cultural Politics of Developmentalism, Patriarchy, and Neoliberalism in South Korea's Popular Music Industry* (Lanham, MD: Lexington Books, 2019).

masculinities arising from South Korea and the various audiences and contexts of the reception of the examined stars.[10] A decade later, *Women We Love* looks at the multifariousness of gender but shifts the lens to femininity. And, like Jung's text, this collection examines audiences worldwide, extending interest into the variations of the Korean Wave that are created outside of South Korea.

Complexities of gender and sexuality are considered within a Chinese popular culture context in Maud Lavin, Ling Yang, and Jing Jamie Zhao's edited volume *Boys' Love, Cosplay, and Androgynous Idols: Queer Fan Cultures in Mainland China, Hong Kong, and Taiwan* (2017).[11] *Women We Love* seeks to embrace a similar examination of queer and androgynous gender and sexuality but takes up different popular subject matter. The result of this shift unfolds through the uniqueness of the Korean Wave's distinct visual output, as well as the global popularity and sensationalism that the stars inspire. Lastly, we are motivated by Catherine Grant and Kate Random Love's approach to fan cultures as methodologies that inspire oppositional practice in their edited text *Fandom as Methodology: A Sourcebook for Artists and Writers* (2019).[12] *Women We Love* takes Grant and Love's sentiment and applies it directly to the Korean Wave, embracing the stars and the fans and demonstrating their powerful symbiotic relationship.

Critics and academics have taken up the Korean Wave phenomenon, responding with rigorous and thoughtful analysis. Since the early 2000s, a plethora of texts on Korean popular culture has been published in English. Within these conversations, however, there is a dearth of analysis on the female-identifying stars and characters who shape and lead this crucial cultural movement. This elision is glaring. Although several texts on the Korean Wave exist, very few focus on gender and none attend to the key female actors, story lines, performers, and consumers that shape this beloved global phenomenon.

In Korean Wave and Korean popular culture literature, several anthologies and source books exist. Chua Beng Huat and Koichi Iwabuchi edited *East Asian Pop Culture: Analysing the Korean Wave* (2008) just as academia was taking notice of the rich scholarly potential of the Korean Wave.[13] This text was followed by Kim Youna's edited volume *The Korean Wave: Korean Media Go Global* (2013) and by Kim Kyung Hyun and Choe Youngmin's *The Korean Popular Culture*

---

10. Sun Jung, *Korean Masculinities and Transcultural Consumption: Yonsama, Rain, Oldboy, K-Pop Idols* (Hong Kong: Hong Kong University Press, 2011).
11. Maud Lavin, Ling Ying, Jing Jamie Zhao, *Boys' Love, Cosplay, and Androgynous Idols: Queer Fan Cultures in Mainland China, Hong Kong, and Taiwan* (Hong Kong: Hong Kong University Press, 2017).
12. Catherine Grant and Kate Random Love, eds., *Fandom as Methodology: A Sourcebook for Artists and Writers* (London: Goldsmiths Press, 2019).
13. Chua Beng Huat and Koichi Iwabuchi, eds., *East Asian Pop Culture: Analysing the Korean Wave* (Hong Kong: Hong Kong University Press, 2008).

Reader (2014).[14] In 2015, Stephen Epstein and Hwang Yun Mi edited a text of primary sources about the Korean Wave, translated into English as *The Korean Wave: A Sourcebook* (2015).[15] Choe Youngmin and Kim Kyung Hyun focus on Korean cinema's transnational reach in their respective texts, and Lee Hark Joon, Jin Dal Yong and Michael Fuhr look at the music industry and popular music.[16]

Gender and sexuality in South Korea have received scholarly attention far beyond the era of the Korean Wave. Jung's focus on masculinity mentioned above is unique, but there are several texts thinking about femininity's relationships to masculinity and nationalism, including edited volumes such as Elaine H. Kim and Choi Chungmoo's book *Dangerous Women: Gender and Korean Nationalism* (1997) and Laurel Kendall's *Under Construction: The Gendering of Modernity, Class, and Consumption in the Republic of Korea* (2002).[17] In the same year, Laura Nelson published *Measured Excess: Status, Gender, and Consumer Nationalism in South Korea* (2000).[18] Although these texts look at femininity within the bounds of Korean gender hierarchy, they set the precedent of showing how femininity can be used to pick apart misogynistic systems. Expanding gender analysis, Todd A. Henry recently edited the text *Queer Korea* (2020), which brings together several essays spanning a broad time frame of South Korean history and queerness.[19]

Attention has been paid to the pluralities of gender and sexuality in Asia, expanding into queer theory. Specific to women, Youna Kim edited an anthology on women in Asia, acknowledging the precarity of the female position.[20] Looking at the propagative and transitive powers of new media and queerness, Chris Berry, Fran Martin, and Audrey Yue edited *Mobile Cultures: New Media in Queer Asia* (2003) as part of the Console-Ing Passions: Television and Cultural

14. Youna Kim, ed., *The Korean Wave: Korean Media Go Global* (London: Routledge, 2013); Kim Kyung Hyun and Choe Youngmin, *The Korean Popular Culture Reader* (Durham, NC: Duke University Press, 2014), https://doi.org/10.2307/j.ctv11smhw7.
15. Stephen Epstein and Hwang Yun Mi, eds., *The Korean Wave: A Sourcebook* (Seongnam-si, Gyeonggi-do: The Academy of Korean Studies Press, 2015).
16. Choe Youngmin, *Tourist Distractions: Traveling and Feeling in Transnational Hallyu Cinema* (Durham, NC: Duke University Press, 2016); Kim Kyung Hyun, *Virtual Hallyu: Korean Cinema of the Global Era* (Durham, NC: Duke University Press, 2011); Lee Hark Joon and Jin Dal Yong, *K-Pop Idols: Popular Culture and the Emergence of the Korean Music Industry* (Lanham, MD: Lexington Books, 2019); Michael Fuhr, *Globalization and Popular Music in South Korea: Sounding Out K-Pop* (New York: Routledge, 2015).
17. Elaine H. Kim and Choi Chungmoo, eds., *Dangerous Women: Gender and Korean Nationalism* (New York: Routledge, 1998); Laurel Kendall, ed., *Under Construction: The Gendering of Modernity, Class, and Consumption in the Republic of Korea* (Honolulu: University of Hawai'i Press, 2001).
18. Laura C. Nelson, *Measured Excess: Status, Gender, and Consumer Nationalism in South Korea* (New York: Columbia University Press, 2000).
19. Todd A. Henry, ed., *Queer Korea*, Perverse Modernities (Durham, NC: Duke University Press, 2020).
20. Youna Kim, ed., *Women and the Media in Asia: The Precarious Self* (Basingstoke: Palgrave Macmillan, 2012).

Power series.[21] Based on a generative conference, Fran Martin, Peter A. Jackson, Mark McLelland, and Audrey Yue edited *AsiaPacifiQueer: Rethinking Genders and Sexualities* (2008), which was followed five years later by another rich volume edited by Mark McLelland and Vera Mackie, *Routledge Handbook of Sexuality Studies in East Asia* (2014).[22] Also inspired by a conference, J. Daniel Luther and Jennifer Ung Loh edited *Queer Asia: Decolonising and Reimagining Sexuality and Gender* (2019) to challenge the boundaries of academic conversation through queer theory, subject matter, and conversation.[23]

Though largely focused on North America and Europe, there are several texts that address popular culture and feminism. These texts acknowledge the importance of popular culture as zeitgeist-forming and therefore a critical and necessary place for analyzing femininities. Anthologies such as Joanne Hollows and Rachel Moseley's *Feminism in Popular Culture* (2005) and Adrienne Trier-Bieniek's *Feminist Theory and Pop Culture* (2019) analyze different moments of feminism and how they apply to popular culture.[24] Andi Zeisler examines the relationship between feminism and popular culture by drawing a historical trajectory in *Feminism and Pop Culture* (2008), and Maria Elena Buszek does this through a rich analysis of pinup girls in *Pin-Up Grrrls: Feminism, Sexuality, Popular Culture* (2006).[25] Focusing on specific kinds of feminism, Rebecca Munford, Melanie Water, Diane Negra, and Yvonne Tasker apply postfeminist politics to popular culture in their respective texts.[26] Most recently—an apt conclusion to this review—Katarzyna Paszkiewicz and Stacy Rusnak edited *Final Girls, Feminism and Popular Culture* (2020), a collection of essays about the "final girl" trope in horror movies.[27]

21. Chris Berry, Fran Martin, and Audrey Yue, eds., *Mobile Cultures: New Media in Queer Asia*, Console-Ing Passions: Television and Cultural Power (Durham, NC: Duke University Press, 2003).
22. Fran Martin, Peter Jackson, Mark McLelland, and Audrey Yue, *AsiaPacifiQueer: Rethinking Genders and Sexualities* (Urbana and Chicago: University of Illinois Press, 2008); Mark McLelland and Vera Mackie, eds., *Routledge Handbook of Sexuality Studies in East Asia* (London: Routledge, 2015).
23. J. Daniel Luther and Jennifer Ung Loh, *Queer Asia: Decolonising and Reimagining Sexuality and Gender* (London: Zed, 2019).
24. Joanne Hollows and Rachel Moseley, eds., *Feminism in Popular Culture* (Oxford, New York: Berg, 2006); Adrienne M. Trier-Bieniek, ed., *Feminist Theory and Pop Culture*, 2nd ed., Teaching Gender 13 (Boston: Brill, 2015).
25. Andi Zeisler, *Feminism and Pop Culture*, Seal Studies (Berkeley, CA: Seal Press, 2008; distributed by Publishers Group West); Maria Elena Buszek, *Pin-Up Grrrls: Feminism, Sexuality, Popular Culture* (Durham, NC: Duke University Press, 2006).
26. Rebecca Munford and Melanie Waters, *Feminism and Popular Culture: Investigating the Postfeminist Mystique* (New Brunswick, NJ: Rutgers University Press, 2014); Yvonne Tasker and Diane Negra, eds., *Interrogating Postfeminism: Gender and the Politics of Popular Culture* (Durham, NC: Duke University Press, 2007).
27. Katarzyna Paszkiewicz and Stacy Rusnak, eds. *Final Girls, Feminism and Popular Culture* (Cham: Palgrave Macmillan, 2020).

Women We Love sits at a unique juncture that occupies the literatures addressed above—it is the multimedia of South Korean popular culture, it is a conversation about gender locally and globally, it is queer, and it is feminist. This collection allows for the ideas explored above to be repositioned to think deeply about the roles of femininity in the Korean Wave and how they function in South Korea, Asia, and globally.

The Chapters

Women We Love brings together a cohort of international thinkers to grapple with representations, impacts, and outcomes of femininities within the Korean Wave. The chapters analyze femininities active in and around the Korean entertainment industry since 2000. The cohort of contributors includes professors, independent scholars, and advanced graduate students from around the world. We are K-pop and K-drama fans, we are queer, we are international, we are academics of Asian histories, sociology, gender and sexuality, art history, and visual culture. The chapters are playful, intersectional, and accessible.

Women We Love is organized into three sections, each devoted to a theme that arose as the contributions took shape. The focus of analysis of the Korean Wave looks closely at moments on the screen or onstage and expands to a macroanalysis via global impacts outside of South Korea. Similarly, femininity is treated as a radical method as well as a passive identifier, crucially showing the multifarious possibilities of the term.

Part I: Characters We Love, looks closely at the female-identifying lead characters we see on-screen. Kate Korroch questions the binary complement of "soft masculinity" through an analysis of the "hard" female leads in relation to their female counterparts in the television dramas *First Shop of Coffee Prince* (2007) and *Secret Garden* (2010). The chapter allows for a recentering of how perceptions of femininity are constructed, shifting away from female-male relationships. Maud Lavin's chapter follows the evolution of the lead in *First Shop of Coffee Prince* as she navigates a romantic relationship that sits at the intersection of heterosexuality and queerness. Lavin unpacks the tomboy trope through analysis of the drama, fans, and autoethnography. Together, Korroch and Lavin's chapters show the significance of the K-drama *First Shop of Coffee Prince*; even over fifteen years after its debut, it remains unique due to its bold treatment of gender and sexuality. SooJin Lee examines the significance of the popular drama *God of the Workplace* (2013) in terms of representation of women in the postindustrial workforce. Through textual and aesthetic analyses of the drama, which she links with statistics and theories of labor and feminism, Lee deconstructs the main character Miss Kim as a persona of ambiguities and ironies that expose the interrelated problems of gender and class in the Korean workforce structure and culture after the financial crisis of 2008.

Part II: More than Girl Groups, offers a plethora of deep dives into K-pop female-only groups. Girl groups are known for their exquisite performances and celebrity prowess, but their impact extends far beyond the stage or screen. Jin Lee and Crystal Abidin's chapter brings together YG Entertainment's group BLACKPINK and social media celebrity Ella Gross, a Korean-American child star who gained fame through her affiliation with BLACKPINK's members. Lee and Abidin's deep analysis of digital participant observation and the content of Gross' Instagram feed investigates the routes and implications of such cross-promotional celebrity. Douglas Gabriel continues the consideration of girl groups through his historical and aesthetic analysis of North Korean girl group Moranbong Band. Gabriel argues that despite being widely ridiculed as an antiquated other to global capitalist entertainment industries, Moranbong Band speaks to a totalitarian element that surreptitiously permeates mass spectacles of all ideological stripes, not only those of the so-called Hermit Kingdom. Jieun Lee and Hyangsoon Yi's chapter stems from a concern about the potential association of masculinity with power, based on the incorporation of masculine tropes in the name of female power. Looking to *ssen-eonni* (*ssen-unni*), or "strong sisters," Lee and Yi examine the empowerment of a new generation and its potential for changing the landscape of what it means to be female in South Korea.

Part III: Fans and Fan-Producers, makes space for an investigation of how fans are the catalyst for Korean Wave transculturation, both in regard to the cultural infiltration and to generations of Korean Wave fan cultures. Stephanie Choi's chapter shows how female-driven fan fiction results in homoerotic performance. Choi teases out the cultural complexities and discrepancies for both the fans and their idols as their mutual engagement influences both written fiction and onstage performances. Reminding readers about the Korean Wave narratives in the non-Western world that make up the understories of Hallyu, Liew Kai Khiun, Malinee Khumsupa, and Atchareeya Saisin discuss new K-pop "frontliners" in Southeast Asia. The authors illustrate increasingly cosmopolitan and women-centric subjects, turning their affections for K-pop into careers and activism, reflecting new forms of feminist mobilities within a more visible trans-pop public that K-pop fans in Southeast Asia have engendered. Moving from the impact in Southeast Asia, Gi Yeon Koo homes in on the Korean Wave fandom through cyberfeminism among women in the Islamic Republic of Iran. Through data collected in Tehran, Koo shows how young Iranian women lead the Korean Wave fandom in Iran and consequently form a community with women around the world. The concluding chapter to this anthology, written by Erik Paolo Capistrano and Kathlyn Ramirez, is aptly titled "Into the New World." Capistrano and Ramirez unpack the rich historical legacy of Girls' Generation (also known as So Nyeo Si Dae and abbreviated as SNSD). As fans and scholars, the authors offer a close look at the history of the decades-old girl group, the members, and their implicit leadership within the Korean Wave. As Girls' Generation arouses a new world for their fans, we hope this text acts as a springboard for allowing the multifariousness of femininity to expand, unfold, and inspire.

Bibliography

Berry, Chris, Fran Martin, and Audrey Yue, eds. *Mobile Cultures: New Media in Queer Asia*. Durham, NC: Duke University Press, 2003.

Buszek, Maria Elena. *Pin-Up Grrrls: Feminism, Sexuality, Popular Culture*. Durham, NC: Duke University Press, 2006.

Chen, Kuan-Hsing. *Asia as Method: Toward Deimperialization*. Durham, NC: Duke University Press, 2010.

Choe, Youngmin. *Tourist Distractions: Traveling and Feeling in Transnational Hallyu Cinema*. Durham, NC: Duke University Press, 2016.

Chua, Beng Huat, and Koichi Iwabuchi, eds. *East Asian Pop Culture: Analysing the Korean Wave*. Hong Kong: Hong Kong University Press, 2008.

Cicchelli, Vincenzo, and Sylvie Octobre. *The Sociology of Hallyu Pop Culture: Surfing the Korean Wave*. Cham, Switzerland: Palgrave Macmillan, 2021.

Epstein, Stephen, and Yun Mi Hwang, eds. *The Korean Wave: A Sourcebook*. Seongnam-si, Gyeonggi-do: The Academy of Korean Studies Press, 2015.

Fuhr, Michael. *Globalization and Popular Music in South Korea: Sounding Out K-Pop*. New York: Routledge, 2015.

Grant, Catherine, and Kate Random Love, eds. *Fandom as Methodology: A Sourcebook for Artists and Writers*. London: Goldsmiths Press, 2019.

Henry, Todd A., ed. *Queer Korea*. Perverse Modernities. Durham, NC: Duke University Press, 2020.

Hollows, Joanne, and Rachel Moseley, eds. *Feminism in Popular Culture*. Oxford: Berg, 2006.

Iseri, Makiko. "Flexible Femininities? Queering *Kawaii* in Japanese Girls Culture." In *Twenty-First Century Feminism: Forming and Performing Femininity*, edited by Claire Nally and Angela Smith, 140–63. London: Palgrave Macmillan, 2015.

Jones, Amelia, and Erin Silver, eds. *Otherwise: Imagining Queer Feminist Art Histories*. Manchester, UK: Manchester University Press, 2015.

Jung, Sun. *Korean Masculinities and Transcultural Consumption: Yonsama, Rain, Oldboy, K-Pop Idols*. Hong Kong: Hong Kong University Press, 2011.

Jung, Sun. "K-Pop beyond Asia: Performing Trans-Nationality, Trans-Sexuality, and Trans-Textuality." In *Asian Popular Culture in Transition*, edited by John Lent and Lorna Fitzsimmons, 108–31. London: Routledge, 2013.

Kelley, Caitlin. "BTS Lead the Growth of Hallyu to Nearly 90 Million Fans Worldwide In 2018." *Forbes*, January 11, 2019. https://www.forbes.com/sites/caitlinkelley/2019/01/11/bts-lead-growth-of-hallyu-90-million-fans-2018/.

Kendall, Laurel, ed. *Under Construction: The Gendering of Modernity, Class, and Consumption in the Republic of Korea*. Honolulu: University of Hawai'i Press, 2001.

Kim, Elaine H., and Chungmoo Choi, eds. *Dangerous Women: Gender and Korean Nationalism*. New York: Routledge, 1998.

Kim, Gooyong. *From Factory Girls to K-Pop Idol Girls: Cultural Politics of Developmentalism, Patriarchy, and Neoliberalism in South Korea's Popular Music Industry*. Lanham, MD: Lexington Books, 2019.

Kim, Ju Oak. "BTS as Method: A Counter-Hegemonic Culture in the Network Society." *Media, Culture and Society* 43, no. 6 (September 2021): 1061–77. https://doi.org/10.1177/0163443720986029.

Kim, Kyung Hyun. *Virtual Hallyu: Korean Cinema of the Global Era*. Durham, NC: Duke University Press, 2011.

Kim, Kyung Hyun, and Youngmin Choe. *The Korean Popular Culture Reader*. Durham, NC: Duke University Press, 2014. https://doi.org/10.2307/j.ctv11smhw7.

Kim, Youna, ed. *The Korean Wave: Korean Media Go Global*. London: Routledge, 2013.

Kim, Youna. *Women and the Media in Asia: The Precarious Self*. Basingstoke: Palgrave Macmillan, 2012.

Kim, Yunmi. "K-Pop Drives Hallyu Craze: Survey." *Korea Herald*, June 13, 2011. http://www.koreaherald.com/view.php?ud=20110613000731.

Kwak, Yeon-soo. "89,000,000 'Hallyu' Fans Worldwide." *Korea Times*, January 11, 2019. http://www.koreatimes.co.kr/www/art/2021/04/732_261877.html.

Lavin, Maud, Ling Yang, and Jing Jamie Zhao. *Boys' Love, Cosplay, and Androgynous Idols: Queer Fan Cultures in Mainland China, Hong Kong, and Taiwan*. Hong Kong: Hong Kong University Press, 2017.

Lee, Hark Joon, and Jin Dal Yong. *K-Pop Idols: Popular Culture and the Emergence of the Korean Music Industry*. Lanham, MD: Lexington Books, 2019.

Luther, J. Daniel, and Jennifer Ung Loh. *Queer Asia: Decolonising and Reimagining Sexuality and Gender*. London: Zed, 2019.

Martin, Fran, Peter A. Jackson, Mark McLelland, and Audrey Yue. *AsiaPacifiQueer: Rethinking Genders and Sexualities*. Urbana: University of Illinois Press, 2008.

McLelland, Mark, and Vera Mackie, eds. *Routledge Handbook of Sexuality Studies in East Asia*. London: Routledge, 2015.

Moon, Seungsook. *Militarized Modernity and Gendered Citizenship in South Korea*. Durham, NC: Duke University Press, 2005.

Moon, Seungsook. "The Production and Subversion of Hegemonic Masculinity: Reconfiguring Gender Hierarchy in Contemporary South Korea." In *Under Construction: The Gendering of Modernity, Class, and Consumption in the Republic of Korea*, edited by Laurel Kendall, 79–114. Honolulu: University of Hawai'i Press, 2002.

Munford, Rebecca, and Melanie Waters. *Feminism and Popular Culture: Investigating the Postfeminist Mystique*. New Brunswick, NJ: Rutgers University Press, 2014.

Nelson, Laura C. *Measured Excess: Status, Gender, and Consumer Nationalism in South Korea*. New York: Columbia University Press, 2000.

Paszkiewicz, Katarzyna, and Stacy Rusnak, eds. *Final Girls, Feminism and Popular Culture*. Cham: Palgrave Macmillan, 2020.

Tasker, Yvonne, and Diane Negra, eds. *Interrogating Postfeminism: Gender and the Politics of Popular Culture*. Durham, NC: Duke University Press, 2007.

Trier-Bieniek, Adrienne M., ed. *Feminist Theory and Pop Culture*. 2nd ed. Boston: Brill, 2015.

Yue, Audrey. "Critical Regionalities in Inter-Asia and the Queer Diaspora." *Feminist Media Studies* 11, no. 1 (March 2011): 131–8. https://doi.org/10.1080/14680777.20 11.537042.

Zeisler, Andi. *Feminism and Pop Culture*. Berkeley, CA: Seal Press, 2008.

Part I

Characters We Love

1

Is Femininity Hard?

Naming Femininities in the Age of Soft Masculinity

Kate Korroch

Introduction: Diverse Femininities

"Is Femininity Hard?" studies two Korean dramas to unpack the potentiality of hard femininity. This is accomplished through scene analysis, the application of soft masculine characteristics, and an understanding of how those tropes are both embodied and rejected within the dramas. I build a nexus of comparison between female characters in the South Korean television dramas *First Shop of Coffee Prince* (2007) and *Secret Garden* (2010) to explore the ways that diverse femininities are depicted through non-romantic homosocial relationship pairings.[1] Engaging discussions central to gender representations and the Korean Wave, in this chapter the characters portrayed as female are released from gender-binary comparisons with their male-portrayed counterparts.

Within scholarship about Korean dramas and popular culture, *soft masculinity* is often employed as a descriptor to discuss characters in South Korean television dramas, evoking a combination of attributes that speak to a gentle yet attractive physique, nostalgic good manners, and (often) neoliberal affluence.[2] Soft masculinity has received significant attention without considering the complementing characters through which soft masculinity is defined. These traits need to be understood as a masculinity that expands the possibilities of embodying that which is masculine, not a seismic shift in the production of masculinity in South Korea. Rather than feminizing masculinity or disrupting binary understandings of gender, soft masculinity points to a type of gender performance that

---

1. The Republic of Korea (South Korea) will be referred to as Korea here on out in this chapter.
2. Sun Jung, "Bae Yong-Joon, Soft Masculinity, and Japanese Fans: Our Past Is in Your Present Body," in *Korean Masculinities and Transcultural Consumption: Yonsama, Rain, Oldboy, K-Pop Idols* (Hong Kong: Hong Kong University Press, 2011).

fits within putatively stable gender formations.[3] Characterizations of soft masculinity are generally thrown into sharp relief within the narrative through comparisons associated with the male lead's relationship to his female counterparts.[4]

Within binary gender constructions, the *other* to soft masculinity would be hard femininity. This chapter asks if that is indeed the case and shows the complexities of hard femininity through the difficulty, the putative stagnation, and the hybridity of femininity. To emancipate female characters and their femininity from binary gender construction, this comparison requires disorientation. In *Queer Phenomenology: Orientations, Objects, and Others* (2007), Sara Ahmed suggests that one does not notice what they are oriented toward until that orientation is disrupted; we must experience disorientation to be able to see orientation.[5] In that spirit, this chapter disorients the narratives of Korean television dramas to parse characters through relationships that are not prioritized within the diegesis; central narratives are propelled by binary heterosexual(ish) entanglements.[6] This text, on the other hand, reorients juxtapositions of binary gender towards the comparison of female characters.

Using queer and feminist methodologies to analyze *Coffee Prince* and *Secret Garden*, I discuss the attributes of the female characters without focusing on their male counterparts as a complement or foil and instead use comparison of the female characters to build this analysis. This works against the commonly followed convention of defining qualities of masculinity and femininity in opposition to each other, but my hope is that it also dismantles the normative expectation of femininity as defined as the other to masculinity. I argue that complex relationships between female characters are required to create an interesting, appealing, and convincing soft-masculine character. By decentering the male characters and heterosexual relationships in the foreground of the narrative, I refocus attention on the female characters' relationships to unveil the portrayal of multiple femininities. In this way, diverse femininities can be articulated through the interconnections of a web of female relationships instead

---

3. Joanna Elfving-Hwang problematizes this in Elfving-Hwang, "Not So Soft After All: Kkonminam Masculinities in Contemporary South Korean Popular Culture" (paper presented at the 7th KSAA Biennale Conference, November 16–18, 2011).
4. These dramas are a large component of the Korean Wave (Hallyu) phenomenon. For further reading, see Chua Beng Huat and Koichi Iwabuchi, eds., *East Asian Pop Culture: Analysing the Korean Wave* (Hong Kong: Hong Kong University Press, 2008) and Stephen Epstein and Hwang Yun Mi, eds., *The Korean Wave: A Sourcebook* (Seongnam-si, Gyeonggi-do: The Academy of Korean Studies Press, 2015).
5. Sara Ahmed, *Queer Phenomenology: Orientations, Objects, Others* (Durham, NC: Duke University Press, 2006), 5.
6. As will be made clear in Chapter 2 of this book and as offered by Maud Lavin, *Coffee Prince* does not offer a normative heterosexual entanglement throughout the entirety of the drama, but heterosexual binaries (and a desire for participating or not participating in said binaries) are still what drive the narrative.

of using male characters as the other to define femininities. I therefore argue for a discussion of femininities that does not depend on binary sexual difference.[7] After introducing the dramas, I employ a three-pronged analysis in my endeavor to define hard femininity through these characters. First, I discuss how these characters are presented as *hard*, meaning both difficult in terms of their personalities and their subversive disregard of idealized femininity. Second, I ask what social dynamics are addressed and possibly levelled through these characters. And third, I consider if and how these female lead roles embody or disorient soft masculinity.

Soft Masculinity and Hard Femininity

My question of hard femininity is an adaptation of Judith Butler's play on words in *Bodies That Matter* (1993). Butler's book draws attention toward ways in which bodies are marked or hailed as important, but also as that which has physicality. I use *hard femininity* to take up Butler's wordplay and ask questions about how femininity might be understood as unmoving and/or difficult.[8] My approach to hard femininity first asks why femininity is putatively stable and fixed, particularly regarding femininity's function as the *other* to masculinity. Second, it responds to the soft masculinity phenomenon specific to Hallyu. Unpacking the hardness of femininity responds to said fixity and association and builds upon and offers multiple under-considered dimensions within the female characters.

In the introduction of *Under Construction: The Gendering of Modernity, Class, and Consumption in the Republic of Korea* (1993), Laurel Kendall references Seungsook Moon's discussion of hegemonic masculinity in South Korea: "Having defended the nation from the omnipresent threat of attack by the Democratic People's Republic of Korea (north Korea) [sic], men are considered 'true citizens,' a status few Korean women obtain."[9] Kendall articulates that there is a desire for nonfixity, but that flexibility and acknowledgment of citizenship is often relegated to the male sex. The privilege to be flexible (read *soft*) is often extended only to those of the male gender. Contrary to that, I provide examples

7. In the late 1990s and early 2000s, there were a number of texts published about gender in South Korea in English: Elaine H. Kim and Choi Chungmoo, eds., *Dangerous Women: Gender and Korean Nationalism* (New York: Routledge, 1998); Laura C. Nelson, *Measured Excess: Status, Gender, and Consumer Nationalism in South Korea* (New York: Columbia University Press, 2000); Laurel Kendall, ed., *Under Construction: The Gendering of Modernity, Class, and Consumption in the Republic of Korea* (Honolulu: University of Hawai'i Press, 2002); Moon Seungsook, *Militarized Modernity and Gendered Citizenship in South Korea*, ed. Julia Adams and George Steinmetz (Durham, NC: Duke University Press, 2005).
8. Judith Butler, *Bodies That Matter: On the Discursive Limits of "Sex"* (Abingdon, Oxon: Routledge, 2011).
9. Kendall, *Under Construction*, 6.

below of flexibility in socioeconomic status through the interactions of the female characters in *Coffee Prince* and *Secret Garden*. Moreover, Moon's articulation speaks to the focus on the male gender within academic literature and mass media when parsing nondiscursive genders in Korean television dramas.

In her talk "Not So Soft After All," Joanna Elfving-Hwang problematizes the presumption that soft masculinity is a step away from traditional masculinity in South Korea.[10] Elfving-Hwang argues that the *kkonminam* (flower-like beautiful men) actually reassert gender binaries in Korea's homosocial order.[11] She states that unlike in the West, there is rarely doubt of "manhood" in Korea.[12]

In contrast to the cosmetic construction and emphasis on outer appearance and demeanor outlined for *kkonminam*, Sun Jung provides an analysis of tender qualities that characterize soft masculinity. In *Korean Masculinities and Transcultural Consumption: Yonsama, Rain, Oldboy, K-Pop Idols* (2011), Jung specifies various formulations of Korean masculinities that are shaped by nationalism, audience reception, and heteronormativity.

As Jung details the traits of soft masculinity in the drama *Winter Sonata*, it becomes evident that soft masculinity is articulated through the character's relationship with his female counterpart. In a 2018 interview, Jung states, "I think the phenomenon should rather be explained through the notion of hybrid or versatile masculinity—soft yet manly at the same time—which is different from effeminized."[13] In agreement with Elfving-Hwang, Jung suggests that the characteristics of soft masculinity are not new but rather repackaged.

Hard femininity takes from these the reliance on surrounding characters to understand the gender of another character as well as the potential of genderedness to be "hybrid or versatile." Femininity is traditionally not allowed that flexibility.[14]

---

10. Elfving-Hwang, "Not So Soft After All," 14.
11. *Kkonminam* (꽃미남) is a combination of the word for "flower" (꽃) and "beautiful man" (미남) in Hangeul. The word likely came into use in conjunction with the proliferation of pretty boys in girls' comics. See Sun Jung, *Korean Masculinities and Transcultural Consumption: Yonsama, Rain, Oldboy, K-Pop Idols* (Hong Kong: Hong Kong University Press, 2011), 58. The term is arguably part of a transcultural flow of masculinities such as the metrosexual, *bishonen* (beautiful young men) in Japan, and *aimei naren* (love beauty men) in China and Taiwan. See Elfving-Hwang, "Not So Soft After All," 2.
12. Elfving-Hwang, "Not So Soft After All," 15.
13. "'Flowerboys' and the Appeal of 'Soft Masculinity,'" BBC News, September 5, 2018, https://www.bbc.com/news/world-asia-42499809.
14. Using J. Jack Halberstam's notion of the transgender look, I discuss gender affirmation's reliance on surrounding characters in a queer South Korean context in my chapter "The Isolated Queer Body: Harisu's Dodo Cosmetics Advertisement" in *Queer Asia*. Kate Korroch, "The Isolated Queer Body: Harisu's Dodo Cosmetics Advertisement," in *Queer Asia: Decolonising and Reimagining Sexuality and Gender*, ed. J. Daniel Luther and Jennifer Ung Loh (London: Zed Books, 2019), 165–83.

The Dramas and Their Leading Characters

The writers of *Coffee Prince* and *Secret Garden* employ similar and familiar formulas from the romance genre to develop the dramas' characters and narratives.[15] The female lead is an unexpected, headstrong person from a disadvantaged background. She is paired with an excessively privileged, overtly confident, tall, and attractive heir who falls for her. And, maintaining romantic tropes, two supporting leads that initially complicate the relationships between the main leads end up falling in love. Notably, within the context of exploring soft masculinity, both Sun Jung and Joanna Elfving-Hwang characterize the initial portrayal of the female characters in the dramas as "ordinary."[16] I bring these dramas together for two reasons: (1) their relevance within the analysis of soft masculinity provides an entry to analyzing them through the lens of hard femininity, and (2) the superficial and performative expansion of gender that occurs within the dramas is created for consumption through mass media platforms, which indicates the assumption that these expansions of gender performance are widely acceptable to potential audiences. The following pages look closely at specific scenes from *Coffee Prince* and *Secret Garden* to build a nonbinary framework of femininity.

First Shop of Coffee Prince is a seventeen-episode drama based on a book of the same name written by Lee Sun-mi. Initially aired on Munhwa Broadcasting Corporation in 2007, the drama is still available on streaming sites. The television script was written by Lee Jung-ah and Jang Hyun-joo and directed by Lee Yoon-jung.

At the start of the drama, the viewer meets the female lead, Go Eun-chan (Yoon Eun-hye). She lost her father in middle school and now works multiple jobs to support her sister (who dreams of becoming a singer) and her mother (who has a problematic penchant for shoes). Her male lead counterpart, Choe Han-gyeol (Gong Yoo), is a food conglomerate heir who harbors a desire to design toys but is forced to run a shabby coffee shop as punishment for floundering and not focusing on the family. Through a series of uncanny events, Eun-chan is hired to work at the coffee shop run by "princes" and dresses in an unassuming drag that does not greatly differ from her regular attire (although in one scene she tapes down her breasts as she prepares for work). As the episodes

---

15. Joanna Elfving-Hwang describes the plot to *Boys Over Flowers* (2009) as such: "The rich main character . . . wins the affection of the less wealthy (yet impossibly cute) girl . . . who initially impresses the male lead with her wit rather than looks. However, and in the tune of the Ugly Duckling, she of course turns out to be unexpectedly beautiful once the male lead's team of stylists have metamorphosed her into nothing short of a fashion icon." Elfving-Hwang, "Not So Soft After All," 10.

16. Sun Jung, "Chogukjeok Pan-East Asian Soft Masculinity: Reading Boys over Flowers, Coffee Prince and Shinhwa Fan Fiction," in *Complicated Currents: Media Flows, Soft Power and East Asia*, ed. Daniel Black, Stephen Epstein, and Alison Tokita (Monash University ePress, 2010).

progress, Eun-chan and Han-gyeol fall in love while working together, but their perceived shared gender presents a social roadblock that is eventually evaded when Eun-chan reveals herself as female toward the end of the series.[17]

Alongside the lead characters, Choe Han-gyeol's cousin Choe Han-seong (Lee Sun-kyun) is a sensitive music producer who first captured Eun-chan's heart. She in fact has a crush on him as she develops her friendship with Han-gyeol. To complete the quartet, Han-seong has an ex-girlfriend, Han Yu-ju (Chae Jung-an), who broke up with him because she fell in love with someone else, but she returns and their on-again, off-again relationship continues. Han-gyeol is infatuated with Yu-ju but knows his cousin is her true love. The drama is propelled by lighthearted antics in the coffee shop punctuated by the personal struggles of the lead characters as they navigate their blossoming and unique relationships. By the end of the series, the lead characters Eun-chan and Han-gyeol have paired up, as have Yu-ju and Han-seong.

Three years after the debut of *Coffee Prince*, *Secret Garden* was released. The twenty-episode drama was aired on Seoul Broadcasting System from 2010 to 2011 and is still available online for streaming. The drama was written by Kim Eun-sook and directed by Shin Wu-cheol and Kwon Hyeok-chan.[18]

Secret Garden's female lead, Gil Ra-im (Ha Ji-won), is an orphan who supports herself as the sole female stunt double on a team of men. She lives with her quirky and effeminate roommate, Im Ah-young (Yoo In-na). The lead male character, Kim Ju-won (Hyun Bin), is the lackadaisical CEO of his family's department store. Ju-won and Ra-im meet coincidentally during the making of an action film in his department store. Throughout the first several episodes they continue to run into each other, in large part due to Ju-won's ploys to lure her to him. In episode five, their lives become entangled; there is a dose of magical realism, with a spell cast that causes Ra-im and Ju-won to switch bodies on and off throughout the series.[19] As the narrative begins in *Secret Garden*, Gil Ra-im's heart belongs to Kim Ju-won's cousin, a famous singer named Choe Wu-young (Yoon Sang-hyun), whose stage name is Oska. Wu-young has an ex-girlfriend, Yun Seul (Kim Sa-rang), who was matched with Ju-won through blind dates

---

17. Maud Lavin addresses this dynamic at length in her essay, which is also included in this volume. Maud Lavin, "Tomboy in Love: Korean and U.S. Views of Heterosexual Eroticism in the K-Drama *First Shop of Coffee Prince*," *Situations* 8, no. 1 (2015): 45–69.

18. Since *Secret Garden*, Kim Eun-sook has written *A Gentleman's Dignity* (2012), *The Heirs* (2013), *Descendants of the Sun* (2016), *Guardian: The Lonely and Great God* (2016–2017), and *Mr. Sunshine* (2018).

19. Since the 1970s, the body-swap or body-switch motif has been employed in manga graphic novels and anime to play with the corporeal bounds of gender, age, time, and more. See Wang (2020), Fraser and Monden (2017) and Dwivedi (2020). With its body-swap theme, the drama *Secret Garden* inspired new takes on the story in *manhwa* (Korean graphical novels).

arranged by their parents.[20] Like the characters in *Coffee Prince*, after various antics and tribulations, the two couples end up paired off at the end of the series.

Hard Femininity: When Femininity Is Difficult

The lead female characters in *Coffee Prince* and *Secret Garden* frequently find themselves struggling against gendered expectations. Audiences are introduced to both characters through situations that emphasize the difficulties that the characters have with standard feminine performances.

The very first scene featuring Eun-chan in *Coffee Prince* shows her being mistaken for a man while doing her job—riding her delivery motorbike to deliver a takeout food order. Outfitted in black sneakers, baggy jeans, and an identity-concealing helmet, the focus is on her speed and control over space as people scramble out of her way; no specifically gendered attributes are highlighted. As she quickly shuffles inside, the camera takes a moment to focus on the rough, scuffed-up sign at the entrance: "목욕합니다," or "Take a bath," indicating the space is a public bathhouse. As Eun-chan saunters in, still sporting her helmet, she deposits containers on a table and partially dressed, middle-aged women look up at her in surprise. When Eun-chan calls out the order, the women all notice her and scurry about yelling at her, scrambling to cover their mostly nude bodies. They throw things at her, and a bather physically forces Eun-chan toward the door—they think she is a man. As the women chat excitedly about a person they perceive to be male-bodied entering the bathhouse, Eun-chan walks back in seeking payment. As the bathers throw more things at Eun-chan, she finally takes off her helmet and yells that she is a girl. The bathers do not believe her and Eun-chan storms out in frustration.

This introductory scene scaffolds Eun-chan's character by showing her trying to do her job while navigating disruptions based on gendered expectations. Eun-chan's femininity is a nuisance, something she embodies with difficulty and only calls upon in desperation to protect herself and procure payment. To announce her gender, she yanks off her helmet and tousles her short, shaggy hair. This move that she begrudgingly undertakes as a gender-reifying gesture is still rejected as an unconvincing performance of femininity by the intentionally feminine, conventionally presented female-bodied people in the bathhouse. Eun-chan huffs and puffs—a signature gesture, as the audience learns throughout the drama—and acts perplexed and frustrated. Femininity seems difficult

---

20. Other similarities in the dramas include both male leads seeking psychotherapy (Han-gyeol for the potential disruption in his self-perceived sexuality and Ju-won for a fear of elevators); a Cinderella moment when the secondary male lead helps the tomboy female lead dress up for a prestigious event; and comedic but fervent resistance to matchmaking dates arranged by parents.

for her to embody, yet she does not suggest that she sees herself as otherwise. From the moment we meet her, the writers contrast Eun-chan with the nearly naked Korean women scrambling and shrieking around her. She plays it cool; her gestures and actions are relatively confident and intentional. Eun-chan never reveals queer or socially unsanctioned desires. She identifies as female but is not locked into the surface presentation of embodying femininity such as clothing or mannerisms that the other characters display.

Secret Garden's female lead, Ra-im, also embodies a female gender performance that does not fit with idealized social expectations. Mere minutes into the first episode, the female supporting lead, Seul, has just finished her first matchmaking date with Ju-won (the male lead). Afterward, she meets her friend for coffee at an exclusive, members-only lounge at Ju-won's family's department store. As Seul imagines her future with Ju-won, she simultaneously criticizes everyone in the lounge, accusing them of overdoing designer clothing and being gold diggers. Framed by this context, Ra-im is introduced as she steps into the lounge. Unlike the other young women outfitted in designer suits, handbags, and ostentatious jewelry, Ra-im sports jeans, a leather jacket, and a plaid shirt around her waist, all topped off with a ball cap and conspicuous headphones. She takes off her leather jacket, revealing a large dragon tattoo (part of her stunt costume for the movie she is filming). Seul is outraged and as the self-appointed future wife of the department store owner, she considers it her duty to quell this disruption. As she steps up to Gil Ra-im, the camera cuts to a view of their shoes, contrasting Ra-im's junky black sneakers and Seul's pristine black suede pumps with an embellished heel. Seul proceeds to call over one of the lounge's staff, Ra-im's best friend and roommate, Im Ah-young. Seul berates her for allowing Ra-im into the lounge and threatens to tell the management, emphasizing this threat by grabbing Ah-young's name tag and strutting out of the lounge. Before Seul physically attacks Ah-young, Ra-im offers to leave, but when Seul threatens her friend, she insists on retrieving the name tag. Ah-young protests and asks Ra-im to just brush the situation aside.

Like Eun-chan in *Coffee Prince*, Ra-im is juxtaposed with a troop of people who embody normative femininity. In Ra-im's case, however, she is contrasted with a specific character who represents the epitome of idealized femininity. Both Eun-chan in *Coffee Prince* and Ra-im in *Secret Garden* remain cool through their encounters; instead of retreating or being shamed, they are direct and stand up for themselves when justified. Unlike Eun-chan, the presentation of Ra-im in *Secret Garden* sets up less of a gender-binary problematic and instead shifts the focus to a difference of socioeconomic status. Seul demonstrates the epitome of successful female embodiment through her smart clothes, fastidious grooming, and intentional mannerisms. Even Ra-im's best friend more closely resembles Seul in her presentation of self, in a smart skirt-suit styled uniform and bright makeup, although she is deferential. In both dramas, the two actors are judged quickly by their appearance and are presented in stark contrast when grouped with their same-gendered peers in feminine homosocial spaces.

Socioeconomic Dynamics of Performing Femininity

Shortly following the moments described above, both *Coffee Prince* and *Secret Garden* present scenes in the first episodes in which a handbag is stolen; both scenes set the tone for how the female characters interact throughout the duration of the drama. In *Coffee Prince*, the male lead Han-gyeol takes Yu-ju on a casual date. When they return to his home, he briefly goes upstairs to retrieve a gift for her. Simultaneously, down the street, Eun-chan is driving her delivery food motorcycle and sees another person on a motorbike weaving in and out of traffic with speed and agility. Her curiosity piqued, she follows the driver, who turns onto a side street where Yu-ju leans on Han-gyeol's car, speaking on the phone and flipping through her datebook. The speedy driver seizes the opportunity and snatches Yu-ju's purse; Yu-ju tumbles to the ground. Eun-chan witnesses the theft and as the driver circles around, she dismounts her motorbike, takes off her helmet, and throws it at the thief, knocking him to the ground. Han-gyeol returns and is very concerned about Yu-ju's minor scrapes and acts aggressively toward Eun-chan.[21] Instead of being accusatory, both women are apologetic and concerned for the other's well-being. Yu-ju wants to pay for Eun-chan's damaged bike; Eun-chan politely refuses the offer but reciprocates worry for Yu-ju's scraped leg.

Through the context of the drama, it is clear that Eun-chan and Yu-ju are of very different socioeconomic means. Yu-ju is an artist who regularly works abroad and runs in the privileged, cosmopolitan circle of Han-gyeol and his cousin, heirs to a large food conglomerate. Eun-chan works multiple jobs to support her family and is swimming in debt. Despite these differences, they treat each other with respect and as equals in this scene.[22] Congenial reciprocity is not demonstrated in the exchange between the female leads in the first episode of *Secret Garden*.

---

21. As Han-gyeol dotes on Yu-ju, Eun-chan discovers that the thief is her acquaintance—a young man who is romantically pursuing her sister, Eun-sae. Earlier in the episode, Eun-chan met this young man and pretended to be Eun-sae's boyfriend to shake him off. He tells Eun-chan that he is stealing the bag to help pay for Eun-sae's music school fees. Eun-chan lets him go, but she (poorly and comedically) acts as though he got away.

22. Yu-ju does not automatically presume Eun-chan's gender, but Han-gyeol immediately genders Eun-chan as a (young) male. The component of age is crucial in Han-gyeol's framing and processing of Eun-chan. The big brother-little brother dynamic that they later adopt to cover for their closeness relies on this gendered misreading—suggesting that her female form is actually that of an adolescent male.

Immediately following the scene in the department store lounge in *Secret Garden*, Ra-im appears to acquiesce to Ah-young's request to ignore Seul's hurtful claims. Upon leaving the lounge and heading for her bicycle, Ra-im sees Seul smugly waiting for a car. Ra-im decides to approach her. The screen flashes back and forth between Ra-im's determined and somewhat haughty stare and Seul, who appears composed but slightly panicked as Ra-im walks toward her. Right as they are about to intersect, Seul's friend's bag gets snatched, causing the friend to start shrieking. There is a moment in which Seul and Ra-im wear similarly annoyed expressions as they turn toward the chaos and watch the thieves run away. Ra-im looks back and forth between the shrieking friend and the departing thieves. She sighs and tells Seul's friend to wait a moment before jumping on her bike to run after them. Optimistic action-style theme music cuts in as Ra-im performs a stunt-like action scene, scaling bridges and weaving through traffic. This culminates in a fight scene in which she single-handedly takes down the four thieves and retrieves the bag. This is all out of sight of Seul, who, upon Ra-im's return, accuses her of being in cahoots with the thieves. When Ra-im returns the bag, she hands it to Seul's friend, but Seul grabs the bag and then hands it to her friend herself. Ra-im, slightly sweaty and glistening from her heroic escapades, tells Seul that they are now even and that she should forget what happened in the lounge and give back the name tag. Seul refuses and says the name tag is in the trash, which reveals Ra-im's short fuse as she grabs Seul by the collar and demands that she hand over the name tag. Ra-im drags Seul inside to a trash can and insists she retrieve the name tag, hence disclosing Seul's bluff.[23] Seul takes the name tag out of her purse and hands it to Ra-im. Not missing a beat, Ra-im politely requests Seul's friend's tear-soaked tissue, grabs Seul's purse, thrusts the tissue into the purse and tosses it back to Seul—she found the true garbage can. With that, she takes the name tag and walks out, leaving Seul irate and her friend blathering in admiration.

Like Eun-chan and Yu-ju's encounter in *Coffee Prince*, socioeconomic difference is presented in stark contrast in *Secret Garden*. Each scene above offers similar glimpses of destabilizing this aspect of socioeconomic social hierarchy, yet they are differently executed. As described above, Eun-chan and Yu-ju achieve this through demonstrating compassion for one another, whereas in *Secret Garden* Ra-im and Seul's mutual disdain levels them to a similar plane. Both characters take turns having the upper hand within their encounters. For example, as Ra-im demands Ah-young's nametag from Seul, she asserts that one of them is a person who spends thousands at a department store and the other may steal coffee from a friend, but the trash stinks to them both.

---

23. Gil Ra-im's treatment of Yun Seul in this scene reflects how male characters often physically drag around their female counterparts.

Socioeconomic status can make the performance of idealized femininity easier or harder to achieve. For example, higher socioeconomic status means being able to afford a feminine marker: a coveted handbag that is worth stealing. Both female leads fall outside of the realm of socioeconomically achievable femininity. Leveling the playing field within the context of socioeconomic disparity shows a flexibility that is offered within femininity. In the introduction to Laurel Kendall's aforementioned book, Kendall argues that as modernity melts into postmodernity, Koreans exhibit a "condition of nonfixity, of gendered constructs in motions with changing politics, emergent classes, new commodities, new ways of talking about and experiencing sexuality, generational conflicts, and economic adjustments."[24] Kendall's notion of nonfixed social status works within the confines of the continued dominance of the male gender. Socioeconomic status and gender are both components in marking social class. The encounters above are an example of the nonfixity Kendall highlights in the postmodern moment, although extended to the female sex. Later in Kendall's edited volume, Nancy Abelmann recalls that in South Korea there is a nostalgia for when everyone was poor together and that "class hierarchy is bound with gender relations."[25] This recent history offers an important perspective on the two scenes discussed above and, in a sense, can relegate gendered engagements into generational eras. On the one hand, Eun-chan and Yu-ju offer a nostalgic relationship as they bond over a hardship. On the other hand, Ra-im and Seul's interaction shows that the fast-paced economic growth in South Korea has had an immense impact on the country at large. Nostalgia for comradery is depicted in the glimmers of flattening socioeconomic hierarchies (either sweetly brushing them aside in *Coffee Prince* or demanding to be valued outside of them in *Secret Garden*). What is exciting here is that female-bodied and identifying characters are doing this outside of the realm of male-bodied and identifying characters.

Female Embodiment of Soft Masculinity

This final section shows the female leads' necessary position as the *other* to soft masculinity, and considers the possibilities of those characters who embody the features of soft masculinity as defined by Elfving-Hwang and Jung.

In her aforementioned talk, Joanna Elfving-Hwang suggests that *kkonminam* can be associated with luxury goods of the high class, who are supposed to take good care of their appearance. They are beautiful, decorative, and pampered.

24. Kendall, *Under Construction*, 18.
25. Nancy Abelmann, "Women, Mobility, and Desire: Narrating Class and Gender in South Korea," in *Under Construction: The Gendering of Modernity, Class, and Consumption in the Republic of Korea*, ed. Laurel Kendall (Honolulu: University of Hawai'i Press, 2002), 34.

These characters are often contrasted with a headstrong woman of the working class, which we see in the examples of *Coffee Prince* and *Secret Garden*. In her analysis of the Korean drama *Boys Over Flowers* (2009), Elfving-Hwang points out that the male lead fluctuates between soft and hard masculinity; like Moon's description of masculinity above, hard masculinity is the nationally propagated form of masculinity that was aggressively established in the 1960s.[26] The title of Elfving-Hwang's essay, "Not So Soft After All," provides an important distinction and highlights a conflation of *kkonminam* and soft masculinity. Characters that fall into these categories may share a similar appearance, but soft masculinity focuses on both appearance and behavior, whereas *kkonmimam* focuses on appearance. In my analysis of *Coffee Prince* and *Secret Garden*, Elfving-Hwang's descriptors of *kkonminam* are useful.

Jung describes soft masculinity through analysis of Hallyu star Bae Yong-joon (BYJ)'s embodiment of his character in *Winter Sonata* (2002).[27] *Winter Sonata* is a melodrama with themes of memory loss and recovery, love, and familial intertwining.[28] BYJ's fans describe him as personifying both masculine rigor and feminine tenderness, particularly in the way he interacts with his female counterpart on-screen.[29]

Taking into account Judith Butler's theory of gender performativity, as Jung puts it, "masculinity is culturally constructed through the repetition of stylized bodily performances."[30] She breaks down BYJ's soft masculinity into three key characteristics: "tender charisma," purity, and politeness.[31] The first component is a combination of self-sacrifice and always putting the needs of his female love interest and costar before his own. This aspect of soft masculinity is also compared to *seonbi* from traditional Confucian ideology—namely, a "man who possesses 'a tender exterior and a strong inner will.'"[32] This is still a desirable trait for Korean men today. The second trait, purity, is constructed through a nostalgic

---

26. Elfving-Hwang, "Not So Soft After All," 11.
27. *Winter Sonata* is part of the *Endless Love* series (2000–2006) directed by Yoon Seok-ho and produced by the Korean Broadcasting System.
28. A brief synopsis of *Winter Sonata*: The main characters, Gang Jun-sang (BYJ) and Jeong Yu-jin (Choi Ji-Woo) briefly fall in love in high school. Joon-sang has an accident and experiences memory loss, then loses contact with Yu-jin. Ten years later, she is engaged to be married and Joon-sang reappears in her life; having suffered the aforementioned memory loss, he does not remember her.
29. Sun Jung, *Korean Masculinities and Transcultural Consumption: Yonsama, Rain, Oldboy, K-Pop Idols* (Hong Kong: Hong Kong University Press, 2011), 45.
30. Judith Butler, "Performative Acts and Gender Constitution: An Essay in Phenomenology and Feminist Theory," *Theatre Journal* 40, no. 4 (December 1988): 519–31, https://doi.org/10.2307/3207893.
31. Sun Jung frames this chapter based on middle-aged Japanese women's enthusiastic reception of BYJ as a Korean masculinity that is tender and gentlemanly rather than their previously conceived understanding of macho and scary masculinity (45).
32. Jung, *Korean Masculinities and Transcultural Consumption*, 48.

first love narrative. Jung uses the example of the female lead surprising her male counterpart with a kiss on his cheek while they build a snowman. His reaction is "innocent and surprised," and the sense of purity is reinforced as the characters are literally surrounded by and frolicking in white, fluffy snow.[33] Lastly, Jung describes politeness in two ways. First, it is demonstrated in Jun-sang's excessive consideration of other people's feelings and putting others' well-being before his own.[34] Second, politeness is further unpacked with an example from the real world: when interacting with fans, BYJ is known for politeness such as "smiling and putting his hands on his chest."[35] These traits, though not necessarily gendered, are not interpreted as feminizing the male character but instead expand the potential performances of desired masculinity.

The male leads in *Coffee Prince* and *Secret Garden* present the superficial and cosmetic markers that Elfving-Hwang articulates—namely, an association with luxury goods and care for their appearance. *Kkonminam* also suggests a soft appearance: "smooth fair skin, silky hair, and a feminine manner."[36] Jung describes BYJ, arguably the most identified symbol of soft masculinity, as follows: "BYJ's soft masculine image is often exemplified through his feminine appearance. In *Winter Sonata*, BYJ's character is a bespectacled architect with dyed brown hair who wears a scarf tied a different way in each scene."[37] These physical attributes are borrowed, and fans and fans' partners would sport the BYJ appearance in a sort of fantasy role-play.

Soft masculinity: Appearance and material indulgence

Within the descriptions of soft masculinity above, it is clear that one can appear that way externally without embodying the internal characteristics. My question then is: Can the female leads in the dramas portray soft masculine attributes? In her chapter "Chogukjeok Pan-East Asian Soft Masculinity," Jung shows how in *Coffee Prince* both Han-gyeol and Eun-chan embody these external physical traits of soft masculinity: "In particular, Eun-chan comes to serve (ironically) as a perfect embodiment of *kkonminam* soft masculinity: 'his' slim feminine face, dewy skin, silky hair, and sweet smile are features that resemble those of a pretty male lead in a *sunjeong manhwa*."[38] In the realm of physical presentation, Eun-chan and Ra-im have tomboyish appearances when compared to their female

---

33. Jung, *Korean Masculinities and Transcultural Consumption*, 49.
34. Jung, *Korean Masculinities and Transcultural Consumption*, 50–51.
35. Jung, *Korean Masculinities and Transcultural Consumption*, 52.
36. Jung, *Korean Masculinities and Transcultural Consumption*, 58.
37. Jung, *Korean Masculinities and Transcultural Consumption*, 57.
38. Jung, "Chogukjeok Pan-East Asian Soft Masculinity."

counterparts.[39] Yu-ju and Seul are petite and graceful; they have long, swooping hair, sweet faces, and feminine manners. Yu-ju wears soft and delicate clothing and Seul sports a tailored power-suit style, but both occupy specifically feminized visualities. Eun-chan and Ra-im present themselves in a way that departs from this idealized embodiment of femininity that Yu-ju and Seul represent. The directors of the dramas intentionally introduce the characters within contexts that exaggerate these differences, though both lead characters are depicted at some point in both series experimenting with more feminine-styled clothing. Ra-im has a bit more grace in these scenes than Eun-chan, but both characters demonstrate awkwardness and confusion with highly feminine fashions.

Another aspect of *kkonminam* soft masculinity is an outward and exaggerated demonstration of capitalistic indulgence, and, as we met them in the beginning of their respective dramas, here Eun-chan and Ra-im appear to depart dramatically. Ra-im explicitly rejects wealth, and Eun-chan is shown struggling to make ends meet. Just hours after the purse theft, Eun-chan begrudgingly calls Han-gyeol for the financial help that he stuffily offers to impress Yu-ju. And although they never move to flaunt their economic and social mobility, by the end of each series, both characters have shifted upward in terms of socioeconomic status through coupling with their male counterparts.

Soft masculinity: Tender, pure, and polite

"Tender charisma"

Jung's definition of BYJ's soft masculinity includes "tender charisma," purity, and politeness. To describe tender charisma, BYJ shows a heightened concern for his female counterpart. In the scenes described in detail above, both Eun-chan and Ra-im do the same and go to great lengths to offer their support. In *Coffee Prince*, when returning Yu-ju's purse, Eun-chan and Yu-ju show more care and concern for each other than for themselves. They demonstrate this care through different, sparsely spaced scenarios throughout the drama that are often mediated through male characters. In *Secret Garden*, Ra-im will not fight for herself, but she is ready to defend her friend. Both Eun-chan and Ra-im would rather cause themselves discomfort than see another person suffer.

---

39. For a close look at Eun-chan's performance, see Maud Lavin's essay included in this volume. See also Lavin, "Tomboy in Love."

Purity of heart

Regarding the second characteristic, purity, both female leads are very slow to have sex with their respective partners in the dramas; but a more complex reading of "purity" is depicted through their female relationships. For example, Eun-chan turns to Yu-ju for complicated relationship advice, situating Yu-ju as more worldly and mature in comparison with herself and framing Eun-chan as innocent or naive. Ra-im's "purity" is demonstrated through her temper and stubbornness. In episode five of *Secret Garden*, Ra-im and Seul meet in unexpected circumstances on Jeju Island, a resort town. When they meet again, Ra-im almost immediately recognizes Seul from their previous encounter, but Seul does not notice. Ra-im sees an opportunity to confront Seul and demand an apology. As this conversation unfolds, Ju-won approaches and Seul feigns a panic attack. Although Ra-im stands her ground and demands an apology for Seul's actions, Ju-won tells Ra-im that she should apologize for using the elite lounge before agreeing with her perspective. This encounter illustrates Ra-im's naivety within class hierarchies, although Ra-im's actions reject this portrayal. Notably, Eun-chan's "purity" is often associated with youthfulness, whereas Ra-im's is usually paired with socioeconomic status. These variations of "purity" demonstrate the complexities and social stigmas that are intertwined with gender representations.

Polite

Eun-chan and Ra-im are generally both deferent and apologetic with the other characters in the television dramas, but their politeness towards their female counterparts varies. Eun-chan maintains this mode of respect with Yu-ju, eventually even calling her *eonni*, a term of both respect and endearment that means "older sister." In the Korean language, a younger sibling that is female would call the older sister *eonni*, but a young sibling that is male would call an older sister *nuna*. Again, Yu-ju's interaction with Eun-chan places Eun-chan back in the female realm rather than in her tomboy, cross-dressing mode through which Han-gyeol sees her. On the other hand, Ra-im does not continue her deferent persona when engaging with Seul. Later in the evening after the scene when they meet again, Ra-im's stunt teammate gets her a meeting with the director of a music video their team is filming (for Oska, Ra-im's crush and Seul's ex-boyfriend!). When Ra-im enters with a polite, somewhat groveling speech, the director turns and it is Seul. Ra-im remains more or less speechless and Seul takes control of the encounter, not missing a beat and remaining polite, formal, and amused by the circumstances. Within Seul and Ra-im's relationship, Ra-im does not maintain the same politeness with her female counterpart as she does with the rest of the characters.

Although Eun-chan nearly perfectly fits Jung's articulations of soft masculinity, through Ra-im, we see a slight shift away from fitting these categories
when it comes to her interactions with other female characters. Within female
relationships, there are moments when Eun-chan and Ra-im embody and
perform soft masculine characteristics as described by scholars such as Jung and
Elfving-Hwang. This not only complicates notions of soft masculinity, which
specifically pushes feminine descriptors aside, but additionally broadens and
diversifies descriptions and relationships related to hard femininity demonstrating potential pluralities.

Queer Gender Strategies and Hard Femininity

In 2011, just a year after *Secret Garden*, Korean Broadcasting System aired a
Korean television show, *Daughters of Club Bilitis*, which was about three lesbian
couples; it was removed from the network three days after airing.[40] This brief
moment shows both that the television network was trying to "[challenge] the
nation's traditionally conservative society and its oft-cited distaste for gay people
and culture," and that a component of Korean society was not prepared for
female queerness and lesbian sexuality.[41] Its release, reception, and quick recall
shows that there is a fine line in the realm of sanctioned non-hegemonic depictions of gender and sexuality in popular culture in South Korea. While *Coffee
Prince* and *Secret Garden* feature characters performing gender in both traditional and flexible ways, they very intentionally do not move into the realm of
non-hegemonic sexuality. The characters can play around with masculinity and
femininity because the audiences "know" that the characters are either male-
bodied or female-bodied, and that they are clearly heterosexual and bound for
heterosexual romantic pairings. With that in mind, in conclusion, I argue that
within the limited context of these Korean dramas, queer gender is required to
locate and parse femininity with the discourse of hegemonic soft masculinity.

At the beginning of this chapter, I reference Sara Ahmed's notion of disorientation to suggest a shifting of the discussion of gender in Korean dramas. Where
Ahmed embraces a *disorientation*, José Esteban Muñoz propagates a *disidentification*, which he expounds through analysis of brown and queer bodied people
in visual culture. In *Disidentifications: Queers of Color and the Performance of
Politics* (1999), Muñoz's disidentification is a survival strategy employed by
racial and sexual minority subjects working against and negotiating dominant

---

40. Charles Junwoo Park, "Lesbians in Drama Test Society's Limits," *Korea JoongAng Daily*, August
     18, 2011, accessed March 4, 2019, http://koreajoongangdaily.joins.com/news/article/article.
     aspx?aid=2940397.
41. Charles Junwoo Park, "Lesbians in Drama Test Society's Limits."

ideology; it is about attempting to locate citizenship in an environment dictated by state power composed through misogyny, white supremacy, and heteronormativity.[42] Muñoz speaks of sites of identification, which impose restrictions on the kinds of identification that can occur; these "normalizing protocols keep subjects from accessing identities."[43] Masculinity, the dominant ideology within the discussions surrounding gender in Korean dramas, has a flattening impact on the richness of femininity. In the spirit of Muñoz, this analysis of female connectivity in *Coffee Prince* and *Secret Garden* allows disentanglement from masculinity as a measuring stick to develop the complexity of femininity.

Although Eun-chan and Ra-im are not sexually queer, their embodiment of hard femininity problematizes, disorients, and disidentifies hegemonic femininity and soft masculinity as framed within the context of the dramas. In both *Coffee Prince* and *Secret Garden*, there is an element of queer gender through dressing as the opposite gender. Eun-chan does so to acquire gainful employment—yes, this is not a huge shift from her usual performance and presentation of self, but this aspect of the drama is central to the narrative. In an even more literal inhabiting, in *Secret Garden*, Ra-im and Ju-won magically and unintentionally swap bodies, being forced to perform another person as they occupy their body. The performances are awkward and clunky, particularly at the beginning of this aspect of the drama, but within this liminal space their performances evolve into compassion and empathy. I therefore pose the open questions: Are these queer performances of disidentification required for the disorientation of soft masculinity? And further, were queer gender performances a precursor to inviting the question of hard femininity? Hard femininity as demonstrated through Eun-chan and Ra-im depicts the complex layers of femininity that demand consideration not only as the other to soft masculinity but as instances of the intersectionality of gender and the potential to disorient gender away from a constantly misogynistic baseline referent.

By proclaiming a soft masculinity, according to hegemonic binary structures of gender, the expected complement is hard femininity. Naming femininity *hard* plays into the suggestion that femininity is inflexible, unchanging, and difficult, juxtaposed with the permitted flexibility of masculinity in Korean dramas. Binary tropes create dangerous slippages where nuance that escapes the binary slides through the cracks in a liminal and queer space. Within the rich intertwining of characters in Korean dramas, this chapter retrieves some of that which has slipped through the cracks.

---

42. José Esteban Muñoz, *Disidentifications: Queers of Color and the Performance of Politics*, Cultural Studies of the Americas, vol. 2 (Minneapolis: University of Minnesota Press, 1999), 5.

43. Muñoz, *Disidentifications*, 8.

In conclusion, I return to the title question: Is femininity hard? In a sense, yes. Femininity is difficult; both to be it and to define it. As an idealized social and cultural marker, achieving femininity is reserved for a select few. But on the other hand, is femininity stagnant and unmoving? The answer is unequivocally no. Rather, femininity offers a range of gender expression and potentiality. Femininity is hard and difficult; it is also complex, intersectional, and a place for resituating social hierarchies.

Bibliography

Abelmann, Nancy. "Women, Mobility, and Desire: Narrating Class and Gender in South Korea." In *Under Construction: The Gendering of Modernity, Class, and Consumption in the Republic of Korea*, edited by Laurel Kendall, 25–54. Honolulu: University of Hawai'i Press, 2002.

Ahmed, Sara. *Queer Phenomenology: Orientations, Objects, Others.* Durham, NC: Duke University Press, 2006.

Berlant, Lauren. "The Female Complaint." *Social Text*, no. 19/20 (Autumn 1988): 237–59. https://doi.org/10.2307/466188.

Butler, Judith. *Bodies That Matter: On the Discursive Limits of "Sex."* Abingdon, Oxon: Routledge, 2011.

Butler, Judith. "Performative Acts and Gender Constitution: An Essay in Phenomenology and Feminist Theory." *Theatre Journal* 40, no. 4 (December 1988): 519–31. https://doi.org/10.2307/3207893.

Chua, Beng Huat, and Koichi Iwabuchi, eds. *East Asian Pop Culture: Analysing the Korean Wave.* Hong Kong: Hong Kong University Press, 2008.

Dwivedi, Ram Prakash. "*Your Name*: A Study of Imagery and Post-postmodernity in Cinema." *International Journal of Culture and Global Studies* 1, no. 2 (August 2020).

Elfving-Hwang, Joanna. "Not So Soft After All: Kkonminam Masculinities in Contemporary South Korean Popular Culture." Paper presented at the 7th KSAA Biennale Conference, November 16–18, 2011.

Epstein, Stephen, and Yun Mi Hwang, eds. *The Korean Wave: A Sourcebook.* Seongnam-si, Gyeonggi-do: The Academy of Korean Studies Press, 2015.

"'Flowerboys' and the Appeal of 'Soft Masculinity.'" BBC News, September 5, 2018, sec. Asia. https://www.bbc.com/news/world-asia-42499809.

Fraser, Lucy, and Masafumi Monden. "The Maiden Switch: New Possibilities for Understanding Japanese *Shōjo Manga* (Girls' Comics)." *Asian Studies Review* 41, no. 4 (2017): 544–61.

Jung, Sun. "Bae Yong-Joon, Soft Masculinity, and Japanese Fans: Our Past Is in Your Present Body." In *Korean Masculinities and Transcultural Consumption: Yonsama, Rain, Oldboy, K-Pop Idols.* Hong Kong: Hong Kong University Press, 2011.

Jung, Sun. "Chogukjeok Pan-East Asian Soft Masculinity: Reading Boys over Flowers, Coffee Prince and Shinhwa Fan Fiction." In *Complicated Currents: Media Flows, Soft Power and East Asia*, edited by Daniel Black, Stephen Epstein, and Alison Tokita. Monash University ePress, 2010.

Jung, Sun. *Korean Masculinities and Transcultural Consumption: Yonsama, Rain, Oldboy, K-Pop Idols*. TransAsia: Screen Cultures. Hong Kong: Hong Kong University Press, 2011.

Kendall, Laurel, ed. *Under Construction: The Gendering of Modernity, Class, and Consumption in the Republic of Korea*. Honolulu: University of Hawai'i Press, 2002.

Kim, Elaine H., and Choi Chungmoo, eds. *Dangerous Women: Gender and Korean Nationalism*. New York: Routledge, 1998.

Korroch, Kate. "The Isolated Queer Body: Harisu's Dodo Cosmetics Advertisement." In *'Queer' Asia: Decolonising and Reimagining Sexuality and Gender*, edited by J. Daniel Luther and Jennifer Ung Loh, 165–83. London: Zed Books, 2019.

Lavin, Maud. "Tomboy in Love: Korean and U.S. Views of Heterosexual Eroticism in the K-Drama *First Shop of Coffee Prince*." *Situations* 8, no. 1 (2015): 45–69.

Moon, Seungsook. *Militarized Modernity and Gendered Citizenship in South Korea*. Durham, NC: Duke University Press, 2005.

Muñoz, José Esteban. *Disidentifications: Queers of Color and the Performance of Politics*. Minneapolis: University of Minnesota Press, 1999.

Nelson, Laura C. *Measured Excess: Status, Gender, and Consumer Nationalism in South Korea*. New York: Columbia University Press, 2000.

Park, Charles Junwoo. "Lesbians in Drama Test Society's Limits." *Korea JoongAng Daily*. August 18, 2011. Accessed March 4, 2019. http://koreajoongangdaily.joins.com/news/article/article.aspx?aid=2940397.

Park, Young-Hai. "Western Feminism and Korean Realities." *Korean Women Today* 5 (1984): 4.

Wang, Yiwen. "The Paradox of Queer Aura: A Case Study of Gender-Switching Video Remakes." *Feminist Media Studies* 20, no. 4 (2020): 496–14.

Yang, Fang-chih Irene. "Rap(p)ing the Korean Wave: National Identity in Question." In *East Asian Pop Culture: Analysing the Korean Wave*, edited by Chua Beng Huat and Koichi Iwabuchi, 191–216. Hong Kong: Hong Kong University Press, 2008.

2

Tomboy in Love

Korean and US Views of Heterosexual Eroticism in the K-Drama First Shop of Coffee Prince

Maud Lavin

In this chapter,[1] I explore the reception in Korea and the US of the hit Korean TV drama *First Shop of Coffee Prince*, first broadcast in 2007 and heavily viewed online since then. Incorporating interviews with viewers and the director, as well as my own reading, I focus on the representation of a feminine-inflected, non-normative heterosexuality in the eroticism and desiring of the drama's tomboy lead: her unique and compelling sexuality.

Countering the prevalence in mainstream American movies and television of a coitus-driven eroticism in romance plots, this K-drama tomboy's polymorphous pleasures—and even a possible misreading of the discretion involved in the courtship between the tomboy and the pretty boy—has appealed to certain US viewers from a range of intersectional identities who self-define as women. With additional and different cultural referents involved in their reception, Korean women viewers at home have been drawn to this hetero-tomboy's eroticism, which for some is intertwined with her hardworking and independent qualities. Overall, *Coffee Prince* is read in this chapter for what it can represent for different women viewers on both sides of the Pacific, in terms of one of

1. An earlier and different version of this chapter was published in *Situations* 8, no. 1 (2015): 45-69, and I appreciate Dr. Terence Murphy's editing on it. An earlier version than that was given as the keynote address for the conference on "Gender & Sexuality: Performance and Representation in Asia" co-sponsored by the Asia Research Institute (ARI), National University of Singapore, and the Wee Kim Wee School of Communication and Information at Nanyang Technological University, Singapore, held at ARI on January 18, 2012, and organized by professors Lucy Davis and Liew Kai Khiun. I am grateful to them and to colleagues SooJin Lee, Karen Morris, and Kate Korroch for their feedback, as well as discussants when I gave this essay as lectures at the School of the Art Institute of Chicago (SAIC) and Bowling Green State University in 2013. At SAIC, I also thank research assistant Somy Kim and SAIC research interns Jackie Cho, Kathleen McCarty, Christl Caspar, and Ensueno Pabon.

many nonnormative heterosexualities not usually depicted in more Hollywood-derived global mainstream culture.

In episode four of the now-classic *Coffee Prince*, there's a sweat-drenched roughhousing scene between the male lead Han-gyeol and tomboy Eun-chan as they compete in basketball under the hot Seoul sun, each refusing to give up. They climb on each other, block each other. The scene has a playfulness that is erotic. For many viewers, this and other tightly physical scenes between Han-gyeol and Eun-chan are romantic in ways that connect friendship with love, and erotic in ways that involve play and the whole body.

Such highlighted roughhousing scenes are unlike the gamboling commonly seen in other popular Korean dramas, where the male protagonist so often grabs the wrist of the female and pulls her into date-like activities like Ferris wheel rides (although admittedly, there are some wrist grabs in *Coffee Prince*, too). In contrast, most of Han-gyeol and Eun-chan's romping is wild, no-holds-barred, and would be traditionally categorized as masculine—like playing casual sports with no referee or letting loose during a drinking night out. Han-gyeol is a man. He thinks Eun-chan is a man, but she's not; she's a woman. Her tomboy style in clothes, aided by disguise elements like binding her breasts, conveys her feminine masculinity. Because we viewers know she's passing as a man, we see how it's socially acceptable for her to sweat and climb on Han-gyeol in public in the middle of the day in Seoul. Because she's living as a tomboy, she's strong and athletic and not used to holding back. The masquerade as a man and the identity as a tomboy: these together give her license for feminine-inflected pleasure in a nonnormative heterosexuality.

In looking at the tomboy in *Coffee Prince* and at the perception of her among female viewers in Korea and the US, I'm employing *Coffee Prince* as a case study for relational comparison around issues of eroticism, reception, and heterosexualities among different viewers who self-define as women (hereafter: women).[2] *Coffee Prince* is well known for its gender-confusion plot and somewhat open discussions by the characters about homosexuality and heterosexuality. It's also recognized as one of the early tomboy-protagonist TV dramas in Korea—others include *You're Beautiful* (2009), *Secret Garden* (2010), *Sungkyunkwan Scandal* (2010), *The Scholar Who Walks the Night* (2015), and *Strong Woman Do Bong Soon* (2017)—following other related plots in Japanese dramas and in *manga* and Korean *manhwa*. Within this context, my analytical goal is to consider how Eun-chan's sexuality exemplifies a nonnormative heterosexuality for mass media and what this might mean for female viewers in Korea and the US.

---

2.   Shu-mei Shih, "Comparison as Relation," in *Comparison: Theories, Approaches, Uses*, ed. Rita Felski and Susan Stanford Friedman (Baltimore: The Johns Hopkins University Press, 2013).

The drama is comprised of seventeen one-hour episodes. *Coffee Prince's* basic plot is that Go Eun-chan, the 24-year-old working-class female protagonist (played by Yoon Eun-hye), masquerades as a young man in order to get a job and earn better money than she could as a woman. We see her in the first episodes cobbling together a living from many part-time jobs. In one discussion in the first episode, her employer at the restaurant tells her he has hired a woman to save money. In fact, money is tight for Eun-chan. Various machinations ensue, and Eun-chan gets hired full-time as a male waiter at a café run by the handsome 29-year-old Choe Han-gyeol (played by Gong Yoo). Han-gyeol is from the rich family that owns both the café and the large Dong-in Foods Company. This would all roll out as a typical Cinderella K-drama plot, except that Eun-chan and Han-gyeol become friends, with Han thinking the cute tomboy is really a man. They cavort together and, gradually and with great sensuality, fall in love, which causes Han-gyeol—who before this had always thought of himself as heterosexual—great distress as he realizes he's falling in love with someone he thinks is a man. We see his longing, his fun, his attraction, his fear, his anger. We also see his friends support him and urge him to adopt a positive attitude toward homosexuality. Meanwhile, Eun-chan stays masqueraded and apparently tongue-tied about her gender, afraid to lose her job and her friendship with Han-gyeol if she speaks up. She also doesn't think she's the kind of woman in terms of class or femininity that would appeal to him. Since its first airing in Korea in 2007, *Coffee Prince* and its stars (carrying the connotations of these characters and those they have played in other dramas) have enjoyed great Korean and international popularity.

In this chapter, both Korean and American viewers are included as recipient examples of contra-flows from a powerful and influential regional media center, Seoul, at one time on the margins of the profitable global entertainment business, to what is still a center (but no longer the only center)—the United States.[3] Primarily, in considering different fields of reception, my questions are these: What might the hetero-tomboy, her physicality and eroticism mean to the primarily female viewers of different cultural backgrounds who watch her? In considering these questions, I use fan-site comments, in-person interviews, interview questionnaires, an exchange with the director of *Coffee Prince*, and autoethnography. The exploration is less about teasing out which elements of this reception montage belong to which culture and much more about considering examples of Korean and US reception of a tomboy figure who is potentially meaningful to viewers as an independent, fresh, appealing, hardworking, and innocent—yet also erotically desiring and physical—woman. I argue that the

---

3. Daya Kishan Thussu, "Mapping Global Media Flow and Contra-Flow," in *Media on the Move: Global Flow and Contra-flow*, ed. Daya Kishan Thussu (London: Routledge, 2007), 10–29.

consumption of *Coffee Prince* can involve, for viewers who so choose, an eroticism of a nonnormative heterosexuality, and that this, along with other instances of expansions and diversifications of mass culture representation of heterosexual desires, is significant in contributing to a redressing of a lack in public discourse around the range of heterosexualities and their pleasures for hetero women.[4]

Clearly promoting heterosexuality in mainstream mass culture can be problematic in its repetitive articulation of a narrow window of possibilities. In mainstream American movies and TV, it is commonly acknowledged that heteroromantic plot developments are so fixed on coitus as a looming goal that the focus on this sexual act can close off a range of alternative erotic sensualities. Of the many examples of the "jumping into bed" plots in American mass media, *Sex and the City* and *Gossip Girls* come quickly to mind. In analyzing *Coffee Prince* for its representation of a polymorphous eroticism, I'm not simply looking at, say, more room for foreplay, but instead a complex and not necessarily goal-oriented polymorphous eroticism. And *Coffee Prince* comes as part of a context of Korean TV depictions of the tomboy.[5]

The Tomboy

In Korea, a tomboy (using the English word) commonly signifies a woman who has a boyish fashion style. In Korean culture, the word *tomboy* does not mean *lesbian*. Regionally, though, and particularly in the different urban cultures of Hong Kong, Mainland China, and Taiwan, the English word *tomboy* or its abbreviation *T*—and related visual styles—can have a spectrum of meanings, from the most alternative (such as butch lesbian) to a merely commodified tomboy look. That spectrum is not comprised of neatly separable identifies, however; overlaps and ambiguities can exist.

In Korean TV dramas, though, the tomboy is usually a twentysomething, short-haired, hardworking heterosexual woman. She is commonly seen as acting in defiance, at least for a certain period of her life, against heteronormative marriage goals; usually she is more interested in working than in landing a fiancé. As the drama unfolds, however, she is nevertheless shown to be attracted to and attractive to the beautiful male lead. She is highlighted as a sturdy, cute, and

4. Hanne Blank, *Straight: The Surprisingly Short History of Heterosexuality* (Boston: Beacon Press, 2012).
5. Interviews, in person and via email, were obtained using the snowballing method through friend networks and also circles at the School of the Art Institute of Chicago, where I have taught, and at Bowling Green State University, where I have lectured. Interviews or interview contact information were obtained as well at pan-Asian-American locales also frequented by white, Latine, and Black people in Chicago, including nail salons and restaurants. Not counting casual conversations, I conducted eight in-person interviews with follow-up emails and nineteen interviews through email questions and responses exclusively, for a total of twenty-seven.

subtly eroticized working girl. A pragmatism is part of her character; short hair can imply a readiness for the workplace. And Eun-chan, the tomboy in *Coffee Prince* (and others modeled after her), is also very sensual and desiring, even exuberantly erotic, although she doesn't seem that way at first. This kind of tomboy, too, is popular abroad.

In February 2012, Arirang TV's *Showbiz Korea*, which is seen in 188 countries, including the US, conducted a three-week poll on its home page asking viewers to pick their favorite Korean TV drama; 2,024 international viewers responded.[6] *Secret Garden* (2010) won first place with 16.1 percent of the vote. Following in descending order were *Boys Over Flowers* (2009), *You're Beautiful* (2009), *Coffee Prince* (2007), *Princess Hours* (2006), and *Sungkyunkwan Scandal* (2010).[7] *Secret Garden*'s female lead is an athletic stuntwoman who has a romance (and changes bodies) with a rich man; the main character in *Boys Over Flowers* is a schoolgirl who is also an athlete and who strongly influences four wealthy private school boys for the better, while two of them fall in love with her; *You're Beautiful* stars a tomboy who has to disguise herself as a man and has a romance with a rock star; *Coffee Prince* stars a tomboy who has to disguise herself as a man to get a job and has a romance with a coffee company heir; *Princess Hours* has a more feminine lead, but she is played by the same actress, Yoon Eun-hye, who plays the tomboy in *Coffee Prince*; and *Sungkyunkwan Scandal* is a historical drama starring a female lead who has to disguise herself as a man in order to get jobs and an education.

In different ways, whether through female athleticism or a boyish look or disguising themselves as men, the main female characters are all tomboys.[8] Although most female K-drama leads are still long-haired and overtly feminine, these are from the subset who are tomboys. These tomboy dramas (among others, particularly historical dramas) are popular internationally. As one 28-year-old

---

6. Arirang TV is produced by the nonprofit Korea International Broadcasting Foundation, and since 2001 DISH Network Satellite TV has transmitted it in the US.

7. hotshotlover30, "Top 7 K-Dramas Chosen by Overseas Fans," Soompi.com, March 12, 2012, accessed August 31, 2013, http://www.soompi.com/2012/03/12/top-7-kdramas-chosen-by-overseas-fans/.

8. These tomboy productions, in their gender-bending plots, commonly refer to many Korean viewers' familiarity with a range of *manhwa*, *manga*, and fan fiction gender-play traditions. Most of these genres do not overtly promote gay rights nor even necessarily homoeroticism, although certainly some episodes of *Coffee Prince* raise the social acceptance of LGBTQ+ and homoeroticism as issues. In terms of what is permissible—and seen as potentially profitable—in mainstream commercial Korean media, it is worth noting that the year before *Coffee Prince* was broadcast marked the stunning commercial success of the internationally acclaimed and nationally popular movie *The King and the Clown*, released at the end of 2005 and a box office hit in 2006. This Korean period drama depicted the homoerotic relationship between two male clowns (jesters) and a mad king's attraction for one of them (Shin 2013). Although homosexuality is not, outside of the military, against the law in Korea, neither is acceptance the rule. (Military service is required for men in South Korea, and the Military Penal Code prohibits sexual behavior between men.)

Vietnamese American fan observed about such female characters in K-dramas, "I like characters that are strong willed and aggressive but can still maintain their charm."[9] Of note, too, the K-drama tomboy heroines, while sometimes infantilized, are very much absorbed in navigating the adult world of work, romance, and sexuality.

What might the tomboy—particularly this Korean-tomboy pastiche—mean to viewers outside as well as inside Korea? The popularity of the tomboy in this Arirang poll parallels my own American taste in K-dramas, as well as that of the interviewees in the US whom I spoke with or polled. Although the strongest audiences for Korean Wave or Hallyu exports are in East Asia and Southeast Asia, as has been well documented, there are now increasing numbers of fans in Latin America, the Middle East, the US, Europe, and around the world.[10] Since the 2000s, English-subtitled Korean TV dramas have become easily available in the United States on web sites such as Viki, YouTube, and Hulu. (Since the 1980s, they have been available on cable TV stations aimed at a Korean diaspora audience; they have also been seen via DISH Network Satellite TV since 2001). With the circulation of English-subtitled Korean dramas online, an American audience once assumed to be a Korean diasporic one has greatly diversified. In fact, in her research on the fan-subbing site Viki (whose most popular content consists of Korean dramas and Mandarin-language dramas), cultural critic Sun Jung reports that 25 percent of Viki's users are Caucasian North Americans.[11] Jung has also analyzed the Korean entertainment news and gossip site allkpop, founded in 2007 by Paul Han and Johnny Noh. Jung quotes Noh when he estimates that about 40 percent of the site's users are from the US, with the other 60 percent spread out across the globe. Of all the site users, "39 percent are Asian, 39 percent Caucasian, 13 percent Hispanic, 8 percent African American, and 1 percent other."[12]

In my own in-person interviews and email exchanges, conducted mainly in 2012 and 2014, with viewers born in Korea and others born in the US, I spoke with a diverse sampling of fans—who, although from a range of

9. An accountant, email message to author, June 20, 2012.
10. Lorna Fitzsimmons and John A. Lent, eds., *Asian Popular Culture in Transition*, 1st ed.(New York: Routledge, 2013); Youna Kim, ed., *The Korean Wave: Korean Media Go Global* (New York: Routledge, 2013); Kim Do Kyun and Kim Min-sun, eds., *Hallyu: Influence of Korean Popular Culture in Asia and Beyond* (Seoul: Seoul National University Press, 2011); Chua Beng Huat and Koichi Iwabuchi, eds., *East Asian Pop Culture* (Hong Kong: Hong Kong University Press, 2008).
11. Fan-subbed sites are websites where dramas are available, usually for free, to viewers, and where fans volunteer to translate and subtitle them. On Viki at present, the English subtitles of a popular Korean drama are usually produced within 24 hours of the drama's original airing in Korea.
12. Jung Sun, "K-Pop beyond Asia: Performing Trans-Nationality, Trans-Sexuality, and Trans-Textuality," in *Asian Popular Culture in Transition*, ed. Lorna Fitzsimmons and John A. Lent, 1st ed. (New York: Routledge, 2013), 113, 119.

different intersectional identities, were all drawn to the tomboy characters. As
one 25-year-old Anglo-American fan in Bowling Green, Ohio, put it, "I love the
dramas where the main female character is a strong girl with personality and
spunk, compared to the dramas where she is a quiet, gentle girl that things just
happen to. *Coffee Prince* and *Secret Garden* are two of my favorites because the
main characters are strong women who take care of themselves and in the case of
Coffee Prince, her mother and sister as well . . . I like to see the female characters
dominating in a man's role and all the entertaining and interesting issues that
arise related to gender and sexuality."[13] A Vietnamese American fan in Chicago
expressed further appreciation for the cross-dressing romance in *Coffee Prince*:
"I like the fact that a heterosexual male fell in love with another person despite
his/her gender. It shows that he truly loves her for her. It is a sweet love story of
his struggle to overcome his denial in order to be with the person he loves."[14] So
there is fan interest not only in the tomboy persona, but also in what the tomboy
does and in the impact she has on others. What is more, Eun-chan can be read
as someone beyond gender, and the love between Eun-chan and Han-gyeol as
one transcending gender. As viewer Kim A. posted on hulu.com/coffee-prince:
"This was a great drama. While watching the drama Go Eun-chan's gender did
not seem to be an issue. The friendship and love she and Choe Han-gyeol had
seemed to transcend gender. They were no longer man and man or man and
woman, but they were two people who genuinely cared about each other and
gender did not dictate their feelings for each other."[15]

Along with the major continued interest in the trans-Asia market and other
regions, Korean mass culture industries also aim at the large US market.[16] And
although there are frustrations and ambivalences here—some products and
launches have been successful, while others have not—there appears to be no
working formula for success in breaking into this market. There is also something
quite satisfying about the growth in popularity of Korean TV dramas and music
groups in the US. This kindles the fantasy that the US economic penetration
of the South Korean market—begun so violently with the Cold War-instigated
Korean War (1950–1953), followed by US aid in the 1950s to the war-torn and
then-poor country—might now be reversed, even if partially. From the 1950s
through to today, in a nonlinear way, South Korea has gone from being one
of the poorest countries in the world to the eighteenth largest economy in the

---

13. A graduate student in education, email to author, May 2012.
14. Interview with a 24-year-old beautician in Chicago, March 2012.
15. May 24, 2011, accessed July 29, 2012. Based on language and syntax, I estimate that Kim A is
    probably American and/or lives in the US.
16. Choe Sang-hun and Mark Russell, "Bringing K-Pop to the West," *New York Times*, March 4, 2012,
    accessed July 9, 2014, https://www.nytimes.com/2012/03/05/business/global/using-social-media-
    to-bring-korean-pop-music-to-the-west.html.

world and the twelfth in purchasing power. US culture in the form of Hollywood movies still dominates East Asia's mass media, and Korea by itself isn't likely to reverse the flow completely.[17] But K-pop—in its massive popularity since the first decade of the 2000s—has suggested to many East Asians that Hollywood is no longer the only production hub for global mass culture.[18]

From my own perspective as an American, I think of these desires for viewing cultural productions from regions other than one's own as opening or reopening imaginaries of erotic desire in the self that, far from Orientalisms past, are not (necessarily—no doubt these desires are different for different viewers) primarily linked to power structures of desiring the exotic other. Instead, these desires function to spotlight explorations and broadenings of the erotic self. Through translating, mistranslating, and fantasizing, they can even be used to imagine a sensibility for the self outside the oppressive hierarchies of one's own home culture. Here, media critic Henry Jenkins's definition of a "pop cosmopolitanism" is useful: "someone whose embrace of global popular media represents an escape route out of the parochialism of her local community."[19] Emphasizing that "a growing proportion of the popular culture that Americans consume comes from elsewhere, especially Asia," Jenkins expresses hope that "[c]osmopolitans embrace cultural difference, seeking to escape the gravitational pull of their local communities in order to enter a broader sphere of cultural experience."[20] In terms of sexualities and genders, we can wonder if this cultural consumption can fuel imaginings outside of localized hierarchies.

For US-based women of a range of ethnicities, how might such self-definitions and/or longing for the cloak of cosmopolitanism function in the consumption of cultural products like dramas? Here, Mica Nava's work exploring the "emotional and libidinal economics of identification and desire" that are "the foundational elements of twenty-first-century urban cosmopolitanism imaginaries" is helpful.[21] Particularly for women who feel marginalized, a desire to identify with an *other* can transcend Orientalism and move toward an affective sense of belonging to an imaginary cosmopolitan culture that seems somehow fairer—or at least open to new possibilities.

---

17. Chua Beng Huat, *Structure, Audience, and Soft Power in East Asian Pop Culture* (Hong Kong: Hong Kong University Press, 2012), 30.
18. Bernhard Seliger, "The Opening of Popular Cultural Markets of South Korea under Economic Nationalism and International Pressure," in *Asian Popular Culture in Transition*, ed. Lorna Fitzsimmons and John A. Lent (New York: Routledge, 2013), 38–56.
19. Henry Jenkins, "Pop Cosmopolitanism: Mapping Cultural Flows in an Age of Media Convergence," in *Fans, Bloggers, and Gamers: Exploring Participatory Culture*, ed. Henry Jenkins (New York: New York University Press, 2006), 152.
20. Jenkins, "Pop Cosmopolitanism," 154–55.
21. Mica Nava, *Visceral Cosmopolitanism: Gender, Culture and the Normalisation of Difference* (Oxford: Berg, 2007), 14.

In applying Nava's ideas to mass culture transnational circulation—a terrain ripe for viewer projections and misreadings—I want to honor those misreadings, at least those that connect to an empathetic cosmopolitanism. In fact, viewing a fantasy drama produced in a culture that seems in some ways far from one's home culture, and that derives from a place one might never travel to, can lead to all sorts of imaginings. The ones that interest me are those that link to an empathetic cosmopolitanism and a desire to escape an unfair gender hierarchy and/or economic system at home. About these, I would argue that authenticity is beside the point; instead, the affective traces of hope that might be stirred from a misreading of a culture and one of its fantasies might be a more useful focus for feminist critical writing. In addition, we can consider how hope is also rooted in the body and connected to eroticism and effect in viewing. Fruitfully, there is a range of eroticisms that the tomboy dramas can elicit, and a range of viewers to which these appeal.

Coffee Prince, Eroticism, and Feminized Androgyny

What kind of eroticisms are suggested in the coupling of the tomboy and the pretty boy? And how might an identification with these foster a kind of empathetic cosmopolitanism? To further explore the kind of erotic and intimate connections available for different viewers, I toggle back and forth between Korea and the US to consider the responses of female viewers in both countries (and to blur categories—a helpful reminder of the contemporary nonstatic condition of both viewers and media texts—Korean citizens studying in the US) as they follow such a couple in the K-drama *Coffee Prince*. In particular, *Coffee Prince* showcases a romance centered on a tomboy protagonist performing a feminine-inflected androgyny—that is, one that mixes feminine and masculine signifiers but is inflected toward femininity in mass entertainment. In Korea, the seeming innocence and playfulness of Eun-chan's character may influence erotic identification with her heterosexual desiring of Han-gyeol in a context where young women are only supposed to admit to inexperience (or relative inexperience) sexually.[22] This can engender its own kind of misreadings of this sexualized romance. As a 30-year-old Korean woman remembers back to her younger reactions when she first watched *Coffee Prince*: "Han-gyeol grew up lonely in a rich family, so Eun-chan has been [able to] play a role of little brother (later sister) to him."[23]

22. James Turnbull, "Korean Women's Sexual Histories: Still a Slippery Subject," The Grand Narrative, June 30, 2014, accessed June 30, 2014, http://thegrandnarrative.com/2014/06/30/korea-virginity-contraception-condom-use/.
23. Anonymous, email to author, June 10, 2014.

That said, not all identifications with Eun-chan, of course, need be about her eroticism. And yet, these identifications are worth considering in that they may enhance identifications with that aspect of her character too. In a Korean context, Eun-chan can appeal to viewers in terms of her personality and brave pragmatism. The same 30-year-old Korean woman, now studying marketing in graduate school in Chicago, wrote in response to questions I emailed her, "Eun-chan appears as a tomboy in 'real life'! Androgynous, independent. Strong and courageous enough to perform another sex to financially support her home."[24] Another Korean graduate student in Chicago, 26 years old and studying media, who remembers watching and liking *Coffee Prince* when it was first broadcast and how much everyone she knew talked about it, describes Eun-chan as "a type of girl who has to pretend to be a man to make a living. Usually, salaries are higher for men and there are more jobs available for males."[25] These comments point to the gendered wage gap in Korea, as well as gender segregation in occupational areas, both of which underline the stark economics of performing gender and earning a living in Korean society.[26]

Aired in 2007 by the media conglomerate MBC (Munhwa Broadcasting Corporation), *Coffee Prince* marked the first time MBC had employed a woman—Lee Yoon-jung—to direct one of its TV dramas.[27] The screenwriter, Lee Jung-ah (pen name for Lee Sun-mi), is also female and the author of the light novel of the same title on which the TV adaptation was based. (The fact that both the director and the writer are female does not necessarily have to result in a complex and engaging approach to femininity in a trendy drama, but as it happened, in the case of *Coffee Prince*, it did.) In an email interview with the director of *Coffee Prince*, Lee Yoon-jung addressed the connections between Eun-chan's masculine attributes and her role as a breadwinner:

> CP started from the writer Lee Sun-mi's novel of the same title. When I first met with LSM, I asked her to tell me about the novels she had written. She . . . talked about CP. I think she started the story like this: "There is this girl with a male-like appearance whose name is Go Eun-chan. She is her family's breadwinner who supports her mother and younger sister—a girl with a strong sense of responsibility. This kid eats a lot and she is strong which betrays her slim body. One day a coffee shop that hires only good-looking men opens in her neighborhood and . . ." Listening to her up to this point I was already convinced

24. Anonymous, email to author, June 19, 2014.
25. The ratio of female to male full-time workers' wages in Korea has been reported as 61 percent in, for instance, *Business Korea*'s June 10, 2014 article, "Gender Wage Gap: Korea Shows Largest Wage Gap between Male and Female Workers in OECD."
26. "Korean TV Drama," VisitKorea, accessed November 7, 2011, http://visitkorea.or.kr/enu/CU/CU_EN_8_5_1_26.jsp.
27. Lee Yoon-jung, email to author, August 3, 2014.

that this would make a very amusing TV drama. The character Eun-chan just jumped into my heart. That she eats a lot unlike average women (she neglects her appearance, which means femininity is not so important to her), that she has a strong sense of responsibility (she's not a weak girl who seeks protection), and that she is physically strong (which suggests the character's humor)—I believed things like these would make a very new kind of drama.[28]

As for interpretations of the eroticisms represented in the drama, the range was greater for the Korean women I interviewed. They understood the transmedia references (such as to Boys' Love *manga* and *manhwa*, with their own kind of boy-on-boy romping) and potential connections to these in the drama; whereas the Anglo-American interviewees, even those with accumulated cultural capital about Korean popular culture, tended not to. As the 26-year-old Korean-born media artist who identifies as heterosexual continues: "I [first] watched it on TV. I was in [Incheon,] Korea, just graduated from high school . . . I liked it. It expanded the visual spectrum of cool urban males. There was the sarcastic, funny one, the innocent macho, the mysterious ponytail, etc., besides an arrogant, rich, handsome prince." As for Eun-chan's character, there was a strong, visible link to Japanese *shōjo* culture and cuteness aesthetics found both there and in Korea. "She is not perfect, rather clumsy. (You want to protect her.) Not beautiful but cute and loveable, typical manga protagonist character for *shōjo manga*. I was busy projecting myself into Eun-chan's character . . . I am sure every girl did . . . And, yes, I did find it erotic."[29] As many have reported, Eun-chan was so popular when the drama was first broadcast that the character started a trend among college girls in Korea to cut their hair short.

With or without a full understanding of the cultural references, though, the androgynous ambiguity of *Coffee Prince*'s eroticism can be appealing to read in a US context. The quick, tightly scripted rush to coitus in many US mass media productions should be seen as hand-in-hand with a tendency to gender and sexual categorical rigidities as performed in public. Despite academic, subcultural, and activist interest in issues of potential gender mutability—and specifically nonbinary gender identities—in everyday life, public practices of highly legible, unambiguous, binary-categorized displays of gender and sexual identities are common in the US.

The relationship between self-articulating sexuality and public visibility of sexual identity is quite different in the US, even accounting for the existence of many different American subcultures, than it is in Korea. While hetero-marital life is a norm in both places, a self-styling of sexual category displayed in public, punctuated by public displays of affection and sexuality, is more common in

---

28. Lee Yoon-jung, email to author, August 3, 2014.
29. Anonymous, email to author, June 26, 2014.

the US In general, for heterosexuals in Korea and elsewhere in East Asia, neo-Confucianist traditions discourage *publicly* articulating and enacting sexuality. This is a complex cultural subject, but a colloquial way of making my point is to simply say that at this cultural moment, a pedestrian in Chicago is more likely to see heterosexual couples making out on park benches than she would heterosexual couples acting similarly in Seoul (although public same-gender physical affection that denotes friendship—such as hand-holding—is more accepted in Korea). Here, I want to note a degree of discretion in Korean culture about public articulations of sexuality for all sexualities—and to think about how such discretion, as it's represented in Korean mass culture, might play out for viewers outside Korea.

In Korean mass culture, this discretion (some might say repression; I mean to articulate nonjudgmentalism in this regard) in public modes of dress and behavior, and the further translation of these to screen fantasies can have, as fans have commented, an unexpectedly liberating impact on an American viewer. Exaggeratedly, in their K-drama world, Eun-chan and Han-gyeol are especially discreet for the majority of *Coffee Prince*'s episodes due to Han-gyeol's confusion about Eun-chan's gender and his own sexuality, so the erotic tension between them is shown with great subtlety. This can be intriguing for American fans. As fan Dakota Harris writes on Hulu.com/coffee-prince: "Hot, hot, HOT! Wow is it just me or is it warm in here? I love these K dramas for the fact they can create such sexual tensions (read: hot!) without resorting to any nudity. It's a refreshing change from American TV, which just throws people into bed. Here they've created more tension, more heat, more excitement and they've barely even kissed!"[30]

The androgynous East Asian representations of tomboys in mainstream media can feel suggestive of nonnormative gender possibilities and can even, in some cases, seem to offer a temporary freedom from sexual categorization. Lived experience in different East Asian cultures suggests otherwise, particularly in light of government and societal prohibitions. But such foreign misreadings of freedoms can be valuable, too; they can stir empathetic cosmopolitanisms. And Eun-chan's tomboy character is appealing to identify with cross-culturally. As a 19-year-old Anglo-American student who identifies as bisexual put it: "I really enjoyed the depth and complexity of her character. I related to her even though I wasn't experiencing the exact same struggles as her."[31]

In an interview with the writer Lee Sun-mi, published online on the Korean *Newsen* site on August 24, 2007, the novelist and scriptwriter explained her priorities in the *Coffee Prince* script: "Female transvestite [*sic*] is not new; it appears

---

30. Dakota Harris, comment on Hulu.com/coffee-prince, February 4, 2011, accessed July 29, 2012.
31. Anonymous, email to author, June 10, 2014.

even in Shakespeare classics. To be honest, it would be more accurate to say that it is used in this drama as an apparatus to show women's fantasy in the process of portraying Eun-chan's love story."[32] She credits director Lee Yoon-jung with creating the romantic details of the beach scene and other more playful interactions, and with involving the actors in these dynamics as well. "Lee Yoon-jung PD, who is known as the Detail Queen, knows exactly what fantasies women want, from their standpoint. She wants to portray feelings of life in more daring and detailed ways by discussing with the actors on the sets."[33] Lee Yoon-jung specifies that "I could really feel their [EC and HG's] playfulness, curiosity, and excitement—perhaps because it was a love made possible by Eun-chan's artlessness. Eun-chan unlike average [heterosexual] women, doesn't only receive and react to men's emotions, but acknowledges and expresses her own emotions as they are—I think this is what gave their romance a fresh charm."[34]

And Lee Sun-mi adds an additional context: "Actually a love story between a tomboy-masqueraded-as-a-man and a *kkonminam* is familiar material in romance novels and *sunjeong* ["pure-love"] *manhwa* that has been reproduced in many ways. Though this is the first time it has appeared in a TV drama on a public network, the audience seems to have received it well and with interest, as it also engages with the code of homosexuality that has recently emerged as a trend in pop culture."[35]

Coffee Prince was one of the first K-dramas to deal with matters of homosexuality, and this is what it's famous for, even though predictably at the end, Eun-chan's gender as a woman is discovered, and, after further machinations, she and Han-gyeol become a heterosexual couple accepted by both of their families. And it's important for spotlighting changing attitudes, ones that have just begun to change publicly in South Korea, toward homosexuality. However, for me as a viewer, the fascination is *Coffee Prince*'s brilliant and less-discussed exploration of how the drama represents erotic feminine-inflected fantasies of a polymorphous heterosexuality not limited to a coitus-dominated heteronormativity.

Polymorphous Heterosexuality

Here, I want to turn to autoethnography, in terms of my own intense enjoyment of the drama, in the context of the eroticisms and views of the depicted romance by Korean-born and US-born interviewees and fan comments discussed. In doing so, I want to trace another thread from the enactment of Eun-chan's seemingly

---

32. Jo Eun Young, "*Coffee Prince* Writer Interview 1," *Newsen*, August 24, 2007, accessed July 24, 2014.
33. Jo, "Coffee Prince Writer Interview 1."
34. Lee Yoon-jung, email to author, August 3, 2014.
35. Jo, "*Coffee Prince* Writer Interview 1."

innocent or playful interactions with Han-gyeol. As an American, a heterosexual woman, and a baby boomer, who came of age just after the sexual revolution and its emphasis on "doing it," i.e., intercourse, what Eun-chan's adventure represents to me is a fantasy of prioritizing the enjoyment of sexuality throughout the whole body.[36] I would hazard that cross-culturally, the connections between recognizing Eun-chan as a desiring heterosexual woman and appreciating her physicality as a tomboy might play out differently for different viewers in different locales. Yet at the same time, to go in-depth into my individual reading may offer a self-reflexive way to enter the range of responses, so as not to be too reductive about any of them. In other words, here I focus the analysis to consider fine-tuned connections between tomboyism in this Korean context and a fantasy of polymorphous heterosexuality. In doing so, I delineate the idea that individual fan responses—as expressed online, or in interviews, or in autoethnography—can also be the tips of a larger iceberg of complex considerations of the erotic and romantic yearnings. I am a fan of *Coffee Prince*, and I love the polymorphous play in it.

In contemporary language, "polymorphous sexuality"—or, in classic Freudian language, "polymorphous perversity"—can be defined as "the ability to find erotic pleasure out of any part of the body."[37] Various writers have associated polymorphous sexuality with infants or with women, or with adults of any gender who tend this way.[38] It can also be seen as a leveler of sexual difference

---

36. This is not to say that American heterosexual baby boomers (who, in terms of Western sexual history, came of age after the invention of the birth control pill and before the spread of HIV), myself included, only perform heterosexuality through intercourse—or that individuals among us don't enjoy intercourse. I do. But generationally I'd say that there has been and continues to be great emphasis on coitus for baby boomers for those historical reasons just mentioned, with perhaps less public-arena attention to other options. (In contrast, sex toys, for instance, have been more discussed at least in the media by other US cohorts; see, for example, the Generation-X-initiated publication *Bust*—in the early years of *Bust*, the affectionate joke was that they never published an issue without at least one article on vibrators. Commercially, sex toys are, of course, available for all cohorts, but each cohort has cultural differences in what is articulated, what habits are formed, and how these might evolve over time. I find it fascinating to note the cohort differences even while granting individual differences and evolutions.) Specific, comprehensive demographic statistics for US viewers of Korean dramas broken down by age as well as gender do not, as far as I've been able to determine, yet exist. Anecdotally, I'd say a similar age spread exists for American female viewers as is commonly assumed for Korean female viewers. And this supposition is supported by a press release from Korean YA Entertainment posted on Newswire on August 8, 2013 (https://www.newswire.co.kr/newsRead.php?no=175617), saying that in the US, Korean dramas are popular with baby boomers as well as younger viewers. And individual websites do show some demographic breakdowns of users—for example, on dramafever.com, aimed at a US and also an international audience, over 75 percent of the audience is female. See Xiaochang Li, "Dramafever.com Full Interview (part 2/5)," Canarytrap.net, April 8, 2009.
37. Dino Franco Felluga, "Polymorphous Perversity," *Introductory Guide to Critical Theory*, accessed December 9, 2011, http://www.cla.purdue.edu/English/theory/psychoanalysis/definitions/polymorphous.html.
38. Sigmund Freud, *Three Essays on the History of Sexuality*, trans. James Strachey (1905; repr., New York: Basic Books, 1962).

and/or associated somehow with homosexuality.[39] Yoon Eun-hye's performance of Eun-chan in *Coffee Prince*, for me, embodies a polymorphous sexuality, and one that can be particularly alluring for those who self-define as heterosexual women.

Eun-chan romps with her whole body at moments throughout *Coffee Prince*. Either alongside or usually engaged with Han-gyeol's body, her erotic play involves many parts of the body and many senses. And I mean *play* here in the most powerful sense of the word—as in British psychoanalyst D. W. Winnicott's elaborate theorizing of play as the transitional space between the self and the outside world; the space of childhood games and of childhood and adult creativity; the space of in-betweenness, delight, and danger.[40] There is a creative intimacy available to people who engage together in such a space—not an innocent intimacy, because, as Winnicott would agree, this space has a way of taking the lid off behaviors and emotions. And in Eun-chan's case—and accessible to viewers who choose to identify with her—the transitional space of play is a very corporeal, very libidinal space.

In her email reply to me, director Lee Yoon-jung also reveals her deft incorporation of play into the production process: "I made many things during rehearsals. When we rehearsed the playful scenes that you mentioned, such as the fountain scene and the basketball scene, the three of us—Gong Yu who played Han-gyeol, Eun Hye who played Eun-chan, and I—played enough in the scenes. It wasn't like shooting scenes by reading learned lines, but we simply *played* within the scenes."[41] Early on, in episode two of the 17-episode run, we see Eun-chan playing with the wind and the speed of the car as she gleefully stands and waves and dances in Han-gyeol's convertible as it speeds across a bridge in Seoul. Combining masculine and feminine, childhood and adult motions, she unleashes physical joy. And it's so much fun to watch.

In episode seven, as things heat up between the main characters, there's a great scene where Eun-chan and Han-gyeol play together in an outdoor fountain. They are drunk. They're roughhousing in a bromance kind of way, since at this point Han-gyeol still believes Eun-chan is a man. But we viewers have never believed this, so we are open to enjoying the eroticism that she as a woman experiences. In fact, *Coffee Prince*'s heterosexual ending, where everyone, including Han-gyeol, realizes Eun-chan is a woman, has been discussed in negative

39. Vatican, "Letter to the Bishops of the Catholic Church on the Collaboration of Men and Women in the Church and in the World," July 31, 2004, accessed October 10, 2013, http://www.vatican.va/roman_curia/congregations/cfaith/documents/rc_con_cfaith_doc_20040731_collaboration_en.html.
40. Donald Woods Winnicott, *Playing and Reality* (1971; repr., New York: Routledge, 2005).
41. Lee, email to author.

terms as defeating the homosexuality-acceptance messages of the drama.[42] That may or may not hold water: I don't think it defeats the earlier message, although it does make the whole drama perhaps unnecessarily safe—and this argument also depends on whether the drama is being read in a Korean or US context. In any case, what is interesting to me is how Eun-chan can be read throughout the drama, particularly by female (and likely majority heterosexual) viewers who choose to identify with her. Importantly, Eun-chan can be read as performing an eroticism that is not dependent on procreation, marriage, or traditionally feminine appropriateness, and above all is not dependent on the goal of coital penetration.

This is important because Eun-chan's eroticism is one that is rarely represented in US-derived globally circulating mass media; and because it has a potential to affirm nonnormative heterosexualities, a range of heterosexualities so many of us who self-define as women are living but which are not often articulated publicly in many Hollywood-template productions. After all, there's so much more to heterosexuality than coitus, and the roles available to exploring and enjoying that so-much-more can also connect to nonnormative roles outside the sexual sphere as well. One option for a nonnormative heterosexuality is one that is not goal-oriented (although it can include that coitus goal if desired); one that involves the whole body and many senses in its range of pleasures, one that is polymorphous. If desired, it can include coitus, but it needn't be dominated by that focus. In that nocturnal scene from episode seven when the two are playing together in a fountain, we see Eun-chan enjoying alcohol, wetness, splashing, and Han-gyeol's body in goalless erotic play.

Such play carries into the domestic space of Han-gyeol's apartment; here he carries and twirls Eun-chan around, and their laughing is also libidinal. And it is included via playful foreplay in his later heterosexual coitus fantasy (his bedroom one in episode fifteen) and their coitus actuality (her seduction of him in episode sixteen). This continuum of polymorphous sexuality into, but not at all limited to, heterosexual coitus is also appealing for a US viewer (in this case, me) from a culture where sexuality is too often squeezed—one might even say "marketed" in the hyper-capitalist US context—into stern categories. Outside subcultures in the US where the word "queer" is popular—as is respect for those who elect to transit or transcend traditional gender categories—women in daily life are commonly considered either heterosexual or lesbian and, if hetero, are then categorized either as "normal" or nonnormative. Those considered nonnormative might even be labeled in a categorical way; for instance, identified or

---

42. "K-dramas and 'Pseudo-Homosexuality': What Gives?" Seoulbeats, September 3, 2012, accessed October 10, 2013, https://seoulbeats.com/2012/09/k-dramas-and-pseudo-homosexuality-what-gives/.

pictured according to specific kinds of kinkiness, like the image of a dominatrix with a whip.

In short, public displays of sexuality in the US tend to be strictly divided into categories. These categories are commonly divided into subcategories. And this categorical organization can be restrictive. In contrast, there can be so much more to sexuality (and sexuality-related identity), so much potential in the wonderful blurring of play and categories, including for those who self-define as heterosexual. In other words, it need not be a matter of simply being categorical or discarding categories. Movement among categories, or those within a given category—say, heterosexuals—can be erotic. And a polymorphous pleasure in its nonrestrictive quality tends to suggest such movement.

In *Coffee Prince*, the viewer always sees Eun-chan as feminine to a degree. In fact, the viewer is led to think about her particular kind of hetero-femininity very often. The viewer also sees Eun-chan as, well, not a lesbian (despite the scene of her binding her breasts early on!), but as still "different" from traditional hetero-femininity. Eun-chan's "new" femininity is overdetermined, and we engaged female viewers can even anguish with her over her functionally androgynous femininity and whether she'll ever be able to deploy it in a heterosexual romance. At the same time, she's seen as heterosexual simply because her desires are explicitly heterosexual (early in the series, when she's still working in food delivery, for instance, we see her getting turned on by a glimpse of Han-gyeol's nearly naked legs). So, she's a feminine-inflected, androgynous, and heterosexual tomboy, and thus, for a US heterosexual female viewer, is subject to heavy categorization and subcategorization; to use the imaginary of Eun-chan is to walk away from these rigidly restrictive categories and right into the arms of joyous, creative, polymorphous heterosexuality.

Appealingly, even apart from her erotic play with Han-gyeol, Eun-chan is marked as a character who does not let corporeal repression stand in the way of her pleasures or her anger. Throughout the drama, we see an astounding number of images of Eun-chan eating as much as she feels like, not only in a masculine way, but in a way considered excessive even for most men. She loves to eat, and she eats a lot. And she regularly becomes irritated or even angry, as evidenced by blowing at her bangs in annoyance, or yelling, or strong-arming some guy into apologizing to her. The corporeal comfort with androgyny, Lee Yoon-jung explains, was intrinsic to the actress's process. Interestingly, Yoon Eun-hye performed at times in her brother's clothes:

> [A]lso that she was wearing her brother's clothes gave her freedom. Though she did practice to walk like a man and make a male voice in the beginning of the filming, she eventually settled down comfortably to be like "a woman who looks like a boyish man"—just like Eun-chan. I think Gong Yu, too, saw Eun Hye

playing Eun-chan not as an actress but as a cute, playful *dongsaeng* ["younger sibling" or a younger close friend]. And this seemed to further strengthen Eun-hye.[43]

At the end, when she comes back from Italy (where she had gone to study to further her barista specialist training), Eun-chan is shown enjoying her own particular negotiation with some feminine traditions—perming her hair, adding a touch of makeup—while retaining her androgyny. In fact, one American viewer remembers liking *Coffee Prince* in part because Eun-chan didn't have "a huge makeover to become a girly girl in the end. She became more feminine [looking], but not extremely so."[44] So there's room in this drama, it seems, for negotiation with different types of femininity.

It's no accident that Eun-chan achieves this, her finally comfortable negotiation, when she leaves her home culture and spends some time for educational and career reasons in a truly foreign one halfway around the world. In Korea, this leaving is associated with the importance of continuing education beyond high school, and other culturally specific connotations concerning some Koreans who go abroad to do so.[45] But a US-born viewer may or may not know those associations—and this is where a critical generosity about misreading is helpful. As a US viewer, what I noticed is that Eun-chan is showing a striking amount of independence and a partial resistance *right* when a Cinderella fairy tale ending appears to be in her grasp. Mainly, Eun-chan's going to Italy (without Han-gyeol; he waits for her in Korea) is portrayed as exciting, even if it's challenging.

The fact that Eun-chan enjoys Italy and learns there, even as she misses people in Korea, also underlines a kind of permission for the American viewer in turn to learn from this *Coffee Prince* fantasy about Korea. Of course, I did not learn a lot about lived experience in Korea from *Coffee Prince*; I learned instead about a Korean-based fantasy cooked up by program director Lee Yoon-jung, writer Lee Jung-ah, the production company MBC, and the actors. But as a fan, I could learn by misreading that fantasy as if it were really (although I know better) a slice of Korean life. Perhaps as a foreigner, it's easier to add a dollop of suspended disbelief when viewing the show to dream that somewhere in Seoul, lives like these are being led. As Nava has argued, for women in Western societies, there can be useful liberatory functions through such dreams and related hopes that encourage feeling cosmopolitan in one's own home—in one's own life (and not necessarily with a plane ticket in hand). As it happens, with or without that suspended disbelief, the *Coffee Prince* fantasy is a wonderfully androgynous

---

43. Lee, email to author.
44. A 25-year-old graduate student in education, email to author, May 2012.
45. Youna Kim, *Transnational Migration, Media and Identity of Asian Women: Diasporic Daughters* (New York: Routledge, 2011).

one that can open all sorts of doors for the pop-cosmopolitan viewer's own fantasies and hopes.

Here, I've articulated my own fan fantasy about a feminine-accented androgyny mixed with a joyously polymorphous heterosexuality. Thus, watching the tomboy as she falls in love, lust, and intimacy activates fantasies for me about my own eroticism and emotions—as well as framing these in broad, sensual ways in relation to public displays and private romps. It encourages me to imagine or remember less categorized ways than are common in everyday circulation in the US to enact my sexuality and my femininity—and my own polymorphous pleasures. So, *Coffee Prince* and other related entertainments can function for me to undergird my cosmopolitanism "at home"—itself a practice of hope and of release from rigid categorizations of gender and sexuality. This can be true for those who inhabit seemingly majoritarian sexual categories, as well as those who identify with minoritarian ones. So, for some American women like me, who "look" heterosexual (that is, are read as hetero) and in fact are heterosexual, a release from rigid legibility that in turn suggests rigid behavioral scripts is desired. In many ways, it doesn't matter to me if these mainstream Korean drama-inspired fantasies are misreadings of daily life in Seoul; the dramas themselves are, after all, fiction. In the case of *Coffee Prince*, what I choose to matter is a reading of the drama as representing and celebrating a feminine-inflected, polymorphous, desiring heterosexuality. In the context of transnational viewing of Korean mass culture, there is a particular kind of sanctioning in its mainstream production and popular narrative qualities. *Coffee Prince* is entertaining and romantic. In suggesting imaginaries of plural heterosexualities, it is also so much more.

Bibliography

Blank, Hanne. *Straight: The Surprisingly Short History of Heterosexuality*. Boston: Beacon Press, 2012.

Choe, Sang-hun, and Mark Russell. "Bringing K-Pop to the West." *The New York Times*, March 4, 2012. Accessed July 9, 2014. https://www.nytimes.com/2012/03/05/business/global/using-social-media-to-bring-korean-pop-music-to-the-west.html.

Chua, Beng Huat. *Structure, Audience, and Soft Power in East Asian Pop Culture*. Hong Kong: Hong Kong University Press, 2012.

Chua, Beng Huat, and Koichi Iwabuchi, eds. *East Asian Pop Culture*. Hong Kong: Hong Kong University Press, 2008.

Fitzsimmons, Lorna, and John A. Lent, eds. *Asian Popular Culture in Transition*. New York: Routledge, 2013.

Freud, Sigmund. *Three Essays on the History of Sexuality*. Translated by James Strachey. New York: Basic Books, 1962. First published in 1905.

Jenkins, Henry. "Pop Cosmopolitanism: Mapping Cultural Flows in an Age of Media Convergence." In *Fans, Bloggers, and Gamers: Exploring Participatory Culture*, edited by Henry Jenkins, 152–72. New York: New York University Press, 2006.

Jo, Eun Young. "*Coffee Prince* Writer Interview 1." *Newsen*, August 24, 2007. Accessed July 24, 2014.

Jung, Sun. "K-Pop beyond Asia: Performing Trans-Nationality, Trans-Sexuality, and Trans-Textuality." In *Asian Popular Culture in Transition*, edited by Lorna Fitzsimmons and John A. Lent, 109–29. New York: Routledge, 2013.

Kim, Do-kyun, and Min-sun Kim, eds. *Hallyu: Influence of Korean Popular Culture in Asia and Beyond*. Seoul: Seoul National University Press, 2011.

Kim, Youna, ed. *The Korean Wave: Korean Media Go Global*. New York: Routledge, 2013.

Kim, Youna. *Transnational Migration, Media and Identity of Asian Women: Diasporic Daughters*. New York: Routledge, 2011.

Nava, Mica. *Visceral Cosmopolitanism: Gender, Culture and the Normalisation of Difference*. Oxford: Berg, 2007.

Seliger, Bernhard. "The Opening of Popular Cultural Markets of South Korea under Economic Nationalism and International Pressure." In *Asian Popular Culture in Transition*, edited by Lorna Fitzsimmons and John A. Lent, 38–56. New York: Routledge, 2013.

Shih, Shu-mei. "Comparison as Relation." In *Comparison: Theories, Approaches, Uses*, edited by Rita Felski and Susan Stanford Friedman, 69–98. Baltimore: The Johns Hopkins University Press, 2013.

Thussu, Daya Kishan. "Mapping Global Media Flow and Contra-Flow." In *Media on the Move: Global Flow and Contra-Flow*, edited by Daya Kishan Thussu, 10–29. London: Routledge, 2007.

Turnbull, James. "Korean Women's Sexual Histories: Still a Slippery Subject." The Grand Narrative, June 30, 2014. Accessed June 30, 2014. http://thegrandnarrative. com/2014/06/30/korea-virginity-contraception-condom-use/.

Winnicott, Donald Woods. *Playing and Reality*. London and New York: Routledge, 2005. First published in 1971.

3
Miss Kim

God of the Workplace

SooJin Lee

This chapter examines the significance of the South Korean television series *God of the Workplace* (직장의 신, aired on KBS2 from April 1 to May 21, 2013, for sixteen episodes) in terms of its representation of women in the postindustrial workforce. Through textual and aesthetic analyses of the drama, and by linking them with statistics and theories of labor and feminism, I will demonstrate the drama's importance as a popular culture construct that critically raised issues with the interrelated problems of gender, class, and workplace power hierarchy in contemporary Korea. My focus here is on deconstructing the main character, Miss Kim (*Miseukim*), and exploring how the show exposes the absurdities of gender and class problems in the Korean workforce structure and culture after the financial crisis of 2008. I will especially highlight how the character performs what I call "cyborg-androgyny." Miss Kim is a thirtysomething single woman who has decided to live an unstable "temp worker" life in the postindustrial workforce, where everyone wants a job that can guarantee social and financial security. During the prolonged economic recession in the 2010s, a fantasy character that is impossible to find in reality, Miss Kim reflected the desires of workforce participants, particularly young female office workers in their twenties and thirties, and exposed the problems of the contemporary Korean workplace that cause such desires.

It should first be noted that *God of the Workplace* is a remake of the Japanese television series *The Pride of the Temp* (ハケンの品格, aired on NTV from January 10 to March 14, 2007, for ten episodes), produced from the original story written by Fujiwara Masahiko. Although heavily based on the Japanese original, *God of the Workplace* is remarkably different in many details that apparently were necessary and considered modifications to reflect and satirize the realities of Korea's workplace, so these differences will be noted and examined in this analysis. It also should be noted that the literal translation of the Korean remake's title is "God of the Workplace," although a gendered translation, *Queen of the Office*, has been more widely used. In respect to the makers' intended twist for the title, I use the literal translation in this chapter. The fact that they decided to call the female protagonist *shin* ("god") instead of *yeoshin* ("goddess"), especially when the word *yeoshin* was in vogue at the time (overused in the popular media to refer to female celebrities with outstanding appearances and talents), signifies their conscious play on gender issues.

Temp Worker Superhero

Every episode of *God of the Workplace* opens with the below voiceover, which is narrated in the same fashion as a superhero movie.

> Sixteen years after the IMF [crisis in 1997], the Republic of Korea is now a country of 8 million temporary workers. Koreans' wish is no longer reunification [of the two Koreas], but permanent employment. While everyone wants a permanent job, there is a person who has chosen to live the life of contract employment. Namely, the nation's very first voluntary temp, Miss Kim. There is no payless work or overtime work in her dictionary. She excludes cumbersome personal relationships, and after completing a three-month contract, travels out of country. It is unknown why she has named herself Miss Kim and why she has entered the world of contract employment.[1]

While South Korea achieved rapid industrial and economic growth since the 1960s, during a period of time called the Miracle on the Han River, the era of spectacular progress and prosperity came to an end with the 1997 economic crisis. At the end of 1997, faced with a currency crisis, South Korea accepted a bailout package from the International Monetary Fund (IMF) on terms that stipulated labor market reforms and opening the economy to foreign investment and ownership, among other requirements. Downsizing became a major social issue, and that's why this economic crisis is called the "IMF Crisis" in Korea. The government officials "encouraged private firms to implement bold restructuring programs, including massive layoffs," resulting in an increase in the unemployment rate from 2.1 percent in October 1997 to almost 9 percent in early 1999.[2] Before then, South Korean jobs typically meant "lifelong arrangements"

---

1. The translation from Korean to English is by this author.
2. Kim Dong-One, Bae Johngseok, and Lee Changwon, "Globalization and Labor Rights: The Case of Korea," *Asia Pacific Business Review* 6, no. 3–4 (2010): 133–53, https://doi.org/10.1080/13602 380012331288502. These scholars in 2010 found that since the 1997 Asian economic crisis, the unemployment rate in Korea was more unstable and much higher than that in Japan. They write that "the lifetime employment principle has been more frequently violated in Korea than in Japan. Despite the recent economic difficulties, Japanese employers have been more conservative than Korean counterparts in conducting massive layoffs by utilizing various substitutes."

that could not be terminated by employers.[3] But following the IMF Crisis, the number of permanent workers significantly decreased as firms sought to rely more on part-time or temporary workers, for whom the employers did not need to pay social insurance.

In *God of the Workplace*, the protagonist, Miss Kim, is indeed portrayed as a superhero in the awfully competitive workforce. She is one of the most in-demand workers in the corporate job market for very ironic reasons: she does not have degrees from prestigious schools, but holds over a hundred certificates and licenses in all sorts of skills, many of which are manual labor skills such as truck driving, aviation maintenance, skydiving, real estate, maternity nursing, hairdressing, and cooking. Unlike most Koreans, who regard permanent and full-time jobs as more secure and desirable than temporary or contract-based jobs, Miss Kim pursues only contract-based temp jobs, taking mostly low-ranking and seemingly trivial but needful and essential roles.

The story of *God of the Workplace* begins as Miss Kim returns to Korea from her vacation in Spain to begin a new contract as an office worker in a food corporation's marketing support team—the main setting of the show. She sits at the end desk to do mostly manual services, such as typing, photocopying, and serving coffee—generally pink-collar tasks expected of so-called "office ladies." However, no matter how small or insignificant Miss Kim's tasks may be, the first episode makes it clear that her efficiency is well known and she is in high demand by employers across Korea. They compete to hire her as a permanent full-timer, but she has her own strict rule that she works for three months at a time without ever renewing a contract. In declining an offer for a permanent position, Miss Kim states that she does not want to become "a slave bound to a company" (episode six).

The protagonist character is thus set up as the "super-*gap* temp," a catchphrase the production team created and used to market the show. Conventionally, in a legal contract in Korea, the word *gap* (甲) is used to introduce the first party, and the word *eul* (乙) to introduce the second party. But in the early 2000s, the phrase "*gap-eul* relationship" began to be used widely in journalism to refer to and critique the unbalanced relationships that often occur between employers (as *gap*) and employees (as *eul*) in the already hierarchical society of Korea.[4] And *gap* and *eul* quickly became commonplace words used to refer to, respectively, those with and those without (relative) power in any kind of relationship or situation. A related neologism in Korea is *gapjil* (made by combining *gap* and *jil*, a

---

3. Steven Borowiec, "IMF's Bitter Medicine Brought Growth, But Also Inequality—Analysis," *Eurasia Review*, February 25, 2018, https://www.eurasiareview.com/25022018-imfs-bitter-medicine-brought-growth-but-also-inequality-analysis.
4. The occurrences of the phrase "*gap-eul* relationship" abruptly increase in number on Korea's popular portal site, Naver, in 2003.

suffix referring negatively to certain actions), which describes abusive conduct or arrogant attitudes of people in positions of power over others.[5] The emergence of *gap* and *eul* in twenty-first-century Korean language and culture reflects an increasingly widespread belief that society is unbalanced and unfair in terms of privilege. In society's common conceptions, temp employees belong in the lowest stratum in a corporate workplace, and they are considered more *eul* than permanent employees.

Such a class distinction between temp and permanent employees is frequently addressed in *God of the Workplace*. In particular, in episode eight's wedding scene, the bride's father refuses to walk down the aisle after finding out the groom is a temp (and the situation is saved by Miss Kim, who walks the bride down the aisle in place of the father). In the fictional world of *God of the Workplace*, the protagonist is a temp but also a *gap*. The character and slogan "super-*gap* temp" is itself a pungent contradiction that immediately speaks to the audience's awareness of the nexus of societal problems related to work, income, status, values of work, and class within the workplace.

The main storyline of *God of the Workplace* revolves around the mystery of why Miss Kim insists on being a contract worker when she could have a permanent position in any company, and everyone else wants a permanent job. Towards the end of the series, it is revealed that she used to be a permanent employee of a bank and experienced the bank's bankruptcy process as part of the global financial crisis of 2007–2008. Having learned that the corporate world is unreliable and that permanent jobs are just as unstable as temp jobs in the increasingly neoliberal workplace, she decided to never again devote her life to work and established herself as a freelance temp worker capable of all odd jobs. Believing in the persistence of such precarity, she decided to change and reinvent herself. The "super-*gap* temp" character is thus built upon a deeply pessimistic view of work and the neoliberal corporate system. For Miss Kim, work is no longer a means of feeling accomplished or achieving social status. When she says, "I work for nobody, I work for pay and lunchtime," she reveals that she doesn't enjoy her work at all (episode two). She works to make a living and that's all.

The pessimism in Miss Kim's character formation is grounded in and reflects the socioeconomic realities of Korea. Throughout the series, the two financial crises that affected contemporary South Korea—the 1997 Asian financial crisis and the global financial crisis of 2007–2008—are constantly referenced; the former crisis in each episode's opening line (quoted above) and the latter as part

---

5. *Gapjil* gained international attention with the "nut rage incident" in 2014 when a Korean Air heiress, dissatisfied with the way she was served nuts on the plane before takeoff, ordered the aircraft to return to the gate. For example, see BBC News, "S Korea Employers Could Face Jail under Harassment Law," July 16, 2019, https://www.bbc.com/news/business-49000046.

of the protagonist's traumatic experience that led her to reinvent herself. *God of the Workplace*'s opening sequence states that back in 2013, when the show was airing, the number of nonregular workers in Korea was 8.6 million, which is 15 percent of the population.[6]

In her early or mid-thirties in 2013, the Miss Kim character represents the so-called "880,000-won generation" most severely affected by the changed employment market and the changing socioeconomic situation in Korea. Even before the global financial crisis of 2007–2008 began to be felt in Korea, in their much-discussed co-authored book of 2007, economist Wu Seok-hun and activist Park Gwon-il famously coined the term "880,000-won generation," referring to the country's first generation of unemployed workers among the highly educated populace;[7] 880,000 won was the estimated average monthly salary that a twentysomething nonpermanent worker made at the time. As the book pointed out, compared to their parents' generation, the current twentysomethings on average had higher education and higher hopes for higher social stability, but they had less chance of getting stable lifelong jobs and made lower income. Commenting on the issue, anthropologist JoHan Hyejeong asserted that the 880,000-won generation is an "anxiety generation" that witnessed the IMF crisis at an early age and grew up sensing a bleak future ahead.[8] In the age of despair, Miss Kim is portrayed as a hero—not because she fights against injustice, but because she has remade herself into a new model worker fit for the neoliberal employment market. Yet she is not played by the system; she uses it to make a living because she needs to, because she has to, for her own survival.

Redefining What It Means to Work Like a Machine

Regarding the protagonist's tasks and position in the workplace, there is a remarkable difference between the Japanese original and the Korean remake. In the Japanese *The Pride of the Temp*, the protagonist, Oomae Haruko, is an office worker and does not do manual labor outside of the office. But Miss Kim in the Korean remake is often portrayed doing various kinds of physical and miscellaneous labor—for example, cleaning the building, delivering heavy equipment,

---

6. This is a much larger demographic than what the original Japanese series *Pride of the Temp* identifies as the number of nonregular workers in Japan in 2007: 3 million, which was 2.5 percent of the population.

7. Wu Seok-hun and Park Gwon-il, *88manwon Sedae: Jeolmang-ui Sidae-e Sseu-neun Himang-ui Gyeonjehak* [888,000-won generation: Writing the economics of hope in the age of despair]. Seoul: Rediang, 2007.

8. JoHan Hyejeong, "IMF Mokgyeokhan Bulhaenghan Cheongnyeon-deul '88manwon Sedae' Wuriga Kkyeoanja" [Let us embrace the "880,000-won generation," the unfortunate youth who witnessed the IMF], *The Kyunghyang Shinmun*, August 28, 2007, https://m.khan.co.kr/view.html?art_id=200708281818411#c2b.

and repairing all kinds of machines. Not only does she do paperwork, but she also does every odd job that usual white-collar office workers don't do, and that is what makes her a top, in-demand temp worker: she is efficient in all things. A particularly crucial layer in the character construction is that Miss Kim does not distinguish between manual and intellectual labor, and she accepts and carries out with dignity the miscellaneous work tasks and duties she has agreed upon in the contract. During work hours, she works nonstop, never taking a break. She spends every minute of her contracted work hours bringing benefits to her employer, finding time to mop the floors and remove staples from used papers so they can be recycled.

Miss Kim works like a machine—efficient, fast, exact, nonemotional, and focused on work while at work. According to the "Miss Kim Operation Manual," which she drew up based on the Labor Standards Act to give to her employers, she works eight hours a day and charges extra pay for any extra work. She begins work exactly at 9:00 a.m., goes out for lunch exactly at 12:00 p.m., resumes work exactly at 1:00 p.m., and leaves work exactly at 6:00 p.m. These are ironclad rules, so she works nonstop during work hours without taking a break and stomps out of a meeting or a conversation when the clock points to 12:00 p.m. or 6:00 p.m. to take a break, often shocking her colleagues and bosses. She never works after hours, during weekends, or on holidays, and she never works on tasks not listed in the contracts. With coworkers, she does not socialize or chitchat, but speaks only on work-related matters.

Miss Kim's own rules, which she obeys, are difficult things to adhere to, especially in a Korean workplace and particularly in Korean corporate culture, where cooperation and collective identity are highly regarded and can in fact influence your work reputation. For example, in Korean offices, the boss should typically be the first one to leave for the day; everyone else must wait, even if the scheduled work hours have long passed—a custom based on the Confucian value of social hierarchy. An open discussion about this issue on Reddit includes comments like, "I can tell most of my colleagues are just wasting time at their desk trying to look busy," and "Companies should all have at least one foreigner to fulfill the role of [leaving on time]."[9] Ingrained in the ethos of Confucianism, the dominant ideology of the Joseon dynasty, such collectivist and hierarchal corporate culture remains influential in contemporary Korea. Within the Confucian mindset, at work as well as at school, it is a virtue to obey elders/seniors and contribute to social harmony. And in the collectivist culture, participation in group outings is deemed essential.

---

9. "Do You Leave the Office before Your Boss?," Reddit discussion, October 18, 2017, accessed October 2019, https://www.reddit.com/r/korea/comments/7749yx/do_you_leave_the_office_before_your_boss/.

Hoesik, the after-hours get-together that normally begins with dinner and ends with a karaoke session involving heavy drinking, is one such group outing, presumably aimed at strengthening relationships among coworkers and facilitating their cooperation for work performance. Active participation in *hoesik* is a tacit requirement of the workplace in Korea. As the male lead of *God of the Workplace*, Jang Gyu-jik (a pun on "regular employment" in Korean) affirms that *hoesik* is considered "a continuation of work" (episode two). "You, as a member of society, don't know such a basic thing?" he scoffs at Miss Kim. We can see that Miss Kim smartly ridicules the culture of *hoesik* by strictly adhering to her contract terms and perfectly excelling in partaking in *hoesik*. In the original Japanese *The Pride of the Temp*, Oomae Haruko continues to refuse, and does not participate in after-hours group outings. But in the Korean remake, and in this particular episode (obviously designed to mock the Korean culture of *hoesik*), Miss Kim at first refuses, calling *hoesik* "a suicidal terror that wastes one's health and time through forced drinking, flattery, and unnecessary fellowship." But she eventually attends it, on the condition that she receives extra pay for "working overtime." During the *hoesik* (episode four), she works and parties hard and tops everyone in flattering her boss with her exceptional skills in grilling barbecue, making tasty *poktanju* (soju mixed with beer), and clichéd karaoke dancing and tambourine-playing that is obviously choreographed to help cheer on fifty-something corporate bosses. The next day, her boss receives an invoice from Miss Kim charging 20,000 won for grilling barbecue and 40,000 won for playing the tambourine. The Korean culture of *hoesik* has since been frequently represented in Korean dramas, but none have critiqued it with such delightful black comedy as Miss Kim.

As such, by strictly following and practicing what is stipulated in her employment contracts, which form the most basic rights for workers, Miss Kim satirizes what are deemed irrational and old-fashioned "customs" deeply rooted in conventional Korean workplace culture. As examined above, the IMF crisis brought rapid changes to the economic structure and employment market of Korea. But the country's workplace culture could not keep up with the pace of the economic structural changes, and the general view that permanent lifelong jobs are stable and better than part-time employment or freelancing remains to this day. Broadcasted in 2013 on national television, Miss Kim was a much-needed black comedy character that critically yet creatively pointed out the outdated absurdities and conflicts between the new economic structure and the old workplace culture.

Problematizing Gender Problems

God of the Workplace not only addresses the problems of Korea's employment market and workplace culture, but also raises questions about gender issues linked with them. During the IMF crisis' massive workforce restructuring in Korea, women were the first to be laid off. In 2013, the year the series aired, it was reported that the country's female employment rate remained "about the same as two decades ago" at just 55 percent, lower than the OECD average of 65 percent and lower than Japan's 62 percent and China's 74 percent.[10] Perceived as a risky investment, as companies fear the cost of maternity and/or early resignation, women and seniors comprise the majority of temp and contract workers. The workplace gender disparity is represented in *God of the Workplace*. Of the twelve workers in the fictional marketing sales department, six are women, all single, in their mid- to late twenties (except Miss Kim, whose age remains unknown but can be inferred to be over 30), and five of them are temps. Socially separated from the rest, these female temps socialize among themselves (excluding Miss Kim, who has no interest in socializing at work), and their dialogues revolve around ongoing concerns with finances and renewing their contracts.

The early 2010s was when the gender inequality of contemporary Korea was unwontedly brought to the table of discussions by a range of outlets, including local and international media. It would be useful to cite some of them to give a glimpse of the historical context in which *God of the Workplace* was produced. In 2010, the National Statistical Office of Korea reported that that year's number of female university graduates (271,773) surpassed that of male graduates (268,223) for the first time in ten years; however, of the new university graduates who got hired by Korea's ten major companies, only 18.5 percent were female.[11] In 2017, *The Economist*'s glass-ceiling index showed that among the OECD countries, South Korea is ranked the "worst" place for working women, with the highest gender wage gap (36.7 percent), the lowest percentage of women in managerial positions (10.5 percent) and on company boards (2.4 percent), and the lowest net childcare costs (0 percent).[12] Compared to the size of the labor market, Korea has developed relatively low social infrastructure and public policies that support women, most notably with childcare. Therefore, while Korea has the lowest birth rate among OECD countries, more and more women give up their

---

10. Song Jung-a, "South Korean Women Face Glass Ceiling in Workforce," *Financial Times*, June 12, 2013, https://www.ft.com/content/50242166-ce60-11e2-8313-00144feab7de.

11. Yim Young-sin and Bae Mi-jeong, "Chui-eop Seongchabyeol Yeodaesaengdeul-ui Nunmul" [Employment gender disparity: Female students' tears], *Maeil Kyungjae*, October 31, 2011, http://news.naver.com/main/ranking/read.nhn?mid=etc&sid1=111&rankingType=popular_week&oid=009&aid=0002564318&date=201111021&type=1&rankingSectionId=102&rankingSeq=10.

12. *The Economist*, "The Economist Releases 2017 Glass-Ceiling Index," August 3, 2017.

jobs after having their first child, or refuse to marry or have kids to avoid the accompanying burdens.[13] Most importantly, it should be remembered that workforce participation is not even an option for many people for whom work means earning a wage rather than pursuing a career.

Episode eight of *God of the Workplace*, which focuses on the issue of pregnancy, received a high rating and several emotional responses, hinting that many viewers identified with the episode. It revolves around Miss Kim's temp coworker Park Bong-hui (a pun on "scarce income"), who hides her pregnancy, worrying that it might have a negative impact on the renewal of her contract. When the secret is revealed by accident, she speaks out in tears: "My contract expires next month and they won't re-contract me if they know I'm pregnant! All my earnings are going into paying debts, so I have to continue to work to make a living for the baby!" After this episode was aired, sympathetic comments flooded social media, including, "It was so realistic I thought it were happening in my office."[14] In Korea, a 90-day maternity leave is protected by law, but a survey in 2013 showed that this was not being observed in reality, and that many pregnant women have experienced discrimination within the workplace and faced pressure to resign of their own accord.[15] When maternity leave is so poorly protected, pregnant temporary workers are in a far more insecure position than regular workers. In fact, data indicates that in 2012, temporary workers took only 37.4 percent of their guaranteed maternity leave, while regular workers took 63.4 percent of theirs, which is still a low rate.[16]

By comparison, however, Miss Kim belongs to the increasing demographic of single, financially independent thirtysomething women. With this in mind, one of the character's crucial peculiarities is that she performs a range of femininities and masculinities, playing with gendered stereotypes related to work and labor. The protagonist's diverse and protean nature is explicitly demonstrated within a few minutes of the drama's first episode. Miss Kim first appears bullfighting in

13. Bang Jun-ho, "South Korean Women Forced to Choose: Give Up Either Your Job or Having Children," *The Hankyoreh*, June 2, 2017, http://english.hani.co.kr/arti/english_edition/e_business/797341.html.

14. Cited in a newspaper article post that is no longer available on the website of *Seoul Shinmun*, http://boom.seoul.co.kr/news/newsView.php?id=20130424050020.

15. The survey by the Korean Women Workers Association is reported in Kim Su-hui, "Moseongboho an hamyeonseo Chulsanryul eojji nopina" [How can the fertility rate increase without protecting maternity?], *Yeoseong Shinmun*, October 10, 2013, http://www.womennews.co.kr/news/61863#.UmXwaiTfZ7w.

16. Lee Jeong-a, "Jinanhae Jikjang yeoseong yusanbiyul jeoneopjubu-boda 1.4-bae nopa" [Last year, the rate of miscarriage among working women was 1.4 times higher than that of full-time housewives], *The Herald Business*, October 8, 2013, http://news.heraldcorp.com/view.php?ud=20131008000429&md=20131011004131_AT. The research was conducted by the office of In Jae-geun, a Democratic Party member of the National Assembly.

Ronda, Spain, hinting at her courageousness and adventurous lifestyle.[17] Next, she is shown flying first class to Seoul wearing a Bohemian-style dress and a wild, glamorous coiffure. She arrives home at a modest, cozy house located on top of a Latin-themed bar, where she occasionally goes on stage to perform a sultry salsa dance. (In fact, the actress Kim Hye-soo is billed as a "glamour star" in Korean media because of her voluptuous body and fashionista image).

In stark contrast, at work, Miss Kim is dressed to work. She has her own uniform for "office work" and she wears it every day to work: a plain black pant-suit with her hair neatly pulled back into a bun. "This is enough for a battlefield," she affirms in episode five. It is not difficult to notice that Miss Kim's "uniform" is actually a common form of corporate workwear worldwide. Miss Kim wears the plainest and humblest version of it, to eliminate her personality or individuality in the corporate workplace. Speaking of gender, what is most interesting about her "uniform" is the mesh hair bun net decorated with feminine ribbons. The ribboned mesh net is the most common type of hair bun net available in Korea and is often decorated with cheap beads. Known as a nurse's or flight attendant's "hair net" in Korea, it is worn by women with long hair in jobs that require uni-forms. In fact, in Korea, you cannot find a nurse or a flight attendant who lets their hair down while dressed in their work uniforms. The fact that Korea makes only ribboned hair nets for those who need hair nets indicates a very ambiguous view of gender roles: women in corporate uniforms are required to hide their hair because of their gender and sexual associations, but those hair nets used to hide the long hair are decorated with highly feminine ribbons or beads. The hair accessory is rendered especially awkward with Miss Kim, whose verbal and facial expressions are exaggeratedly unfeminine.

Performance of Cyborg-Androgyny

As observed above, Miss Kim thoroughly minimizes her gender and sexual iden-tity to emphasize her efficiency and productivity as an office worker. This does not mean that the character performs masculinities, but that she is portrayed as consciously and strategically minimizing femininities in her everyday perfor-mances and verbal and facial expressions, to an extent that she talks and acts like a robot or computer. Miss Kim's machine-like performance of identity can be connected to Donna Haraway's postfeminist notion of the cyborg. In her seminal essay "A Cyborg Manifesto," published in 1985, Haraway used the metaphor of the cyborg in conceptualizing a postgender identity.[18] Through the metaphor

---

17. In the Japanese original, the protagonist makes her first appearance socializing with Romani people around a bonfire in Spain's Andalusia region.
18. See Donna Haraway, *Simians, Cyborgs, and Women: The Reinvention of Nature* (New York: Routledge, 1991).

of the cyborg, she was able to argue for a completely new identity beyond the conventional terms of identity politics established during second-wave feminism and other civil rights movements of the 1960s and 1970s. Haraway made an argument that is theoretically perfect, important, and attractive, but while using the cyborg as a metaphor, she gave no concrete examples of how her "A Cyborg Manifesto" can be brought into practice or realization. And like many other theories, it offered no pragmatic solution that can help change our reality. It is for the same reason that Judith Butler's theory of gender as performativity has been very influential but has also been received as impractical and inaccessible.[19] But when a fictional character on television strategically acts out an ironic mix of masculinities and femininities in an explicitly artificial manner, the novelty can have a strong impact and the aftereffect is immeasurable.

Miss Kim's performance of what I would call *cyborg-androgyny* renders some of the gendered expectations and stereotypes commonly held in the Korean workplace absurd. Most obviously, her in-office duties as specified in the Miss Kim Operation Manual include repairing office supplies such as photocopiers and computers (a duty usually assigned to male workers) and serving coffee and collecting garbage (a duty usually assigned to female workers), thus transcending the traditionally gender-specific or gender-divided work categories. She is shown at times cleaning restrooms like a cleaning maid, but also carrying on her shoulder eighteen-liter bottles for water purifiers like a burly, muscular man. With an assortment of skills from operating industrial machinery to nursing, playing sports and dancing, Miss Kim's background defies the conventional gendering of occupational roles.

Miss Kim's verbal and facial expressions point to subtler, more severe gendered expectations for women at work. Hers are non-expressions rather than expressions. She never smiles and she speaks like a robot, uttering her words in a staccato manner and without intonation. When her male coworker presses her to smile—"Hey, can't you smile?"—in episode two, she gives him an awkward, almost comical, feigned smile. Her obstinate stiffness is a great challenge to the Korean workplace culture, where suavity and submissive amiability are unspoken requirements of sorts for job applicants, especially young women interviewing for temporary or assistant positions. As *The Wall Street Journal*'s "Korea Realtime" blog reported in August 2013, "the need to smile all day at work" in Korea was such a huge stress that in the early 2010s, there was "a sudden rise in demand for the so-called smile surgery this year among men and women in their 20s and 30s, most of whom are concerned about facing criticism at work because

---

19. See Judith Butler, *Gender Trouble: Feminism and the Subversion of Identity* (New York: Routledge, 1990). Rosemarie Tong and Tina Fernandes Botts, *Feminist Thought: A More Comprehensive Introduction* (New York and London: Routledge, 2018).

of their expressionless miens."[20] Originally developed as an antiaging face-lifting method, the smile surgery lifts up the lips' edges at the cost of about $2,000 to give it a "natural" smile even when the person is not smiling, preventing them from appearing as though they were frowning with drooping lip edges.

Regarding the intersecting issues of age, class, and gender in Korean workplace culture, there's something significant about Miss Kim's name. In Korean public culture, the appellation "Miss" is associated with young women serving at *dabang* (modern Korean teahouses). The English word is known to have come into use in Korea in the 1950s, amid the postwar influx of Western influences, to describe publicly sociable modern women—a new phenomenon at the time. As women's workforce participation grew in the following decades, the appellation was extended to the other, male-dominated workplaces, including company offices, where the few female employees were expected to serve coffee to their male bosses and coworkers and take care of all the photocopying and similar menial tasks within the office. Currently, the appellation has been ousted in Korean workplaces due to public awareness of its negative connotations and the increase of female participation in the workforce. But media representations of women with the appellation (e.g., Miss Kim, Miss Lee, Miss Park) have long been mostly derogatory, portraying them as lowly, uneducated working women dressed in garish miniskirts and cheap jewelry while loudly chewing gum. Miss Kim's name is thus intentionally regressive and contradictory. Miss Kim is a novel character who volunteers to make and serve coffee, only because she wants to drink tasty coffee and she knows she can make the best coffee in the office. The name immediately signals the character's disinterest in social recognition and connotes the crooked history of the particular appellation in Korea.

Lastly, it should be noted that *God of the Workplace* is a rare example of a Korean drama where the female lead's nemesis is a man, Jang Gyu-jik, who later develops a romantic interest in Miss Kim. The drama ends suggesting their future together. Jang Gyu-jik is no Prince Charming, just like Miss Kim is no Cinderella. At the climax of the series' final episode, she comes to save him when he is captured in an explosive container factory. As such, Miss Kim is a personification of seeming incongruities and contradictions, aimed at unraveling and exposing irrationalities in contemporary Korean society and workplace culture.

Concluding Remarks

Since the drama's airing in 2013, the rise of concepts such as "YOLO" (you live only once) and "work-life balance" (*worabel*) in society and popular culture

---

20. Jeyup S. Kwaak, "Surgeons Defend 'Smile Surgery,'" *Wall Street Journal*, August 27, 2013, http://blogs.wsj.com/korearealtime/2013/08/27/surgeons-defend-smile-surgery/?mod=e2fb.

indicate a changed attitude toward work among millennials. But recent statistics have revealed that in 2019, even before the COVID-19 pandemic struck, South Korea still had a comparatively high rate of women leaving the workforce in their thirties to raise children and dedicate themselves to their families,[21] which demonstrates the ongoing relevance of the issues effectively raised by *God of the Workplace*. In this chapter, my textual and aesthetic reading of the drama has entailed discussions of Korea's economic history, workforce situation, workplace culture, hierarchical society, gender inequality, and problems of class, which turn out to all be intertwined. By interweaving my interpretation with statistics and theories of labor and gender, my exploration above has focused on deconstructing the protagonist character as it exposes problems of gender, class, and workplace power hierarchy in Korea during the prolonged economic recession. Miss Kim is a fantasy character, impossible to find in reality. But we need more unique, vital, and complicated superheroines like her that offer pleasure, reflection, and critical consideration as well as creative exploration. It will enrich our culture and inspire change.

Bibliography

Bang, Jun-ho. "South Korean Women Forced to Choose: Give Up Either Your Job or Having Children." *The Hankyoreh*, June 2, 2017. http://english.hani.co.kr/arti/english_edition/e_business/797341.html.

BBC News. "S Korea Employers Could Face Jail under Harassment Law." July 16, 2019. https://www.bbc.com/news/business-49000046.

Borowiec, Steven. "IMF's Bitter Medicine Brought Growth, But Also Inequality— Analysis." *Eurasia Review*, February 25, 2018. https://www.eurasiareview.com/25022018-imfs-bitter-medicine-brought-growth-but-also-inequality-analysis.

Butler, Judith. *Gender Trouble: Feminism and the Subversion of Identity*. New York: Routledge, 1990.

Haraway, Donna. *Simians, Cyborgs, and Women: The Reinvention of Nature*. New York: Routledge, 1991.

JoHan, Hyejeong. "IMF Mokgyeokhan Bulhaenghan Cheongnyeon-deul '88manwon Sedae' Wuriga Kkyeoanja" [Let us embrace the "880,000-won generation," the unfortunate youth who witnessed the IMF]. *The Kyunghyang Shinmun*, August 28, 2007. https://m.khan.co.kr/view.html?art_id=200708281818411#c2b.

Kim, Dong-One, Bae Johngseok, and Lee Changwon. "Globalization and Labor Rights: The Case of Korea." *Asia Pacific Business Review* 6, no. 3-4 (2010): 133-53. https://doi.org/10.1080/13602380012331288502.

---

21. "Female Employment Rate in Korea Is M-shaped," *The Dong-A Ilbo*, March 19, 2021. The reporter's name is not indicated. The statistics research is by the Korea Economic Research Institute. https://www.donga.com/en/article/all/20210319/2511793/1.

Kim, Su-hui. "Moseongboho an hamyeonseo Chulsanryul eojji nopina" [How can the fertility rate increase without protecting maternity?]. *Yeoseong Shinmun*, October 10, 2013. http://www.womennews.co.kr/news/61863#.UmXwaiTfZ7w.

Kwaak, Jeyup S. "Surgeons Defend 'Smile Surgery.'" *Wall Street Journal*, August 27, 2013. http://blogs.wsj.com/korearealtime/2013/08/27/surgeons-defend-smile-surgery/?mod=e2fb.

Lee, Jeong-a. "Jinanhae Jikjang yeoseong yusanbiyul jeoneopjubu-boda 1.4-bae nopa" [Last year, the rate of miscarriage among working women was 1.4 times higher than that of full-time housewives]. *Herald Business*, October 8, 2013. http://news.heraldcorp.com/view.php?ud=20131008000429&md=20131011004131_AT.

Song, Jung-a. "South Korean Women Face Glass Ceiling in Workforce." *Financial Times*, June 12, 2013. https://www.ft.com/content/50242166-ce60-11e2-8313-00144feab7de.

Tong, Rosemarie, and Tina Fernandes Botts. *Feminist Thought: A More Comprehensive Introduction*. New York and London: Routledge, 2018.

The Economist. "The Economist Releases 2017 Glass-Ceiling Index." August 3, 2017.

Wu, Seok-hun, and Park Gwon-il. *88manwon Sedae: Jeolmang-ui Sidae-e Sseu-neun Himang-ui Gyeonjehak* [888,000-won generation: Writing the economics of hope in the age of despair]. Seoul: Rediang, 2007.

Yim, Young-sin, and Bae Mi-jeong. "Chui-eop Seongchabyeol Yeodaesaengdeul-ui Nunmul" [Employment gender disparity: Female students' tears]. *Maeil Kyungjae*, October 31, 2011. http://news.naver.com/main/ranking/read.nhn?mid=etc&sid1=111&rankingType=popular_week&oid=009&aid=0002564318&date=20111021&type=1&rankingSectionId=102&rankingSeq=10.

Part II

More than Girl Groups

4
Ella Gross and Child Social Media Stars

Rising to Fame through K-Pop Idol Trainee Systems, Mixed-Raceness, and Tabloid Cycle Controversies

Jin Lee and Crystal Abidin

Introduction

The K-pop industry has been gaining global momentum in recent years, in part due to the growing prominence of idols and artists between the Korean and American markets, with members of the Korean diaspora in the United States returning to South Korea to launch their music careers.[1] The cross-cultural flows and ties between South Korea and the US has lent the K-pop industry a more cosmopolitan image. Successful K-pop groups are also signing with American labels to assist with their expansion into the Global North.[2] Against this backdrop, K-pop artists of mixed-race descent are often heralded among the stars of the industry for their cultural flexibility and exotic appearance. In this vein, and considering the very young age at which tweens are being enrolled as trainees in the K-pop industry, this chapter turns its attention to Korean-American Ella Gross (b. 2008), who is among the most famous child stars in the K-pop industry with almost 4 million Instagram followers at the time of writing.[3]

Born and based in Los Angeles, California, Gross was initially a child model who starred in print ads in the US from age two. She swiftly rose to international fame at age eight, especially because of her mixed-race features, when her pictures became widely circulated on the internet. At age ten, she signed on with The Black Label, a subsidiary of South Korean media giant YG Entertainment.

---

1. For example, singer-songwriter Eric Nam from Atlanta, Georgia, rapper Jessi from New York, BOBBY of iKON from Fairfax, Virginia, and soloist Chungha from Dallas, Texas.
2. BTS with Universal Music Group and BLACKPINK with Interscope Records.
3. Child Influencers like Ella Gross are increasing and receiving great attention on social media. For example, four-year-old identical twins Taytum and Oakley Fisher have 3 million followers, and Bentley Hammington, a three-year-old son of Australian media personality Sam Hammington (based in Korea), has 1.3 million followers (both as of April 1, 2021).

She was widely touted in K-pop forums and online communities to be specially groomed for the next generation of K-pop idols. Shortly after she became famous, mainly in K-pop online communities, Gross's name and face made the headlines and front covers of tabloids in June 2019 when a Baskin-Robbins TV and YouTube commercial featuring her encountered backlash for sexualizing her through apparent visual innuendos. Despite being just eleven years old at that time, Gross is shown wearing adult-like makeup in the ad as the camera zooms in on her lips and her mouth licking a spoon of ice cream. Audiences accused the ad of sexualizing a minor, reinforcing a beauty norm even for children, and borrowing visual innuendos from pornography. The scandal went viral to the extent that many people were posting harsh comments to Gross's official Instagram account and her mother's personal Instagram account.

By tracing the short history of Ella Gross's fame from a child Instagram star to the next K-pop star and an internet celebrity enmeshed in a scandal, this research builds on the legacy of studies on the K-pop industry and on child Influencers in the age of social media. We consider Gross's milestones and strategic practices to be making headway in the rising intercultural partnerships and collaborations between the K-pop industry in America and Korea and focus on the teething issues that have emerged thus far.

The Industrial and Racial Context of K-Pop

In this section, we provide some context on the different environments and settings that contributed to Gross's rapid rise to stardom on social media and presence within K-pop. We focus especially on the K-pop industry's idol trainee system, celebrity culture, and perceptions of mixed-raceness in Korea.

The K-pop industry's idol trainee system

It is widely known that K-pop idols are manufactured by the media industry, in the same manner that stars are created as cultural objects by star systems.[4] But a unique characteristic of the star manufacturing system of the K-pop industry is the idol trainee system, which has drawn some attention from academia.[5] The

---

4. Chris Rojek, *Celebrity* (London: Reaktion Books, 2001).
5. Joanna Elfving-Hwang, "K-Pop Idols, Artificial Beauty and Affective Fan Relationships in South Korea," in *Routledge Handbook of Celebrity Studies*, ed. Anthony Elliott (London and New York: Routledge, 2018), 190–201; Jennifer M. Kang, "Rediscovering the Idols: K-Pop Idols Behind the Mask," *Celebrity Studies* 8, no. 1 (2017): 136–41, http://dx.doi.org/10.1080/19392397.2016.127 2859; Ho-young Kim and Tae-Jin Yoon, "How the Idol System in Korean Pop Culture Works: An Explorative Study on the Dual Structure of Production/Consumption of Idol Culture," *Broadcasting and Communication* 13, no. 4 (2012): 45–82; Lee Jong-im, *Aidol Yeonseupsaeng-ui Ttamgwa Nunmul* [Idol trainees' sweat and tears], Seoul: The Seoul Institute, 2018.

media have also paid attention to it, at times with a critical perspective[6] and at other times in the form of celebratory TV shows.[7] What is noticeable here is how the K-pop system has evolved in light of social media cultures, including influencer ecologies.

The idol-trainee system in Korea has been flourishing since the late 1990s, run by entertainment agencies, especially by the three top firms: SM Entertainment, YG Entertainment, and JYP Entertainment.[8] The age range to enter into contracts with such entertainment agencies as trainees has been lowered as the years pass to now include preteens to late teens,[9] but the basic system remains the same: a person is recruited or auditions to be a trainee of the entertainment agencies, and undergoes years of training and grooming to eventually become an idol star. After contracting with an agency, the trainee lives in a dorm with other trainees and experiences a wide range of intensive training programmes, including singing, acting, dancing, and beauty training that includes fitness and cosmetic surgery.[10] Trainees' lives are monitored and strictly regulated (e.g., no dating, no meeting with friends during the training session), and their media personas are scripted and manufactured as characters by agencies, until they debut as stars.[11]

When a trainee is considered ready for the market, they are often grouped with other trainees and debuted as an idol group. However, big entertainment agencies tend to unofficially debut their trainees as public figures through modelling engagements and features in other established K-pop stars' songs, so that the public can become familiar with them before they officially debut as an idol group. Such prominent trainees are known as "celebrity trainees." When a celebrity trainee who already has a significant number of fans is debuted as a member

---

6. "[Nonjaeng] Aidol yukseong siseutem idaero joeunga?" [Is the idol training system good as it is?], *The Hankyoreh*, June 17, 2011, http://www.hani.co.kr/arti/opinion/argument/483303.html; Kim Jee-hye, "[The Dark Side of K-Pop] They Said I Could Debut Right Away, But . . . Left with 600 Million Won of Debt, Depression, and a Bunch of Lawsuits after 8 Years as a Trainee," *The Kyunghyang Shinmun*, October 6, 2020, http://english.khan.co.kr/khan_art_view.html?artid=2 02010061751247&code=710100; Lee Byeongjun, "Aidolgwa yeonseupsaeng-i sseureojinda . . . Gyeyakseo sseugo ilhaneun nodongja gwolli isseo" [Idols and trainees are collapsing . . . they also have a laborer's right to work under a contract], *JoongAng Ilbo*, January 26, 2020, https://www.joongang.co.kr/article/23690218#home.
7. For example, see the documentary *9 Muses of Star Empire* (dir. Lee Hark-joon, 2012) and reality TV shows like *Produce 101* (Mnet, 2016–2017).
8. Kang, "Rediscovering the Idols," 136–37.
9. Lee Eunjeong, "Yeonseupsaeng Jedowa Bulgongjeong Gyeyagi Choraehaneun Aidol Ingwonmunje" [Idol human rights problems caused by the trainee system and unfair contracts], *Hallyu Now*, March 28, 2019, http://kofice.or.kr/b20industry/b20_industry_03_view.asp?seq=7991.
10. Elfving-Hwang, "K-Pop Idols, Artificial Beauty," 193; Lee, *Tears and Sweat of Idol Trainees*, 71–80.
11. Elfving-Hwang, "K-Pop Idols, Artificial Beauty," 194; Lee, *Tears and Sweat of Idol Trainees*, 71–80; Lee Jong-im, "Munhwanodongjaroseo-ui aidol/yeonseupsaeng-ege piryohan geot" [What idols/trainees need as cultural laborers], *Cultural Media*, no. 98 (2019): 232–46.

of an idol group, it is highly likely for their group to instantly garner more popularity and achieve market success through fan networks.

The big entertainment agencies—like SM, YG, and JYP—have long advertised their trainees by filming their lives for lifestyle vlogs and documentaries, entering them in reality-style singing auditions and competitions,[12] featuring them alongside other prominent idol groups in music videos, and even showcasing them on social media via networks of other idol groups and prominent K-pop celebrities.[13] Agencies have also been known to seek out social media viral stars and internet celebrities and recruit them as trainees to consolidate their social media fandoms and capitalize on their organic virality. It is not uncommon for many of these celebrity trainees to be of mixed-race descent.

Celebrity culture and mixed-race perceptions in Korea

Mixed-raceness is a characteristic that is often found in the media industry in Korea, especially in the K-pop industry. Historically, mixed-race people in South Korea often experience social prejudice for being "dirty" and "impure," as evidenced in the "tragic mulatto" discourse that has been dominant in the country since the Korean War.[14] After the Korean War, the South Korean government institutionally offered prostitution to the US military as a "diplomatic gesture," and the prostitutes in the US camptowns (un)officially served as "personal ambassadors."[15] In turn, the population of mixed-race people increased, mostly found around the camptowns of the US military and born to American soldiers and Korean prostitutes. As such, Korean prostitutes in the camptown areas were also denigrated as sexual wantons who did not abide by Confucianist values because they had lost their virginity and were thus perceived as "agents of sexual and national betrayals."[16] Mixed-race bodies in Korea were thus stigmatized as a symbol of sexual promiscuity and national betrayal. But the hierarchy among mixed-race bodies was also established in line with the US race system. Prostitutes who slept with white men were perceived to be in the upper class, as opposed to those who had associated with Black men.[17] Similarly, mixed-race

---

12. For example, *Sixteen* (Mnet, 2015) and *Produce 101* (Mnet, 2016–2017).
13. Maria Scott, "10+ K-pop Idols Who Made Pre-Debut Appearances on Other Artists' Music Videos," *Kpop Starz*, June 11, 2022, https://www.kpopstarz.com/articles/307076/20220611/10-kpop-idols-pre-debut-appearances-music-videos.htm.
14. Oh Mi-Young, "A Study on the Stigma of Mixed-Race: Factors Affecting Stigma on Mixed-Race and Stigma Effect," *Korean Journal of Social Welfare* 61, no. 2 (May 2009): 215–46.
15. Mary Lee, "Mixed Race Peoples in the Korean National Imaginary and Family," *Korean Studies* 32 (2008): 66, https://doi.org/10.1353/ks.0.0010.
16. Lee, "Mixed Race Peoples in the Korean National Imaginary and Family," 67.
17. Katherine H. S. Moon, *Sex Among Allies: Military Prostitution in U.S.-Korea Relations* (New York: Columbia University Press, 1997), 72.

bodies were also hierarchically categorized with reference to their skin color, although they were still marked as "impure" and "dirty"[18] for polluting the "pure bloodline" of the Korean ethnicity.[19]

For instance, several middle-aged celebrities, such as Black Korean singers Insooni and Park Il-joon (alias Park Ilchun), were publicly condemned as *kkamdungi* [깜둥이, the n-word in Korean] for their "exotic" looks and for having been born to Korean mothers and African American fathers.[20]

Of late, mixed-race representation in the Korean celebrity industry is increasingly framed in a celebratory manner, albeit applying mostly to white-Korean mixed-race individuals, or mixed-race Koreans with "white" phenotypic features, such as blue eyes, blonde hair, fair skin color, and a Caucasian skull shape. This is in part due to the global expansion of the Korean economy and culture from the mid-2000s, propelled by a handful of prolific cases of "successful" white Korean celebrities. Prominent examples include Korean Irish American actor Daniel Henney, who is prominent in both Hollywood and the Korean media industry, and Korean Dutch Canadian singer and model Jeon Somi, who starred in several Korean reality TV singing competitions and game shows.

Media scholar Ahn Ji-Hyun explains that this pivot to embracing images of white Korean mixed-race in the media industry is a mark of globalization in celebrity culture.[21] For instance, Daniel Henney's white Korean mixed-raceness is often referred to as an "Amerasian" look, and is strategically employed in celebrity culture to demonstrate white desirability to symbolize that Korea has well embraced globalization in accordance with white standards—albeit only nominally and through a focus on visuality.[22] The cultural meaning of whiteness in Korea is frequently found in the different vocabularies and perspectives of mixed-race persons in the country. For example, white Korean people and their families are usually referred to as "global families," connoting globalization and metropolitanism, whereas Korean Southeast Asian or Korean African people and their families are usually called "multicultural families," implying multiculturalism as an object to tolerate and embrace.[23]

18. Lee, "Mixed Race Peoples in the Korean National Imaginary and Family," 69.
19. Oh, "A Study on the Stigma of Mixed-Race," 219–21.
20. Lee Huiyong, "Insuni-ui sangcheoga amullyeomyeon" [To heal Insooni's wounds], *Yonhap News*, August 17, 2016, https://www.yna.co.kr/view/AKR20160812164800371.
21. Ahn Ji-Hyun, *Mixed-Race Politics and Neoliberal Multiculturalism in South Korean Media* (Cham: Palgrave Macmillan, 2018).
22. Ahn, *Mixed-Race Politics*, 103–28; Lee Hee-Eun, You Kyung-Han, and Ahn Ji-Hyun, "Strategic Multiculturalism and Racialism in Television Advertising," *Korean Journal of Communication and Information*, no. 39 (August 2007): 473–505.
23. Ahn, *Mixed-Race Politics*, 154; Claire Lee, "Defining Racism in Korea," *Korean Herald*, September 4, 2014, http://www.koreaherald.com/view.php?ud=20140904001088.

In this manner, mixed-race bodies are differently mobilized along the lines of racial hierarchies, where white-mixed bodies are favorably racialized and frequently employed in media scenes through the lens of "Asianized (Western) cosmopolitanism."[24] This plays a key role in the global expansion of K-pop. Using the markers of *globalness* while maintaining some *Koreanness* is crucial to demonstrate the twin aspects of globalized and cosmopolitan Korean culture.[25] Thus, elements of Anglo-centric Western culture are added to K-pop as marketing strategies of cultural hybridity, which includes the use of English words in K-pop lyrics,[26] including "foreign" members from other countries (e.g., Japan, China, Taiwan),[27] and showing "exotic" but "metropolitan" faces through mixed-race K-pop artists.[28] The recent increase and high endorsement of white Korean idols in the industry demonstrates the symbolic value and function of whiteness in the current global culture and economy.

Methodology

The case study of Ella Gross emerges at a time where there is a confluence of the rising power of the influencer industry, a growing presence of mixed-race Koreans in K-pop, and an increasingly lowered age range for trainees in the industry. As such, Gross's rapid rise in fame warrants an in-depth study for pioneering phenomena and practices that will grow to become more mainstream in the years to come. To investigate the structures and norms of the K-pop industry, the influencer industry, and social media that have assisted in her rapid celebrification, we take up press archival research and social media sentiment scoping in our study.

Press archival research

Press archival research in the English and Korean languages informs our understanding of the corporate and popular discourse around Gross. We conducted archival research on the press coverage of Ella Gross by Google searching the

24. Ahn, *Mixed-Race Politics*, 109.
25. Park Gil-Sung, "Manufacturing Creativity: Production, Performance, and Dissemination of K-Pop," *Korea Journal* 53, no. 4 (2013): 14–33, http://doi.org/10.25024/kj.2013.53.4.14.
26. Jin Dal Yong and Ryoo Woongjae, "Critical Interpretation of Hybrid K-Pop: The Global-Local Paradigm of English Mixing in Lyrics," *Popular Music and Society* 37, no. 2 (2014): 113–31, https://doi.org/10.1080/03007766.2012.731721.
27. Ahn Ji-Hyun and Tien-wen Lin, "The Politics of Apology: The 'Tzuyu Scandal' and Transnational Dynamics of K-pop," *International Communication Gazette* 81, no. 2 (2019): 158–75, https://doi.org/10.1177/1748048518802947.
28. Mun Se-eun, "Inhyeonggateun mimoro paenege 'eolgul gonggyeok' haneun 'honhyeolgye' aidol 5in" [5 mixed-race idols who attack fans with their Barbie-like faces], *Insight*, April 14, 2019, https://www.insight.co.kr/news/219861.

keywords *Ella Gross* and 엘라그로스 (Ella Gross in Korean) in October 2020. We chose Google instead of local platform Naver to search both English and Korean articles, given the increasing global attention to K-pop scenes. Excluding duplicates and spam, we narrowed the results down to a corpus of the top seventy news articles offered by Google, ranked by the algorithm through a combination of recency and relevance. This corpus included sixteen English-language and fifty-four Korean-language articles. Each article was read by one of the (bilingual Korean and English) coauthors, and the images included were also studied. Key snippets of data were translated into English as we searched for themes and patterns in the media discourse around Ella Gross.

In our analysis, we paid attention to significant happenings and milestones that shaped the discourse in different directions, such as Gross being signed to YG Entertainment in June 2018 and her Baskin-Robbins advertising controversy in June 2019. Additionally, we also focused on how Ella Gross's social media activities became newsworthy and how such coverage subsequently links her back to idol group BLACKPINK via proximate celebrification.[29]

Sentiment scoping on social media

Targeted searching of keywords on social media platforms popularly used in South Korea and internationally, especially within K-pop fandom, informs our understanding of some of the vernacular sentiment toward Ella Gross. As in the previous section, we searched for the keywords *Ella Gross* and 엘라그로스 (Ella Gross in Korean) on different platforms in October 2020. The Korean-language corpus focused on Twitter and theqoo (theqoo.net). Twitter was selected on the basis of being the most active site for the consumption and discussion of K-pop fandoms in Korea, in the form of sharing news articles and expressing opinions via the platform's function of tweeting, retweeting, quote tweeting, and the like.[30] theqoo was selected for being the biggest and most popular online community for K-pop fandom locally in South Korea. This is especially so among women, where discourses on K-pop stars and the entertainment industry are circulated and reproduced through the consumption of rumors and tabloidesque news

29. Crystal Abidin, "Introduction to Panel: Fame and Microcelebrity on the Web," AoIR 16th Annual Meetings Proceeding, https://spir.aoir.org/ojs/index.php/spir/article/view/8596/6845.
30. Kim Su-a, "Yeongyeolhaengdong (Connective Action)? Aidol Paendeomui Teuwiteo Haesitaegeu Undong-ui Myeong-am" [Connective action? Critical review of Twitter hashtag activism and Korean idol fandom], *Munhwawa Sahoe* [Korean Journal of Cultural Sociology] no. 25 (December 2017): 297–336, http://dx.doi.org/10.17328/kjcs.2017.25..007; Ko Hyeri and Yang Eunkyung, "Korean Boy Group's Misogyny and Division between Female Fandom," *Journal of the Korea Contents Association* 17, no. 8 (August 2017): 506–19, https://doi.org/10.5392/JKCA.2017.17.08.506.

coverage.[31] For example, theqoo members post news articles and other social media postings about K-pop stars; the site is often treated as another "resource" for news items by tabloids.

The English-language corpus focused on Reddit and three popular K-pop tabloid websites: Allkpop (allkpop.com), Koreaboo (koreaboo.com), and Soompi (soompi.com). Reddit was selected as it has been identified in social media discourse as a key forum for international and English-speaking K-pop fans to congregate. It has also been identified as one of the key platforms that K-pop fans use to generate, market, and consume content within their fandoms.[32] We focus especially on the subreddit r/BlackPink (a community for fans of BLACKPINK), where Reddit discussions on Ella Gross tend to accumulate based on a top-level search on the forum. Although the most popular subreddit dedicated to K-pop is r/kpop, at the time of writing there were no relevant articles. Allkpop, Koreaboo, and Soompi were selected as they were often represented in social media discourse—through memes, viral posts, and forum discussions—as the trio of K-pop tabloid forums that offer the most up-to-date news in the industry.

However, it should be noted that while the veracity of the content is often dubious, as the sites are believed to offer fan opinions more than factual news updates, they are still critical sites of study, as they tend to reflect the opinions of the general public. Of the three, Soompi is perceived to be the most reliable. It has facilitated international K-pop fandom identity-making for over a decade.[33] Allkpop has been noted as an early player in facilitating K-pop fandom discourse.[34] Excluding duplicates and spam, our keyword searches accumulated twenty-two posts (and 637 comments) from theqoo, forty-two tweets from Twitter, fourteen posts (and ninety-eight comments) from r/BlackPink, seven articles (and 205 comments) from Allkpop, five articles from Koreaboo (and no comments, as that feature is not enabled on the platform), and one article from Soompi (and one comment). These searches were last performed on October 20, 2020.

Tabloids—also called celebrity journalism—often facilitate online discussions and contribute to community-building on online platforms. By sharing tabloid coverage of celebrities with online communities, online users gossip

31. Kim Hyojeong, "theqoo, daehanminguk daepyo 'yeocho' keomyuniti" [theqoo, the most popular 'female-dominant' community in Korea], *Weekly Chosun*, October 28, 2019, http://weekly.chosun.com/client/news/viw.asp?ctcd=C01&nNewsNumb=002580100002.
32. Everest Christine Xu, "Marketing Plan for a Kpop Fan Artist" (honors thesis, Arizona State University, 2018), https://repository.asu.edu/items/48489.
33. Stephanie Parker, "Soompi and the 'Honorary Asian': Shifting Identities in the Digital Age," *Stanford Journal of Asian American Studies* II (October 2009), https://www.academia.edu/800498/Soompi_and_the_Honorary_Asian_Shifting_Identities_in_the_Digital_Age.
34. Cassie Kwon, "Who Is Your Bias? The Symbolic Interactions and Social Solidarity of the K-Pop Fan Community" (paper presented at the Humanities and Creative Projects, 2012).

about celebrities whom they like or hate, develop their fanship and identity, and negotiate social norms embedded in the discourses around celebrities.[35] Audience participation and production in the consumption and sharing of celebrity journalism constitutes a crucial part of Korean social media, particularly related to the K-pop industry. The volume and content of online community posts about K-pop stars and tabloids are valued as key barometers to measure the popularity of stars and the market situation in the entertainment industry.[36] Indeed, the majority of our data collected from theqoo and Twitter came from fans engaging with tabloid news articles, by reposting the articles in the forums and retweeting them with their comments.

Thus, in our analysis, we focused on fans' sharing and reading of tabloids about Gross, alongside their "original" posts about her, and what main discourses emerge from their consumption of Gross. Specifically, we paid attention to the headlines, reposts, and embedded social media posts in the articles, descriptions of Gross, and the overall sentiment of the discourse in each comments section. In particular, the threads, articles, and forum-like threaded comments were studied for their tonality in relation to Gross's internet celebrity, her mixed-race background and appearance, and her relationship to BLACKPINK.

Star-Making through the Tabloid News Cycle

In our press archival research analysis, we found that Gross was mostly mentioned in tabloids, with her biracial physical appearance often highlighted. Tabloids played a key role in familiarizing people with her name by simply reproducing her modeling shots and social media posts in their articles. The cycle of tabloid news coverage peaked around two events: one, Gross joining the "YG family" after her contract with The Black Label; and two, her Baskin-Robbins controversy. We found four dominant themes: endorsing Gross' biracial (white Korean) appearance; Gross's involvement with YG Entertainment and The Black Label as joining the "YG family"; Gross being dubbed a "little Jennie from BLACKPINK";[37] and Gross' Baskin-Robbins controversy. Notably, these four themes were not mutually exclusive of each other, but rather, were often used in tandem to introduce and explain Gross's internet celebrity.

35. Kathleen A. Feeley, "Gossip as News: On Modern U.S. Celebrity Culture and Journalism," *History Compass* 10, no. 6 (2012): 467–82.

36. Kim Sanghwa, "'Ipsomun' jal tamyeon daebak? 'Jeonjaeng' sujunui aidol SNS hongbo" [Is it great if you ride "word of mouth" well? "War"-like SNS promotion of idols], *Ohmynews*, May 14, 2019, http://star.ohmynews.com/NWS_Web/OhmyStar/at_pg.aspx?CNTN_CD=A0002536283.

37. Ji Miyeong, "YG-ga deryeogan olhae 9sal 'hangukgye honhyeol' kijeumodel Ella-ui sejerye mimo" ["Korean mixed," 9-years-old Ella's world-most-beautiful appearance whom YG picked], *Insight*, July 14, 2018, https://www.insight.co.kr/news/166249.

Biracial Ella Gross as a "Little Jennie" in the "global" YG family

The K-pop industry has exercised various strategies to expand its global market, such as including foreign national members in idol bands and mixing English with predominantly Korean lyrics. Within this context, recruiting the biracial Gross, who had risen to stardom on Instagram in the US, contributed to YG Entertainment's branding of itself as a global company. Concurrently, Gross's fame was also localized for the Korean entertainment industry, and she was slowly solidified as a "Korean star" beyond mere Instagram fame. Tabloid news provided a place for people to get to know her name, and Gross's biracial body and beauty became a commodity to attract people's attention and emphasize the global image of YG Entertainment.

Although news outlets began to show interest in Gross in late 2017, when modeling shots and social media selfies of her went viral on the internet, about half of our news data corpus was dated back to the period when Gross had joined The Black Label and entered the "YG family." When reporting on this recruitment, news stories endorsed Gross's mixed-race heritage and beautiful appearance, often reiterating her racial background (born to a Korean American mother and a white American father). Media reports described her as being the "perfect harmony of East and West"[38] and pointed to her beauty as a result of her mixed-race heritage, going so far as to describe her as "the world's most beautiful girl with an already perfectly made appearance."[39] Many articles also endorsed her *visuals* (K-pop fan lingo for an idol's appearance; the best-looking member of a group is usually affectionately known as the *visual* of the group) and dubbed her a "living Barbie" with a "unique and mature aura,"[40] for appearing grown-up despite her relative youth.

Many news articles explicitly racialized Gross, at times even commodifying her racial identity and appearance, by noting her mixed-raceness in their headlines,[41] and even by using the hashtag #혼혈 (*honhyeol*, meaning "mixed-race") or #미국+한국 혼혈 (*Miguk + Hanguk honhyeol*, meaning "America + Korea mixed-race").[42] Juxtaposing her biracial identity with her recent enlistment

38. *Segye Ilbo*, "Dongseoyang-ui wanbyeokan johwa . . . SNS-seo nallinan kijeu model" [A perfect harmony of East and West . . . a kid model taking SNS by storm], November 15, 2017, http://m. segye.com/view/20171115002320.
39. Ji, "White-Korean Mixed."
40. Hwang Jiyeong, "'Kijeu model' Ella Gross, The Black Label gyeyak . . . Teddy hansotbap" ["Kid model" Ella Gross, contracting with The Black Label, now family with Teddy], *Ilgan Sports*, July 23, 2018, https://news.jtbc.joins.com/article/article.aspx?news_id=NB11669462.
41. Kim Minjeong, "Ella Gross nugu? Hangugin honhyeol segyejeok kijeu model" [Who is Ella Gross? The white-Korean mixed race, world-class kid model], *Kukje Shinmun*, July 27, 2018, http://www. kookje.co.kr/news2011/asp/newsbody.asp?code=0500&key=20180727.99099013654.
42. Ji, "White-Korean Mixed."

in the YG family reinforced YG's cosmopolitan image and increasing diversity, as evidenced through their expanding roster of international and foreign talents.

Gross being a member of the YG family was emphasized in tabloids' report on her sisterhood with its star group, BLACKPINK. The news articles that we collected indicated either her resemblance to Jennie from BLACKPINK through physical appearance and fashion style, or her close friendship with other members of the group. Many articles introduced Gross as a "little Jennie,"[43] and reposted Instagram pictures by Gross or Jennie featuring both of them.[44] The articles also quoted the terms of endearment exchanged between Gross and Jennie, such as Jennie calling Gross "my lil baby♥" on her Instagram[45] and Gross calling Jennie "unni" (*eonni*, meaning "older sister").[46] In this manner, the intimate interaction between Gross and BLACKPINK became a subject of public discussion, and the celebrity status of Gross is (re)assured by her star network.

Co-branding is a "strategic alliance that connects two or more brands in the marketplace" to bolster brand identities.[47] While this practice is widely executed in the brick-and-mortar industry, a similar tactic is also found in the celebrity industry, particularly to promote a new star or a new trainee using the established idol stars in Korea. Gross's close relationship with BLACKPINK helps fans imagine and construct a narrative about her and BLACKPINK as sisters in relation to the YG brand image of being a family, which further serves to validate her celebrity quality and brand her as a global K-pop star.

Ella Gross as "the girl" in the Baskin-Robbins ad controversy

When the Baskin-Robbins ad starring Ella Gross—which was only aired in South Korea in 2019—was criticized for sexualizing her, various news articles introduced her as a person of interest in a media scandal, thus extending her presence in the news cycle. Only a few non-tabloid mainstream news agencies covered the scandal seriously, by pointing out the tendency of child sexualization in South Korean media and reiterating the Korean government's decision

43. Ji, "White-Korean Mixed."
44. Kim Mijin and Nam Hyeonji, "Segyejeogin eorini model Ella Gross" [World-class kid model Ella Gross], *Vogue Korea*, July 27, 2018, https://www.vogue.co.kr/2018/07/27/%ec%84%b8%ea%b3%84%ec%a0%81%ec%9d%b8-%ec%96%b4%eb%a6%b0%ec%9d%b4-%eb%aa%a8%eb%8d%b8-%ec%97%98%eb%9d%bc-%ea%b7%b8%eb%a1%9c%ec%8a%a4/.
45. Kang Sohyeon, "'Jennie dalmeunkkol' Ella Gross, jinjja Jenniewa jjigeun injeungsyat hwaje 'My Little Baby'" ["Jennie-like" Ella Gross's real photo with Jennie becomes viral "My Little Baby"], *Money S*, July 1, 2019, https://moneys.mt.co.kr/news/mwView.php?no=2019070109228034111.
46. "BLACKPINK Introduce Jennie's Younger Version in a Live Broadcast," *Women Journal*, October 30, 2019, [link deleted].
47. Søren Askegaard and Anders Bengtsson, "When Hershey Met Betty: Love, Lust and Co-Branding," *Journal of Product & Brand Management* 14, no. 5 (August 2005): 322–29, http://doi.org/10.1108/10610420510616359.

to issue warnings to the TV channels that aired the advertisement.[48] However, most online news sites plainly emphasized the racializing of Gross's body in their repetitive coverage of the issue. Some news articles focused on Gross's adult femininity—as implied in the focus on her lips and tongue licking ice cream— despite her still being a child, by repeating the coverage of her successful career in the modeling industry and reposting images of her photoshoots for fashion magazines.[49]

Buzz marketing—also called *noise marketing* in Korea[50]—refers to a marketing strategy that garners attention by generating buzz through eye-catching content or practices on various media.[51] In tandem with the attention economy, media companies—including celebrity agencies—intentionally make scandals and produce controversial content concerning misogyny, online hatred, and sex to raise the profile of their content or new stars.[52] This practice was also found in the Baskin-Robbins scandal, as it was the moment when Gross's fame rose to some level of stardom and people began to recognize her face and name as YG's new asset.[53]

The controversy around the ad developed into a scandal, as Gross's mother objected to the public's criticism of the commercial and backlash by posting her response on Instagram: "honestly meant to be a fun commercial . . . [but was] perceived . . . as something disgusting and horrific . . . To those that are rallying against the Baskin-Robbins commercial, stop saying that you are doing this 'for

---

48. Chu Inyeong, "Eorini iyonghae seongjeok hwansang Baskin-Robbins gwanggo chaeneore 'gyeonggo'" [Baskin-Robbins ad channel received a warning for "giving sexual fantasies using a child"], *JoongAng Ilbo*, August 26, 2019, https://www.joongang.co.kr/article/23562397#home; Sim Yunji, "Baskin-Robbins 'adong seongsangpumhwa' nollan . . . haeweyeotdamyeon jejae daesangieosseulkka" [Baskin-Robbins' controversial ad for sexualizing children . . . would it be punished overseas?], *Kyunghyang Shinmun*, July 3, 2019, http://news.khan.co.kr/kh_news/khan_art_view.html?art_id=201907031650001#csidxe6f3bf0c39cec99886bcfed32239c73.

49. Kim Hayeon, "Ella Gross, hwaryeohan deureseu-edo dotboineun bijueol 'shin' hwabo jang-in" [Ella Gross: A new master of photoshoots with amazing beauty and gorgeous dress], *Top Star News*, July 12, 2019, http://www.topstarnews.net/news/articleView.html?idxno=645361.

50. Kim Ha-Yeon and Lee Soo-Bum, "The Effect of Curiosity about New Menus on Customers' Emotions and Intention to Buy in Food Service Companies," *International Journal of Tourism and Hospitality Research* 33, no. 5 (May 2019): 63–76.

51. Dhiraj Murthy, "Twitter and Elections: Are Tweets, Predictive, Reactive, or a Form of Buzz?" *Information, Communication & Society* 18, no. 7 (2015): 816–31, https://doi.org/10.1080/1369118X.2015.1006659.

52. Kim Sooah, "Misogynistic Cyber Hate Speech in Korea," *Issues in Feminism* 15, no. 2 (October 2015): 279–317.

53. Since 2003, Baskin-Robbins Korea has often used Korean white mixed-race child models in its TV commercials, especially around the Christmas season. Although Gross's Baskin-Robbins ad was broadcast in the summer, it is notable that Baskin-Robbins' Christmas editions are branded through exoticism, manifested in the TV commercials featuring Korean white mixed-race child models.

Ella."[54] Gross's mother's Instagram post sparked further controversy, and tabloids likewise reported the conflict between Gross's mother and internet users who had criticized the commercial. But even such news coverage of the conflict covered the scandal as a kind of ancillary item to introduce Ella Gross as "the girl" of the Baskin-Robbins ad scandal by centering her name in the news title and showing her Instagram pictures in the news content:

엘라 그로스 배스킨라빈스 광고, '아동 성적 대상화' 논란 → 사과에도 '시끌'
[Ella Gross's Baskin-Robbins advertisement, controversy over "child sexualization" → still "noisy" despite apology][55]

배스킨라빈스 '엘라 그로스', '성 상품화 논란' 광고 내보낸 방송사, 심의 받는다 [Ella Gross in the Baskin-Robbins ad, child sexualization: TV broadcasters that aired the commercial will undergo deliberation][56]

In the meantime, [despite the controversy,] Ella Gross is a child actress and fashion model. Her dad is American and mother is assumed to be 1.5 generation Korean-American . . . She started her career by contracting with The Black Label. She is very popular, with more than 3.21 million Instagram followers.[57]

In this manner, Gross—not Baskin-Robbins nor the ad agency—became the center of the controversy; she began to be called "the girl from the Baskin-Robbins scandal."[58] Regardless of the issues around the ad's child sexualization and the South Korean government's stance and warning,[59] it was evident that

---

54. Lee Changgyu, "Ella Gross eomma, seongsangpumhwa nollane ipjang balkyeo . . . 'Gwanggo bandaehaneun saramdeul, Ellareul wihandago malhaji malgil'" [Ella Gross's mother states her stance on a controversy around her child of sexualization . . . "To those who don't disagree with the ad, don't say you are for Ella"], *Top Star News*, July 2, 2019, http://www.topstarnews.net/news/articleView.html?idxno=641566.

55. Kim Soyeon, "Ella Gross Baskin-Robbins gwanggo, 'adong seongjeok daesanghwa' nollan→Sagwaedo sikkeul" [Ella Gross's Baskin Robbins ad became a center of controversy for child sexualization → despite apology, still controversial], *Star Today*, July 1, 2019. https://www.mk.co.kr/star/hot-issues/view/2019/07/473379/.

56. Park Jeongmin, "Baskin-Robbins 'Ella Gross', seong 'sangpumhwa nollan' gwanggo naebonaen bangsongsa, simui banneunda" ["Ella Gross" in the Baskin-Robbins ad, child sexualization: TV broadcasters that aired the commercial will undergo deliberation], *Top Star News*, July 29, 2019, http://www.topstarnews.net/news/articleView.html?idxno=651566.

57. Lee Changgyu, "Ella Gross eomma" [Ella Gross's mother].

58. Yun Huijeong, "Choding-I . . ." Gwanggo hanaro nalli natdeon "Ella Gross" geunhwange baneung gallyeotda" [The girl from the Baskin-Robbins scandal, Ella Gross's recent Instagram received differently], Wikitree, May 16, 2020, https://www.wikitree.co.kr/articles/532947.

59. South Korean media regulation agency Korea Communications Commission issued a warning to the broadcasting channels that ran the Baskin-Robbins TV commercial, stating, "Broadcasting channels should take social responsibilities to protect children's welfare and well-being. Thus, airing a TV commercial that can imply sexual fantasies of children with images of a child with makeup is a serious issue of dismissing their public responsibility as broadcasting channels, in which legal sanction is unavoidable." Broadcasting systems and channels receive annual reports from the Commission, and they may be fined or their broadcasting rights can be reconsidered by

the scandal was exploited by tabloids and news media as a resource for buzz marketing to channel more traffic to these news sites, which helped the public memorize her name and helped her to accrue fame.

(Anti-)Fan Labors over Children in K-Pop (Social) Media

In our social media sentiment scoping analysis, we found four main practices undertaken by fans (and anti-fans) in relation to children in K-pop (social) media via the case study of Gross: constructing a mythic discourse around Gross's lineage and mixed-race appearance; using the halo effect from BLACKPINK to extrapolate positive qualities about Gross; defending Gross from accusations by redirecting criticism to the systemic faults of the K-pop and media industries; and calling out Gross's parents for their (lack of) responsibility over their child. We weave together our analyses from both the Korean- and English-language corpuses, with a focus on fan reactions and practices through user-generated articles and associated comment sections and threads on forums. The section ends with a brief discussion on the legal status and issues regarding child stars in K-pop (social) media.

"Mythic discourse" around lineage

The first practice of fans in both English- and Korean-language social media is the construction of a mythic discourse around Gross's lineage and mixed-race appearance, wherein discussions of her origins are idealized and discussed as extraordinary. On Reddit, conversations refer to Gross's "biracial Eurasian"[60] appearance as the primary reason that local Koreans are "fawning" over her,[61] with many users complimenting her "looks."[62] On Allkpop, this sentiment is echoed in posts that attribute Gross's popularity to her "half German (American) and half Korean"[63] origins and user comments asserting that "mixed ethnicities tend to inherit the best from both sides."[64] On theqoo, Gross was praised for

the Commission when they have received several warnings or similar sanctions. See Chu, "Baskin-Robbins Ad received a warning."

60. u/ft1231, "190327 Ella Gross Instagram Story Update with Lisa," Reddit, March 26, 2019, https://www.reddit.com/r/BlackPink/comments/b5t14j/190327_ella_gross_instagram_story_update_with_lisa/.
61. u/ft1231, "190327 Ella Gross Instagram Story Update with Lisa."
62. haydn-an, "This YG Entertainment Trainee Is Being Called the 'Second Jennie,'" Allkpop, October 7, 2020, https://www.allkpop.com/article/2020/10/this-yg-entertainment-trainee-is-being-called-the-second-jennie.
63. haydn-an, "This YG Entertainment Trainee."
64. haydn-an, "This YG Entertainment Trainee."

being "perfectly pretty despite her young age."[65] Many users posted a number of her photos and complimented her "natural star quality", which was assessed from "her gorgeous mixed-race look" and "unique aura." By doing so, they reproduced the mythic discourse that celebrities are born with their talent through "lineage"[66]—that is, her biological makeup (her Korean mother and white father).

In fact, Gross's apparent beauty at her very young age was subject to so much mythic discourse that anti-fans and naysayers began to speculate whether she had "depend[ed] on plastic surgery to enhance [her] looks," only to be corrected by other commenters that her beauty was all-natural from her mixed-race background.[67] An article on Koreaboo grouped Gross under "foreign artists"[68] who were signed to the "Big 3" K-pop companies—YG, JYP, and SM—despite her not having formally debuted as an artist.

"Halo effect" via BLACKPINK

Throughout all the platforms we surveyed, fans consistently used the halo effect from BLACKPINK to extrapolate positive qualities about Gross, wherein positive impressions of BLACKPINK had the potential to spill over to Gross. On theqoo, users would consistently share news articles about Gross, including news of her joining YG and her closer proximity to BLACKPINK as a result. There were often photos of Gross and Jennie of BLACKPINK cross-posted on the forum as well, as users discursively shaped Gross's backstory as a rising star based on their imagined intimacies between both public figures. Speculations (translated from Korean) include: "BLACKPINK also often tend to post pictures with her"; "Do you know the new YG trainee Ella Gross? She totally has the Jennie vibe"; "Think Ella Gross absolutely can be an idol group's member." The coverage of Instagram posts featuring Gross and Jennie on Allkpop featured handfuls of commenters who were visibly confused over whether both of them were "genuinely" sisters or "half-sisters."[69] By connecting pieces of information that were scattered across her Instagram, BLACKPINK's Instagram, and news articles, K-pop fans labored over a coherent star narrative of Ella Gross.

On Reddit, most of the threads on Gross included users cross-posting Instagram posts by Gross and BLACKPINK members featuring each other. This

65. We are intentionally omitting the source URLs to posts hosted on theqoo, because it is a members-only platform. We are also intentionally omitting source URLs to Twitter posts to avoid the identification of specific users.
66. Rojek, *Celebrity*, 17–18.
67. haydn-an, "This YG Entertainment Trainee."
68. Koreaboo, "Here Is Every Foreign Artist Signed under the Big 3," Koreaboo, August 9, 2020, https://www.koreaboo.com/lists/every-foreign-artist-signed-big-3/.
69. u/bk1155, "190208 Rosé IG Update with Ella Gross," Reddit, February 8, 2019, https://www.reddit.com/r/BlackPink/comments/aojra7/190208_ros%C3%A9_ig_update_with_ella_gross/.

unofficial archiving of K-pop idols' content is a mainstay of fandom practices and serves as a form of documentary and newsworthiness. In several Reddit threads featuring such reposts, fans would reiterate their nicknames for Gross, often comprising portmanteaus of the names of the women in BLACKPINK. For example, in a thread documenting BLACKPINK member Rosé's Instagram Live that featured a short conversation with Gross, commenters referred to Gross as the "daughter" of "Chaennie," the "ship" name for Rosé and Jennie. In another April 2019 thread featuring an Instagram post from Gross showcasing her visiting BLACKPINK backstage at their concert, fans referred to Gross as the unofficial fifth member of the group. Fan sentiments on similar Reddit posts observed that Gross is "almost the only IG [Instagram] account" they have seen the BLACKPINK members comment on regularly. One Reddit thread focused on an April 2019 Instagram post of Gross and Rosé sharing food in a restaurant; it featured a particularly astute comment from a fan, noting that YG has "well played" Gross's appearances alongside BLACKPINK "so much" that her increased visibility and the public's rising interest in her has been good for her career.[70]

Fans' cross-posted archives of K-pop idols' content and the idols' social media accounts function as secondary spaces for fans to discuss, interpret, and dissect the minutiae of minor photographic details. For instance, in a March 2020 Reddit thread that reposted Gross' TikTok challenge, users observed that Gross had "nominated" BLACKPINK and six other prominent YG-related staff (e.g., Soon Ho Choi, VINCE, Zion.T, R.Tee) to partake in the "See 10 Do 10" challenge. It was noted by hawkeyed fans that Gross had even mentioned BLACKPINK producer Teddy, even though he is not on social media and did not have an account that she could tag. Resulting discussions focused on how Gross had direct access and intimate working relationships even with the staff and crew who work behind the scenes with BLACKPINK, thus highlighting her proximity to the idols and her exclusivity in the entertainment industry.

Defense via criticism of systemic faults

In the wake of Gross's Baskin-Robbins ad scandal, fans were observed defending Gross from accusations by redirecting criticism to the systemic faults of the K-pop and media industry. On Twitter, many posts criticized the Korean media convention of sexualizing children, Influencer culture, and the K-pop industry

---

70. u/LesBleusFFF, "190420 Ella Gross IG update: sharing food with ROSÉ," Reddit, April 20, 2019, https://www.reddit.com/r/BlackPink/comments/bfi2jr/190420_ella_gross_ig_update_sharing_ food_with_ros%C3%A9/.

at large.[71] Users specifically pointed out that Gross's entertainment agency, YG, had a part to play in approving her heavy makeup and the camera movements that led to impressions of child sexualization (e.g., the closeup of her lips in the ad). During that period, YG's founder Yang Hyun-suk and other YG singers were accused of prostituting and spycamming women, including their trainees,[72] in what became known as the Burning Sun scandal. To this end, some Twitter users connected the scandal to Gross's campaign and registered their worry that she might have been another victim of the media industry. Such tweets analyzed a longer trajectory of Gross's modeling work, including screengrabs of her past photoshoots for a fashion magazine, and problematized the sexualizing gaze placed on her even in her career as a child model, as evidenced by her clothes, makeup, and facial expressions in the photos. Other comments on Twitter and Allkpop threads chided Baskin-Robbins for not picking up on the troubling angle of the commercial at the storyboard stage, and for not issuing a formal apology.

However, fan discourse on Allkpop also pointed to "Knetz"—internet slang for "Korean netizen" or internet users—as the culprits for being oversensitive and taking screenshots of the video commercial "out [of] context."[73] Some fans asserted that the commercial was not at all sexual, and was only framed to appear as such by "YG haters."[74] Others speculated that the visibility and internet traffic generated by news items headlined by Gross and BLACKPINK were often utilized as clickbait by various media outlets. Regardless of who they felt were the actual culprits of Gross's Baskin-Robbins scandal, these fans and followers tended to employ discursive tactics to displace the blame away from Gross—by suggesting that fans needed to protect her from such harmful discourse—and to distance her from the decision-making processes.

Call-out of parental responsibility

The final stream of fan labors involved users calling out Gross's parents for their (lack of) responsibility over their child. This sentiment converged on two main

71. Kang Yewon, "A Study of Popularization of Feminism and Becoming a Teenage Feminist in the Digital Era," (master's thesis, Ehwa Womans University, 2019), http://www.riss.kr/search/detail/DetailView.do?p_mat_type=be54d9b8bc7cdb09&control_no=36b04877c03df75effe0bdc3ef48d4 19.

72. Matthew Campbell and Kim Sohee, "The Dark Side of K-Pop: Assault, Prostitution, Suicide, and Spycams," Bloomberg Businessweek, November 6, 2019, https://www.bloomberg.com/news/features/2019-11-06/k-pop-s-dark-side-assault-prostitution-suicide-and-spycams?srnd=premium-asia.

73. Choi Ji-won, "Baskin-Robbins Korea Hit by Claims of Sexualizing 11-Year-Old," Allkpop, July 1, 2019, https://www.allkpop.com/article/2019/07/baskin-robbins-korea-hit-by-claims-of-sexualizing-11-year-old.

74. Choi, "Baskin-Robbins Korea Hit by Claims."

topics: the overall social media presence and visibility of Gross, and Gross's involvement in the Baskin-Robbins scandal.

In one Reddit thread discussing a March 2019 Instagram story of Gross wishing BLACKPINK member Lisa a happy birthday, one commenter noted that Gross's mother, who manages her Instagram account, "reacts to everything BP [BLACKPINK]" specifically for Gross to be noticed by the public and to "constantly get the Jennie comparisons."[75] Another sentiment from Twitter notes that Gross's mother appears to be "using BP [BLACKPINK] to grow her daughter's followers" to be an Instagram Influencer, and that Gross's visibility with BLACKPINK members on Instagram is an overt "business strategy."[76] There are also lengthy discussions about the ethics of Gross's mother "showing" her on social media, as she is still a minor and her mother is already profiting off of her image. On the topic of the Baskin-Robbins scandal, commenters on Allkpop referred to Gross's mother as a stage parent and accused her of making money off of her daughter's successes.

However, a handful of commenters on Allkpop state their appreciation of Gross's mother for defending her daughter on social media while remaining polite toward even the most obnoxious anti-fans. In a similar vein, an article on Koreaboo reposted the public statement from Gross' mother, clarifying the intentions of the Baskin-Robbins ad through a lengthy explanation.

On Twitter, commenters problematized parents' lack of gender awareness and lack of understanding about how child influencers are consumed and sexualized, especially in the Korean media industry. They criticized Gross's mother's Instagram post in which she states:

> I pray she will be a role model for other girls . . . To those that are rallying against the Baskin Robbins commercial, stop saying that you are doing this "for Ella." She is surrounded and loved by many strong and powerful women who wholeheartedly have her best interests at heart.[77]

On Twitter, users raised awareness of the complex issues surrounding Gross's scandal, refocusing attention away from individualized blame and toward the systemic issues at play. For instance, users questioned how gendered and hyperfeminized images of a young child can inspire other girls, apart from socializing them to abide by beauty norms. They further pointed out various child welfare issues in the influencer industry, in which child influencers are physically and mentally abused by audiences and even by their parents for the media, including

75. u/ft1231, "190327 Ella Gross Instagram Story Update with Lisa."
76. From theqoo. We intentionally omit the source of theqoo citations since it is a members-only community.
77. From Twitter. We anonymize the source of Twitter citations to avoid the identification of specific users.

their YouTube channels and Instagram accounts, by being objectified at their early age and laboring for media content. In all of these instances, fans were partaking in instances of calling out—to assess the well-being of Gross, to attribute blame to parties whom they felt were not assuming responsibility for Gross's missteps, and to demonstrate concern toward Gross by performing outrage on her behalf.

Conclusion

In this essay, we showed how Gross, a child influencer, rose to stardom, strategically displaying her relationship with an established K-pop idol group and her mixed-race appearance. The process of her obtaining celebrity status, however, raised concerns regarding child sexualization, child labor, racialization, and commercialism, in which minor celebrities are treated as assets of the entertainment industry and clickbait for the attention economy of tabloidesque scenes. Although she became famous as a new member of the YG family through perceived intimacies with BLACKPINK and through the Baskin-Robbins scandal, we argue that Gross's body has been objectified and racialized. Further, she and her mother encountered online hate for "using BLACKPINK" and for "exploiting a child for money."

In our data, we found many posts and comments within online communities that focus on the issue of child labor in the broader media industry. Some criticized the Baskin-Robbins scandal for portraying Gross as an adult model and demanded that Baskin-Robbins Korea formally apologize. Similarly, others emphasized how legal and institutional changes are necessary to protect children who are "exploited" for the media, from social media platforms like YouTube and Instagram to the K-pop industry, including star agencies like YG.

Although many criticize the sexualization of children and women in the K-pop and influencer industries, the relevant laws and policies are lacking and the media industry itself has not shown an attempt to resolve these problems. The Korea Communications Commission published a guideline to protect children (under age fourteen) and adolescents (under age nineteen) who appear on internet-based personal media broadcasting on June 30, 2020,[78] in response to increasing cases of child exploitation in social media.[79] The guideline states that children's guardians, content creators, and MCN channels should protect the

---

78. Korea Communications Commission, Inteonetgaeinbangsong Churyeon Adongcheongsonyeon Boho Jichim [A guideline to protect children and adolescents on internet personal broadcasting], Korea Communications Commission, 2020.

79. Kim Kyung-jin, "Gov't Guidelines Suggest Limits on Underage Live-Streaming," *JoongAng Daily*, July 1, 2020, https://koreajoongangdaily.joins.com/2020/07/01/business/industry/kid-youtuber-youtube/20200701190000417.html.

health of children and adolescents through content themes (e.g., not to sexualize them and not to insert advertisements in content) and in the broadcasting
process (e.g., to prevent children from livestreaming at night during the hours of
10:00 p.m. to 6:00 a.m. and from broadcasting for more than three consecutive
hours without breaks).[80] However, this is only a guideline and has no force of law.

The Child Welfare Act states that media content and advertising must not
sexualize children, and that any persons who violate the law can be subject to
imprisonment (maximum ten years) or fine (maximum KRW 50 million).[81]
However, the criteria with which to judge child sexualization are vague and
uncertain, and the online activities of child sexualization, including social media
posts, are rarely monitored. Furthermore, as evidenced in the news coverage of
Ella Gross, media industries, including news outlets, continue their business as
usual by simply repeating the problematic discourse through tabloidesque coverage to generate traffic and views, rather than inviting any meaningful dialogue
about the situation.

Indeed, despite the controversy around the scandal, many who consumed
the tabloids were endorsing Gross's mixed-race body. Additionally, as opposed
to several posts reproaching her parents' lack of parental responsibilities and
gender awareness, we could not find posts that criticized the media convention
of celebrating the norms of whiteness and for exoticizing her mixed-race body.
Rather, Gross was still being endorsed as the perfect mixture of West and East,
and people widely shared and reposted the photos of her face and body, despite
her being a minor. On social media, where such norms are reinforced through
the number of likes, comments, and subscriptions, child influencers are exposed
without any protection to such conventions and norms of racialization and gendering. Even their parents may not recognize how toxic the environment is for
their children. Thus, it is crucial to raise an urgent need to discuss and bring
institutional changes to protect the welfare issue of children on social media. We
conclude this paper by emphasizing a necessity for academia, industry, and government to collaborate to develop protective measures for child influencers on
social media against racialization, sexualization, and commodification of their
bodies.

Bibliography

Abidin, Crystal. "Introduction to Panel: Fame and Microcelebrity on the Web." AoIR 16th
    Annual Meetings Proceeding, Phoenix, AZ, October 21–24, 2015. https://spir.aoir.
    org/ojs/index.php/spir/article/view/8596/6845.

---

80. Korea Communications Commission, 2020.
81. Ministry of Health and Welfare, *Child Welfare Act*, 2014, Seoul. https://www.law.go.kr/%EB%B2%
    95%EB%A0%B9/%EC%95%84%EB%8F%99%EB%B3%B5%EC%A7%80%EB%B2%95.

Ahn, Ji-Hyun. *Mixed-Race Politics and Neoliberal Multiculturalism in South Korean Media*. East Asian Popular Culture. Cham: Palgrave Macmillan, 2018.

Ahn, Ji-Hyun, and Tien-wen Lin. "The Politics of Apology: The 'Tzuyu Scandal' and Transnational Dynamics of K-Pop." *International Communication Gazette* 81, no. 2 (2019): 158–75. https://doi.org/10.1177/1748048518802947.

Askegaard, Søren, and Anders Bengtsson. "When Hershey Met Betty: Love, Lust and Co-Branding." *Journal of Product & Brand Management* 14, no. 5 (August 2005): 322–29. http://doi.org/10.1108/10610420510616359.

Busse, Kristina. "'I'm Jealous of the Fake Me': Postmodern Subjectivity and Identity Construction in Boy Band Fiction." In *Framing Celebrity: New Directions in Celebrity Culture*, edited by Su Holmes and Sean Redmond, 41–56. London: Routledge, 2006.

Campbell, Matthew, and Kim Sohee. "The Dark Side of K-Pop: Assault, Prostitution, Suicide, and Spycams." *Bloomberg Businessweek*, November 6, 2019. https://www.bloomberg.com/news/features/2019-11-06/k-pop-s-dark-side-assault-prostitution-suicide-and-spycams?srnd=premium-asia.

Chu, Inyeong. "Eorini iyonghae seongjeok hwansang Baskin-Robbins gwanggo chaene-ore 'gyeonggo'" [Baskin Robbins ad channel received a warning for "giving sexual fantasies using a child"]. *JoongAng Ilbo*, August 26, 2020. https://www.joongang.co.kr/article/23562397#home.

Elfving-Hwang, Joanna. "K-Pop Idols, Artificial Beauty and Affective Fan Relationships in South Korea." In *Routledge Handbook of Celebrity Studies*, edited by Anthony Elliott, 190–201. London and New York: Routledge, 2018.

Feeley, Kathleen A. "Gossip as News: On Modern U.S. Celebrity Culture and Journalism." *History Compass* 10, no. 6 (2012): 467–82. https://doi.org/10.1111/j.1478-0542.2012.00854.x.

Hankyoreh. "[Nonjaeng] Aidol yukseong siseutem idaero joeunga?" [Idol training system, is this okay?]. June 17, 2011. http://www.hani.co.kr/arti/opinion/argument/483303.html.

Hwang, Jiyeong. "'Kijeu model' Ella Gross, The Black Label gyeyak . . . Teddy hansotbap" ["Kid model" Ella Gross, contracting with The Black Label, now family with Teddy]. *Ilgan Sports*, July 23, 2018. https://news.joins.com/article/22824002.

Ji, Miyeong. "YG-ga deryeogan olhae 9sal 'hangukgye honhyeol' kijeumodel Ella-ui sejerye mimo" ["Korean mixed," 9 years-old Ella's world-most-beautiful appearance whom YG picked]. *Insight*, July 14, 2018. https://www.insight.co.kr/news/166249.

Jin, Dal Yong, and Ryoo Woongjae. "Critical Interpretation of Hybrid K-Pop: The Global-Local Paradigm of English Mixing in Lyrics." *Popular Music and Society* 37, no. 2 (2014): 113–31. https://doi.org/10.1080/03007766.2012.731721.

Jo, Min-sun, and Chung EunHye. "A Study on the Transmedia Storytelling of Korean Idol Content: Focusing on EXO and BTS." *Humanities Contents* no. 52 (March 2019): 223–46. https://doi.org/10.18658/humancon.2019.03.52.223.

Kang, Jennifer M. "Rediscovering the Idols: K-Pop Idols Behind the Mask." *Celebrity Studies* 8, no. 1 (2017): 136–41. http://dx.doi.org/10.1080/19392397.2016.1272859.

Kang, Sohyeon. "'Jennie dalmeunkkol' Ella Gross, jinjja Jenniewa jjigeun injeungsyat hwaje 'My Little Baby'" ["Jennie-like" Ella Gross's real photo with Jennie becomes viral "My Little Baby"]. *Money S*, July 1, 2019. https://moneys.mt.co.kr/news/mwView.php?no=2019070109228034111.

Kang, Yewon. "A Study of Popularization of Feminism and Becoming a Teenage Feminist in the Digital Era." Master's thesis, Ewha Womans University, 2019. http://www.riss.kr/search/detail/DetailView.do?p_mat_type=be54d9b8bc7cdb09&control_no=36b04877c03df75effe0bdc3ef48d419.

Kim, Hayeon. "Ella Gross, hwaryeohan deureseu-edo dotboineun bijueol 'shin' hwabo jang-in" [Ella Gross: A new master of photoshoots with amazing beauty and gorgeous dress]. *Top Star News*, July 12, 2019. http://www.topstarnews.net/news/articleView.html?idxno=645361.

Kim, Ha-Yeon, and Lee Soo-Bum. "The Effect of Curiosity about New Menus on Customers' Emotions and Intention to Buy in Food Service Companies." *International Journal of Tourism and Hospitality Research* 33, no. 5 (May 2019): 63–76. http://doi.org/10.21298/IJTHR.2019.5.33.5.63.

Kim, Hoyoung, and Yoon Tae Jin. "How the Idol System in Korean Pop Culture Works: An Explorative Study on the Dual Structure of Production/Consumption of Idol Culture." *Broadcasting and Communication* 13, no. 4 (December 2012): 45–82. http://doi.org/10.22876/bnc.2012.13.4.002.

Kim, Hyojeong. "theqoo, daehanminguk daepyo 'yeocho' keomyuniti" [theqoo, the most popular 'female-dominant' community in Korea]. *Weekly Chosun*, October 28, 2019. http://weekly.chosun.com/client/news/viw.asp?ctcd=C01&nNewsNumb=002580100002.

Kim, Jee-hye. "[The Dark Side of K-Pop] They Said I Could Debut Right Away, But . . . Left with 600 Million Won of Debt, Depression, and a Bunch of Lawsuits after 8 Years as a Trainee." *The Kyunghyang Shinmun*, October 6, 2020. http://english.khan.co.kr/khan_art_view.html?artid=202010061751247&code=710100.

Kim, Mijin, and Nam Hyeonji. "Segyejeogin eorini model Ella Gross" [World-class kid model Ella Gross]. *Vogue Korea*, July 27, 2018. https://www.vogue.co.kr/2018/07/27/%ec%84%b8%ea%b3%84%ec%a0%81%ec%9d%b8-%ec%96%b4%eb%a6%b0%ec%9d%b4-%eb%aa%a8%eb%8d%b8-%ec%97%98%eb%9d%bc-%ea%b7%b8%eb%a1%9c%ec%8a%a4/.

Kim, Minjeong. "Ella Gross nugu? Hangugin honhyeol segyejeok kijeu model" [Who is Ella Gross? The white-Korean mixed race, world-class kid model]. *Kukje Shinmun*, July 27, 2018.

Kim, Sanghwa. "'Ipsomun' jal tamyeon daebak? 'Jeonjaeng' sujunui aidol SNS hongbo" [If you ride "word of mouth" well, it's a jackpot? Idol social media promotion at the level of "war"]. *Ohmynews*, May 14, 2019. http://star.ohmynews.com/NWS_Web/OhmyStar/at_pg.aspx?CNTN_CD=A0002536283.

Kim, Sooah. "Misogynistic Cyber Hate Speech in Korea." *Issues in Feminism* 15, no. 2 (October 2015): 279–317.

Kim, Soyeon. "Ella Gross Baskin-Robbins gwanggo, 'adong seongjeok daesanghwa' nollan→Sagwaedo sikkeul" [Ella Gross's Baskin-Robbins advertisement, controversy over 'child sexualization' → still 'noisy' despite apology]. *Star Today*, July 1, 2019. https://www.mk.co.kr/star/hot-issues/view/2019/07/473379/.

Kim, Su-a. "Yeohyeolhaengdong (Connective Action)? Aidol Paendeomui Teuwiteo Haesitaegeu Undong-ui Myeong-am" [Connective action? Critical review of Twitter hashtag activism and Korean idol fandom"]. *Munhwawa Sahoe* [Korean Journal of Cultural Sociology] 25, no. 2 (December 2017): 297–336. http://dx.doi.org/10.17328/kjcs.2017.25..007.

Ko, Hyeri, and Yang Eunkyung. "Korean Boy Group's Misogyny and Division between Female Fandom." *Journal of the Korea Contents Association* 17, no. 8 (August 2017): 506–19. https://doi.org/10.5392/JKCA.2017.17.08.506.

Korea Communications Commission. Inteonetgaeinbangsong Churyeon Adongcheongsonyeon Boho Jichim [A guideline to protect children and adolescents on internet personal broadcasting]. Korea Communications Commission, June 30, 2020. https://kcc.go.kr/user.do?boardId=1113&page=A05030000&dc=K00000200&boardSeq=49655&mode=view.

Kwon, Cassie. "Who Is Your Bias? The Symbolic Interactions and Social Solidarity of the K-Pop Fan Community." Paper presented at the Humanities and Creative Projects, 2012. https://digitalcommons.linfield.edu/cgi/viewcontent.cgi?referer=&httpsredir=1&article=1041&context=studsymp_cr.

Lee, Byeongjun. Aidolgwa yeonseupsaengi sseureojinda . . . gyeyakseo sseugo ilhaneun nodongja gwolli isseo" [Idols and trainees are collapsing . . . they also have a laborer's right to work under a contract]. *JoongAng Ilbo*, January 26, 2020. https://www.joongang.co.kr/article/23690218#home.

Lee, Changgyu. "Ella Gross eomma, seongsangpumhwa nollane ipjang balkyeo . . . 'Gwanggo bandaehaneun saramdeul, Ellareul wihandago malhaji malgil'" [Ella Gross's mother states her stance on a controversy around her child of sexualization. "To those who don't disagree with the ad, don't say you are for Ella"]. *Top Star News*, July 2, 2019. http://www.topstarnews.net/news/articleView.html?idxno=641566.

Lee, Claire. "Defining Racism in Korea." *Korean Herald*, September 4, 2014. http://www.koreaherald.com/view.php?ud=20140904001088.

Lee, Dong Eun, and Son So Hee. "The Study on Image Storytelling to Maintain the Identity of Idol through <Beast> and <Highlight>." *Cartoon and Animation Studies*, no. 53 (December 2018): 523–56.

Lee, Eunjeong. "Yeonseupsaeng jedowa bulgongjeong gyeyagi choraehaneun aidol ingwonmunje" [Idol human rights problems caused by the trainee system and unfair contracts]. *Hallyu Now*, March 28, 2019. http://kofice.or.kr/b20industry/b20_industry_03_view.asp?seq=7991.

Lee, Hee-eun, You Kyung-Han, and Ahn Ji-Hyun. "Strategic Multiculturalism and Racialism in Television Advertising." *Korean Journal of Communication and Information*, no. 39 (August 2007): 473–505.

Lee, Huiyong. "Insooni-ui sangcheoga amullyeomyeon" [To heal Insooni's wounds]. *Yonhap News*, August 17, 2016. https://www.yna.co.kr/view/AKR20160812164800371.

Lee, Jong-im. *Aidol Yeonseupsaeng-ui Ttamgwa Nunmul* [Idol trainees' sweat and tears]. Seoul: The Seoul Institute, 2018.

Lee, Jong-im. "Munhwanodongjaroseoui aidol/yeonseupsaengege piryohan geot" [What idols/trainees need as cultural laborers]. *Cultural Media* no. 98 (2019): 232–46. https://www.dbpia.co.kr/journal/articleDetail?nodeId=NODE08749010.

Lee, Mary. "Mixed Race Peoples in the Korean National Imaginary and Family." *Korean Studies* 32 (2008): 56–85. https://doi.org/10.1353/ks.0.0010.

Ministry of Health and Welfare. *Child Welfare Act*. Ministry of Health and Welfare, 2014. Seoul. https://www.law.go.kr/%EB%B2%95%EB%A0%B9/%EC%95%84%EB%8F%99%EB%B3%B5%EC%A7%80%EB%B2%95.

Moon, Katharine H. S. *Sex Among Allies: Military Prostitution in U.S.-Korea Relations.* New York: Columbia University Press, 1997.

Mun, Se-eun. "Inhyeonggateun mimoro paenege 'eolgul gonggyeok'haneun 'honhyeolgye' aidol 5in" [5 mixed-race idols who attack fans with their Barbie-like faces]. *Insight*, 14 April 2019. https://www.insight.co.kr/news/219861.

Murthy, Dhiraj. "Twitter and Elections: Are Tweets, Predictive, Reactive, or a Form of Buzz?" *Information, Communication & Society* 18, no. 7 (2015): 816–31. https://doi.org/10.1080/1369118X.2015.1006659.

Oh, Mi-Young. "A Study on the Stigma of Mixed-Race: Factors Affecting Stigma on Mixed-Race and Stigma Effect." *Korean Journal of Social Welfare* 61, no. 2 (May 2009): 215–46.

Park, Gil-Sung. "Manufacturing Creativity: Production, Performance, and Dissemination of K-Pop." *Korea Journal* 53, no. 4 (2013): 14–33. http://doi.org/10.25024/kj.2013.53.4.14.

Park, Jeongmin. "Baskin-Robbins 'Ella Gross', seong 'sangpumhwa nollan' gwanggo naebonaen bangsongsa, simui banneunda" ["Ella Gross'" in the Baskin Robbins ad, child sexualization: TV broadcasters that aired the commercial will undergo deliberation]. *Top Star News*, July 29, 2019. http://www.topstarnews.net/news/articleView.html?idxno=651566.

Parker, Stephanie. "Soompi and the 'Honorary Asian': Shifting Identities in the Digital Age." *Stanford Journal of Asian American Studies* II (October 2009). https://www.academia.edu/800498/Soompi_and_the_Honorary_Asian_Shifting_Identities_in_the_Digital_Age.

Rojek, Chris. *Celebrity*. London: Reaktion Books, 2001.

Scott, Maria. "10+ K-pop Idols Who Made Pre-Debut Appearances on Other Artists' Music Videos." *Kpop Starz*, June 11, 2022. https://www.kpopstarz.com/articles/307076/20220611/10-kpop-idols-pre-debut-appearances-music-videos.htm.

Segye Ilbo. "Dongseoyang-ui wanbyeokan johwa . . . SNS-seo nallinan kijeu model" [A perfect harmony of East and West . . . a kid model taking SNS by storm]. November 15, 2017. http://m.segye.com/view/20171115002320.

Sim, Yunji. "Baskin-Robbins 'adong seongsangpumhwa' nollan . . . haeweyeotdamyeon jejae daesang-ieosseulkka" [Baskin-Robbins' controversial ad for sexualizing children . . . would it be punished overseas?]. *Kyunghyang Shinmun*, July 3, 2019. http://news.khan.co.kr/kh_news/khan_art_view.html?art_id=201907031650001#csidxe6f3bf0c39cec99886bcfed32239c73.

Women Journal. "BLACKPINK Introduce Jennie's Younger Version in a Live Broadcast." October 30, 2019. [Link deleted.]

Xu, Everest Christine. "Marketing Plan for a Kpop Fan Artist." Honors thesis, Arizona State University, 2018. https://repository.asu.edu/items/48489.

Yun, Huijeong. "Choding-I . . . Gwanggo hanaro nalli natdeon "Ella Gross" geunhwange baneung gallyeotda" [The girl from the Baskin-Robbins scandal, Ella Gross's recent Instagram received differently], Wikitree, May 16, 2020, https://www.wikitree.co.kr/articles/532947.

5

Girl Groups in Uniform

Moranbong Band and the Staging of NK-Pop in and out of North Korea

Douglas Gabriel

Introduction

On July 6, 2012, the Pyongyang Grand Theatre swelled with a resplendent dia-pason as some eighteen young female musicians and vocalists of a newly formed pop group graced the stage. Illuminated by the flare of pyrotechnic sparklers, Moranbong Band (*Moranbong Akdan*) instantaneously became icons of popular culture in the Democratic People's Republic of Korea (DPRK, North Korea's official designation).[1] They have subsequently dominated television screens throughout the country with their eccentric showmanship and infectious anthems. NK-pop, you might call it.

On the surface, the group comes across as the latest cultural sensation through which the North Korean regime seeks to indoctrinate the populace, packaging its ideological precepts as entertaining media spectacles. There is ample reason to see it this way. Moranbong Band undoubtedly follows in the immediate footsteps of so-called light music groups established in North Korea since the 1980s. Early examples included the Wangjaesan Light Music Band (*Wangjaesan Gyeongeumakdan*) and the Pochonbo Electronic Ensemble (*Bocheonbo Jeonja Akdan*), acts that combined electronic, orchestral, and traditional Korean instru-ments.[2] These groups stood apart from the massive choirs and symphonies that

---

1. Translating as "Moran Hill," Moranbong refers to a park in Pyongyang that sits in close proximity to a number of sites that are significant within North Korean historical narratives. Chief among these is the Kaeson Revolutionary Site, which commemorates Kim Il-sung's return to Pyongyang in October 1945 following the liberation of Korea from Japanese colonial rule at the end of World War II.

2. Peter Moody, "From Production to Consumption: The Socialist Realism/Personality Cult Divide in North Korean Popular Music," *European Journal of Korean Studies* 19, no. 2 (2020): 22–24, https://doi.org/10.33526/ejks.20201902.7.

otherwise dominated the landscape of North Korean music at the time. They played a leading role in refashioning revolutionary songs and introducing them to a younger generation. The logic was simple: the core messages of the old standards could be more effectively transmitted to the youth when set to foxtrot rhythms and disco beats. Moreover, these bands functioned as a form of cultural diplomacy, embarking on extensive tours of China and Japan.[3] Hyon Song-wol, vocalist and de facto leader of Moranbong Band, previously sang with Pochonbo Electronic Ensemble, establishing a direct overlap between the two generations of pop music in North Korea.

Keith Howard conveys the general perception of Moranbong Band's political function when he writes that in totalitarian states,

> Songs become tools. Songs service the mass media, broadcasting ideology to the millions. Songs reinforce control, but if they can be made genuinely popular, they normalize authority. Songs generate change by altering social behavior, just as public displays of loyalty coerce compliance through mass spectacles, games, and festivals. Totalitarian states regard creators and performers—the writers, artists, musicians, and dancers—as workers of the state. They are rendered subservient to designated others—the people, audiences, and spectators (as they become part of spectacles)—who consume what is produced, and to the ruling elite who claim to represent the consumers.[4]

It is difficult to envision anyone arguing against any of these points—at least, so long as a group like Moranbong Band is considered solely within a caricaturized domestic context in which their music and performances are imagined to be consumed only by North Korean audiences, who uncritically absorb all propagandistic media directed their way.[5] However, such an oversimplified conception ignores the unruly ways in which North Korean popular culture has proliferated domestically and globally since the foundation of the state in 1948. It conforms to what Andre Schmid has identified as a pervasive tendency to characterize the North Korean government as having an omnipresent bearing on cultural production. Describing this perspective as adopted by scholars of North Korea, Schmid writes: "Nowhere is the state subjected to analysis precisely because it

---

3. Peter Moody, "Before the Korean Wave, the Ripple: North Korea's Music Diplomacy in East Asia in the 1970s–90s," paper presented for the National Committee on North Korea's "Emerging Scholars Roundtable Series," Zoom lecture, August 18, 2020.
4. Keith Howard, Songs for "Great Leaders": Ideology and Creativity in North Korean Music and Dance (New York: Oxford University Press, 2020), 241.
5. Howard is hardly alone in considering Moranbong Band solely within the contours of North Korean state ideology. See also Kang Dong-Wan and Mun Da-Hye, "Moranbongakdan 'Sinjageumakhoe Gongyeon' Uimi-wa Sisajeom" [Implications of Moranbong Band's "new music concert"], Dongbugayeongu [Northeast Asia Research] 30, no. 1 (2015): 273–304.

is everywhere."[6] Of course, part of the problem is the perceived lack of access to points of view that deviate from the state. Whether cultural producers have any intention, realized or not, of subverting the dictates under which they work remains a mystery to us because of the dearth of outlets through which any such view could be openly expressed. I contend, however, that this limitation does not inevitably lead to the conclusion that the state alone arbitrates over the meaning of the cultural artifacts that emerge under its banner. To hold such a view would be to ignore post-structuralism's lessons on the fundamentally precarious foundation of meaning in cultural texts. Notwithstanding the entrenchment of post-structuralist frameworks across disciplines in the humanities, when it comes to objects and texts that are perceived as belonging to a totalitarian milieu, the working assumption of many scholars is that such aesthetic forms can have no meaning outside the boundaries set by an all-controlling state.[7]

Breaking with this discursive precedent, the present chapter winds through three vignettes, each of which explores a distinct staging of Moranbong Band in geopolitical contexts that range from North Korea to China to Japan. While the North Korean and Chinese contexts involve the group directly, the Japanese context provides a useful contrast in that it entails an example of a Tokyo-based fan club of all things North Korean, which has assimilated elements of Moranbong Band's sartorial trademarks, choreography, and overall affect in their various activities. In adopting this approach, I build on the limited scholarship that has considered North Korean cultural production in light of its reception by both domestic and international audiences. Representative of this methodology is the work of performance and communication studies scholars David Terry and Andrew Wood, who have studied the Arirang Mass Games—a spectacle involving thousands of North Korean citizens and professionals in a breathtaking display of acrobatics and synchronous visual effects.[8] Terry and Wood analyze the event in terms of the tension it produces between different messages directed towards and received by audiences of disparate cultural and linguistic backgrounds. The Arirang Mass Games indeed provides a cogent case study on this head, as the event is one of North Korea's foremost tourist attractions and draws a relatively wide range of demographics. Yet it is hardly the only instance

---

6. Andre Schmid, "Historicizing North Korea: State Socialism, Population Mobility, and Cold War Historiography," *American Historical Review* 123, no. 2 (2018): 455–56, http://doi.org/10.1093/ahr/rhy001.
7. I think here of Michel Foucault's classic description of the author as "the ideological figure by which one marks the manner in which we fear the proliferation of meaning." Michel Foucault, "What Is an Author?" in *The Foucault Reader*, ed. Paul Rabinow (New York: Pantheon Books, 1984), 119.
8. David P. Terry and Andrew F. Wood, "Presenting Juche: Audiencing North Korea's 2012 Arirang Mass Games," *Text and Performance Quarterly* 35, no. 2–3 (2015): 177–201, https://doi.org/10.108 0/10462937.2015.1036110.

in which North Korean culture is consumed and interpreted by international audiences. The diffuse range of responses to Moranbong Band demonstrates as much. More than their music, their image has become an object of attention and appropriation around the world, and it is for this reason that I focus primarily on the visual dimensions of the group.

A caveat: this chapter makes no pretense of giving a complete picture of the group's reception by the diverse audiences that feature in the episodes discussed herein. Read it instead as a conceptual reckoning. Deliberately impressionistic, this chapter aims to rescript Moranbong Band's emergence and evolution by foregrounding the multiple effects their image has produced as it has cleaved through an extraordinary spectrum of ideological and political hues.

Comeback Stage: The Revitalization of NK-Pop circa 2012

Moranbong Band's debut took place before an audience that included Chairman Kim Jong-un, who at the time had occupied the office less than a year, following the death of his father, Kim Jong-il, in December 2011.[9] Adding to the intensity of the spectacle, the event doubled as the first public appearance of Chairman Kim's wife, who was revealed to be Ri Sol-ju, a singer herself and a former member of the earlier light music group Unhasu Orchestra (*Eunhasu Gwanhyeonakdan*).[10] This dual unveiling of North Korea's latest musical phenomenon and the First Lady evinced the deep imbrications of pop music and politics in North Korea, effectively telegraphing that one might perform as a vocalist one day and ascend to the highest echelons of the ruling hierarchy the next, even in the context of North Korea's highly patriarchal political system.[11] It likewise underscored the emphatic role of visuality in North Korean politics, where the act of making an appearance often generates more hype and repercussions than verbal or textual articulations.[12]

According to the official telling, Kim had played a direct role in forming Moranbong Band in March 2012. Early news reports on the group portrayed

---

9.   A video of Moranbong Band's debut performance, rebroadcast on North Korean television, can be viewed at https://www.youtube.com/watch?v=JkH8u39DW2g (last accessed October 17, 2020).
10. Howard, *Songs for "Great Leaders"*, 260.
11. In fact, by 2017, Hyon Song-wol would be elected to the Central Committee of the Workers' Party of Korea and travel to South Korea as part of the delegation responsible for representing North Korea's intent to participate in the 2018 Winter Olympics in Pyeongchang. See Howard, *Songs for "Great Leaders"*, 266.
12. A peculiar feature of North Korean newspaper articles, for instance, is that they regularly dedicate more space to listing the names of officials who appeared at a given political or cultural event than they do to any description of the content of the speeches made on the occasion. Moreover, charting public appearances (or lack thereof) is one of the primary means by which outside observers attempt to track the standing of high-ranking officials in North Korea.

Kim's creation of the ensemble as inaugurating a new era of popular music in keeping with the demands of the contemporary moment. The day after Moranbong Band's debut, for example, the Korea Central News Agency (KCNA) rhapsodized that Kim had "organized the Moranbong band as required by the new century, prompted by a grandiose plan to bring about a dramatic turn in the field of literature and arts this year in which a new century of Juche Korea begins."[13] In more measured terms, the historian Jeon Jong-hyeok wrote in a 2015 article detailing the group's formation that, in founding the group, Kim had insisted upon the necessity of "shedding established forms and molds" so as to cut a clear path for "the constant creation of new things."[14] Jeon specifies that this directive stemmed not from an infatuation with novelty for its own sake but rather from Kim's discerning realization that the coming era should be greeted by "a new rhythm in our style," with the possessive determiner here referring to aesthetic sensibilities that the state broadly attributes to the Korean people.[15] Intuiting the political dimensions of this push for newness, Pekka Korhonen and Adam Cathcart suggest that such rhetoric worked to demonstrate that Kim Jong-un's leadership "stays in tune with the changing times and is itself capable of navigating the revolution into the future."[16]

The band was thus tasked with updating the style and sound of the afore-mentioned light-music groups that had been established under Kim Jong-il in the 1980s and 1990s. While continuing in the general strain of previous light-music groups, Moranbong Band's contemporaneity was put on full display at their first concert, a performance Korhonen and Cathcart see as emblematic of the group's "early liberal style."[17] During this period, Moranbong Band's concerts comprised a diverse repertoire of instrumental pieces, which showcased the virtuosity of the musicians, and vocal performances, which ran the gamut from laudatory ballads to Chinese and even Western covers. Throughout the debut performance, the five

13. Korea Central News Agency (KCNA), "Kim Jong Un Appreciates Demonstration Performance of Newly Organized Moranbong Band," July 7, 2012, accessed September 21, 2020, http://www.kcna.co.jp/item/2012/201207/news07/20120707-09ee.html. "Juche" refers to the official ideology promoted by the state. Translating as "self-reliance," it emphasizes the centrality of human agents in what the state conceives as a teleological unfolding of history. See Bruce Cumings, *Korea's Place in the Sun: A Modern History* (New York: W.W. Norton, 2005), 413.
14. Jeon Jong-hyeok, "Moranbongakdan-eul Juchehyeongmyeong-ui Saesidae Bonbogiakdaneuro Ganghwabaljeonsikisin Gyeongaehaneun Kim Jong-un Dongji-ui Bulmyeorui Eopjeok" [Moranbong Band, strengthened and developed as a model band of the new era of the Juche Revolution—an immortal achievement of Dear Comrade Kim Jong-un), *Yeoksa Gwahak* [Historical Science] 4 (2015): 47. (All translations from Korean are my own.)
15. Jeon, "Moranbongakdan-eul," 47.
16. Pekka Korhonen and Adam Cathcart, "Tradition and Legitimation in North Korea: The Role of the Moranbong Band," *Review of Korean Studies* 20, no. 2 (2017): 25, http://doi.org/10.25024/review.2017.20.2.001.
17. Korhonen and Cathcart, "Tradition and Legitimation," 23.

vocalists of the group worked the stage in tinseled outfits, which complemented what proved to be a multimedia extravaganza. Pyrotechnics flashed as videos, synced to each song, projected from nine towering digital screens punctuating the rear of the stage.

The most energized moment came near the end of the program, when the group ran through a lengthy medley of songs from various Disney soundtracks. For this segment, performers costumed as Disney characters paraded on stage and danced while the background screens showed scenes culled from the corresponding animations. This aspect of the performance would have been astonishing had it not been preceded by an even more ironic incorporation of American popular culture. Earlier in the set, the group had performed Bill Conti's "Gonna Fly Now," better known as the theme song from the movie *Rocky* (1976) and its many sequels and spin-offs. The background screens in this case showed a run of decontextualized clips from the series, including the dramatic scene from *Rocky IV* (1985) in which Sylvester Stallone's character lands a knockout punch on his Soviet rival, Ivan Drago. Due to its negative portrayal of the Soviet Union, *Rocky IV* is widely perceived as one of the most blatant examples of American Cold War propaganda.[18] Incorporated into Moranbong Band's performance twenty-seven years after its release, the film was inexplicably assimilated by the very country often described as one of the last holdouts of Soviet-style socialism.

This absorption of ostensibly antagonistic foreign elements by Moranbong Band aligns with what Lisa Burnett describes in her reading of the Arirang Mass Games as the state's desire to project a future in which national boundaries give way to a prospect of utopian universalism. In this worldview, "music breaks free of issues of cultural origin, ownership, and authenticity that so often accompany discourse on aesthetics and nationalism."[19] Indeed, the abovementioned KCNA article described Moranbong Band's debut performance as having constituted a momentous demonstration "before the world."[20] Although situated in North Korea and among North Koreans, the performance was represented in the state media as directed towards an imagined global constituency undivided by ideological rifts. The music and video clips from the *Rocky* movies were, in this context, stripped of any impactful connection to Cold War ideology. Instead, the world on the stage modeled a cosmos of free-floating signifiers unfettered from outmoded referents to a bygone world order. The splintering of Hollywood movie clips across divided screens in the background could not have been more

18. William J. Palmer, *The Films of the Eighties: A Social History* (Carbondale: Southern Illinois University Press, 1995), 219.
19. Lisa Burnett, "Let Morning Shine over Pyongyang: The Future-Oriented Nationalism of North Korea's Arirang Mass Games," *Asian Music* 44, no. 1 (2013): 5, http://doi.org/10.1353/amu.2013.0010.
20. KCNA, "Kim Jong Un."

appropriate, lending a spatial emphasis to the fractured spate of signs projected indiscriminately from the stage.

There is no doubt that, on one level, the dynamics of the performance were funneled into the service of upholding the Kim regime.[21] The whirlwind of semiotic drift that coursed through Moranbong Band's showcase set in relief the stability attributed to Kim's leadership, with the intervallic praises to the Respected Marshal in Moranbong Band's songs coming to appear as the only constant in a world of signs denuded of any substantive meaning. At the same time, the event foreshadowed the uncontrollable range of readings and uses to which Moranbong Band—considered here as a semiotic set of aural and imagistic functions—would be put when disseminated abroad. Before we follow the group's discursive odyssey internationally, however, it bears considering the impact of their performances on the domestic front.

The emergence of Moranbong Band as the pinnacle of pop music in North Korea had marked effects outside of the performance hall. The proliferation of media images of the members in sequined skirts and high heels was accompanied by a rise in demand for ostentatious clothing and accessories. They became influential trendsetters for a generation of young women who enjoy a newfound degree of economic power by dint of the now quasi-legal market economy.[22] That the North Korean regime became apprehensive of the power that had begun to accumulate around Moranbong Band upon their emergence is strongly suggested by the group's sudden disappearance from the public eye in July 2015. That is not to say that their music ceased to be heard. Rather, television broadcasts that normally would have featured clips of the group's live performances now played their music over stock footage of nature scenes and shots of Pyongyang.[23] It was not so much Moranbong Band's sound, but rather the visual influence of the group that led to their hiatus and, as we will see, a conspicuous rebranding of their image.

Adding plausibility to the notion that the group was pulled from public appearances for political reasons is the fact that their disappearance overlapped with the debut of another all-female group called Chongbong Band (*Cheongbong Akdan*) in August 2015. This "rival" group was rumored to have been formed under the direction of Chairman Kim's wife, Ri Sol-ju, who, as Tai Wei Lim suggests, "may have strategically positioned herself as the ultimate arbiter of the

21. David Zeglen, "Rockin' in the Unfree World: North Korea's Moranbong Band and the Celebrity Dictator," *Celebrity Studies* 8, no. 1 (2017): 142–50, https://doi.org/10.1080/19392397.2016.1272861.
22. Bronwen Dalton and Jung Kyungja, "Women's Image Transformed: Femininity in North Korea," *East Asia Forum Quarterly* 8, no. 2 (April–June 2016): 31.
23. "N. Korea's All-Female Music Band Disappears from Broadcasts," *Korea Herald*, September 7, 2015, http://www.koreaherald.com/view.php?ud=20150907000683.

fates of cultural groups in North Korea."[24] Lim is led to this hypothesis in part
because of widespread reports that Kim Jong-un had been romantically involved
with Hyon Song-wol, the leader of Moranbong Band, prior to the formation
of the group—a presumable cause for jealousy on Ri's part. More broadly, this
speculation emerges from a framework that conceives of Moranbong Band as
participating in a patron-client relationship with the state, one in which the
group receives the rewards of fame, social status, and a relatively comfortable
standard of living in return for their work in bolstering the legitimacy of the
leader and propagating the state's doctrine. From this perspective, temporarily
sidelining the group became a means of reminding Moranbong Band of their
place in the hierarchical system.

When Moranbong Band returned to the stage in September 2015, their
appearance and the format of their concerts had appreciably changed. Out
were the glittery garments, and in were outfits modeled on military uniforms.[25]
Cavorting cartoon characters no longer adorned the stage for elongated medleys
of foreign songs. Instead, a single background screen projected video footage of
Kim Jong-un at regular intervals, in this way directing the audience's behavior
by prompting them to stand and clap. The band members themselves displayed a
regimented and unified appearance, having adopted nearly identical short hair-
styles that stood out in contrast to the distinct cuts they had previously sported.
Moreover, they held solemn facial expressions for the duration of their performances, adding to the militaristic air of their refashioned image.

The break between the respective phases of the band before and after their
hiatus is obvious on the surface. Yet North Korean sources published after the
group's reformation in late 2015 describe nothing of the sort. Commentators
have instead reframed the band's early performances in light of their conservative overhaul. A 2018 article in the general interest magazine *Chollima* implies
that Moranbong Band's early performances functioned less to update preexisting
models of popular music than to uncover forgotten songs of the past. The article
focuses on the group's October 2012 performance for Foundation Day, a national
holiday marking the founding of the Workers' Party of Korea (WPK). On this

---

24. Tai Wei Lim, "State-Endorsed Popular Culture: A Case Study of the North Korean Girl Band
    Moranbong," *Asia and the Pacific Policy Studies* 4, no. 3 (2017): 605, https://doi.org/10.1002/
    app5.195.
25. Focusing specifically on the group's outfits, Huh Jungsun and Kim Awon perceive two separate
    phases since the group's return to the stage, the first of which involved costumes inspired by air
    force and navy uniforms, and the second of which involved the use of actual uniforms worn by
    navy personnel. Each of these can be seen in contrast to the earlier extravagant style of 2012
    through early 2015. Huh Jungsun and Kim Awon, "Moranbongakdan Mudaeuisang-ui Seutail
    Teukseong mit Sangjing" [Style characteristics and symbolism of the Moranbong Band's stage
    costumes], *Boksik* [Journal of the Korean Society of Costume] 68, no. 4 (2018): 23–35, http://doi.
    org/10.7233/jksc.2018.68.4.023.

occasion, they had debuted a rendition of a piece titled "Mother and Father's Days of Youth," a song which had originally been released in 1995 but received scant attention at the time.[26] Relating the aesthetic and ideological beauty of the work, and the degree to which it purportedly touched Kim Jong-un, the article proposes that aspects associated with the conservative reinvention of the group were in fact already present in their early performances. In this reading, to meet the demands of the times does not necessarily require supplanting earlier cultural works with untested models. New melodies need not be devised out of thin air. Rather, the past offers itself as a cornucopia of musical ideas awaiting recuperation. By singling out a song that had been written in 1995 but which only received its due appreciation in 2012, the author is able to link the regimes of Kim Jong-il and Kim Jong-un via a recursive temporality, wherein Moranbong Band answers the demands of the present by reviving the past.

All of this goes to show that, even within North Korea, there has hardly been a single narrative of Moranbong Band's entrance onto the scene of state-sanctioned pop music. The range of approaches North Korean authors have taken in casting the group as representative of Kim Jong-un's contributions to cultural advancement attests to Moranbong Band's unsteady role in facilitating the grand propaganda schemes devised by the state.

To be sure, our knowledge of Moranbong Band is steeped in a morass of hearsay. The group's standing vis-à-vis the North Korean leadership, and their function as a formative influence on the contours of fashion and taste in the country, remain opaque. But it is this uncertainty that has propelled audiences outside of North Korea to discursively frame and repurpose Moranbong Band's music and image in dynamic ways, expanding the horizons of the group's impact and import.

Pariah Pop Stars under the Paparazzi Gaze

In December 2015, Moranbong Band made headlines across the world when they traveled by train to Beijing for what would have been their first international concert, only for the event to be cancelled and the group members recalled to Pyongyang. Speculation abounded as to whether the cancellation had resulted from a diplomatic snub on China's part in response to Kim Jong-un's recent assertion of North Korea's capacity to build a hydrogen bomb, or because of internal deliberations on the appropriateness of the concert, given that North Korea was about to engage in collective mourning to mark the fourth anniversary of Kim Jong-il's death.

---

26. "17nyeonmane dasi Chajajusin Norae" [A song discovered again after seventeen years], *Chollima*, no. 10 (2018): 21.

Whatever the cause for their premature departure, Moranbong Band had arguably given one of their biggest performances to date simply by journeying to Beijing. The sight of North Korean pop stars in flesh and blood, alighting and ambulating through the Chinese metropolis, mesmerized the international media. Some accounts fetishized the Cold War vintage outfits exhibited by the members upon their arrival. As Edward Wong and Owen Guo exclaimed in the *New York Times*, "Paparazzi photographs posted online showed band members being whisked through the streets on a bus, dressed in old-school socialist fashion: furry hats with a red star and long olive military-style winter coats."[27] The images referenced by Wong and Guo include photographs circulated by Reuters and other news outlets.[28] They show the group members at close range and from candid angles typical of paparazzi photos, occasionally capturing other photographers in the background positioning themselves for the perfect shot. While the members display a heightened awareness of performing for the camera eyes that

Figure 5.1: Hyon Song-wol (far right) carrying a Chanel handbag as Moranbong Band members leave for a rehearsal, Beijing, December 11, 2015. Photograph by Imaginechina Limited, provided by Alamy Stock Photo.

---

27. Edward Wong and Owen Guo, "North Korea Sends Its Leader's Chosen Pop Band to Beijing," *New York Times*, December 11, 2015, https://www.nytimes.com/2015/12/12/world/asia/china-north-korea-moranbong-girl-band.html.
28. For a slideshow of the images published by Reuters, see "North Korean Moranbong Band Prepare for China Performance," Reuters, December 11, 2015, accessed October 16, 2020, https://www.reuters.com/news/picture/north-korean-moranbong-band-prepare-for-idUSKBN0TU1YH20151211.

surround them, they seldom meet the gaze of any photographer, adding to the mysterious aura that enveloped their visit.

In contrast to reports that focused on the peculiar dress of the ensemble, several editorials expressed bewilderment at how closely the members of Moranbong Band resembled any other tabloid-worthy celebrities in their behavior—particularly in their apparent predilection for high-end commodities. Yi Whan-woo of the *Korea Times* related, for instance, that Hyon Song-wol "was seen carrying an extravagant Chanel handbag."[29] Perhaps even more than the band's performance of Western covers in their early performances, Hyon's sartorial coupling of socialist chic and haute couture perplexed onlookers, confounding all expectations of how the North Korean idols would present themselves.

Amid the awe expressed in coverage of the group's abbreviated Beijing trip, media outlets made frequent parallels between Moranbong Band and global pop sensations, from South Korean K-pop groups like Girls' Generation to Western pop groups like the Spice Girls. And yet, in the same breath, these accounts habitually cast Moranbong Band as an absolute other to the sphere of global culture, infusing their descriptions of the North Korean troupe with references to the abominations with which North Korea has become synonymous in the international media: namely, human rights perils and the pursuit of nuclear weapons. Writing for the British tabloid the *Daily Mail*, Jamie Fullerton epitomized this phenomenon, likening Moranbong Band to the Spice Girls while proposing that they take nicknames similar to the members of the 1990s UK sensation, but ones appropriate to the conditions of North Korea. The writer's suggestions included such grotesque variations as "Military Spice, Prison Camp Spice, Execution Spice, Starving Spice and Gross Violation Of Human Rights Spice."[30]

This interplay between the familiar and the repulsive suggestively recalls Sigmund Freud's well-rehearsed concept of the uncanny, or "something which is familiar and old-established in the mind and which has become alienated from it only through the process of repression."[31] In the case of Moranbong Band, the group members reminded the international media of girl groups like the Spice Girls while also appearing as an unsolicited return of aesthetics associated with

29. Yi Whan-woo, "NK Girl Band Becomes Rumor Mill," *Korea Times*, December 14, 2015, https://www.koreatimes.co.kr/www/news/nation/2015/12/485_193139.html.

30. Jamie Fullerton, "Short Skirts, High Heels and DIY Double Eyelid Surgery at HOME: The Beauty Secrets of North Korean Women Braving the Fashion Police to Look Like Rogue State's Own 'Spice Girls' (and Kim's Mysterious Wife)," *Daily Mail*, February 12, 2015, https://www.dailymail.co.uk/news/article-2950718/North-Korean-fashion-changing-thanks-country-s-Spice-Girls.html. Fullerton's quip plays on the nicknames by which the members of the Spice Girls identified themselves: Baby Spice, Ginger Spice, Posh Spice, Scary Spice, and Sporty Spice.

31. Sigmund Freud, "The 'Uncanny,'" in *The Standard Edition of the Complete Psychological Works of Sigmund Freud, Vol. XVII (1917–1919): An Infantile Neurosis and Other Works*, trans. James Strachey (London: Hogarth Press, 1955), 241.

totalitarian regimes of the early twentieth century. Thus, press coverage invoked the familiar gossipy terms of celebrity culture—as if the fact that one member had carried a Chanel bag constituted news at all—only to definitively jettison Moranbong Band from the ranks of global pop by twinning them with references to famine and firing squads.

Far from isolated to their Beijing appearance, the perception of Moranbong Band as an uncanny anomaly has characterized international coverage of the group since their debut. Decidedly darker than the flippant appellations attributed to the members in the *Daily Mail*, much speculation on the group has turned on actual matters of life and death. All the more apt, then, is the concept of the uncanny, for as Freud notes, "Many people experience the feeling [of the uncanny] in the highest degree in relation to death and dead bodies, to the return of the dead, and to spirits and ghosts."[32] To take an exemplary case, in August 2013, rumors ran amok that Hyon Song-wol had been executed by firing squad along with eleven members of the Unhasu Orchestra and the Wangjaesan Light Music Band. South Korean reports based on an anonymous source claimed that the convicted musicians had produced and distributed pornographic videos, which had been discovered on the black market in China.[33] Adding to the abhorrence of the situation, the unidentified source alleged that members of Moranbong Band were made to witness the execution.

Nine months after Hyon had been presumed executed, however, she suddenly reemerged, speaking at a rally for the nation's art workers in May 2014. Thereafter, she participated in Moranbong Band's performances, apparently having resumed her role as leader of the band. Against this background, Hyon's glamorous strut through the streets of Beijing before crowds of befuddled paparazzi becomes a scene redolent with political implications.[34] Whether voluntarily or not, in these appearances, Hyon presented herself as having risen from the dead, upending assumptions about the absolute brutality of the North Korean regime. In doing so, she came to embody the uncanniness that has accompanied Moranbong Band's image and reputation outside of North Korea. In the international context, the group registers as strangely familiar in terms of their image. And at the same time, they emblematize a despotic model of communism otherwise considered a historical phenomenon, a throwback to the dark days before the downfall of the Soviet Union. To quote Freud on Friedrich Wilhelm Joseph Schelling's definition of the uncanny, Moranbong Band materializes as "something which ought to have remained hidden but has come to light."[35]

---

32. Freud, "'Uncanny,'" 241.
33. Ahn Yong-hyun, "Kim Jong-un's Ex-Girlfriend 'Shot by Firing Squad,'" *Chosun Ilbo*, August 29, 2013, http://english.chosun.com/site/data/html_dir/2013/08/29/2013082901412.html.
34. Lim, "State-Endorsed Popular Culture," 606.
35. Freud, "'Uncanny,'" 241.

In these encounters with the international media, Moranbong Band assumes an unwittingly critical function, tacitly implying that Western popular culture itself might be shot through with a totalitarian impulse. In academic circles, such ideas are typically associated with the Frankfurt School of critical theory. By now, Theodor Adorno and Max Horkheimer's classic pronouncements have come to ring out as the complaints of so many Marxist curmudgeons. Think of such lines as: "The blind and rapidly spreading repetition of designated words links advertising to the totalitarian slogan."[36] This appraisal succinctly encapsulates the thrust of what Adorno and Horkheimer term the "culture industry," or the conditions of late capitalism that transmogrify the sphere of culture into insipid forms of entertainment, which distract passive consumers from the otherwise blatant abuses of power that bear upon their lives. With Moranbong Band, these old charges are given a new face. Looking at the group, one begins to sense that the mass propaganda of an authoritarian regime does not differ so much from the waves of commercial culture that saturate our own lives. Down come the safeguards that would ensure an impenetrable divide between North Korea's propagandistic displays and the global entertainment industry. The embankments denying any point of tangency between the two no longer hold. Military coats aside, the group looks all too ordinary. The band underscores just how much we rely on othering North Korea's cultural and political spectacles to convince ourselves that our own mass phenomena belong to a higher order, or at least a less devastating one.

Marching in and out of Lockstep: The Military-First Girls

Meet "Chunhun," the sobriquet of a Japanese internet sensation who fronts a largely anonymous community styled *Sengun Joshi*, or the "Military-First Girls."[37] A veritable fan club of North Korean culture, the group was formed in 2014 when Chunhun convened a party with five other women in their twenties and thirties who, like the host, harbored an interest in North Korea. In the years since their inaugural meeting, the six women have maintained an online presence via an official Twitter page and their respective personal accounts.[38] As we will see, they have also occasionally given public performances.[39]

36. Theodor Adorno and Max Horkheimer, "The Culture Industry: Enlightenment as Mass Deception," in *Dialectic of Enlightenment: Philosophical Fragments*, ed. Gunzelin Schmid Noerr, trans. Edmund Jephcott (Stanford: Stanford University Press, 2002), 135.
37. I thank Zachary Trebellas for his research assistance and help in translating the Japanese sources referenced in this section.
38. The Military-First Girls' Twitter page can be found at https://twitter.com/sengunjoshikai (last accessed October 17, 2020).
39. My sketch of the group is based primarily on Tomohiro Osaki, "Drawn to North Korea's Culture, Japanese Internet Star Looks beyond the Saber-Rattling," *Japan Times*, August 16, 2017, https://

Figure 5.2: Chunhun of Sengun-Joshi rehearsing Moranbong Band's choreography for a fan event in Tokyo, October 29, 2017. Image by Toru Nahai of Reuters, provided by Alamy Stock Photo.

Chunhun's interest in North Korea originated through visual experiences. As a studio art major, she encountered reproductions of North Korean propaganda posters and found herself enticed by the impeccably detailed work of illustrators associated with Pyongyang's Mansudae Art Studio. To this day, a pinned post on Chunhun's Twitter page links to images of her personal sketchbooks scribbled with exhaustive notes on the compositions of various North Korean socialist realist paintings.[40] This fascination eventually led her to take an internship at the *Daily NK*, a South Korean-based news outlet that focuses on North Korea. All the while, she has incorporated elements of North Korean aesthetics into her everyday life, extending her commitment on this score to procuring and using North Korean makeup purchased from stores in Dandong, a Chinese city just north of the border with the DPRK. Germane to our purposes, she likewise remains enthralled by Moranbong Band, relating: "Even if I have a really tough day coming up, I can easily switch into a very aggressive mood when these songs

www.japantimes.co.jp/news/2017/08/16/national/drawn-north-koreas-culture-japanese-internet-star-looks-beyond-saber-rattling/.

40. Chunhun, Twitter post, November 1, 2019, 10:12 a.m., https://twitter.com/pomhyanggi/status/1190270313210114048. Please note that since the initial writing of this article, Chunhun's account has been made private and is therefore only available to approved followers.

encourage me to 'annihilate enemies' or assure me that I have the 'Great Marshal' on my side."[41]

Chunhun is quick to emphasize that the Military-First Girls do not support North Korea's development of nuclear weapons. Nor do they turn a blind eye to human rights issues in the country. Rather, their express mission lies in revealing to the Japanese public that the messaging and actions of the Kim regime do not define the people and culture of North Korea. "By introducing North Korea's culture, like its fashion, music and arts," Chunhun explains, "I want the Japanese public to realize there are good people living there and that they can't be blamed for what their government does."[42]

Yet the Military-First Girls' activities have hardly amounted to anything like a conventional campaign to influence public opinion. Rather than distributing educational tracts, for instance, the group's textual output has taken the form of a thirty-six-page North Korea-themed magazine called *Sengun* (Military-First), which was limited to 100 copies and sold out by February 2020. With such a limited print run, the document has taken on the aspect of a rarified underground zine, rather than that of a methodical attempt at reaching the wider public. In begging the question of what the group hopes to accomplish through their publicized actions, the magazine points to how the Military-First Girls often deliberately obfuscate any sense of a clear agenda.

A whimsical example of the Military-First Girls' enigmatic attitude toward North Korea comes from the Twitter account of Risesshu, who is the only member to identify as *Zainichi*—a permanent resident of Japan of Korean background. In February 2020, Risesshu posted what otherwise would have been a mundane photographic account of her experience at a dessert café that offers a "coffee print" service, whereby customers can have an image of their choice reproduced on the surface of their drink.[43] Staring back at visitors to Risesshu's page is the grinning face of Kim Jong-un. Risesshu's comment relates that she, "of course," elected to have the "loved and respected supreme majesty" imprinted on her caffeine fix of the day. A series of images follows, showing a straw placed through Kim's mouth and the disintegration of his portrait as the drink is consumed. Risesshu's final comment proclaims that Kim will "live on in our hearts foreverrrr." This intermixing of sloganeering and social media-speak hits on the emphatic evasion of the Military-First Girls in their treatment of North Korean ideological paraphernalia. While such gestures would seem to suggest that the

41. Quoted in Osaki, "Drawn to North Korea's Culture."
42. Quoted in Osaki, "Drawn to North Korea's Culture."
43. Risesshu, Twitter post, February 26, 2020, 2:50 a.m., https://twitter.com/resesh_DPRK/status/1232573667390844930. Since my initial access of this Twitter post on October 14, 2020, Risesshu's account has been suspended, perhaps speaking to the pronounced tension that surrounds the Military-First Girls in Japan.

group members engross themselves in a purely ironic appropriation of loaded imagery, other activities they have engaged in cast the group in a different light— one that has provoked a vitriolic reaction from the Japanese public.

In 2017, the Military-First Girls staged a public performance that might best be described as North Korean cosplay. In truth, it baffles all characterization. I hazard a sketch here based on the scant video footage of the performance that has circulated online.[44] In a venue that looks like a subterranean karaoke joint, the members of the Military-First Girls take the stage in front of a screen on which one of Moranbong Band's concert videos is projected. Chunhun and her fellow travelers do not sing themselves but, dressed in white navy outfits, perform dance routines in sync with the concert footage. The visual effect is one of a dramatic *mise en abyme*. The video of the Pyongyang performance seems to leap out of the projection and into the space of the live event, bridging the distance between the North Koreans on-screen and the audience in Japan.

The performance had been anticipated by a series of photographs published by international media outlets showing the Military-First Girls practicing Moranbong Band's choreography.[45] Adding to the uncertainty regarding the group's attitude toward North Korea, these images capture the members in a small living space adorned with reproductions of the portraits of Kim Il-sung and Kim Jong-il that are ubiquitous in North Korea, along with assorted DPRK-themed memorabilia. Amid these props, the women of the Military-First Girls study Moranbong Band's concert videos and run through their dance routines.

Far from an innocuous indulgence, the Military-First Girls' dance with Moranbong Band ignited a wave of backlash, primarily from the far-right wing of Japan's political continuum. That the group has struck such a nerve is largely due to the outrage that persists over North Korea's kidnapping of Japanese citizens during the 1970s and 1980s—abductions that were long suspected, and for which Kim Jong-il made a rare public apology in September 2002. Details remain shadowy, and it is unclear how many Japanese citizens were directly abducted against their will and how many were otherwise talked into traveling to North Korea and subsequently detained. What is clear, however, is that once in North Korea, the Japanese citizens held there underwent intense indoctrination, so much so that erstwhile members of the New Left movement came to believe that the revolution they had formerly envisioned carrying out in Japan could only come to fruition through the promotion of ideology modeled on North Korea's

44. See, for example, the video clip that accompanies Kelly-Ann Mills, "North Korea's All-Female Fan Club Dress Up in Military Uniforms and Recreate Songs by Kim Jong-un's Favourite Pop Band," *Mirror*, November 2, 2017, accessed October 8, 2020, https://www.mirror.co.uk/news/world-news/north-koreas-female-fan-club-11454430.

45. Emil Lendof, "Inside Japan's North Korea Fan Club," *New York Post*, November 2, 2017, accessed January 23, 2021, https://nypost.com/2017/11/02/inside-japans-north-korea-fan-club/#2.

political system and the Kim leader cult.[46] As part of the indoctrination process, these revolutionaries were kept in isolation and subjected to constant reiterations of North Korea's political platitudes. They were also made to watch North Korean films that used graphic imagery to stress the brutality of the Japanese during the colonial period.[47] That the Military-First Girls would choose to dance beneath portraits of the Kim leaders flies in the face of the anti-North Korean stance that has become widespread in Japan due to these abductions.[48]

Consequently, Chunhun receives voluminous hate mail messages and faces relentless speculation that she might be a North Korean defector or a spy.[49] Additionally, since leaving her post at the *Daily NK*, she has struggled to land employment because of her unfavorable reputation.[50] In the face of this adversity, however, Chunhun keeps her poise, insisting on the normality of her engagement with North Korean culture. "I'm the same as girls who like K-pop and love the culture of Seoul," she pleads, "or the girls who wear the same makeup as America's Taylor Swift."[51] The ordinariness of North Korea is reiterated by a 23-year-old member of the Military-First Girls, who has explained to the Japanese media that she became interested in North Korea after taking a tour of Pyongyang out of curiosity.[52] While aware that the experiences afforded to tourists hardly represent the complete picture of life in North Korea, she nevertheless found herself surprised by the degree to which the people she encountered seemed to be living lives not so different from her own.

As the above episodes demonstrate, the Military-First Girls' approach to North Korea wavers wildly: now appearing as a campy gag, and now a genuine attempt to understand the people and culture of this inscrutable place. The equivocality of the fan club cuts against the pervasive notion that to celebrate any facet of North Korea is to make a sweeping endorsement of the country in all its particulars. By this logic, in which the part and the whole become indistinguishable, one must either condone or condemn North Korea on all grounds. By permitting themselves to take pleasure in North Korean culture and its attendant sign systems in ways that confound classification, the Military-First Girls model

46. Patricia Steinhoff, "Kidnapped Japanese in North Korea: The New Left Connection," *Journal of Japanese Studies* 30, no. 1 (2004): 123–42, http://doi.org/10.1353/jjs.2004.0035.
47. Steinhoff, "Kidnapped Japanese in North Korea," 128.
48. Osaki, "Drawn to North Korea's Culture."
49. Simon Osborne, "North Korea's All-Girl Fan Club REVEALED: Japanese Group Devoted to Kim Jong-un's Regime," *Express*, November 2, 2017, https://www.express.co.uk/news/world/874650/japan-north-korea-fan-club-sengun-joshi-military-first-girls-chunhun.
50. Osborne, "North Korea's All-Girl Fan Club."
51. Quoted in Mills, "North Korea's All-Female Fan Club."
52. "No Bunka Ni Mune Kyun . . .? 'Sengun Joshi' No Sekai" [Their hearts skip a beat over North Korean culture . . .?! The world of "Sengun Joshi"], *Chunichi Shimbun*, June 11, 2017, https://www.chunichi.co.jp/article/34862.

alternative postures. In their cosplay reenactments, Moranbong Band is neither critically *détourned* nor mobilized as a means of indoctrination. The Military-First Girls, masquerading as Moranbong Band, present themselves as playing by other rules than those that define the perpetual deadlock between North Korea and the rest of the world.

Conclusion

At the time of this writing, reports are emerging that suggest Moranbong Band may soon undergo a significant turnover in membership. In mid-2020, Kim Jong-un's sister, Kim Yo-jong, who holds a high-ranking position in Pyongyang's Propaganda and Agitation Department (PAD), ordered the recruitment of female vocalists and instrumentalists.[53] The move has been interpreted as preparation for the instatement of a new generation of Moranbong Band members. This is hardly a far-fetched scenario, given that most current members are approaching their late twenties and early thirties and are thus likely to get married in the near future. It remains to be seen whether this will in fact take place, or whether any such shuffling of members will be accompanied by perceptible changes to the band's stature and function in North Korea's cultural orbit. But the fact that we can so easily imagine the group members being replaced and the band itself carrying on virtually uninterrupted underscores how Moranbong Band is in many ways designed to accommodate a vast interchangeability of parts, so long as the unit as a whole continues to produce desirable ideological effects in the form of captivating aural and visual stimuli.

As much as Moranbong Band comes across as a monolithic machine ventriloquized by the state, however, this chapter has aimed to convey the prodigious outpouring of readings and perceptions that have amassed around the band, especially in cases where they have entered global circuits of diplomacy and consumption. In light of their international intersections, the interpretive scope demanded by Moranbong Band eclipses conventional frameworks that would portray North Korea's cultural apparatuses as ensconced within a tightly sealed system wherein they are meticulously stage-managed by the state. By taking a more expansive view, we are pushed to adopt new ways of interfacing with the multifaceted dimensions of North Korea, and to move beyond the perception that every engagement must amount to a full-fledged endorsement or denouncement of North Korea in its entirety. To look anew at North Korean society and politics, we might begin by quite literally facing the music.

---

53. Ha Yuna, "North Korea May Select New Members for Moranbong Band," *Daily NK*, July 17, 2020, accessed October 17, 2020, https://www.dailynk.com/english/north-korea-may-select-new-members-moranbong-band.

Bibliography

"17nyeonmane dasi Chajajusin Norae" [A song discovered again after seventeen years]. *Chollima*, no. 10 (2018): 21–22.

Adorno, Theodor, and Max Horkheimer. "The Culture Industry: Enlightenment as Mass Deception." In *Dialectic of Enlightenment: Philosophical Fragments*, edited by Gunzelin Schmid Noerr, translated by Edmund Jephcott, 94–136. Stanford: Stanford University Press, 2002.

Ahn, Yong-hyun. "Kim Jong-un's Ex-Girlfriend 'Shot by Firing Squad.'" *Chosun Ilbo*, August 29, 2013, http://english.chosun.com/site/data/html_dir/2013/08/29/2013082901412. html.

Burnett, Lisa. "Let Morning Shine over Pyongyang: The Future-Oriented Nationalism of North Korea's Arirang Mass Games." *Asian Music* 44, no. 1 (2013): 3–32. http://doi. org/10.1353/amu.2013.0010.

Chunichi Shimbun. "No Bunka Ni Mune Kyun . . .? 'Sengun Joshi' No Sekai" [Their hearts skip a beat over North Korean culture . . .?! The world of "sengun-joshi"], June 11, 2017. https://www.chunichi.co.jp/article/34862.

Cumings, Bruce. *Korea's Place in the Sun: A Modern History*. New York: W. W. Norton, 2005.

Dalton, Bronwen, and Kyungja Jung. "Women's Image Transformed: Femininity in North Korea." *East Asia Forum Quarterly* 8, no. 2 (April–June 2016): 30–31. https://search. informit.org/doi/abs/10.3316/informit.337815787537618.

Foucault, Michel. "What Is an Author?" In *The Foucault Reader*, edited by Paul Rabinow, 101–20. New York: Pantheon Books, 1984.

Freud, Sigmund. "The 'Uncanny.'" In *The Standard Edition of the Complete Psychological Works of Sigmund Freud, Vol. XVII (1917–1919): An Infantile Neurosis and Other Works*, 219–53. Translated by James Strachey. London: Hogarth Press, 1955.

Fullerton, Jamie. "Short Skirts, High Heels and DIY Double Eyelid Surgery at HOME: The Beauty Secrets of North Korean Women Braving the Fashion Police to Look Like Rogue State's Own 'Spice Girls' (and Kim's Mysterious Wife)." *Daily Mail*, February 12, 2015. https://www.dailymail.co.uk/news/article-2950718/ North-Korean-fashion-changing-thanks-country-s-Spice-Girls.html.

Ha, Yuna. "North Korea May Select New Members for Moranbong Band." *Daily NK*, July 17, 2020. Accessed October 17, 2020. https://www.dailynk.com/english/ north-korea-may-select-new-members-moranbong-band.

Howard, Keith. *Songs for "Great Leaders": Ideology and Creativity in North Korean Music and Dance*. New York: Oxford University Press, 2020.

Huh, Jungsun, and Awon Kim. "Moranbongakdan Mudaeuisang-ui Seutail Teukseong mit Sangjing" [Style characteristics and symbolism of the Moranbong Band's stage costumes]. *Boksik* [Journal of the Korean Society of Costume] 68, no. 4 (2018): 23–35. http://doi.org/10.7233/jksc.2018.68.4.023.

Jeon, Jong-hyeok. "Moranbongakdan-eul Juchehyeongmyeong-ui Saesidae Bonbogiakdaneuro Ganghwabaljeonsikisin Gyeongaehaneun Kim Jong-un Dongji-ui Bulmyeorui Eopjeok" [Moranbong Band, strengthened and developed as a model band of the new era of the Juche Revolution—an immortal achievement of Dear Comrade Kim Jong-un]. *Yeoksa Gwahak [Historical Science]* 4 (2015): 47–48.

Kang, Dong-Wan, and Da-Hye Moon, "Moranbongakdan 'Sinjageumakhoe Gongyeon' Uimi-wa Sisajeom" [Implications of Moranbong Band's "new music concert"]. *Dongbugayeongu* [Northeast Asia Research] 30, no. 1 (2015): 273–304.

Korea Central News Agency (KCNA). "Kim Jong Un Appreciates Demonstration Performance of Newly Organized Moranbong Band." July 7, 2012. Accessed September 21, 2020. http://www.kcna.co.jp/item/2012/201207/news07/20120707-09ee.html.

Korea Herald. "N. Korea's All-Female Music Band Disappears from Broadcasts." September 7, 2015. http://www.koreaherald.com/view.php?ud=20150907000683.

Korhonen, Pekka, and Adam Cathcart. "Tradition and Legitimation in North Korea: The Role of the Moranbong Band." *Review of Korean Studies* 20, no. 2 (2017): 7–32. http://doi.org/10.25024/review.2017.20.2.001.

Lendof, Emil. "Inside Japan's North Korea Fan Club." *New York Post*, November 2, 2017. Accessed January 23, 2021. https://nypost.com/2017/11/02/inside-japans-north-korea-fan-club/#2.

Lim, Tai Wei. "State-Endorsed Popular Culture: A Case Study of the North Korean Girl Band Moranbong." *Asia and the Pacific Policy Studies* 4, no. 3 (2017): 602–12. https://doi.org/10.1002/app5.195.

Mills, Kelly-Ann. "North Korea's All-Female Fan Club Dress Up in Military Uniforms and Recreate Songs by Kim Jong-un's Favourite Pop Band." *Mirror*, November 2, 2017. Accessed October 8, 2020. https://www.mirror.co.uk/news/world-news/north-koreas-female-fan-club-11454430.

Moody, Peter. "Before the Korean Wave, the Ripple: North Korea's Music Diplomacy in East Asia in the 1970s–90s." Paper presented for the National Committee on North Korea's "Emerging Scholars Roundtable Series," Zoom lecture, August 18, 2020.

Moody, Peter. "From Production to Consumption: The Socialist Realism/Personality Cult Divide in North Korean Popular Music." *European Journal of Korean Studies* 19, no. 2 (2020): 7–35. https://doi.org/10.33526/ejks.20201902.7.

Osaki, Tomohiro. "Drawn to North Korea's Culture, Japanese Internet Star Looks beyond the Saber-Rattling." *Japan Times*, August 16, 2017. https://www.japantimes.co.jp/news/2017/08/16/national/drawn-north-koreas-culture-japanese-internet-star-looks-beyond-saber-rattling/.

Osborne, Simon. "North Korea's All-Girl Fan Club REVEALED: Japanese Group Devoted to Kim Jong-un's Regime." *Express*, November 2, 2017. https://www.express.co.uk/news/world/874650/japan-north-korea-fan-club-sengun-joshi-military-first-girls-chunhun.

Palmer, William J. *The Films of the Eighties: A Social History*. Carbondale: Southern Illinois University Press, 1995.

Reuters. "North Korean Moranbong Band Prepare for China Performance." December 11, 2015. Accessed October 16, 2020. https://www.reuters.com/news/picture/north-korean-moranbong-band-prepare-for-idUSKBN0TU1YH20151211.

Schmid, Andre. "Historicizing North Korea: State Socialism, Population Mobility, and Cold War Historiography." *American Historical Review* 123, no. 2 (2018): 439–62. http://doi.org/10.1093/ahr/rhy001.

Steinhoff, Patricia G. "Kidnapped Japanese in North Korea: The New Left Connection." *Journal of Japanese Studies* 30, no. 1 (2004): 123–42. http://doi.org/10.1353/jjs.2004.0035.

Terry, David P., and Andrew F. Wood. "Presenting Juche: Audiencing North Korea's 2012 Arirang Mass Games." *Text and Performance Quarterly* 35, no. 2–3 (2015): 177–201. https://doi.org/10.1080/10462937.2015.1036110.

Wong, Edward, and Owen Guo. "North Korea Sends Its Leader's Chosen Pop Band to Beijing." *New York Times*, December 11, 2015. https://www.nytimes.com/2015/12/12/world/asia/china-north-korea-moranbong-girl-band.html.

Yi, Whan-woo. "NK Girl Band Becomes Rumor Mill." *Korea Times*, December 14, 2015. https://www.koreatimes.co.kr/www/news/nation/2015/12/485_193139.html.

Zeglen, David. "Rockin' in the Unfree World: North Korea's Moranbong Band and the Celebrity Dictator." *Celebrity Studies* 8, no. 1 (2017): 142–50. https://doi.org/10.1080/19392397.2016.1272861.

6

Ssen-Unni in K-Pop

The Making of "Strong Sisters" in South Korea

Jieun Lee and Hyangsoon Yi

Introduction[1]

In 2018, the all-female K-pop group BLACKPINK released their music video titled "DDU-DU DDU-DU," in which all four members (Jennie, Jisoo, Rosé, and Lisa) perform their own individual segments and also as a group. This music video broke the prevalent innocent-girl-group image, replacing it with that of a more in-your-face performance.[2] The first scene of the music video instantly sets the group's rebellious tone through Jennie's opening lyrics: "I may look sweet, but I don't act like it / My slender figure hides twice the volume / I give it to them straight / Don't care what people think / Black to the Pink / We're pretty and savage."[3] The dominantly black and dark blue hues of the visuals of the video reinforce the idea of a tough woman with a serious aspect, with the sets accentuating sharp angles and the main platform being made of solid gray stone akin to inverted steps. Performing within this jagged space are the four women. With "DDU-DU DDU-DU" BLACKPINK confirmed their popularity, which they had enjoyed as the first all-female K-pop band to reach the 55th spot on the *Billboard* Hot 100 chart on June 30, 2018.[4] With this important landmark in K-pop history,

---

1. An earlier and different version of this chapter was published in *Korea Journal* 60, no. 1 (Spring 2020).
2. Before BLACKPINK's success in terms of their *ssen-unni* performance, other girl groups like 2NE1 and Miss A had steered away from a demure girl image. This paper discusses 2NE1 in a later section.
3. BLACKPINK, "BLACKPINK - '뚜두뚜두 (DDU-DU DDU-DU)' M/V," June 15, 2018, video, 3:35, https://youtu.be/IHNzOHi8sJs.
4. Xander Zellner, "BLACKPINK Makes K-Pop History on Hot 100, Billboard 200 & More With 'DDU-DU DDU-DU,'" *Billboard*, June 25, 2018, https://www.billboard.com/articles/columns/chart-beat/8462635/blackpink-k-pop-history-hot-100-billboard-200.

BLACKPINK foregrounds the strong female image as their trademark.[5] This image, termed *"ssen-unni"*[6] (strong sister) in the entertainment industry, is now widely circulated in Korean popular culture at large.

Yet before BLACKPINK's accomplishment, solo female artists such as Lee Sang-eun and Kim Wan-sun in the late 1980s, Uhm Jung-hwa in the 1990s, BoA and Lee Hyori in the 2000s, and Jessi from the 2010s to the present had already paved the way, marking an important change in direction for all-female K-pop groups and solo artists by embodying the concept of *ssen-unni*, which has recently gained popularity with K-pop fans. Messages of women's empowerment have thus been produced by women performers in South Korea (hereafter Korea) from the beginning of Hallyu, but more prominently in the current wave of K-pop music.[7] But *ssen-unni* in K-pop is in and of itself a performative embodiment of contradictory elements. It is our contention that women K-pop performers are showing a strong female image through their music videos and stage performances as a way of fighting the sexist and normalized idea of a weak femininity that inscribes women as docile and innocent. In the process of engendering this strong femininity, however, these performances insinuate the underlying message that power is derived from what society views as masculine, reaffirming patriarchal and hierarchical perceptions. This conflicted notion of *ssen-unni* utilizes images of women imitating hypermasculine mannerisms, wearing male-identified clothing, and using objects such as baseball bats and

---

5. According to Elaine Ramirez, BLACKPINK's huge success engendered a 2019 global tour "aiming to take the West by storm." Elaine Ramirez, "BlackPink: The All-Girl K-Pop Group Following BTS's Footsteps and Taking over the U.S.," *Forbes*, April 1, 2019, https://www.forbes.com/sites/elainer-amirez/2019/04/01/blackpink-the-all-girl-k-pop-group-following-btss-footsteps-and-taking-over-the-u-s/?sh=1929445b3e25. Jeff Benjamin sees this as an indication of female K-pop groups' strong worldwide appeal, with artists such as Red Velvet performing in the United States, Canada, Mexico, Japan, and even North Korea. Jeff Benjamin, "Red Velvet Gears Up for North Korea: 10 Things to Know before the Historic K-Pop Performance," *Billboard*, March 30, 2018, https://www.billboard.com/articles/columns/k-town/8275948/red-velvet-south-korean-kpop-group-get-to-know-10-facts. Benjamin also mentions the group TWICE, whose album *Fancy You* debuted in fourth place on *Billboard*'s World Albums chart. Jeff Benjamin, "TWICE's 'Fancy' Revamp Leads to Biggest U.S. Sales Week for an Album Yet," *Billboard*, May 3, 2019, https://www.billboard.com/articles/columns/k-town/8510028/twices-fancy-you-world-albums-chart-biggest-us-sales-week.

6. This term should be transcribed as either *ssen eonni* (Ministry of Culture system) or *ssen ŏnni* (McCune-Reischauer system), according to scholarly conventions within Korean studies. In popular media, however, *ssen-unni* is extensively used, and we adopt this transcription throughout this article.

7. The term *Hallyu* was coined in 1999 by the Korean Ministry of Culture and Tourism in an effort to improve Korean Chinese public relations through the use of Korean popular music. The ministry produced a music CD titled *Hallyu—Song from Korea* (Hánliú 韓流 in Chinese), and the term *Hallyu* became widely popular as "Chinese newspapers represented the success of Korean singers in China as hallyu." Jin Dal Yong and Yoon Tae-Jin, "The Korean Wave: Retrospect and Prospect: Introduction," *International Journal of Communication* 11 (2017): 2241–49, https://ijoc.org/index.php/ijoc/article/viewFile/6296/2047.

machine guns, symbols of masculinity,[8] especially "associated with hierarchical social roles (father, protector) and with . . . values such as patriarchy."[9] If the only way to turn the tables on a male-dominated society is by appropriating toxic masculine symbols, the message is bound to be questionable and loses the potentiality of *ssen-unni* appeal. Consequently, performing hypermasculinity and gender hierarchy in female K-pop music videos is likely to undermine the potential sociocultural impact of *ssen-unni* on empowering a new generation of young women, thereby failing to effectively address the chronic problem to which they attempt to demonstrate resistance—that of patriarchy beyond the performance space.

Yet, from a Western feminist perspective, one could think of the current *ssen-unni* phenomenon in light of third-wave feminism.[10] Defying the categorical and essentialist views in the way that women and men reveal their feminist ideologies, third-wave feminists envision multiplicity and ambiguity, claiming that diverse aspects of female expression should be embraced in their theorizing endeavors.[11] Moreover, Jennifer Baumgardner and Amy Richards note how "prizing, acknowledging, or valuing the 'feminine'—be it the domestic sphere, being a mom, or a talent for adornment—is within the scope of feminist history and future" and how "using makeup isn't a sign of our sway to the marketplace and the male gaze; it can be sexy, campy, ironic, or simply decorating ourselves

---

8. Paul Kline, *Fact and Fantasy in Freudian Theory* (New York: Routledge, 1972), 280. Evelyne Accad, "Sexuality and Sexual Politics: Conflicts and Contradictions for Contemporary Women in the Middle East," in *Third World Women and the Politics of Feminism*, ed. Chandra Talpade Mohanty, Ann Russo, and Lourdes Torres (Bloomington: Indiana University Press, 1991), 237–50.
9. Bruno Chauvin, "Individual Differences in the Judgment of Risks: Sociodemographic Characteristics, Cultural Orientation, and Level of Expertise," in *Psychological Perspectives on Risk and Risk Analysis: Theory, Models, and Applications*, ed. Martina Raue, Eva Lermer, and Bernhard Streicher (Cham, Switzerland: Springer, 2018), 37–61.
10. The periodization of waves of feminism is derived from the American feminist movement. First-wave feminists predominantly focused on female suffrage, whereas the goal of second-wave feminists was to achieve social change for equal rights in terms of jobs, education, and reproductive rights (see Rory Cooke Dicker, *A History of U.S. Feminisms* [Berkeley: Seal Press, 2008], 103). Third-wave feminism, which began to appear in the United States in the mid-1980s, embraced "pluralistic thinking within feminism . . . [working] to undermine narrow visions of feminism and their consequent confinements, through in large part the significantly more prominent voice of women of color and global feminism." Amber E. Kinser, "Negotiating Spaces for/through Third-Wave Feminism," *NWSA Journal* 16, no. 3 (2004): 124–53, http://www.jstor.org/stable/4317084. It is important to note that this periodization is arbitrary, not fully addressing concerns in between the waves and leaving out the many different voices of women of color within and outside the US. Above all, this periodization is hardly applicable to contextualizing the experiences of women and the emergence of feminism in the history of Korea.
11. Rebecca Walker, *To Be Real: Telling the Truth and Changing the Face of Feminism* (New York: Anchor Books, 1995).

without the loaded issues."[12] Indeed, the performances of *ssen-unni* could be understood as a possible dialogue with these feminist thoughts of espousing the heterogeneous ways in which femininity can be embodied in Korea.

All in all, the prevalence of this concept in the K-pop world is indicative of a great complexity in the ways in which young generations of Korean women navigate the conventional mold of womanhood that perpetuates characteristics of silence, demureness, submissiveness, and dependency. It is highly conceivable that *ssen-unni* might serve as an effective force for bringing various women's issues to light, such as prevalent marital and relationship abuse and sexual violence, among others.[13] In this sense, the image of *ssen-unni* can potentially participate in changing the landscape of what it means to be a woman in contemporary Korea. If this is the direction in which the concept is evolving, its seemingly contradictory messages on gender dynamics need to be thoroughly examined.

Korean "Strong Sisters": Contextualizing *Ssen-Unni* in Changing Korean Society

The term *unni* literally translates as "older sister"—a female family member or person who must be respected within the Korean kinship hierarchy and societal age structure. In the context of Korean feminist practices, the use of the word *unni* has become an exercise to actualize feminist ideology. For example, members of the feminist activist group UNNInetwork, founded in 2004, use the appellation *unni* among themselves not only as a way of expressing their mutual familiarity and ease, but also to show their sisterhood. According to UNNInetwork, such usage reveals their priority of pursuing solidarity, support, and empathy among women. The members of another feminist group known as *Jeongchihaneun eommadeul* (Political Mamas)—which was founded in 2017 with the specific aim of redressing social inequalities and systemic discrimination through the political engagement of Korean mothers—also use the term *unni* to refer to one another as a way of challenging the patriarchal and hierarchical relationship and treating all group members equally. The members of this feminist activist group consider that the use of the term has affected their democratic way of communicating

---

12. Jennifer Baumgardner and Amy Richards, "Feminism and Femininity: Or How We Learned to Stop Worrying and Love the Thong," in *All about the Girl: Culture, Power, and Identity*, ed. Anita Harris (New York: Routledge, 2004), 59-67.

13. Grace A. Chung and Ok Sun-Wha, "Marital Violence in South Korea," in *Family Violence from a Global Perspective: A Strengths-Based Approach*, ed. Sylvia M. Asay, John DeFrain, Marcee Metzger, and Bob Moyer (Los Angeles: Sage Publications, 2014), 81-92. See also Kim Hyun Mee and Jamie Chang, "'Sexuality and Public Politics': Temporality of the #MeToo Movement in Contemporary South Korea," *Azalea: Journal of Korean Literature & Culture*, 14 (2021): 243-60.

their opinions and decision-making process.[14] In this vein, *unni* is more than a technical reference on an interpersonal communication level; it functions as a cultural signifier conveying specific meanings of womanhood and sisterhood that are geared toward social change.

The adjective *ssen* means "strong," "tough," and "powerful," but this illustrative expression has been gendered within the contemporary Korean sociocultural milieu. For instance, if a man is described as *ssen*, his personality or actions are positively interpreted as powerful, fearless, and fierce. By contrast, when used for a woman, this adjective often takes on pejorative connotations of boldness and arrogance. Thus, while *ssen-unni* literally means *strong sister*, in a social context it implies a brazen woman who embodies rebellious characteristics, thus remaining outside of the feminized norms. Jung-Youn Lim points out that in Korean women's literature, consuming alcohol and tobacco symbolizes an act of resistance against a patriarchal and sexist power structure.[15] In some cases, women *perform* as outlaws when drinking and smoking in public spaces, exposing their *ssen* quality by doing what men are allowed to do but women are not. The underlying message of the *ssen* actions by these women is an outright opposition to the traditional patriarchal ideology and a projection of themselves as independent, assured, unapologetic, and rebellious. The adjective, therefore, refers to their determined stance for their own desire and voice.

The *ssen-unni* appellation is a designation in the present K-pop world for a charismatic female star who can be trusted and looked up to, someone who will serve as a role model with her fearlessness. This image of a strong sister stands in direct contrast to that of *oppa*. This term literally means "elder brother," but it can also mean "boyfriend" or "older male friend." The use of *oppa* in Korean popular culture nowadays conjures up the image of a young man whose younger sisters need entertainment or help, and who makes them feel whole as a person. But the popular media construction of the image of the *ssen-unni* results in the replacement of the male *oppa* figure as a subject of desire. It is quite intriguing to observe that while the male figure evaporates, the *ssen-unni* replaces the position of the *oppa*, and in so doing, she becomes the object of admiration as the epitome of female strength and stability for younger sisters. This subversion of the traditional power dynamics in gender and the hijacking of the female gaze to redirect it from male to female K-pop performers renders *ssen-unni* the object of desire in and for their younger fans. Unlike the male gaze, which connects

---

14. Baek Un-Hui et al., *Na-neun ireoke bullineun geot-i bulpyeonhamnida* [I'm uncomfortable being called in this way] (Seoul: Hanibook, 2019).

15. Lim Jung-Youn, "Yeoseong munhak-gwa sul/dambae-ui gihoron" [Semiotics about alcohol/cigarette in women's literature], *Yeoseong munhak yeongu* [Feminism and Korean Literature] 27 (2012): 213–40, https://www.kci.go.kr/kciportal/ci/sereArticleSearch/ciSereArtiView.kci?sereArticleSearchBean.artiId=ART001677402.

to a fantasized sexual desire,[16] the female gaze searches for the strong sister in a nonsexual girl crush way. Although a girl crush can be associated with lesbian feelings, the expression "girl crush" is also defined as platonic emotions of fondness and admiration that a woman has for another woman, or as a "passionate friendship."[17] According to Caitlin Kelley, the notion of girl crush specifically in K-pop "functions more as a descriptor of both visuals and message, to varying degrees," and one can identify a girl crush song through certain signifiers such as sports sweaters, fishnet stockings, less colorful palettes, and a fierceness in women sometimes "masculinized" in dress, haircut, and an attitude that steps "outside the expectations of hyperfemininity," amounting to more "abstract ideas of relatability, aspiration and female empowerment."[18]

The shift of the female gaze from male to female performers is rather ironic and conflicted in the way that many singers in their *ssen-unni* performance disclose their rebelliousness by incorporating sexualized female stylistics: mini-skirts, high-heeled shoes, perfect hair and makeup, highly sensuous dance movements, and overtly sexual lyrics. In music video narratives, these elements usually purport to tease a male target, creating attractive images of women specifically for the male gaze in the audience. In our view, however, *ssen-unni* performances somewhat detach this male gaze from its "erotic basis for pleasure in looking at another person as object."[19] Consequently, it seems that a complicit compromise occurs in the meaning of the *ssen-unni* image. On the one hand, it distances the male gaze by performing outside of the cherished patriarchal feminine norms. On the other, it highlights a sexualized connotation to reinvite the male gaze. This duality generates an inconsistent view of what it means to be an independent, strong, and empowered woman. The complexity of gaze hijacking unveils *ssen-unni*'s inherent contradiction: the image of the strong sister embodies women artists' fear of losing male fans, while simultaneously attracting female fans to the message of women's empowerment.

A Genealogy of *Ssen-Unni*: Before and after the Rise of the Korean Wave

In the summer of 1988, the Seoul Olympics took place and put Korea in the world spotlight. International television crews were filming both the Olympic

---

16. Laura Mulvey, *Visual and Other Pleasures* (Bloomington: Indiana University Press, 1989), 19.
17. Erin Blakemore, "How Women Crushed on One Another Back in the Day," *JSTOR Daily*, June 29, 2017, https://daily.jstor.org/how-women-crushed-on-one-another-back-in-the-day.
18. Caitlin Kelley, "How 'Girl Crush' Hooked Female Fans and Grappled with Feminism as K-pop Went Global in 2018," *Billboard*, December 27, 2018, https://www.billboard.com/articles/events/year-in-music-2018/8491604/girl-crush-k-pop-feminism-2018.
19. Mulvey, *Visual and Other Pleasures*, 17.

Summer Games and the everyday lives of Korean citizens. The phrase "Miracle on the Han River" was heard and described in many foreign TV newscasts. As Brian Bridges states, "[t]he 1988 Olympic Games in Seoul were a coming out party for South Korea—a culmination of its efforts to be recognized as an accomplished economic power and a serious international actor."[20] A decade later, in 1997, the IMF financial crisis had a powerful impact on the entire nation, and Korea's music industry was not spared. After the Seoul Olympics and the IMF crisis, and as one of the main components of Hallyu, K-pop became "inextricably intertwined with the very fabric of South Korean economy, society, and culture [. . . as well as] an explicit export-oriented culture industry."[21] More specifically, due to a severe decline in CD sales and a highly restricted national market, in addition to the digitization of music, mainly starting in the late 1990s, the viable path for the entertainment industry was the export market, where a new breed of music entrepreneurs used the technological breakthroughs of digitized music and video to cost-efficiently promote their groups outside of Korea.[22] By most accounts, the boy band H.O.T., with its debut in 1996, is considered the first group on the K-pop music scene, followed by the first K-pop girl group, Baby V.O.X in 1997.[23]

As a proto-Hallyu K-pop model, a trio called Seo Taiji and Boys created a new sound with the release of their 1992 song "Nan Arayo" (I Know), which not only innovatively blended rap and hip-hop musical tones with Korean pop music, but also incorporated rap and hip-hop movements as a main dance component.[24] K-pop emerged from this innovative sound and enhanced its hybridity by incorporating certain American popular music elements such as rhythm and blues, electronic music, and rap,[25] as well as, according to Timothy Laurie, "1980s Hi-NRG and its cousins J-Pop dance culture, 1990s Cantonese pop idols (Cantopop), and mainland Chinese performers (Mandopop), as well as fashion elements reworked from mid-1960s Motown and Japanese V-Kei ('visual style')."[26] K-pop thus forms a contact zone by utilizing not only music and dance

20. Brian Bridges, "The Seoul Olympics: Economic Miracle Meets the World," *The International Journal of the History of Sport* 25, no. 14 (2008): 1939–52, http://doi.org/10.1080/09523360802438983.
21. John Lie, "What Is the K in K-pop? South Korean Popular Music, the Culture Industry, and National Identity," *Korea Observer* 43, no. 3 (2012): 339–63. https://www.tobiashubinette.se/hallyu_1.pdf.
22. Lie, "What Is the K in K-Pop?," 353–54.
23. Lie, "What Is the K in K-Pop?," 351–52.
24. Lie, "What Is the K in K-Pop?," 349.
25. Kim Gooyong, "Between Hybridity and Hegemony in K-Pop's Global Popularity: A Case of Girls' Generation's American Debut," *International Journal of Communication* 11 (2017): 2367–86, https://ijoc.org/index.php/ijoc/article/view/6306/2054.
26. Timothy Laurie, "Toward a Gendered Aesthetics of K-Pop," in *Global Glam and Popular Music: Style and Spectacle from the 1970s to the 2000s*, ed. Henry Johnson and Ian Chapman (New York: Routledge, 2016), 214–31.

but also cultural imaginings from other countries and recontextualizing their significances.

Going back to the 1980s, the world witnessed an increasing global pressure for gender equality after the United Nations declared a "decade of women."[27] In the earlier part of that decade, several international symposiums on women took place in Korea, addressing international feminist thoughts, issues, and actions to Korean women.[28] Buoyed by the global phenomenon of feminism and an increasing anger toward the establishment regarding violence and sexual assaults against women by the police, as well as workers' exploitation by manufacturing and heavy industry companies, "women's involvement in the prodemocracy movement . . . affected the goals and the strategies of progressive women's-movement groups formed in the 1980s [which] contributed to the processes of breaking down military rule in the late 1980s."[29]

These social changes in Korea—from a military dictatorship where popular music was censored in form and content, to a democratic government (still with a censorship process, though more liberalized) that financially supports the K-pop industry in its exporting endeavors[30]—were reflected in the music industry, particularly in Japanese pop music's and American music's "corrupting effects."[31] In the wake of the spirit of change, the freedom of expression, and the economic affluence of the late 1980s and early 1990s, Korea encountered a greater spectrum of performing femininity. It was in this changing sociocultural climate that women performers with different femininities—such as Kim Wan-sun, Lee Sang-eun, Lee Sun-hee, and Uhm Jung-hwa—appeared on the music scene. Each one of these performers had their own style, with Kim Wan-sun gaining the nickname "the Korean Madonna," Lee Sang-eun sporting a boyish and androgynous style, Lee Sun-hee having a commanding operatic voice and a non-provocative, "chaste girl-next-door" image,[32] and Uhm Jung-hwa embracing erotics through her choreography, daring costumes, and powerful lyrics about taking revenge as a woman wronged in love. All of these solo performers' characteristics exuded the air of *ssen-unni*, which blended into several K-pop women singers' performances in the next decades.

27. Nam Jeong-Lim, "Gender Politics in the Korean Transition to Democracy," *Korean Studies* 24 (2000): 94-112, https://www.jstor.org/stable/23719707.
28. Nam, "Gender Politics in the Korean Transition to Democracy," 96.
29. Nam, "Gender Politics in the Korean Transition to Democracy," 94.
30. Oh Ingyu and Lee Hyo-Jung, "K-Pop in Korea: How the Pop Music Industry Is Changing a Post-Developmental Society," *Cross-Currents: East Asian History and Culture Review* 3, no. 3 (2014): 72-93, http://doi.org/10.1353/ach.2014.0007.
31. Lie, "What Is the K in K-Pop?," 347.
32. Keith Howard, "Exploding Ballads: The Transformation of Korean Pop Music," in *Global Goes Local: Popular Culture in Asia*, ed. Timothy J. Craig and Richard King (Vancouver: University of British Columbia Press, 2002), 80-95.

If a liberalization in Korean society allowed changes in the representations of women in K-pop to some extent, one needs to also consider the moneymaking nature of the industry that creates artists as products that need to appeal to consumers in the neoliberal post-1997 era. K-pop agencies such as SM Entertainment are artistic corporations sorting out the best candidates via an arduous training period in which "only 20–30 out of 1,000 trainees ever appear professionally."[33] To maximize profit, agencies commonly create groups, which are less expensive to train than solo performers, with each group member farmed out for individual appearances in TV dramas or fan meetings, all to the benefit of the group and its agency.[34] Yet the performing talent still toils under the firm control of the K-pop industry's structure, which remains predominantly male-dominated. In this context, it is also important to mention that although some male executives work closely with group members, supporting women artists in their creative input, the songs, videos, and public images of these performers are still mainly being produced from a male perspective.[35]

In the highly competitive K-pop music scene, aside from an agency's option to diversify its assets, showcasing a "difference" is a strategy to entice viewers who have become accustomed to repetitive images and performances by women artists. However, innovations that find profitability are quickly copied for financial gain. Certain women performers tend to mechanically reproduce the *ssen-unni* image as an embodiment of difference but do not contribute to formulating a different kind of discourse of femininity, resulting in performances conveying weaker and limited messages about what it means to be a strong woman. *Ssen-unni* is an embodied performance reflecting the changes in the bifurcated depictions of female identities in which, as Michael Fuhr states, "the innocent-yet-cute 'girl-next-door' and the sexually enticing imageries figure prominently at the respective ends."[36] In this sense, defining *ssen-unni* in K-pop is a challenge, as it could denote a female performer's all-encompassing concept—such as BLACKPINK's, as previously mentioned—or making a visual statement such as embracing the "corset-free movement" rejecting lookism, as Mamamoo did by performing in sweatshirts, baggy pants, and white sneakers.[37] *Ssen-unni* could also be a means of affirmation—for example, a temporal stand for queer performativity, as in AOA's broadcast performance that included voguing dancers,

33. Lie, "What Is the K in K-Pop?," 357.
34. Lie, "What Is the K in K-Pop?," 357–58.
35. Lonnie, "Women Empowerment: The Girl Crush Anthem," *Seoulbeats*, April 22, 2019, https://seoulbeats.com/2019/04/women-empowerment-the-girl-crush-anthem.
36. Michael Fuhr, "K-Pop Music and Transnationalism," in *Routledge Handbook of Korean Culture and Society*, ed. Youna Kim (Abington: Routledge, 2017), 283–96.
37. Park Jin-hai, "Girl Bands Join 'Corset-Free Movement,'" *Korea Times*, March 26, 2019, https://www.koreatimes.co.kr/www/art/2020/02/732_266077.html.

a first on TV in Korea, where homosexuality is still not fully accepted.[38] All of these performances embody the notion of *ssen-unni* due to their courage to break with patriarchal values in style and content, forging a way to an acceptance and solidarity in diversity. With more Hallyu female groups and solo performers embracing the image of a strong woman, a discussion of the mechanisms in which *ssen-unni* is engendered and repeated can elucidate the complexity as well as the limitations of this critical concept.

The Contemporary Makings of *Ssen-Unni*: Materialistic Hypermasculinization and Sketchy Resistance

Regarding the repetitive constructions of *ssen-unni* in female K-pop artists' works between the 2000s and 2010s, two distinct features can be identified and conceptualized via two works by solo women performers CL and Lee Hyori. The first prominent element in the representation of women in K-pop can be found in the hypermasculinization of images, objects, and actions that seem to achieve a strong performance by utilizing the concept of *ssen-unni*, but that expose a misconception of power by appearing masculine. Next, it presents the idea of women as political beings resisting, but resistance is left disconnected from contingent issues; hence, a missed opportunity for women's solidarity.

Materialistic hypermasculinization

The group 2NE1 debuted in 2009 and was composed of four women: CL, Dara, Park Bom, and Minzy. According to Kelley, their 2011 hit music video, "I Am the Best" (*Naega jeil jal naga*), has an "abrasive" stylistic choice in props and costumes such as baseball bats, leather jackets with studs and spikes, and "gravity-defying haircuts."[39] The video is full of assertive and fearless attitudes, with unashamedly boastful lyrics about the four women being fabulous and no one else being as good. Regarding their *ssen-unni* performance, the members of 2NE1 even recognize their faithful women fans in the lyrics that Park sings: "Girls are following me." Yet no matter how proud the group claims to be of their coterie of female fans, their representations of *ssen-unni* characters invite further consideration of the ways in which they perform their strength. From the first frame of the music video, the image shows one of the group members clad in boxing shorts, wearing a boxing robe with a hood, and holding a large, iconic boxing championship belt.

---

38. SLY, "Ranking the Queendom Part 2 performances from AOA to Mamamoo," *OH!PRESS*, September 20, 2019, https://blog.onehallyu.com/espressoh-ranking-the-queendom-part-2-performances-from-aoa-to-mamamoo/.
39. Kelley, "'Girl Crush.'"

Further on, another member arrives in a futuristic black car, and a third member dances in between two moving locomotive pistons. More than halfway through the video, all four singers take on the persona of gang members—wearing baseball bats, chains, and thick black leather jackets and gloves—and smash glass window cases. The last segment of the video is set in front of a large black pyramid surrounded by a band of blindfolded women in black uniforms who beat on hybrid traditional Korean drums. At the very end, the four 2NE1 members take up machine guns and shoot at the pyramid. These images, and certainly the violent behavior toward the end of the video, suggest hypermasculine symbols. Indeed, the segment with the uniformed women around the pyramid, with their precision drumbeating choreography, brings unquestionably to mind the idea of a militarized masculinity.

If not so overtly militaristic, CL adopts a repetitive style of hypermasculinity with her 2013 initial solo music debut, "The Baddest Female" (*Nappeun gizibae* or *Nappeun gijibae*), a mixture of hip-hop and electronica viewed by over 1 million people in less than 24 hours on the 2NE1 YouTube channel.[40] The first part of the video is filled with images of herself as a successful, rich, and famous woman that are crosscut with shots of her in hip-hop clothing, wearing a gold plate across her left knuckles with the word "UNNIE" (*unni*) and another gold plate with the word "GIZIBE" over her right knuckles. The second section of the video switches to her as part of a gang, and the last segment briefly shows her in a militaristic outfit holding a black flag atop a jagged mountaintop before the scene transitions to one of tropical scenery. Moving through this lush vegetation, CL discovers a hidden space, complete with a hair salon, populated almost exclusively by women who happily hip-hop dance and play with her as she joins the pseudo-paradise.

The lyrics themselves give the sense that this is more of a manifesto than a song. The English words she declares with megaphone effect on the mountain summit, with a flag flapping in the wind, attest to this:

> This is for all my bad girls around the world
> Not bad meaning bad, but bad meaning good, you know?
> Let's light it up and let it burn like we don't care
> Let 'em know how it feels damn good to be bad.[41]

This declaration of self-assuredness produces a feeling of catharsis and a sense of empowerment for young women, giving them the right to be "bad" in the sense

---

40. Jeff Benjamin, "2NE1's CL is 'The Baddest Female' in Solo Video," *Billboard*, May 28, 2013, https://www.billboard.com/music/music-news/2ne1s-cl-is-the-baddest-female-in-solo-video-1565006/.

41. 2NE1 Official YouTube Channel, "CL-Nappeun gijibae M/V" (CL-THE BADDEST FEMALE M/V), YouTube video, 04:02, posted May 27, 2013, https://www.youtube.com/watch?v=7LP4foN3Xs4&ab_channel=2NE1.

of rejecting patriarchal discriminatory labels and affirming their right to define themselves. Through this declaration and throughout the song, CL is speaking directly to her fans—more precisely, to her female fans—as she calls out to them with her refrain ("Where all my bad gals at?") while positioning herself as their big sister ("Girls call me *unni*").

The Korean title of the song uses the word "*gizibe*" (*gijibae*), a colloquial term to describe girls and young women. Adding the adjective "bad" to *gizibe*, however, implies a disparagement in which the English title "The Baddest Female" becomes comparable to the meaning of *bitch*. This reclamation of a derogatory term for women finds a connection to what feminist author Jo Freeman (under the name Joreen) wrote in the seminal article "The BITCH Manifesto," defining a "bitch" as a self-determined proud, strong, and militant woman.[42] This redefinition of bitch is found in a current cultural and literary production in Korea: the four-cut webtoon entitled *Ssyangnyeon-ui mihak* (A Bitch's Aesthetics) by Min Seo-Young.[43] In this cartoon, *ssyangnyeon* (bitch) is redefined as a woman who prioritizes her desires over others' demands and voices her opinions about her lifestyle choices without being subservient or apologetic.[44] CL utilizes the word *gizibe* in a similar way, bestowing upon herself this iconic title in her *ssen-unni* performance.

There is no doubt that 2NE1's and CL's performances manage to express their empowerment, but through the adoption of a male-imbedded lens; consequently, their choices of imagery perpetuate the idea of a pervasive male supremacy in society. In both music videos, objects are infused with hypermasculinity, an exaggerated pattern of manners and actions within cultural norms commonly viewed in men: baseball bats, chains, thick fighting gloves, machine guns, gold-plated metal knuckles, clubs, gold chains, and even one shot of CL with her mouth open to reveal sharp gold teeth, evoking a militant fighter. All of these objects embody the elements that define hypermasculinity, but here are appropriated by the women artists. Moreover, not only are both videos saturated with objects, but the focus of the objects is the women artists themselves, who either wear them, hold them, or wield them, so that they become an extension of their bodies.

---

42. Jo (Joreen) Freeman, "The BITCH Manifesto," in *Notes from the Second Year: Women's Liberation: Major Writings of the Radical Feminists*, ed. Shulamith Firestone and Anne Koedt (New York: Radical Feminism, 1970), 5–9.

43. Distributed through the web-based cartoon platform Justoon, *Ssyangnyeon-ui mihak* discloses candid expressions of women's experiences of encountering numerous discriminatory and absurd situations by mere fact of being a woman in Korea. This cartoon became a monumental feminist work, recording an accumulative 4 million views. It was subsequently published as a book in 2018, with a sequel in 2019 and additional plans for a web-based drama adaptation.

44. Min Seo-Young, *Ssyangnyeon-ui mihak* [A bitch's aesthetics] (Seoul: Wisdom House, 2018).

These hypermasculinized performances embodied through decorative objects, however, do not enhance a discourse on the radical enhancement of women's feelings of liberation strongly enough to dismantle the culture of misogyny and gendered norms. Another issue with the depictions is that their implication—that power is attainable through the consumption of these excessive hypermasculine objects—sends confusing signals to female teenage fans, who constitute the majority of fans for both women and men K-pop singers. By so doing, the women artists infuse their *ssen-unni* performances with visual imitations of exaggerated performances of maleness, which rarely disrupt a patriarchal capitalism that entraps women in a society of consumerism and sexism and are prone to pass down the restricted view of empowerment to the next generation of women.

Sketchy resistance

Whereas 2NE1 in "I Am the Best" and CL in "The Baddest Female" use materialistic hypermasculinity to present strength, self-assurance, and self-reliance, the solo performer Lee Hyori expresses the power of *ssen-unni* performance through narratives of resistance. Michel Foucault states that "where there is power, there is resistance."[45] Applying Foucault's statement to Lee's music video, it is eye-opening to see how women are shown as forces of resistance through protest. Authority is represented by either the state, family, teachers, or police, but apart from directly targeting her anger and actions against that corrupted authority, Lee's dissension does not, in the end, imagine solidarity among women through highly politicized acts.

As the Korean Wave progressed, most women K-pop groups in the 1990s shed their initial images of innocence and cuteness, such as Fin.K.L with "To My Boyfriend" and "Everlasting Love," and S.E.S. with "I'm Your Girl" and "Oh, My Love," songs that recount fairy-tale stories of girlfriends in need of affirmation from their *oppas*. Departing from this image, Lee Hyori, a member of the pioneering K-pop girl group Fin.K.L from 1998 to 2005, began a solo career with her album *Stylish . . . E* in 2003 and immediately found success with the hit single "10 Minutes." Over the years, Lee has expanded her career from singer to record producer, actor, television host, and animal rights activist. Released in 2013, her "Bad Girls" music video is shot in a cartoonish fashion, complete with comic book-style pop-up text bubbles. The story follows the life of a fictional Lee Hyori from birth, during which her mother dies in a campy hospital birthing scene punctuated by a 1960s-style "Monster Mash" Halloween music, through her experience of having a stepmother, then through schooling up to high school. At

---

45. Michel Foucault, *The History of Sexuality*, vol. 1 (New York: Pantheon Books, 1978), 95.

every stage in her life, Lee is mistreated by family members, classmates, teachers, job interviewers, and eventually the police. She reacts to all this with rebellious and vengeful behavior, but in a cartoonish way: when she blows up her mean classmates with a stick of dynamite, they only wind up with blackened faces and smoking hair. In the chain of episodic performances of her rebelliousness, one of the cathartic moments in "Bad Girls" occurs when a woman is sexually harassed in a public restroom; Lee takes revenge on the male perpetrator in a humorous way by disrobing the man in public. At the end of the video, Lee takes part in protests, provokes a policewoman into a car chase, and gets arrested. The last scene features her during her mug shot photo, making an insulting gesture at the camera.

The idea of resistance in *ssen-unni* performance here connects Lee's rebelliousness with the group of protesters at the end. In that sequence, Lee is up in front of a wire fence while protesters hold up placards reading "Don't Touch Me," "Even If You Wear [*sic*] So Sexy You Can't Touch Me," "Don't Hate Me," and other important messages regarding sexual harassment in particular that are difficult to make out due to fast movements and quick editing. The fact that the camera does not focus on any particular sign reveals Lee's indifference to protest as an act of social justice or civil disobedience, while the collective voices of the politicized activities of the protesters demanding social justice for women produce only a vague resistance. Whereas Lee is foregrounded in these shots, the public and their act of resistance merely become a backdrop.

As a positivity of performance exists within the staging of dissent, making protests into spectacular scenery in "Bad Girls" seemingly defeats the purpose. In the history of feminism, protest as dissent has been an effective tool for the public to demand sociopolitical and cultural change. From the suffragette movement in early twentieth-century America to protests in the 1960s and 1970s for equal rights, to the worldwide Women's March in January 2017, women's protests have served to express their discontent over marginalization. In Korea as well, protests have been part of the fabric of Korean society. In particular, women workers' formation of resistance in the 1970s was significantly vocal and visible.[46] More recently, protests have been staged by women against sexual abuse in the entertainment industry, at school, and in public places—especially against sexism and spy-camera digital sexual violence.[47] Indeed, resistance "alerts us to the feminist insistence on the importance of collective as well as individual action

---

46. Kim Mikyoung, "Gender, Work and Resistance: South Korean Textile Industry in the 1970s," *Journal of Contemporary Asia* 41, no. 3 (2011): 411–30, http://doi.org/10.1080/00472336.2011.582 711.

47. See Kim Jinsook, "Sticky Activism: The Gangnam Station Murder Case and New Feminist Practices against Misogyny and Femicide," *JCMS: Journal of Cinema and Media Studies* 60, no. 4 (2021): 37–60, http://doi.org/10.1353/cj.2021.0044.

in order to transform social relations that systematically disempower women."[48] In this context, with "Bad Girls," K-pop is enfranchising the potential resistance that has been embodied through the *ssen-unni* performance, but it falls short of disseminating the idea of women's actualization for social transformation and remains a sketchy, kitschy gesture.

Conclusion

If female empowerment can only be demonstrated in materialistic, hypermasculine ways through consumption or as sketchy rebelliousness, then the meaning of empowerment certainly becomes abstruse. The next stage of Hallyu might see new K-pop narratives and innovative approaches to bringing women's experiences of liberation and freedom from compulsory structures regarding gender and sexuality to the forefront, thus strengthening the "power" of K-pop.

The word "feminism" is no longer estranged from our everyday lives. From the popularity of Cho Nam-Joo's bestselling feminist novel *82-nyeonsaeng Kim Jiyoung* (Kim Jiyoung, born 1982), published in 2016,[49] to movements like #MeToo in Yonghwa Girls' High School and at a number of Korean universities in 2018, Korean girls and women have become more vocal and visible in public in the face of blatant sexism, misogyny, and sexual violence, such as that witnessed in the sordid 2019 Burning Sun scandal that shattered "K-pop's innocent image."[50] No longer feeling isolated, women can band together through social media and public protests to find expression and solidarity with one another, while using technological and activist networks as platforms for change.

Within this contemporary wave of feminism, *ssen-unni* performances in the Korean Wave possess the great potential to engender even bigger waves, communicating the variety of women's voices in more powerful and different ways. For instance, the group Mamamoo, which debuted in 2014, has recently disrupted gender norms in their work and publicly supported the Seoul Queer Culture Festival in 2017, showing how *ssen-unni* can be reincarnated by incorporating the female as an empowered performer and fearless agent for equality within and beyond the screen and stage.

48. Nickie Charles, "Feminist Practices: Identity, Difference, Power," in *Practising Feminism: Identity, Difference, Power*, ed. Nickie Charles and Felicia Hughes-Freeland (London: Routledge, 1996), 14–15.
49. Presently, the film adaptation of this novel is covered by Korean media as an unexpected box-office hit. This is a surprising feat given the large negative campaign against it on social media. The popularity of the film is a compelling testimony to growing societal awareness and acceptance of women's issues as no longer the agenda of a small group of radical feminists.
50. August Brown, "K-Pop's Innocent Image Is Shattered by the 'Burning Sun' Scandal," *Los Angeles Times*, April 5, 2019, https://www.latimes.com/entertainment/music/la-et-ms-burning-sun-20190319-story.html.

Will the performance of *ssen-unni* become embedded in the hearts and minds of young Korean women and girls to contribute to a growing feminist movement that is seen as a performative threat to traditional values dominated by patriarchy? Or will *ssen-unni* be relegated to a fad of the Hallyu brand for mere national and international commercialism? In either case, the power of K-pop has shown that innovative concepts can be transmitted to the public at large. We hope that *ssen-unni* performances in K-pop will keep embracing the meaningful empowerment of women to actualize their liberation in Korea and beyond, thereby contributing to the growth of Hallyu. We choose to imagine *ssen-unni* as daring, strong, fearless, and entirely relatable to issues afflicting Korean women and men who admire an ever-changing K-pop.

Bibliography

2NE1. "CL - 나쁜 기집애 (THE BADDEST FEMALE) M/V" (CL-THE BADDEST FEMALE M/V). May 28, 2013. Video, 4:02. https://www.youtube.com/watch?v=7LP4foN3Xs4&ab_channel=2NE1.

Accad, Evelyne. "Sexuality and Sexual Politics: Conflicts and Contradictions for Contemporary Women in the Middle East." In *Third World Women and the Politics of Feminism*, edited by Chandra Talpade Mohanty, Ann Russo, and Lourdes Torres, 237–50. Bloomington: Indiana University Press, 1991.

Baek, Un-Hui et al. *Na-neun ireoke bullineun geot-i bulpyeonhamnida* [I'm uncomfortable being called in this way]. Seoul: Hanibook, 2019.

Baumgardner, Jennifer, and Amy Richards. "Feminism and Femininity: Or How We Learned to Stop Worrying and Love the Thong." In *All about the Girl: Culture, Power, and Identity*, edited by Anita Harris, 59–67. New York: Routledge, 2004.

Benjamin, Jeff. "Red Velvet Gears up for North Korea: 10 Things to Know before the Historic K-Pop Performance." *Billboard*, March 30, 2018. https://www.billboard.com/articles/columns/k-town/8275948/red-velvet-south-korean-kpop-group-get-to-know-10-facts.

Benjamin, Jeff. "TWICE's 'Fancy' Revamp Leads to Biggest U.S. Sales Week for an Album Yet." *Billboard*, May 3, 2019. https://www.billboard.com/articles/columns/k-town/8510028/twices-fancy-you-world-albums-chart-biggest-us-sales-week.

Benjamin, Jeff. "2NE1's CL is 'The Baddest Female' in Solo Video." *Billboard*, May 28, 2013. https://www.billboard.com/music/music-news/2ne1s-cl-is-the-baddest-female-in-solo-video-1565006/.

BLACKPINK. "BLACKPINK - '뚜두뚜두 (DDU-DU DDU-DU)' M/V." June 15, 2018. Video, 3:35. https://youtu.be/IHNzOHi8sJs.

Blakemore, Erin. "How Women Crushed on One Another Back in the Day." *JSTOR Daily*, June 29, 2017. https://daily.jstor.org/how-women-crushed-on-one-another-back-in-the-day.

Bridges, Brian. "The Seoul Olympics: Economic Miracle Meets the World." *The International Journal of the History of Sport* 25, no. 14 (2008): 1939-52. http://doi.org/10.1080/09523360802438983.

Brown, August. "K-Pop's Innocent Image Is Shattered by the 'Burning Sun' Scandal." *Los Angeles Times*, April 5, 2019. https://www.latimes.com/entertainment/music/la-et-ms-burning-sun-20190319-story.html.

Charles, Nickie. "Feminist Practices: Identity, Difference, Power." In *Practising Feminism: Identity, Difference, Power*, edited by Nickie Charles and Felicia Hughes-Freeland, 1–37. London: Routledge, 1996.

Chauvin, Bruno. "Individual Differences in the Judgment of Risks: Sociodemographic Characteristics, Cultural Orientation, and Level of Expertise." In *Psychological Perspectives on Risk and Risk Analysis: Theory, Models, and Applications*, edited by Martina Raue, Eva Lermer, and Bernhard Streicher, 37-61. Cham, Switzerland: Springer, 2018.

Chung, Grace A., and Ok Sun-Wha. "Marital Violence in South Korea." In *Family Violence from a Global Perspective: A Strengths-Based Approach*, edited by Sylvia M. Asay, John DeFrain, Marcee Metzger, and Bob Moyer, 81-92. Los Angeles: Sage Publications, 2014.

Dicker, Rory Cooke. *A History of U.S. Feminisms.* Berkeley: Seal Press, 2008.

Foucault, Michel. *The History of Sexuality*, Vol. 1. Translated by Robert Hurley. New York: Pantheon Books, 1978.

Freeman, Jo (Joreen). "The BITCH Manifesto." In *Notes from the Second Year: Women's Liberation: Major Writings of the Radical Feminists*, edited by Shulamith Firestone and Anne Koedt, 5-9. New York: Radical Feminism, 1970.

Fuhr, Michael. "K-Pop Music and Transnationalism." In *Routledge Handbook of Korean Culture and Society*, edited by Youna Kim, 283-96. Abington: Routledge, 2017.

Howard, Keith. "Exploding Ballads: The Transformation of Korean Pop Music." In *Global Goes Local: Popular Culture in Asia*, edited by Timothy J. Craig and Richard King, 80-95. Vancouver: University of British Columbia Press, 2002.

Jin, Dal Yong, and Yoon Tae-Jin. "The Korean Wave: Retrospect and Prospect: Introduction." *International Journal of Communication* 11 (2017): 2241-49. https://ijoc.org/index.php/ijoc/article/viewFile/6296/2047.

Kelley, Caitlin. "How 'Girl Crush' Hooked Female Fans and Grappled with Feminism as K-Pop Went Global in 2018." *Billboard*, December 27, 2018. https://www.billboard.com/articles/events/year-in-music-2018/8491604/girl-crush-k-pop-feminism-2018.

Kim, Gooyong. "Between Hybridity and Hegemony in K-Pop's Global Popularity: A Case of Girls' Generation's American Debut." *International Journal of Communication* 11 (2017): 2367-86. https://ijoc.org/index.php/ijoc/article/view/6306/2054.

Kim, Hyun Mee, and Jamie Chang. "'Sexuality and Public Politics': Temporality of the #MeToo Movement in Contemporary South Korea." *Azalea: Journal of Korean Literature & Culture* 14 (2021): 243-60.

Kim, Jinsook. "Sticky Activism: The Gangnam Station Murder Case and New Feminist Practices against Misogyny and Femicide." *JCMS: Journal of Cinema and Media Studies* 60, no. 4 (2021): 37-60. http://doi.org/10.1353/cj.2021.0044.

Kim, Mikyoung. "Gender, Work and Resistance: South Korean Textile Industry in the 1970s." *Journal of Contemporary Asia* 41, no. 3 (2011): 411–30. http://doi.org/10.108 0/00472336.2011.582711.

Kinser, Amber E. "Negotiating Spaces for/through Third-Wave Feminism." *NWSA Journal* 16, no. 3 (2004): 124–53. http://www.jstor.org/stable/4317084.

Kline, Paul. *Fact and Fantasy in Freudian Theory*. New York: Routledge, 1972.

Laurie, Timothy. "Toward a Gendered Aesthetics of K-Pop." In *Global Glam and Popular Music: Style and Spectacle from the 1970s to the 2000s*, edited by Henry Johnson and Ian Chapman, 214–31. New York: Routledge, 2016.

Lie, John. "What Is the K in K-Pop? South Korean Popular Music, the Culture Industry, and National Identity." *Korea Observer* 43, no. 3 (2012): 339–63. https://www.tobiashubinette.se/hallyu_1.pdf.

Lim, Jung-Youn. "Yeoseong munhak-gwa sul/dambae-ui gihoron" [Semiotics about alcohol/cigarette in women's literature]. *Yeoseong munhak yeongu* [Feminism and Korean Literature] 27 (2012): 213–40.

Lonnie. "Women Empowerment: The Girl Crush Anthem." *Seoulbeats*, April 22, 2019. https://seoulbeats.com/2019/04/women-empowerment-the-girl-crush-anthem.

Min, Seo-Young. *Ssyangnyeon-ui mihak* [A bitch's aesthetics]. Seoul: Wisdom House, 2018.

Mulvey, Laura. *Visual and Other Pleasures*. Bloomington: Indiana University Press, 1989.

Nam, Jeong-Lim. "Gender Politics in the Korean Transition to Democracy." *Korean Studies* 24 (2000): 94–112. https://www.jstor.org/stable/23719707.

Oh, Ingyu, and Lee Hyo-Jung. "K-Pop in Korea: How the Pop Music Industry Is Changing a Post-Developmental Society." *Cross-Currents: East Asian History and Culture Review* 3, no. 1 (2014): 72–93. http://doi.org/10.1353/ach.2014.0007.

Park, Jin-hai. "Girl Bands Join 'Corset-free Movement.'" *Korea Times*, March 26, 2019. https://www.koreatimes.co.kr/www/art/2020/02/732_266077.html.

Ramirez, Elaine. "BlackPink: The All-Girl K-Pop Group Following BTS's Footsteps and Taking over the U.S." *Forbes*, April 1, 2019. https://www.forbes.com/sites/elaineramirez/2019/04/01/blackpink-the-all-girl-k-pop-group-following-btss-footsteps-and-taking-over-the-u-s/?sh=1929445b3e25.

SLY. "Ranking the Queendom Part 2 Performances from AOA to Mamamoo." *OH!PRESS*, September 20, 2019. https://blog.onehallyu.com/espressoh-ranking-the-queendom-part-2-performances-from-aoa-to-mamamoo/.

Walker, Rebecca. *To Be Real: Telling the Truth and Changing the Face of Feminism*. New York: Anchor Books, 1995.

Zellner, Xander. "BLACKPINK Makes K-Pop History on Hot 100, Billboard 200 & More with 'DDU-DU DDU-DU.'" *Billboard*, June 25, 2018. https://www.billboard.com/articles/columns/chart-beat/8462635/blackpink-k-pop-history-hot-100-billboard-200.

Part III

Fans and Fan-Producers

7

Alpeseu (RPS) and Business Gay Performance in the Korean K-Pop World

Stephanie Jiyun Choi

In the reality TV show *BRANDNEWBOYS*, which promoted the K-pop group AB6IX, five male idols played the paper kiss game, one of the most popular games performed by K-pop idols on variety shows.[1] One scene, accompanied by Leonard Cohen's song "I'm Your Man," features the five beautiful young men, divided into two teams, passing a piece of paper from mouth to mouth. The purpose of the game was for the idols to entertain the audience by accidentally dropping the paper and ending up touching each other's lips. Fans' reactions included, "I can't stop laughing because of Woojin and Youngmin," "Daehwi just went for it without even hesitating!" and "Woojin was kissed by Donghyun and Youngmin, so lucky!"[2] Some fans collected and edited such homoerotic moments—a compilation video entitled, "KPOP IDOLS GAY MOMENTS," for instance, earned more than 6.1 million views within a year and a half of being posted on YouTube.[3] A female idol version, "the most lesbian moments in kpop," also earned more than 1.8 million views within just a few months.[4]

Despite the popularity of these homoerotic games, South Korean society and its entertainment industry are far from LGBTQ-friendly. Conservatives and evangelical Christians have gone out of their way to disrupt Pride festivals every year and have continued to condemn anti-discrimination bills for supporting

---

1. Mnet K-POP, "BRANDNEWBOYS 5-hoe *Wiheomdo 522%* Ibeuro jong-i omgigi! 190516 EP.5" (BRANDNEWBOYS ep.5 *Risk level 522%* Transferring a piece of paper from lips to lips! 190516 EP.5), May 16, 2019, video, 4:35, https://www.youtube.com/watch?v=UFpyddWyJaw.
2. Mnet K-POP, "BRANDNEWBOYS EP.5." See the comment section.
3. KPOP MXB, "KPOP IDOLS GAY MOMENTS (BTS,MONSTA X,EXO,IKON,STRAY KIDS,KNK, 14U, NCT AND MORE) #1," March 17, 2019, video, 6:59, https://youtu.be/SWWMzwiZdxg.
4. ggsnation, "The Most Lesbian Moments in Kpop," February 4, 2021, video, 3:34, https://youtu.be/4c3Ms-SKA-A.

same-sex marriage since 2007.[5] Despite active discussions on the anti-discrimination law during Moon Jae-in's liberal administration (2017–2022), Yoon Suk-yeol's election led the Ministry of Gender Equality and Family to withdraw its support for the related bills and announce that it will maintain the previous heteronormative Framework Act on Healthy Families, which defines family as "the fundamental group unit of society formed by marriage, blood or adoption" and excludes other forms of non-traditional families, including same-sex partnerships.[6] When actor Hong Seok-cheon came out as gay in 2000, he was unable to find work until 2003 and was shunned by many of his famous friends.[7] Two decades later in 2018, K-pop idol Holland declared he was gay. Although entertainment companies serve as powerhouses for K-pop idols, Holland made his debut without a company because none of the companies would sign him when he insisted on publicly supporting sexual minorities.[8] Harisu, one of South Korea's very few openly transgender entertainers, explained that lesbian, gay, and transgender entertainers in South Korea have to stay in the closet if they want to continue working in show business.[9] Transgender YouTuber Pungja only recently began to appear on public television shows, thanks to her exceptional popularity among youth on digital media platforms. If the South Korean entertainment industry has traditionally discriminated against LGBTQ entertainers, how should we understand K-pop idols' commonly-performed homoerotic gestures and performances before their Korean audience? How do these idols articulate their sexuality in these performances? How do fans understand these homoerotic performances, and how is gender equity connected to these performances?

This chapter explores the fan-made alternative universe of RPS ("real person slash," a fictional setting in which fans imagine same-sex relationships between media personalities) and the idol-made "business gay performances" in K-pop. K-pop RPS has a lot in common with other global fan-writing practices, such

---

5.   Jung Da-min, "Anti-Discrimination Law Back on Table at National Assembly," *Korea Times*, July 3, 2020, https://www.koreatimes.co.kr/www/nation/2020/07/356_292216.html.

6.   Michael Lee, "Gender Ministry Switches Sides on 'Healthy Family' Issue," *Korea JoongAng Daily*, September 22, 2022, https://koreajoongangdaily.joins.com/2022/09/22/national/socialAffairs/Korea-samesex-family/20220922184656179.html.

7.   Shin Seong-a, "Hong Seok-cheon, 'Keoming-aut ihu chinan namja yeoneindeul modu yeollak kkeuneo" [Hong Seok-cheon states, "All of my close male celebrity friends were no longer in touch with me after I came out"], *NewDaily*, January 3, 2013, http://www.newdaily.co.kr/site/data/html/2013/01/03/2013010300001.html.

8.   Ryu In-ha, "Inteobyu: 'Seongsosuja sinin-gasu Hollaendeuimnida'" [Interview: I am the sexual minority rookie singer, Holland], *The Kyunghyang Shinmun*, February 4, 2018, http://news.khan.co.kr/kh_news/khan_art_view.html?art_id=201802040927001.

9.   *Kyunghyang Shinmun*, "Harisu 'Yeonegye sumeun dongseongaeja, teurenseujendeo itta' gobaek" [Harisu confesses, "There are closeted gay/lesbian and transgender entertainers"], November 28, 2007, http://news.khan.co.kr/kh_news/khan_art_view.html?art_id=200711281725201.

as slash fiction in the West and manga genres, *yaoi* (Boys Love or BL) and *yuri* (Girls Love or GL), in Japan. All three genres encourage female participation in fan communities.[10] Unlike slash fiction and manga narratives that feature fictional characters and/or supplement the narratives of the original productions, K-pop RPS borrows idols' physical appearances and names but transforms their ages, personalities, residences, occupations, sexualities, and other elements of their identities with new temporal and spatial settings. As if they were responding to the RPS fantasy, idols have presented various homoerotic moments by holding hands, caressing and kissing each other, and playing paper kiss games in public. From the early 2010s, Korean fans started to call this *bijeuniseu gei peopomeonseu* (*bigepeo*), or "business gay performance," understanding such behaviors as a marketing tactic in the K-pop business world.

As a resistance discourse against the academic legacy of pathologizing female fans as abnormal, fandom scholars have claimed fan fiction and yaoi/BL writing activities as women's productive activities linked to their identity formation, often with a feminist motivation of subverting gender hierarchies.[11] While celebrating fan fiction practices as liberating and celebratory for women, scholars are also concerned with identity (re)presentations of gay men whose lives are fantasized and commodified by female writers. As fan fiction scholar Kristina Busse notes: "Simply reading and writing about gay sex and enjoying the depiction of gay characters is not necessarily an act of subversion; in fact, it may

---

10. There are disagreements over whether *yaoi* is the same as Boys Love (BL). However, the terms *yaoi* and Boys Love are often used interchangeably in South Korean fandom.

11. Henry Jenkins, "Star Trek Rerun, Reread, Rewritten: Fan Writing as Textual Poaching," *Critical Studies in Mass Communication* 5, no. 2 (1988), 85–107, https://doi.org/10.1080/15295038809366691; Constance Penley, "Feminism, Psychoanalysis, and Popular Culture," in *Cultural Studies*, ed. Lawrence Grossberg, Cary Nelson, and Paula Treichler (New York: Routledge, 1992), 479–500; Michael Jindra, "Star Trek Fandom as a Religious Phenomenon," *Sociology of Religion* 55, no. 1 (1994) 27–51, https://www.jstor.org/stable/3712174; Henry Jenkins, "'Out of the Closet and into the Universe': Queers and Star Trek," in *Science Fiction Audiences: Watching Star Trek and Doctor Who*, by John Tulloch and Henry Jenkins (London: Routledge, 1995), 237–65; Ann K. McClellan, *Sherlock's World: Fan Fiction and the Reimagining of BBC's Sherlock* (Iowa City: University of Iowa Press, 2018); Sharalyn Orbaugh, "Creativity and Constraint in Amateur 'Manga' Production," *U.S.-Japan Women's Journal*, no. 25 (2003): 104–24, https://www.jstor.org/stable/42771905; Akiko Mizoguchi, "Male-Male Romance by and for Women in Japan: A History and the Subgenres of Yaoi Fictions," *U.S.-Japan Women's Journal*, no. 25 (2003): 49–75, https://www.jstor.org/stable/42771903; Kazumi Nagaike,"Perverse Sexualities, Perverse Desires: Representations of Female Fantasies and 'Yaoi Manga' as Pornography Directed at Women," *U.S.-Japan Women's Journal*, no. 25 (2003): 76–103, https://www.jstor.org/stable/42771904; Kim So-won, "Geunyeodeureun wae sonyeondeureui sarang-e yeolgwanghaneunga? Yamaoka Shigeyuki hujyosi-eui simnihak" [Why they are enthusiastic about boys' love? Yamaoka Shigeyuki's *The Psychology of Hujyosi*]. *Daejungseosayongu* [Popular Narrative Research] 24, no. 2 (2018): 275-303; Yang Sungeun, "Yeoseongsimnihak gwanjeomeseo bunseokhan namseongdongseongae-manhwa-eui yuhijeok suyong" [A feminist psychological analysis on the playful embrace of boys' love manga], *The Journal of the Korean Contents Association* 18, no. 9 (2018): 510-20, https://doi.org/10.5392/JKCA.2018.18.09.510.

become its opposite when such an engagement occurs completely divorced from any realistic context and in the absence of awareness of sexual politics in general and gay rights in particular."[12] This chapter will provide an ethnographic exploration of the local history of K-pop RPS, with the question of how interactions between RPS activities and business gay performances have reshaped gender relations among fans, K-pop idols, and the LGBTQ community in South Korea.

Although K-pop RPS is a global phenomenon widely appreciated by fans of all sexualities and gender identities, I focus on Korean female fans and their male idols, whose RPS activities have cultural and political influences on the queer visibility in South Korea. For this reason, I will use the Korean word *alpeseu* instead of *RPS* and *paenpik* or *fanfic* instead of *fan fiction* to respect fans' use of terminologies and the local context of the K-pop RPS. The direct translation of the fandom term *dongseong paenpik* is "homosexual fanfic"; however, because of the pathologizing connotation of the English term *homosexual*, I will use *dongseong paenpik* in romanized Korean to refer to same-sex fanfics. While *dongseong paenpik* refers to the same-sex fanfic genre, *alpeseu* encompasses a broader spectrum of memes, social media content, fan art, and fanfics that adopt the alternative universe of same-sex romance. My interviewees in this chapter include two Korean heterosexual male idols in their twenties, one gay fan in his twenties, and six Korean female fans in their twenties and thirties who identified either as heterosexual or bisexual. At their request, I am protecting their anonymity.

K-Pop *Alpeseu* Goes Underground

The first K-pop idol group H.O.T. made its debut in 1996 under President Kim Young-sam's regime (1993–1998), the first civilian government to promote the *segyehwa* (globalization) campaign as a way of democratizing and reformulating South Korea's neoliberal relations with the world. The South Korean government lifted restrictions on overseas travel in 1989 and gradually removed its ban on Japanese cultural products from 1998 to 2004. Japanese *yaoi* culture was introduced in South Korea in the 1980s and became popular in the 1990s on the pre-web internet (PC *tongsin*), providing a model for the early K-pop fanfic culture.[13] Because of the popularity of K-pop idols and the underground nature of the *dong-in* (self-published works) culture, female consumers of *yaoi*

12. Kristina Busse, "'I'm Jealous of Fake Me': Postmodern Subjectivity and Identity in Boy Band Fan Fiction," in *Framing Celebrity: New Directions in Celebrity Culture*, ed. Su Holms and Sean Redmond (London: Routledge, 2006), 211.
13. Kim Hyojin, "Hanguk dong-inmunhwawa yaoi: 1990nyeondaereul jungsimeuro" [Korean Dong-in culture and yaoi: Focusing on the changes in the 1990s]. *Cartoon and Animation Studies* 30 (2013): 263-91, https://doi.org/10.7230/KOSCAS.2013.30.263.

and fanfics were often denigrated in the mass media as *ppasuni* (a derogatory term for "fangirls").[14]

K-pop 1.0 (from the late 1990s to the early 2000s) was an era of adopting and exploring the fanfic culture.[15] Teenage female fans shared their fanfics through online fan communities. The genres included *iseong paenpik* (heterosexual fanfic) and *dongseong paenpik* (homosexual fanfic), both of which covered mainly romance, but also comedy, horror, historical heroism, mystery, and sci-fi.[16] The mass media often covered controversies surrounding *dongseong paenpik*, discussing whether one should understand the fanfic culture as a juvenile problem that "instills distorted ideas of gender and sexuality to teenagers," or as a new type of literature movement that "encourages communication and cultural diversity."[17] Some teenage fans first encountered same-sex romance via *dongseong paenpik* and took the opportunity to explore their sexuality. Some teenagers, who learned about LGBTQ culture through *dongseong panpik*, called themselves *paenpik iban* (fanfic-oriented sexual minority), drawing criticisms from the LGBTQ community who proclaimed themselves as "authentic."[18]

Dongseong paenpik stood out as a social issue, especially when the Ministry of Information and Communication (*Jeongbotongsinbu*) added the Internet Content Rating System (*Inteonetnaeyong Deunggeupje*) to its newly proposed bill in July 2000. A month later, the ministry designated South Korea's first lesbian and gay community website, exzone (http://exzone.com), as a "Harmful Media Content for Minors" (*Cheongsonyeon Yuhaemaechemul*). The decision was based on the Minor Protection Law (*Cheongsonyeonbohobeop Sihaengnyeong*), which defined Harmful Media Content for Minors as anything "describing and promoting socially unacceptable sexual relations, such as zooerastia, group sex, incest, homosexuality, perverted sexual behaviors such as sadomasochism,

---

14. Kim Hyojin, "Dong-innyeo-eui balgyeon-gwa jaehyeon: Han-guk sunjeongmanhwa-ui sarereul jungsimeuro" [Discovering and representing 'Dong-in-nyo' in Korea: Focusing on examples from Korean girls' comics], *Asiamunhwayeongu* [Asian cultural studies] 30 (2013): 43–75.
15. The K-pop 1.0 generation includes groups like H.O.T., S.E.S., Baby V.O.X, Sechs Kies, Fin.K.L, Shinhwa, g.o.d, BoA, and Rain.
16. Kim Minjeong, "Saibeo yeoseong munhwaroseo paenpik yeon-gu: Hwantajiwa seongjeongch'eseong-eui yeonkwanseong-eul jungsimeuro" [A study on fanfic as a women's cyber subculture: Focusing on the relations between fantasy and gender identity] (master's thesis, Ewha Womans University, 2002), 32.
17. *Weekly Donga*, "Oppaneun naegeosiya!" [Oppa is mine!], May 27, 2005, https://weekly.donga.com/List/3/all/11/64208/1.
18. Lee Jieun, "Sipdae yeoseong-iban-ui keomyuniti gyeongheom-gwa jeongchaeseong-e gwanan yeongu" [A study of teenage iban girls' community experience and identity] (master's thesis, Yonsei University, 2005). http://anthro.yonsei.ac.kr/bbs/board.php?tbl=data2&mode=VIEW&num=2&category=&findType=&findWord=&sort1=&sort2=&page=5.

and prostitution."[19] Netizens, especially adolescent females, strongly opposed the proposal, fearing that same-sex fanfic and *yaoi* would also be considered "harmful content."[20] About 210 websites added a banner declaring "No (Internet) Censorship" (*geomyeolbandae*); about 30 percent of these websites were fanfic and *yaoi* websites.[21] A 16-year-old female fan of pop ballad singer Jo Sung-mo stated, "All of my friends actively post comments against the censorship and participate in online protests."[22] Some female fans joined offline rallies near Myeongdong Cathedral and Shinchon in Seoul. In 2004, *dongseong-ae* (homosexuality) was removed from the Criteria for Examination of Media Products Harmful to Juveniles (*Cheongsonyeonyuhaemaechemul Simeuigijun*) after the National Human Rights Commission of Korea advised the government to remove it for the human rights of lesbian and gay citizens.[23] However, the operator of exzone, who filed a lawsuit against the ministry in 2002 for categorizing the website content as harmful, lost the case in 2007.[24] The Seoul High Court's ruling stated that "it is possible to consider the decision of including gay content in the Criteria for Examination of Media Products Harmful to Juveniles as unconstitutional or unlawful . . . However, there is no precedent ruled by the Supreme Court that such regulation is unconstitutional . . . it is not objectively clear or unquestionable whether it is unconstitutional or invalid."[25]

Until the end of K-pop 2.0 (from the early 2000s to the early 2010s), it was easy to find fanfic boards on fan community websites, and entertainment companies also encouraged fan fiction writing. The membership of Ddeotta Shinhwa, a fanfic community website of boy band Shinhwa, for example, once

19. Lee Sanghui, "Dongseong-aeja-eui gomindo 'eumnanmul' ideon geuttae" [Those years when the LGBTQ community's agony was considered pornographic media content], *Hankyoreh 21*, May 10, 2013, http://h21.hani.co.kr/arti/society/society_general/34481.html.
20. Shinyun Dong-uk, "'Urin mauseuro jeohanghanda'" ["We resist with our computer mouse"], *Hankyoreh 21*, September 6, 2000, http://h21.hani.co.kr/arti/special/special_general/447.html.
21. Shinyun, "Urin mauseuro." The websites included *Seongmo Cheonsa* (Angel Sungmo), *Chyotiyeonghon* (H.O.T. Spirit), *Shinhwa Changjo* (Shinhwa's Fan Club), *Neohiga Jekireul Aneunya* (Do You Know Sechs Kies), *Yaoi Sarangbang* (Yaoi Salon), *Ryano-eui Yaoi Soseolbang* (Ryano's Yaoi Novel Room), and *Yaoi Milgyo* (Yaoi Mystic Scripture).
22. Shinyun, "Urin mauseuro."
23. "Cheongsonyeon bohobeop sihaengryeong" [The Enforcement Ordinance for the Juvenile Protection Act], Korea Ministry of Government Legislation, accessed November 14, 2018, http://www.law.go.kr/LSW/lsRvsRsnListP.do;jsessionid=TU5Zbo9EBMBPjArdIFwGU-0-.LSW2?lsId=005209&chrClsCd=010102&lsRvsGubun=all.
24. Jeong Seongyun, "Dongseong-ae saiteu 'exzone' yuhaemaechaemul gyeoljeong-eun jeongdang" [It is just to define homosexual website 'exzone' as harmful media content], *Law Times*, June 28, 2007, https://www.lawtimes.co.kr/Case-Curation/view?serial=29742&page=5.
25. The National Law Information Center, "Cheongsonyeonyuhaemaechaemulgyeoljeongmitgosi cheobunmuhyohwagin" [A confirmation of the invalidity of the decision and announcement of the harmful media content for minors], https://www.law.go.kr/LSW/precInfoP.do?precSeq=78304.

exceeded 300,000.[26] SM Entertainment held fanfic contests for fans of TVXQ and Super Junior in 2006 and offered prize money, autographed CDs, and an opportunity to meet the idols.[27] Idols also started to materialize the *dongseong paenpik* fantasy on television shows in humorous ways, acknowledging fanfic as part of the K-pop culture. Famous examples include boy band Big Bang's parody of the kissing scene in Korean drama *Secret Garden*, and H.O.T.'s appearance on *SNL Korea*, where the members parodied the same-sex romance of their fanfics, appealing to the nostalgia of first-generation fans.

In the K-pop 3.0 era (from the early 2010s to the late 2010s), fans began to use the term *alpeseu* as an umbrella term encompassing all sorts of media content with the alternative universe of same-sex romance.[28] The nondialectical representation of the first-generation idols on mass media enabled fans to fantasize about their idols and create new fanfic characters and narratives. In contrast, social media has facilitated mutual communications between third-generation idols ad fans. P. David Marshall argues that, unlike how celebrity culture as a representational culture retains its function of parasociality and pedagogical role in the discourse of the "production of the self," social media as presentational media demands an engagement that "implicates the celebrity themselves in the interpersonal flow of communication."[29] Social media has changed fans' perception of their idol as a real person who may actually read fanfics, as idols started to express excitement or irritation about fanfics.[30] This mutual communicative nature of social media has led fans to make their fanfic activities invisible from their idols.

The changes in gender relations between idols and fans have also caused the fanfic culture to go underground. Most fans of first-generation idols in the 1990s entered the fandom as adolescent females whose fan activities were financially

26. Lee Hwajin, "Saibeo paenpik (fan-fiction) eul tonghae bon '10dae yeoseongdeureui ijung-eogapgwa dae-an mosaek" [A study on teenager female's double suppression and their exploration of alternative space in cyber fan fiction—with a focus on 'Ddeotta Shinhwa', a singing group Shinhwa's fanfic web site] (master's thesis, Hanyang University, 2003), 4.
27. Kang Sujin, "Dongbangsinki 'paenpik gongmojeon' yeonda" [TVXQ will hold a "fanfic contest"], *Kyunghyang Shinmun*, February 3, 2006, http://sports.khan.co.kr/entertainment/sk_index.html?art_id=200602031330193&sec_id=540201.
28. The K-pop 3.0 era features idol groups such as EXO, Mamamoo, VIXX, Red Velvet, BTS, GOT7, GFRIEND, WINNER, OH MY GIRL, iKON, Seventeen, TWICE, MONSTA X, DAY6, BLACKPINK, NCT, and (G)I-DLE.
29. P. David Marshall, "The Promotion and Presentation of the Self: Celebrity as Marker of Presentational Media," *Celebrity Studies* 1, no. 1 (2010): 43–44, http://doi.org/10.1080/19392390903519057.
30. For example, Super Junior and NU'EST mentioned that they have read fanfics written by their fans. See Bigeulbigeul Shupeojunieo, "Paenpigeun sireohajiman siljero boneungeoneun joahaneun Yeseong" [Yesung hates fanfic but likes to watch his members performing it], September 6, 2020, video, 2:13, https://youtu.be/GM_jOwAfM4E; see also macyNoodles, "130904 After School Club EP21 NU'EST 뉴이스트," September 4, 2013, video, 54:51, https://youtu.be/gSZm6_0Xtig.

and physically restricted by their parents. By the early 2010s, however, these fans became young adults who could financially support their third-generation teenage idols. In the ever-saturated idol market, male idols are infantilized as vulnerable boys who cannot sustain their careers without the sponsorship of their adult female fans. The consumer power of these women is implied in the fandom terminologies—fans nowadays call their idols *aedeul* (kids) or *nae saekki* (my child), and such nomenclature is widely used even among teenage fans who are younger than their favorite idols. Idols are not expected to grow a beard, smoke, or date in public, and are expected to shave their legs and wear cute costumes. Fans, in return, promote their idols by streaming and bulk-buying the latest albums, voting for the idols to receive music awards, sending lunch boxes to the idols' workplaces, and advertising the idols in public and online spaces.

By the late 2010s, fanfic had become *eumji munhwa*—an underground culture. The contradiction between fans' perception of idols as premature boys and their sexual depictions of these boys in fanfics have driven the fanfic culture underground. An idol fan, who finds *dongseong paenpik* offensive, states: "Imagine your fan depicting you as a gay man who has sex with your friend [another group member of the idol]. How would you feel? You don't have to be rude, so just enjoy it behind his back if you want to."[31] Fan communities no longer provide boards dedicated to fanfics; instead, fanfics have moved to closed fanwork community websites that require registrations, logins, age verifications, and charges for some contents. When they share their fanfics on personal blogs, fans upload them in a TXT file format so their idols do not come across the content on the internet by accident.

The Heteronormative Foundation of *Alpeseu*

While the direct interactions between idols and fans in social media and offline events have established *yangji munhwa* (overground culture), fans have also developed *eumji munhwa* (underground culture) on their own, using strategies that keep them invisible from idols and the public on the internet. The term "underground" often indicates the community's minority status, anti-commercial drive, geographic enclave, and/or political connotation of alterity or stylistic marginality followed by subcultural authenticity, in opposition to the mainstream media.[32] The term *eumji munhwa* in K-pop, however, does not refer to the

---

31. Fan B, in discussion with the author, July 10, 2016.
32. Sarah Thornton, *Club Cultures: Music, Media, and Subcultural Capital* (Middletown, CT: Wesleyan University Press, 1996), 181; Anna Szemere, *Up from the Underground: The Culture of Rock Music in Postsocialist Hungary* (University Park: Penn State University Press, 2001), 16; Falu Bakrania, *Bhangra and Asian Underground: South Asian Music and the Politics of Belonging in Britain* (Durham, NC: Duke University Press, 2013), 34.

fans' marginalized status, resistance to commercialism, and/or physical/virtual enclave, but rather implies its invisibility and absence of acknowledgement in the mutual communications between idols and fans, because of the queer sexualities that fans adopt in fanfic narratives and their economic activities that appropriate idols' publicity. For this reason, there is a tacit agreement that fans will never talk about *alpeseu* in front of their idols.

Paul Booth defines the blogging practices of fan fiction as a "textual freedom," as individuals "in a carnivalesque atmosphere subsume their identities."[33] Although fans assume that their male idol is heterosexual, they transform him into a man who cannot maintain a sexual relationship with anyone but his group member. Just like Boys Love (BL), K-pop fans call the assignment of fictional roles as same-sex lovers *keopeuling* or "CP" ("coupling," also known in English as "shipping"—as in "relationshipping"). Until the mid-2010s, K-pop fans called the "masculine" penetrator, who dominates the relationship, *gong* and the "feminine" penetrated, who is more emotional and passive in the relationship, *su*.[34] From the late 2010s onward, K-pop fans started to replace *gong* and *su* with *oen* and *reun*, following the recent trend in BL; yet unlike BL, K-pop fans reject the conventional heteropatriarchal relationship between *gong/oen* and *su/reun*. Fan C, a bisexual female fan in her mid-thirties, explains the difference between *yaoi* and *alpeseu*:

> I think creative writing reflects the current condition of our society. I heard from BL fans that misogynistic BL novels are still popular on major BL platforms such as Joara and Ridibooks. I think [K-pop] fanfic/*alpeseu* is more progressive than BL. This difference comes from whether you're a full-time writer or not. Many BL writers are full-time writers, so it is important for them to gain popularity to make a living. So even if they wish to talk about progressive ideologies, they must tone it down. But fanfic/*alpeseu* writing is a hobby for most writers, so they are free from such restrictions. This is why I like fanfic/*alpeseu*. I hate all those misogynistic narratives of the privileged written by men. I think fanfic/*alpeseu* is a genre where you find the most progressive writers who candidly write their thoughts from the point of sexual minorities.[35]

According to Fan C, the commercial milieus of BL and fanfic affect the gender politics of each culture. Both BL and K-pop *alpeseu* in South Korea share many elements, including the universe and character settings that adopt same-sex romance. When the *dongseong paenpik* culture in K-pop emerged in the mid-1990s, same-sex romance was a controversial topic in South Korean society. Mass media's interest was in teenage fans' exploration of, or "deviation" toward,

---

33. Paul Booth, *Digital Fandom: New Media Studies* (New York: Peter Lang, 2010), 62.
34. The terms *gong* and *su* are direct translations of *seme* and *uke* in Japanese Boys Love.
35. Fan C, in discussion with the author, August 13, 2020.

LGBTQ lifestyles through fanfic. Early studies of fanfic also focused on adolescent fangirls' exploration of queer sexuality through fanfic.[36] While naming the gay romance fantasy created and actualized by straight women as "FANtasy," fandom scholar Kwon Jungmin argues:

> The gay body is romanticized by Korean FANtasy fans (and by extension, by Korean women) because gay men are believed to have features that straight men do not. In other words, Korean women tired of strong, manly, and patriarchal Korean men project their male fantasy—a soft appearance and sweet personality, responsiveness to female desire, and egalitarianism—onto the gay body . . . In the 1990s, the preference for such male types was combined with soft masculinity and metrosexuality and led to the emergence of the flower-boy syndrome . . . That is, the flower boy represents a new type of ideal man based on FANtasy culture's gay imagery . . . Hallyu (Korean Wave) singing groups popular across the world, such as Big Bang, TVXQ, Super Junior, and EXO, include many flower-boy members. In brief, FANtasy culture's gay imagination contributed to demolishing the standard of manliness and complicating the ideal male image in Korean society.[37]

While I agree that K-pop fans' sexual desire is consistent with a rejection of patriarchal masculinity, I argue the following: first, a gay man is not the opposite concept of a patriarchal straight man; moreover, the fictional character found in same-sex romance in *alpeseu* is not the same as a gay man. A bisexual female fan explains why idols are seemingly gay men in *alpeseu*: "First, *napeseu* [a fanfic universe that describes a romance between the idol and the reader] is a taboo. It's like, 'Are you going to monopolize our idol?' Second, it comes from a lack of gender awareness. It's like, 'Because he has a penis [and loves a man], he is a gay man.' But what is really important is that *alpeseu* must be realized only within the group that I like."[38] Another fan also comments, "Why would I long for a gay man? I'm a heterosexual woman and won't date a gay man anyway. What I like is my idol, not a gay man."[39] A gay fan notes,

36. Kim Hunsun and Kim Minjeong, "Paenpigeui saengsan-gwa sobireul tonghae bon sonyeodeureui seong hwantaji-wa jeongchijeok hameui" [A fantasy of fanfic and the politics], *Korean Journal of Journalism & Communication Studies* 48, no. 3 (2004): 330-53; Ryu Jinhee, "Paenpik: Dongseong(seong)ae seosa-eui yeoseong gonggan" [Fanfics: The women's space of homosexual narratives], *Feminism and Korean Literature* 20 (2008): 163-84; Park Sujin, "Cheongsonyeon paenpikmunhwawa dongseong-ae-e daehan taedo yeongu" [A study on teenagers' fanfic culture and attitudes toward homosexuality—focusing on middleschool girls] (master's thesis, Ewha Womans University, 2003); Lee Jieun, "Sipdae yeoseong-iban-ui keomyuniti gyeongheom-gwa jeongchaeseong-e gwanan yeongu" [A study of teenage iban girls' community experience and identity] (master's thesis, Yonsei University, 2005).
37. Kwon Jungmin, *Straight Korean Female Fans and Their Gay Fantasies* (Iowa City: University of Iowa Press, 2019), 10-11.
38. Fan E, in discussion with the author, August 13, 2020.
39. Fan F, in discussion with the author, August 14, 2020.

The biggest charm of *dongseong paenpik* is that it fulfills my fantasy, because it shows events that will hardly happen to me in real life. But every time I read fanfics, I'm not happy with [the writers] making *su* extremely feminine. They're just creating a pleasurable setting for themselves by applying the heterosexual framework. The *su* role is so much like a female protagonist in a [Korean] drama.[40]

Because an idol should remain as public property to which each fan can purchase access (e.g., by paying for concerts and fanmeets), a one-on-one dating relationship between the idol and an individual fan is discouraged, even in a fanfic setting. The safest way for millions of fans to claim equal ownership over an idol's body is to make the character incapable of falling in love other than with their group members.

K-pop fans' consumption pattern of *alpeseu* has changed in the 2010s for two reasons. First, the adolescent females of the 1990s had become adult women by the 2010s. Both *dongseong paenpik* and gay masculinity were new for adolescent females to explore in the 1990s; by the 2010s, however, fanfic writing had become more of a form of entertainment than an exploration of sexuality. Fans make it clear that their depiction of *alpeseu* has nothing to do with gay men and gay masculinity by using *alpeseu*-exclusive terminologies—such as *oen* and *reun*—in describing the characters' gender and sexuality. Second, as the adult fans became their idols' promoters, *alpeseu* went underground because fans knew that they were violating their idols' publicity rights by deploying imaginary sexualities— especially queer sexualities—in the idols' bodies. Fans eventually shied away from publicly consuming *alpeseu*.

In other fandoms, RPS (real person slash) is often believed to be real and gives rise to activism for LGBTQ rights. The shippers of English-Irish boy band One Direction, for example, claim their RPS shipping of Harry Styles and Louis Tomlinson to be real and use the opportunity to promote LGBTQ issues and activism.[41] Korean fans, however, engage in *alpeseu* imagination under the belief that their idols have acquired hegemonic masculinity as heterosexual males, even if they arbitrarily imagine and craft the idols' sexuality in *alpeseu*. Because the purpose of *alpeseu* is to fantasize a relationship between two idols, not gay masculinity per se, idols as *alpeseu* characters can personify all types of gender and sexuality. *Aromul*, or omegaverse, is an example of recreating a male persona through a feminine gaze. The omegaverse genre was created by fans of the American television series *Supernatural*, and Korean fans adopted the genre in the mid-2010s. In *aromul*, a male idol in the "omega" role can become pregnant. This does not mean that fans fantasize a male who can have a child; it only

---

40. Fan G, in discussion with the author, May 27, 2016.
41. Southerton and McCann, "Queerbaiting," 162.

implies that female writers can readily apply their life experiences and cultural values to the fictional character that they create. In other words, *alpeseu* activities are focused on the romantic/sexual creation of an idol-exclusive universe, not on fantasizing gay masculinity or a man who is able to conceive. No outsiders are allowed to join the *alpeseu* universe, whether it be a woman or even a man if he is not a member of the writer's favorite idol group.

"Business Gay Performance": Publicly Responding to Underground Desires

A popular sentiment in K-pop fandom regarding *dongseong paenpik* and *alpeseu* is that "what's underground should stay underground." Paul Booth argues that fan fiction subverts the "political power of the established media oligarchy" by rewriting and rereading copyrighted materials, while media producers unofficially and passively support this act of copyright infringement as a way of advertising the product.[42] But what if the media texts—K-pop idols, in this case—are real people? How should we position the idols' agency between the media oligarchy and fans' subversion of it? Can we still celebrate fans' subversion of political power if it comes at the cost of the sexual objectification of human subjects, let alone the violation of publicity rights? Legally, *dongseong paenpik* and *alpeseu* violate K-pop idols' publicity rights.[43] However, because the K-pop idol system encourages a cultivation of intimacy between idols and fans, idols and their entertainment companies have reappropriated *alpeseu* imaginings instead of suing the creators.

The essence of the K-pop idol system lies in the development of intimate relationships between idols and fans.[44] While fans emotionally and financially support and promote their idols for years, idols, in return, provide "fan service" (*paenseobiseu*)—musical, verbal, textual, and/or physical performances that provide pleasure to their fans. Idols talk about their daily habits and personal tastes and confess their love to their fans on social media. At their fans' requests, idols make cute faces or gestures called *aegyo* during live streams. Idols share information about their private lives with their fans (e.g., by holding a birthday party with their fans), but are also surveilled by their fans. The idol body is a

---

42. Booth, *Digital Fandom*, 73.
43. According to the Seoul Eastern District Court's 2006 ruling, the "right of publicity" is the exclusive right that allows a person to commercially use and control their name, portrait, or other types of identity. An idol whose publicity right is violated by others can legally claim for damages based on article 750 of the Civil Code. See https://easylaw.go.kr/CSP/CnpClsMain.laf?popMenu=ov&csmSeq=530&ccfNo=4&cciNo=4&cnpClsNo=2.
44. Stephanie Choi, "Gender, Labor, and the Commodification of Intimacy in K-pop" (PhD diss., the University of California, Santa Barbara, 2020).

product in which fans have invested. Fans expect their idols to be celibate, or at least keep their sexual relationships out of public view. Thus, the idol body can also become a site in which fans' sexual desire in *alpeseu* can be materialized. From K-pop 2.0 onward, idols have adopted the imagined gender relations in *alpeseu* and have performed the so-called *bigepeo*, the "business gay performance," which is celebrated as a form of fan service by the K-pop industry and fandom.

A video clip of the idol group Shinhwa's 2012 concert in Seoul is a good example of how same-sex romance becomes entertainment. While Hyesung talks to the audience, Eric shows his affection for Hyesung, holding his arm while pushing other members of the group aside.[45] Eventually, Eric gives Hyesung a big hug and shouts, "Everyone, Ricsyung is the best!" The fans are excited to hear Eric calling himself and Hyesung "Ricsyung," the term that indicates Eric and Hyesung's *alpeseu* relationship. Fans and other members demand that the Ricsyung couple kiss, but Eric tries to compromise by hugging Hyesung again. As Eric and Hyesung hesitate, Jun Jin, another member of the group, tells them: "Since everyone wants it, please do it so that we can move on." Eric awkwardly kisses Hyesung's cheek, and Hyesung bursts out laughing.

Sometimes, *bigepeo* is sophisticated enough to make the viewers believe that the situation is real. My interviewee Idol A showed me a television interview where his group member Idol B touched Idol C's leg during other members' interview. It looked very natural and private to me, but Idol A told me that it was staged:

> They don't even talk to each other when the camera is off. They obviously know that fans are watching them. They know how to behave before their fans. We had a pre-recording session [for a television show] when I injured my leg, and all of the members went up to the stage without helping me out during the rehearsal. But when the pre-recording session began and fans came into the studio, they knew that our mics were on, so they whispered on the mic, "Take care of yourself," as if they were worried about me. Then they assisted me when I went up to the stage. But none of them came to my brother's wedding when I invited them.[46]

The physical touch that is not too obvious yet homoerotic straddles homosocial friendship and same-sex romance. Such moments often circulate as memes within fandom, contributing to the character relationships in the *alpeseu* universe.

No matter how much *bigepeo* is sophisticated enough to look natural, there is a rule among fans that *bigepeo* should be understood only as a deliberately

---

45. FLASHBACK4shs, "RicShung_Riksheong-i jjang-iraneun edaepyo-ui soyuyok" [Eric says RicShung is the best], April 9, 2012, video, 1:43, https://www.youtube.com/watch?v=htQiJcZUOx0.
46. Idol A, in discussion with the author, August 2, 2017.

staged performance by heterosexual idols and that it should not develop into a public assumption that the idols are gay, as such an assumption can jeopardize the idols' publicity and career in heteropatriarchal Korean society. Through snippets of paparazzi photos and rumors that the idols are dating women, fans are convinced that Eric and Hyesung are straight men. Fan D insists that the idols cannot be gay:

> It's so obvious that they like women when you see them on talk shows. I think it's natural for them to kiss each other's cheeks since they've been friends for 16 years. [If it's true that they're gay,] I'd be okay, but I don't think I can say, "I'm so happy for you! Hope you have a lovely relationship!" I think they should rather get married [with women]. Considering that I enjoy reading homosexual fanfics, I know it is ironic, but I'm a Christian and I think homosexuality is wrong.[47]

In a society where the LGBTQ community is compelled to remain silent, *bigepeo* cannot serve as an assertion of gay masculinity; it only offers an opportunity for the idols to assert their heterosexuality. After kissing other male performers on a 2009 concert tour, Super Junior member Heechul stated in several interviews that he was "not gay at all" and that onstage kissing was "a new type of performance."[48]

Until the mid-2010s, it was not uncommon for the host of a TV show to ask male entertainers if they were gay and for the entertainers to deny it. It has now become less frequent as activists and supporters of the post-2015 feminist movement have criticized it.[49] But when idols are asked to perform *bigepeo*, many of them perform it with feigned awkwardness or discomfort by grimacing or screaming in shock and anger. In AB6IX's paper kiss game that I mentioned in the beginning of this chapter, the idols scream before putting their lips on the paper and shout, "How do you want us to do this?" Then they drop to their knees or fall to the ground when they accidentally kiss each other. Other members shout, "Did they kiss? Eww!" and pretend to be disgusted.[50]

When Holland, who debuted as a gay idol, was asked about fanfic, he explained his limitations on performing *bigepeo*:

47. Fan D, in discussion with the author, December 14, 2014.
48. Lee In-gyeong, "Inteobyu 2: Shupeojunieo Hicheol, dongseong kiseu haepeuning 'Twieoboryeoneun peopomeonseu'" [Interview 2: Super Junior Heechul, same-sex kiss event was "an eye-catching performance"], *JoongAng Sunday*, March 11, 2009, http://article.joins.com/news/article/article.asp?ctg=&Total_ID=3525642.
49. From the mid-2010s, self-proclaimed radical feminists have performed "mirroring" (*mireoring*), a resistance discourse that emulated misogynistic discourse. The activists have brought up various topics including femicide, sexual abuse, the LGBTQ community, the gender pay gap, the #MeToo movement, the Korean patriarchy, dating violence, and abortion in public discourses.
50. Mnet K-POP, "BRANDNEWBOYS EP.5."

I knew about the [fanfic] culture because I used to like various celebrities when I was younger. I don't really know why they do it either, but I can only guess fans probably wouldn't want to see their favorite idols going out with anyone else. Instead, they want to see them going out with another idol they like. I think that's how the [fanfic] culture started. I'm particularly cautious about [performing *bigepeo*], because many people can misjudge my intentions. Even if I simply say hi or make some gestures to other idols without any intentions, people can still misinterpret my behavior [because of my sexuality], so I'm cautious [about my behavior].[51]

Holland's statement demonstrates how the commercial setting of idols' homo-erotic games can be realized only under the assumption that all participants are heterosexual males and that *bigepeo* only confirms the heteronormative system of the K-pop industry. A gay fan states, "Whether the idol is gay or not, he earns money off of public attention, so I understand if he denies that he's gay," in South Korean society where queer visibility as a way of empowering the LGBTQ community may risk one's career and societal membership.[52]

Discussing Human Rights in *Alpeseu* Culture

There is no question about the heteronormative configuration of *alpeseu* and *bigepeo*. Fans reject or negotiate with the *alpeseu* culture based on their attitudes toward the commodification of idols' sexuality and appropriation of gay masculinity. On the one hand, those who refuse to consume the *alpeseu* fantasy see it as sexual harassment of idols and an incorrect depiction of gay men. On the other hand, those who acknowledge the heteronormative setting of *alpeseu* offer a discourse in which participants in the culture can consider the impact of their productions on the idols, gay men, and the LGBTQ community.

Some idols contemplate their influence on the general perception of the LGBTQ community. Idol D, who presented a homoerotic performance with his group member at their concert, stresses the irrelevance between his *bigepeo* and gay masculinity:

Me: Do you remember how your performance with Idol E was a shock to your fans?

Idol D: Because it was a "homosexual performance"? I do remember.

Me: Was it planned or rehearsed?

---

51. sbspopasia, "EXCLUSIVE: Sam Hammington Talks to the First Openly Gay K-Pop Idol Holland," April 10, 2018, video, 12:48, https://youtu.be/xZhT5Q29aTQ. I used the interview translation on the video subtitled by sbspopasia and modified slightly for accuracy.
52. Fan G, in discussion with the author, May 27, 2016.

Idol D: It wasn't planned. I wanted to give a sensual feeling but didn't intend
          to give homosexual feelings. It was just the energy that came out from
          the chemistry between me and Idol E. When there was a controversy
          around my "homosexual performance," I only felt how much our
          country was a closed society, but I never thought, "I should be careful
          from now on."

Me: What do you mean by "closed"?

Idol D: [During our interview,] I previously mentioned that the statement "I
          support homosexuality (dongseong-ae)" is wrong. Homosexuality is
          not a thing that you can support or not, because it already exists. So
          there's nothing to support over its existence. If someone asks me, "Are
          you gay?" I won't even say "no," because I'm worried if I look like I'm
          denying it only to avoid any disadvantages that I will get due to the
          social prejudice against homosexuality. So if someone asks, "Are you
          gay?" I will ask back, "What do you think? Think whatever you want."
          Because homosexuality is not wrong, I don't care if they think of me as
          a gay man. Apparently, there are many people who respond like this.

Me: Many people? Who are you referring to? Idols?

Idol D: Oh, foreigners, obviously. There is no Korean who would answer
          like that. That's why I think [our society] is closed. I think it can be
          oppressive to sexual minorities when a celebrity who has a great deal
          of social influence says, "I support homosexuality," even if that was not
          his intention. So I didn't really care when I got such responses after my
          performance. I was okay with being seen as a gay man, because I'm not.
          But I think I'm okay with it perhaps because I have never experienced
          such oppression.[53]

Idol D separates his homoerotic performance from his sexuality. However, one
can never be free from doing gender; even if it is not easily recognized, gender
functions as a background identity in a social relational context.[54] In the interview, Idol D attempts to separate his *alpeseu/bigepeo* masculinity from gay masculinity. At the same time, he is aware of the visibility of gay masculinity in his
performance.

Some fanfic writers depict gay men in more respectful ways. Fan A, a female
in her mid-thirties, added more "realistic" stories to her fanfics and depicted her
idol as a closeted gay man: "Even if it happened in fanfic, I was not happy with
depicting the idols as openly gay characters in this Confucian country [a sarcastic

53. Idol D, in discussion with the author, September 10, 2015.
54. Candace West and Don H. Zimmerman, "Doing Gender," *Gender and Society* 1, no. 2 (1987):
     125–51, http://links.jstor.org/sici?sici=0891-2432%28198706%291%3A2%3C125%3ADG%3E2.0.
     CO%3B2-W; Cecilia L. Ridgeway and Shelley J. Correll, "Unpacking the Gender System: A
     Theoretical Perspective on Gender Beliefs and Social Relations," *Gender and Society* 18, no. 4
     (2004): 510–31, https://www.law.berkeley.edu/php-programs/courses/fileDL.php?fID=9833.

reference to conservatism in South Korea]. It requires a huge paradigmatic shift for a person to realize his identity, accept it, face a new world, and build new relationships with people . . . As a bisexual person, I wanted to cover those issues."[55] While fanfic writers like Fan A incorporate the marginalization of gay men into their narratives, fanfic readers censor those who contain negative stereotypes of gay men. Fan E occasionally asks fanfic writers to revise their narratives. One time she read a fanfic that "described homosexuality as unethical as adultery."[56] Later, the writer responded to her complaint and revised the narrative.

Conclusion

In South Korea, where openly gay entertainers are disadvantaged, if not discriminated against, by their industry and by the public, *bigepeo*, as a materialization of *alpeseu*, only confirms idols' heterosexuality, because K-pop idols' homoerotic behaviors can only be tolerated as a staged performance. Being a gay idol only signals the impossibility of constructing a heterosexual bond between the idol and his fans and becomes a threat to other heterosexual male idols. Despite the rigid heteronormative structure of *alpeseu* and *bigepeo*, a growing number of idols and fans attempt to publicize issues of gender equality and visibility of sexual minorities. Although I have discussed a small portion of the K-pop *alpeseu* culture limited to the interactions between male idols and female fans in South Korea, I believe future studies on female-idol fanfics, lesbian and gay writers and readers, and interactions between K-pop idols and international fanfic writers will contribute to diverse case studies of gender performativity in the global fanfic world of K-pop.

Bibliography

Bakrania, Falu. *Bhangra and Asian Underground: South Asian Music and the Politics of Belonging in Britain*. Durham, NC: Duke University Press, 2013.

Booth, Paul. *Digital Fandom: New Media Studies*. New York: Peter Lang, 2010.

Busse, Kristina. *Framing Fan Fiction: Literary and Social Practices in Fan Fiction Communities*. Iowa City: University of Iowa Press, 2017.

Busse, Kristina. "'I'm Jealous of Fake Me': Postmodern Subjectivity and Identity in Boy Band Fan Fiction." In *Framing Celebrity: New Directions in Celebrity Culture*, edited by Su Holms and Sean Redmond, 253–68. London: Routledge, 2006.

Busse, Kristina. "My Life Is a WIP on My LJ: Slashing the Slasher and the Reality of Celebrity." In *Fan Fiction and Fan Communities in the Age of the Internet: New Essays*,

---

55. Fan A, in discussion with the author, August 13, 2020.
56. Fan E, in discussion with the author, August 13, 2020.

edited by Karen Hellekson and Kristina Busse, 207-24. Jefferson, NC: McFarland & Co., 2006.

Choi, Stephanie. "Gender, Labor, and the Commodification of Intimacy in K-Pop." PhD diss., University of California, Santa Barbara, 2020. https://escholarship.org/uc/item/5xj1r230.

Jenkins, Henry. "'Out of the Closet and into the Universe': Queers and *Star Trek*." In *Science Fiction Audiences: Watching Star Trek and Doctor Who*, by John Tulloch and Henry Jenkins, 237-65. London: Routledge, 1995.

Jenkins, Henry. "*Star Trek* Rerun, Reread, Rewritten: Fan Writing as Textual Poaching." *Critical Studies in Mass Communication* 5, no. 2 (1988): 85-107. https://doi.org/10.1080/15295038809366691.

Jindra, Michael. "Star Trek Fandom as a Religious Phenomenon." *Sociology of Religion* 55, no. 1 (1994): 27-51. https://www.jstor.org/stable/3712174.

Kim, Hunsun, and Kim Minjeong, "Paenpigeui saengsan-gwa sobireul tonghae bon sonyeodeureui seong hwantaji-wa jeongchijeok hameui" [A fantasy of fanfic and the politics]. *Korean Journal of Journalism & Communication Studies* 48, no. 3 (2004): 330-53. https://www.kci.go.kr/kciportal/ci/sereArticleSearch/ciSereArtiView.kci?sereArticleSearchBean.artiId=ART000974870.

Kim, Hyojin. "Dong-innyeo-eui balgyeon-gwa jaehyeon: Han-guk sunjeongmanhwa-ui sarereul jungsimeuro" [Discovering and representing "Dong-in-nyo" in Korea: Focusing on examples from Korean girls' comics]. *Asiamunhwayeongu* [Asian Cultural Studies] 30 (2013): 43-76. https://www.kci.go.kr/kciportal/ci/sereArticleSearch/ciSereArtiView.kci?sereArticleSearchBean.artiId=ART001779207.

Kim, Hyojin. "Hanguk dong-inmunhwawa yaoi: 1990nyeondaereul jungsimeuro" [Korean Dong-in culture and yaoi: Focusing on the changes in the 1990s]. *Cartoon and Animation Studies* 30 (2013): 263-91. https://doi.org/10.7230/KOSCAS.2013.30.263.

Kim, So-won. "Geunyeodeureun wae sonyeondeureui sarang-e yeolgwanghaneunga? Yamaoka Shigeyuki hujyosi-eui simnihak" [Why they are enthusiastic about boys' love? Yamaoka Shigeyuki's *The Psychology of Hujyosi*]. *Daejungseosayongu* [Popular Narrative Research] 24, no. 2 (2018): 275-304. https://doi.org/10.18856/jpn.2018.24.2.009.

Kwon, Jungmin. *Straight Korean Female Fans and Their Gay Fantasies*. Iowa City: University of Iowa Press, 2019.

Marshall, P. David. "The Promotion and Presentation of the Self: Celebrity as Marker of Presentational Media." *Celebrity Studies* 1, no. 1 (2010): 35-48. http://doi.org/10.1080/19392390903519057.

McClellan, Ann K. *Sherlock's World: Fan Fiction and the Reimagining of BBC's Sherlock*. Iowa City: University of Iowa Press, 2018.

McLelland, Mark J. "The Love between 'Beautiful Boys' in Japanese Women's Comics." *Journal of Gender Studies* 9, no. 1 (2000): 13-25.

Mizoguchi, Akiko. "Male-Male Romance by and for Women in Japan: A History and the Subgenres of Yaoi Fictions." *U.S.-Japan Women's Journal*, no. 25 (2003): 49-75. https://www.jstor.org/stable/42771903.

Nagaike, Kazumi. "Perverse Sexualities, Perversive Desires: Representations of Female Fantasies and 'Yaoi Manga' as Pornography Directed at Women." *U.S.-Japan Women's Journal*, no. 25 (2003): 76-103. https://www.jstor.org/stable/42771904.

Orbaugh, Sharalyn. "Creativity and Constraint in Amateur 'Manga' Production." *U.S.-Japan Women's Journal*, no. 25 (2003): 104-24. https://www.jstor.org/stable/42771905.

Penley, Constance. "Feminism, Psychoanalysis, and Popular Culture." In *Cultural Studies*, edited by Lawrence Grossberg, Cary Nelson, and Paula Treichler, 479-500. New York: Routledge, 1992.

Ridgeway, Cecilia L., and Shelley J. Correll. "Unpacking the Gender System: A Theoretical Perspective on Gender Beliefs and Social Relations." *Gender and Society* 18, no. 4 (2004): 510-31. https://www.law.berkeley.edu/php-programs/courses/fileDL.php?f ID=9833.

Ryu, Jinhee. "Paenpik: Dongseong(seong)ae seosa-eui yeoseong gonggan" [Fanfics: The women's space of homosexual narratives]. *Feminism and Korean Literature* 20 (2011): 163-84. https://www.kci.go.kr/kciportal/ci/sereArticleSearch/ciSereArti View.kci?sereArticleSearchBean.artiId=ART001306103.

Southerton, Clare, and Hannah McCann. "Queerbaiting and Real Person Slash: The Case of Larry Stylinson." In *Queerbaiting and Fandom: Teasing Fans through Homoerotic Possibilities*, edited by Joseph Brennan, 161-63. Iowa City: University of Iowa Press, 2019.

Szemere, Anna. *Up from the Underground: The Culture of Rock Music in Postsocialist Hungary*. University Park: Penn State University Press, 2001.

Thornton, Sarah. *Club Cultures: Music, Media, and Subcultural Capital*. Middletown, CT: Wesleyan University Press, 1996.

West, Candace, and Don H. Zimmerman. "Doing Gender." *Gender and Society* 1, no. 2 (1987): 125-51. http://links.jstor.org/sici?sici=0891-2432%28198706%291%3A2%3 C125%3ADG%3E2.0.CO%3B2-W.

Winter, Rachel. "Fanon Bernie Sanders: Political Real Person Fan Fiction and the Construction of a Candidate." In "Fandom and Politics," edited by Ashley Hinck and Amber Davisson, special issue, *Transformative Works and Cultures* 32 (2020). https://doi.org/10.3983/twc.2020.1679.

Yang, Sungeun. "Yeoseongsimnihak gwanjeomeseo bunseokhan namseongdongseongae-manhwa-eui yuhijeok suyong" [A feminist psychological analysis on the playful embracement of boys' love manga]. *The Journal of the Korean Contents Association* 18, no. 9 (2018): 510-20. https://doi.org/10.5392/JKCA.2018.18.09.510.

8

Females, Frontliners, Fringes

K-Pop's Performers and Protesters from Southeast Asia

Liew Kai Khiun, Malinee Khumsupa, and Atchareeya Saisin

Introduction: Southeast Asia, K-Pop's Understory

Debuted in 2016 under the YG Entertainment label, the all-women K-pop group BLACKPINK rapidly shot to global stardom, rivaling their male counterparts BTS on the world stage. Among the group's four members is Lalisa Manoban (Lisa) from Thailand. Non-Korean members of K-pop groups have become common as the industry seeks to broaden their talent pool. In one segment of her self-titled solo music video, released on September 10, 2021, Manoban dons a sabai-style shirt and sarong wrap skirt that pay homage to Thai artistry and fabrics. For the native of the Thai province of Buri Ram Buriram, the efforts to incorporate Thai heritage with contemporary fashion designs and dance choreography stemmed from the desire to conjure the "Thai-style melody line within the song to the music video sets, styling album design and choreography."[1] With more than 70 million views on YouTube within 24 hours of its release, the song "Lalisa" set a new record for the most viewed solo artist on the platform in a day. The video has more than 400 million views at the time of writing this chapter; through K-pop, Lisa has projected Thai cultural aesthetics and heritage onto the world stage.[2]

Using the analogy of a forest, if the American market represents the canopy of K-pop's globalization, Southeast Asia would be its often-neglected understory. As much as it places the region in the global spotlight, the music video is perhaps

---

1. Janelle Okwodu, "With 'Lalisa,' Blackpink's Brightest Star Steps into the Spotlight," *Vogue*, October 22, 2021, https://www.vogue.com/article/lisa-blackpink-lalisa-pop-breakthrough.
2. Angela Patricia Suacillo, "BLACKPINK's Lisa Breaks Taylor Swift's YouTube Record with 'Lalisa,'" NME, September 14, 2021, https://www.nme.com/en_asia/news/music/blackpink-lisa-lalisa-break-youtube-record-most-viewed-24-hours-taylor-swift-3045185.

the tip of the iceberg with how it rides on the Korean Wave (Hallyu), where entertainment careers, community networks, and social activism have evolved from the engagement with K-pop. Predominately female-fronted and youth-oriented, these activities have created new publics and frontliners.

From artists to fandom and political activism, this chapter surveys the ongoing trends in the inter-Asia intersectionality of K-pop in Southeast Asia. K-pop performers and social and political activism leveraged from the social networks of K-pop fandom in the public and political spheres. The occupation of multiple positionalities by mainly female subjects reflects upon feminist mobilities, defined by Lilian Chee as the flexibilities in moving between the center and margins and between the domestic and public discourses.[3] Such mobilities of contemporary K-pop fandom consciously carve out their public presences simultaneously within the K-pop industry and the sphere of national politics.

Case studies will include those in the following categories of *performers*, *promoters*, and *protesters*. The first category, performers, covers performers from Southeast Asia in both the mainstream K-pop industry and its local adaptations, while the discussion of the second category of promoters comes in the case study of the fan-organized public commemorations of the death of the celebrity Jonghyun from the K-pop group SHINee. The front line is given a new meaning in the case of Thailand, and more recently Myanmar, where K-pop fandom is brought to the forefront of national politics in the recent youth- and women-led pro-democracy protests in the third category of protesters. This regional survey allows for more macro discursive trends to be identified for Southeast Asia, not just as a peripheral consumer market for Hallyu but as dynamic trans-pop cultural frontliners.

ASEAN Fueling Hallyu: Mobilities, Technologies, Demography

Southeast Asia has been serving as a crucial springboard for the transnationalization of East Asia's modern entertainment culture and the formations of more undercurrent Pan-Asian cultural commonalities. With Abrahamic, Indic, and Confucian cosmologies embedded in diverse political models of governmentalities compressed within the monsoon zone, the region is both a vehicle and a reflection of globalization. Beginning in the early twentieth century, modern transnational popular culture interactions between East and Southeast Asia have

---

3.   Lilian Chee, "The Domestic Residue: Feminist Mobility and Space in Simryn Gill's Art," *Gender, Place & Culture: A Journal of Feminist Geography*, 19, no. 6 (2012): 750-70, https://doi.org/10.108 0/0966369X.2012.674924.

been facilitated by Indian and Chinese diasporas, linking new colonial commercial and cultural networks with developments in media technologies.[4]

Although globalization's momentum still rests in the northern hemisphere in terms of market and cultural dominance, Southeast Asia's role in globalizing Hallyu is critical as well. Covering close to one-third of genres watched on streaming sites, Korean television dramas are integral to households across the region, inspiring sustained tourism waves to South Korea for close to two decades.[5] National chapters of K-pop fandom and related communities spread across Southeast Asia, from recently reopened Myanmar to the Philippines. As they started being visibly present in Twitter estimates,[6] social media activities from Southeast Asia region became the more significant factor in the 2010s in terms of augmenting K-pop's global prominence. In terms of consumption, a K-pop fan in Southeast Asia spends an estimated US$1,000 on fan merchandise,[7] a significant sum for the developing Global South.

The significant digital presence of the region in the K-pop cyberspace is probably buttressed by the rapid adoption of mobile internet by a burgeoning youth population for the otherwise developing economies of Southeast Asia to achieve radical momentum.[8] A slightly higher percentage of women—51

4.   Chan Kwok-bun and Yung Sai-shing, "Chinese Entertainment, Ethnicity, and Pleasure," *Visual Anthropology* 18 no. 2-3 (2005): 103-42, https://doi.org/10.1080/08949460590914813; Chua Beng Huat, "Pop Culture China," *Singapore Journal of Tropical Geography* 22, no. 2 (2001): 113-21; Liew Kai Khiun, *Transnational Memory and Popular Culture in East and Southeast Asia* (London: Rowman & Littlefield, 2016); Nissim Otmazgin and Eyal Ben-Ari, eds., *Popular Culture Co-productions and Collaborations in East and Southeast Asia* (Singapore: NUS Press, 2013); Rachmah Ida, "Consuming Taiwanese Boys Culture: Watching Meteor Garden with Urban Kampung Women in Indonesia," in *Popular Culture in Indonesia: Fluid Identities in Post-Authoritarian Politics*, ed. Ariel Heryanto (London: Routledge, 2008), 93-110.

5.   Kim Hyelin and Kim Hwaya, "SE Asian Interest in Visiting Korea Rises for Five Straight Years," Korea.net, March 20, 2019, https://www.korea.net/NewsFocus/Society/view?articleId=169385; Nadirah H. Rodzi, Tan Hui Yee, and Raul Dancel, "Streaming Battle: Who's Watching What in South-east Asia," *Straits Times*, September 20, 2020, https://www.straitstimes.com/asia/se-asia/whos-watching-what-in-south-east-asia-0.

6.   Adobo Magazine, "Digital: Kpop Continues to Rise on Twitter with 6.1 Billion Tweets Globally in 2019, Philippines Makes Top 5 Tweeting Countries," January 14, 2020, https://www.adobomagazine.com/digital-news/digital-kpop-continues-to-rise-on-twitter-with-6-1-billion-tweets-globally-in-2019-philippines-makes-top-5-tweeting-countries/; Tamar Herman, "10 Years On, Twitter Is Shaping the Spread of K-Pop," *Forbes*, September 21, 2020, https://www.forbes.com/sites/tamarherman/2020/09/21/10-years-on-twitter-is-shaping-the-spread-of-k-pop/?sh=2da00d5399a7.

6.   Jung Joo-ri and Lee Jihae, "Map Showing K-Pop's Popularity by Global Region Released," Korea.net, August 27, 2019, https://www.korea.net/NewsFocus/Culture/view?articleId=174587.

7.   Franchesca Judine Basbas, "New Research Says Southeast Asian K-Pop Fans Spend over $1,400 for Their Favourite Groups," *Bandwagon Asia*, November 26, 2020, https://www.bandwagon.asia/articles/new-research-says-k-pop-bts-army-twice-blackpink-blinks-fans-spend-over-us-1400-for-their-favourite-groups-iprice-november-2020.

8.   For a region where four-fifths of the populace had no internet connectivity in 2010, more affordable smartphones have added around 100 million users a year—the current number stands at 350

percent—in the region also suggests a relatively more women-oriented economy and society.⁹ Historically more autonomous and mobile,¹⁰ this demographic has been fueling the Hallyu industry since the early 2000s. Led predominantly by young women as audiences, fans, and even performers, the K-pop trends in the region take on a dynamic gender dimension toward transnational and inter-Asia circulation of popular culture.¹¹

Creating the Frontliners

In terms of gender issues, creative practices and performances can be used here to gauge the reinterpretative communities in reshaping gender identities, discourses, exhibitions, and mobilities through Hallyu. As part of the broader subaltern fandom publics weaved in part through cyberspace's digital networks, fan communities are integral to the K-pop entertainment scene. Until recently, their presence is often confined to the intimate feminine sphere of what Sun Jung calls the cosmopolitan trans-pop prosumers, with international mobilities predicated upon their purchasing powers and information access.¹² Like its global counterparts, the evolution of K-pop fandom in Southeast Asia has taken a radical turn in the past decade, with K-pop fans leveraging the networks and communities to take center stage in multiple publics in the capacity of performers, promoters, and protesters.

million users—during a decade that saw Southeast Asia's internet economy balloon from US$32 billion in 2015 to US$100 billion in 2019 and a projected US$300 billion in 2025. An estimated 213 million youths, or close to 30 percent of the region's population, comprise a significant portion of this increase in the region, with 10 million users between 15 and 19 years old joining the mobile age on an annual basis. ASEAN Secretariat, "First ASEAN Youth Development Index," 2017, https://asean.org/wp-content/uploads/2017/10/ASEAN-UNFPA_report_web-final-05sep.pdf.

9. ASEAN Secretariat, "ASEAN Statistical Yearbook," 2019, https://www.aseanstats.org/wp-content/uploads/2020/10/ASYB_2019-rev20201031.pdf.

10. Barbara Andaya, "Studying Women and Gender in Southeast Asia," *International Journal of Asian Studies* 4, no. 1 (2007): 113–36, https://doi.org/10.1017/S147959140700054X; Michael Pletez, "Neoliberalism and the Punitive Turn in Southeast Asia and Beyond: Implications for Gender, Sexuality, and Graduated Pluralism," *Journal of the Royal Anthropological Institute* 26, no. 3 (2020): 612–32, https://doi.org/10.1111/1467-9655.13317; Clara Sarmento, "Culture, Politics and Identity: Critical Readings on Gender in Southeast Asia," *Indian Journal of Gender Studies* 19, no. 3 (2012): 437–67, https://doi.org/10.1177/097152151201900305.

11. Ubonrat Siriyuvasak and Shin Hyunjoon, "Asianizing K-Pop: Production, Consumption and Identification Patterns among Thai Youth," *Inter-Asia Cultural Studies* 8, no. 1 (2007): 109–36, https://doi.org/10.1080/14649370601119113. See also ASEAN Secretariat, "ASEAN Statistical Yearbook," 2019, https://www.aseanstats.org/wp-content/uploads/2020/10/ASYB_2019-rev20201031.pdf.

12. Weiyu Zhang, *The Internet and New Social Formations in China: Fandom Publics in the Making* (London: Routledge, 2016); Jung Sun, *Korean Masculinities and Transcultural Consumption: Yonsama, Rain, Oldboy, K-Pop Idols* (Hong Kong: Hong Kong University Press, 2011), 75–76.

Frontliners 1: Performers

Since debuting in 2016, BLACKPINK has surged rapidly in global popularity. Reflecting the group's phenomenal ascent was a Netflix original documentary, *BLACKPINK: Light Up the Sky* (dir. Caroline Suh, 2020), which featured spontaneously presented interviews with its members. Here, Manoban displayed her cosmopolitan linguistic abilities as she switched spontaneously between English, Korean, and Thai. With her image on countless billboards on the streets of Bangkok, her fame comes as a new peak for artists from Southeast Asia, leveraged on K-pop's global projections. The transnational presence of these artists parallels that of the industry's international ascension with Nichkhun of the Thai boy band 2PM, as well as Sandara Park of 2NE1, who spent her formative years in the Philippines. Park continues to move comfortably between the local Tagalog and K-pop entertainment scenes, even after the disbanding of the group in 2014.

Rather than isolated examples from local K-pop fans to international K-pop idols, the participation of artists from Southeast Asia has become increasingly generational. Thai national Minnie (Nicha Yontararak) is part of the multinational lineup of the K-pop group (G)I-DLE that debuted in 2018 under the aegis of Cube Entertainment. Recounting her experiences, she stated: "Previously, I just wanted to be a singer, even in Thailand is okay. But I was an Elf [a Super Junior fan] since I was young. When I and Yuqi [a Chinese member from the same group] first met, we discussed about Super Junior a lot because we're both fans. Actually, I used to think about being K-pop singer but in that time it seemed impossible."[13]

Cube Entertainment has also brought on board another Thai artist, Sorn (Chonnasorn Sajakul), as a member of the girl group CLC, which debuted in 2015. Consisting of Chinese and Taiwanese members as well, the female idol group is one of the few K-pop groups outside the "Big Three" labels—YG, JYP, and SM Entertainment—to have made some headway in the industry. The male Thai American idol Nichkhun (Nitchakhun Horawetchakun) set a precedent for the Southeast Asia presence in K-pop when he debuted in JYP's 2PM in 2008 at the tender age of twenty. Within a decade, together with Lisa, Minnie and Sorn, the newer generation of female artists that are now maintaining the presence of Thai performers in the K-pop industry has emerged.

The performativity of Southeast Asia's interaction with Hallyu and K-pop can be described in two broad areas. In the first area, within the industry, there is the

---

13. Susan-Han, "Yuqi & Minnie Touch MC Eunhyuk by Proving They're Real E.L.Fs + (G)I-DLE Try to Make Up Their Own 'Random Play Dance' Rules on 'Weekly Idol,'" *Allkpop*, May 6, 2020, https://www.allkpop.com/video/2020/05/yuqi-minnie-touch-mc-eunhyuk-by-proving-theyre-real-elfs-gi-dle-try-to-make-up-their-own-random-play-dance-rules-on-weekly-idol.

participation of Southeast Asian nationals as both professional K-pop artists and amateur hobbyist cover dancers. The second area has come about more recently with the appropriation and creative transformation of K-pop texts, aesthetics, and dance choreographies into performative protests by otherwise previously anonymous fans turned publicly visible political activists and frontline demonstrators. While the trajectories of the two areas may be divergent, both segments of K-pop subjects have placed K-pop audiences at the active center stage.

Lalisa Manoban and Sandara Park are internationally identifiable K-pop idols from Southeast Asia. They are, however, just two entertainers among a multitude of artists and performers from the region in various professional and amateur capacities. The latter—consisting of trainees from televised auditions, cover dancers, and dance instructors—contribute to the popularity of the genre.

The survey here focuses on case studies in the categories of *aspiring K-pop artists* and *K-pop inspired groups*. Sandara Park, Lisa, Minnie, and Sorn have reached the canopy of the global K-pop industry. But it is the transient precarity and creative rearrangements and localization of the genre by their less prominent counterparts that holistically make up the undergrowth of the entire cultural forest of K-pop. One of the earlier instances of aspiring K-pop artists from the region is that of SKarf, a female group comprised of both Korean and Singaporean artists that was formed in 2012 under the new Alpha Entertainment company, which collaborated with JYP in a competitive audition in Southeast Asia in 2010. Then teenagers, the duo, Tasha Low and Ferlyn Wong, were the first in the Republic of Singapore to enter the industry.[14]

As ethnic Chinese people with a bilingual education in both English and Mandarin, Singaporean artists could potentially be of value in forging bicultural and regional linkages to the K-pop industry, especially with that of the lucrative Chinese market. The generation of artists before Low and Wong became regionally popular Cantopop and Mandopop artists when they made their music careers in Hong Kong and Taiwan starting in the 1990s.[15] Due to its novelty, SKarf was featured all over Singaporean media platforms with performances on both national television and in one of the country's main events, the National Day Parade. However, the momentum of their group was not sustained; SKarf was disbanded by 2015 and its members rejoined the industry as trainees on different entertainment platforms. Returning to Singapore, Wong went into the

14. "SKarf Members Profile," KProfiles, updated April 11, 2019, https://kprofiles.com/skarf-members-profile/.
15. Liew Kai Khiun, "Symbolic Migrant Workers: Southeast Asian Artists in the East Asian Entertainment Industry," in *Pop Culture Formations across East Asia*, ed. Shim Doobo, Ariel Heryanto, and Ubonrat Siriyuvasak (Seoul: Jimoodang, 2010), 181-208.

Mandopop market with the release of her mini-album *FIRST* in 2019.[16] Low is currently more active on TikTok, doing dance skits, as well as being involved in the local mainstream television and film industries.[17]

Just as the K-pop careers of the Singaporean aspirants became history, over in Malaysia, a new all-female quartet group, DOLLA, debuted in March 2020 with their first song "Dolla Make You Wanna." With their fast-paced filming, dance choreographies, and colorful fashion aesthetics resembling that of a K-pop group, the members of DOLLA—Angel, Sabronzo, Tabby, and Syasya—were also brought together by an audition similar to that of other groups in the genre.[18] Unlike their Singaporean counterparts, the members are completely homegrown artists under the label of Universal Music Malaysia.[19] DOLLA represents the localization of the globalizing trends of K-pop that are being appropriated and reproduced autonomously outside the Seoul-centric entertainment industry. While not making a splash in the mainstream K-pop industry, DOLLA is distinguished in Malaysia for their more cosmopolitan ethno-gender outlook.

While Malaysian society is still defined amid the continuously tense ethno-religious politics of the Bumiputra Malay-Muslim majority, opposing those of their fellow ethnic Chinese and Indian citizens, the members of DOLLA come from both Malay and Chinese backgrounds. Three decades of the politics of Islamization in Malaysia have given Islamist politics legal and theological predominance over public morality that overshadows the previously more cosmopolitan social fabric.[20] Gender and sexuality have been placed at the forefront of the arising tensions, which run into the areas of fashion and public expression, with the wearing of the hijab/tudung asserting itself as the exhibition of religious piety for women.[21] The increasingly exclusivist and severe interpretation and application of Islamic laws have also led to greater segregation of the non-Muslim segments of the Malaysian population.

16. Wu Qi, "Lack of Opportunities Drove Ferlyn G out of SKarf," *8days*, December 27, 2019, https://www.8days.sg/sceneandheard/entertainment/lack-of-opportunities-5201298.

17. Bryan Lim, "Once a K-Pop Idol, Ex-SKarf Member Tasha Low Became a Sales Manager and Is Now Making Her Comeback," *Asiaone*, October 26, 2019, https://www.asiaone.com/entertainment/once-k-pop-idol-ex-SKarf-member-tasha-low-became-sales-manager-and-now-making-her.

18. "DOLLA Members Profile and Facts," *KProfiles*, updated November 5, 2020, https://kprofiles.com/dolla-members-profile-facts/.

19. Yahoo! News, "Malaysian Girl Group Dolla Says Similarities with K-Pop's Blackpink Just a 'Coincidence,'" October 23, 2020, https://malaysia.news.yahoo.com/malaysian-girl-group-dolla-says-045422536.html?guccounter=1.

20. Joseph Chinyong Liow, "Political Islam in Malaysia: Problematising Discourse and Practice in the UMNO-PAS 'Islamisation Race,'" *Commonwealth and Comparative Politics* 42, no. 2 (2004): 184–205.

21. Humairah Zainal, "The Irony of Islamization: Sexuality, Piety and Power on Malaysian Screens," *Continuum* 33, no. 1 (2019): 16–36.

In this respect, despite its popularity, Hallyu, and K-pop in particular, has been negatively framed by its naysayers as un-Islamic.[22] Apart from the occasional public condemnation of K-pop followers by religious figures, one striking moment of such tension was the disciplining of several hijabi-clad female Malaysian fans by the religious authorities for been seen in video footage hugging the K-pop group B1A4 in an otherwise closed-door fan event. The incident was also commented upon by Malaysia's former youth minister, Khairy Jamaluddin, pondering aloud that Malaysian women should be adoring "tall, dark and handsome" men over the pale-skinned and feminine-looking K-pop idols.[23] This is a case of K-pop's soft masculinity coming into conflict with the normalized "hard" masculinity in Malaysia and Asia in general.[24]

Given this context, DOLLA's relatively smooth debut in 2020 is considered here to be unexpected. The two ethnic Malay women (who are also predominantly Muslim in Malaysia and Singapore), Sabronzo (Wan Sabrina Wan Rusli) and Syasya (Noor Syasya Afiqah Shahrizal), created stage personas without the hijab and with tight-fitting wardrobes and urban dance styles, personas that seem more aligned with K-pop than Islamic aesthetics and fashion sensibilities. However, the main criticism leveled against DOLLA was their resemblance to BLACKPINK in terms of member composition, dance choreographies, and fashion aesthetics, as part of the general suspicion surrounding the originality of K-pop-inspired groups in the region.

Two of their main songs, "Dolla Make You Wanna" and "Impikan," are sung in Bahasa Melayu (Malay), and a cursory survey of comments from their music videos posted on YouTube reflect general support, with many defending their authenticity as a K-pop-inspired local group in a genre reputed for hybridizing an assortment of musical styles. In fact, one commentator, "奇乐七Ki," on the "Impikan" music video on YouTube felt:

> As a Malaysian, I can see that they did not exactly copy BlackPink, since I can hear the Malaysian influenced music beats in the song. TBH im impressed my country can produce a good girl group like them, and I think it will inspire many young girls that it okay not to be milky white or must look a certain way to be called beautiful/ BA since I had been insecure too before in the past (but

22. Ivany Atina Arbi, "K-Pop Promotes LGBT Lifestyles, Free Sex, Famous Preacher Tells Muslim Fans," *Jakarta Post*, February 27, 2019, https://www.thejakartapost.com/news/2019/02/27/k-pop-promotes-lgbt-lifestyles-free-sex-famous-preacher-tells-muslim-fans.html.
23. *Straits Times*, "K-Pop Boy Band at Centre of Controversy over Hugging Three Muslim Girls," January 18, 2015, https://www.straitstimes.com/asia/se-asia/k-pop-boy-band-at-centre-of-controversy-over-hugging-three-muslim-girls.
24. Mary Ainslie, "Korean Soft Masculinity vs. Malay Hegemony: Malaysian Masculinity and Hallyu Fandom," *Korea Observer* 48, no. 3 (2017): 609–38.

artist like HWASA, youtubers like vivikatt and jella helped me a lot in loving my appearance).[25]

The responses to DOLLA's productions reflect a broadening acceptance of and more intimate identification with K-pop-inspired initiatives within the genre's repertoire. Joining this transnational musicological dialogue in Malaysia are the more Islamist renditions of K-pop's trends—specifically, the pop nasyid movement that has been modernizing Islamic-themed music through appropriating contemporary popular music styles since the 1990s.[26] More recent prominent songs include "Hatiku" (My Heart) from the Malay-Muslim male band Rabithah's acoustic cover of BLACKPINK (feat. Selena Gomez)'s "Ice Cream." Under the pop nasyid-inclined label, Tarbiah Sentap, "'Hatiku' was meant to offer a more clean-cut Islamic version of what was considered otherwise to be a racy foreign music video."[27] The efforts to present more genteel representations of Islam by the group pitch a softened, religious, and localized masculinity in response to K-pop global gender discourses.

Based on YouTube views alone as indicators of the popularity of K-pop-appropriated productions, "Hatiku"'s views currently sit at around 360,000 from its premiere in October 2020.[28] "Dolla Make You Wanna," which debuted earlier in March of the same year, has registered approximately 4.5 million views.[29] These figures reveal the significant gulf between the Islamized rendition of BLACKPINK's "Ice Cream" and that of the seemingly more localized variation of the girl group.

Accompanying this identification is also a celebration of more cosmopolitan sociocultural identities that transcend defensively narrower ethnocentric claims. With the discussion shifting from the politics of authenticity and mimesis to that of representation, the K-pop-inspired local idol groups become increasingly acknowledged for their creative agencies and cultural leveraging of recipients turned performers. K-pop's reproducibility has given greater access to new platforms for women in Southeast Asia. The next section is about the widening of

25. DOLLA, "DOLLA – Impikan (Official Music Video)," October 30, 2020, video, 4:04, https://www. youtube.com/watch?v=RwVM0jo_0JI&lc=Ugyqoo4BkbMulhEKk_V4AaABAg.

26. Margaret Sarkissian, "'Religion Never Had It So Good': Contemporary Nasyid and the Growth of Islamic Popular Music in Malaysia," *Yearbook for Traditional Music* 37 (2005): 124–52.

27. Marco Ferrarese, "Blackpink's Ice Cream without the Sexual Overtones? Malaysian Bands Release Islamic-Friendly K-Pop Covers Less Likely to Upset Muslims," *South China Morning Post*, January 10, 2021, https://www.scmp.com/lifestyle/entertainment/article/3116962/blackpinks-ice-cream-without-sexual-overtones-malaysian.

28. Rabithah (feat. Fitri Haris), "Rabithah Ft. Fitri Haris – HATIKU (ICE CREAM BLACKPINK VERSI DAKWAH)," October 16, 2020, video, 5:19, https://www.youtube.com/watch?v=a_c1z PMMs2I&t=1s.

29. DOLLA, "@DOLLA – Dolla Make You Wanna (Official Music Video)," March 20, 2020, video, 2:58, https://www.youtube.com/watch?v=OvTqxSuN9go&ab_channel=UniversalMusicMalaysia.

K-pop fandom into the public space with the case study of fan communities that transformed public spaces into sites of public commemoration over the death of K-pop idol Jonghyun in 2016. Other than making their presence visibly felt in these public memorials and in raising social issues like mental health and suicide, as *promoters*, the local K-pop fan communities have also started to display greater social consciousnesses.

Frontliners 2: Promoters

With the momentum generated by social media, which has networked otherwise individual consumers into more collective groupings, it is also in the 2010s that we witness the advent of more intensive and innovative fan practices, producing fans that often come across to the larger public as obsessive fans or *sasaeng*.[30] Going beyond individualized private consumption to more public affirmations, especially of K-pop idols, are an emerging generation of digital natives from their adolescence, leveraging social media's connectivities and algorithms to globalize the groups they support. At this stage, too, the affirmations move beyond collective displays of celebrity adoration (alongside a creative economy of DIY fan-made memorabilia, literature, and public billboards celebrating their idols' birthdays) to more public and social-oriented events. Apart from charity projects and donations, we see the beginning of more publicly conscious debates and interventions into male-related industry practices, idol reputations, and behavioral track records.

One prominent milestone was the events surrounding the death of Kim Jonghyun, a member of the K-pop group SHINee, on December 18, 2017. Formed in 2009 under the SM Entertainment label, SHINee was one of the company's more globally popular groups. Reports that Kim had died from suicide driven by depression shocked the group's fan community, commonly known as "Shawols."[31] Apart from South Korea, there were fan-organized public memorials for Kim, whose experiences with mental health challenges resonated intimately with his youthful fans.

Singapore hosted witnessed Kim's memorial, the first of its kind for K-pop artists, at the republic's Speakers' Corner in Hong Lim Park, the only legally designated public site for permitted protests in the tightly regulated city-state. Commonly a place for civil society activists to stage demonstrations on a range

---

30. Jasmine Ong, "The Dark Side of the K-Pop Phenomenon: When Fans Turn Obsessive," *Nylon*, January 6, 2020, https://www.nylon.com.sg/2020/01/the-dark-side-of-the-k-pop-phenomenon-when-fans-turn-obsessive/.
31. Justin McCurry, "K-Pop Singer Jonghyun's Death Turns Spotlight on Pressures of Stardom," *Guardian*, December 19, 2017, https://www.theguardian.com/world/2017/dec/19/k-pop-singer-jonghyun-death-shinee-pressures-of-stardom.

of municipal and sociopolitical issues, the use of the premises for the memorial, organically organized by teenage female Shawols, was unprecedented. Held in the evening as a candlelight memorial, the event was attended by an estimated several thousand people and came across as orderly and coordinated, with volunteers ushering mourners clad uniformly in black and holding candles and flowers, moving in neat lines to pay their respects to a portrait of Kim on a makeshift stage.[32] Similar memorials were also held in the prominent public areas of cities in the region, visibly attended by hundreds of mourners. It was the memorial that brought K-pop fandom to the forefront of the national imagination, as news of the event was published together with both international and local political stories on the front pages of the local dailies the following morning. At the same time, Shawols used the events surrounding Kim's death to raise awareness of otherwise taboo issues in the region, such as suicide, depression, and other mental health challenges.

With the provision of relevant health information and local telephone hotlines for social services and fan-support groups, Jonghyun's memorial as a campaign for greater awareness of mental health challenges gained momentum. In Indonesia, the Shawol community responded to a callous online tweet accusing fans of prioritizing a singer's suicide over the plight of Palestinians by raising a "kindness campaign" fundraising campaign. Led by twenty-year-old university student Wina Andana Putri, it aimed to raise donations by bringing people together in remembrance of Jonghyun. The proceeds went both to local animal welfare charities and to Palestine under the banner "From Jonghyun to Indonesia and Palestine."[33] SHINee may no longer be at the forefront after Jonghyun's death and the enlistment of its other members into military service. Being in the Shawol fandom may come to be remembered as an adolescent transition for SHINee's supporters. In the case of Jonghyun's memorial, this transition has also created fan communities and publics; as the next section will demonstrate, the transition also becomes a political rite of passage, with K-pop fandom being part of youth-led public protests.

Frontliners 3: Protesters

K-pop fans in Thailand are known as *ting* or *ting Korean* (Accent Ting Koalee). Associated with the national school regulations concerning the hair length of

---

32. Wai Yee Yip, "A Black and White Memorial for Shinee's Jonghyun by Singaporean Fans at Hong Lim Park," *Straits Times*, December 21, 2017, https://www.straitstimes.com/lifestyle/ entertainment/a-black-and-white-memorial-for-shinees-jonghyun-by-singaporean-fans-at-hong.
33. Liza Yosephine, "K-Pop Fans Unite in Viral Charity Campaign after Jonghyun's Death," *Jakarta Post*, December 21, 2017, https://www.thejakartapost.com/life/2017/12/21/k-pop-fans-unite-in-viral-charity-campaign-after-jonghyuns-death.html.

female students, this "ting" became synonymous with the archetype of the fanatical young female fan of K-pop idols.[34] However, by 2019, the tings became more visible in the mainly youth-led protest movements for monarchical reforms in the kingdom. Encapsulating the politicization of the otherwise predominantly feminine sphere of K-pop fandom, in an interview with Reuters, a ting by the pseudonym of Suphinchaya noted: "K-pop fans would love to just fangirl over our 'oppas' and care about nothing else, but with our country like this, we as citizens have to call for better things."[35]

The K-pop fandom in Thailand is witnessing generational diversity with a mix of youths in schools and universities and those in their twenties who are now working adults with more disposable income. In terms of emotional investment, the former has more time while the latter has greater financial means to sustain their K-pop fan activities. Meanwhile, the younger generation of K-pop fans, mostly students in university and high school, is now at the forefront of Thai politics.

Dating back to the 1970s, student-led pro-democracy movements have been part of the evolution of Thailand's political tensions surrounding that of the monarchy, military, and parliament.[36] In this respect, the youth-dominated public protests from 2019 calling for the removal of Prime Minister Prayuth Chan-ocha (who had staged a military coup in 2014)[37] and constitutional reforms to the monarchy are part of this political continuum.[38]

The role of popular music and culture in political protests is not new. What is novel here in the context of Thailand's history is the spontaneous, smooth repurposing of digital networks and communities engendered from the otherwise commercialized K-pop industry by fandom into political spearheads. Compared to their predecessors—traditionally centered in student unions on campus grounds—the modus operandi of the current youth social movements, cultivated from K-pop fandoms, are more decentralized, autonomous, and diffused. Unlike the more hierarchical nature of mainstream civic organizations, which are also increasingly divided along generational and political lines, the

34. Terry Fredrickson, "Like K-Pop? Then You're a 'Ting,'" *Bangkok Post*, May 12, 2013. https://www.bangkokpost.com/learning/advanced/349605/like-k-pop-then-you-re-a-ting.

35. Patpicha Tanakasempipat, "K-Pop's Social Media Power Spurs Thailand's Youth Protests," Reuters, November 2, 2020, https://www.reuters.com/article/us-thailand-protests-k-pop-idUSKBN27I23K.

36. Prajak Kongkirati, "Thailand: The Cultural Politics of Student Resistance," in *Student Activism in Asia: Between Protest and Powerlessness*, ed. Meredith Weiss and Edward Aspinall (Minneapolis: University of Minnesota Press, 2012), 229-58.

37. Britannica.com, Prayuth Chan-o-cha (n.d.), https://www.britannica.com/biography/Prayuth-Chan-ocha.

38. Kanokrat Lertchoosakul, "The White Ribbon Movement: High School Students in the 2020 Thai Youth Protests," *Critical Asian Studies* 53, no. 2 (2021): 206-18.

relationships in K-pop fandom are more horizontal and open.[39] Analogous to blockchain technologies, the protest movement has become a complex network of peer-to-peer nodes or groups of protesters and activists, linked by digital and mobile media.[40] As such, the momentum of the protest has not been crippled by the traditional police measures of arresting key leaders or forceful crowd dispersion.

Two areas are identified here for further discussion: namely, financing and supporting the protests at the front lines, and occupying the cyberspace. Thailand's otherwise predominantly apolitical tings, previously operating away from the public eye in the feminine confines of local K-pop fan communities, have developed organizational expertise and experiences in mobilizing and channeling resources. Applied to the political arena, the otherwise fragmented K-pop fan clubs organized around different groups have bankrolled donations to support and finance the protest movements and maintained fundraising campaigns.

Table 8.1 is a compilation of the estimated 4 million Thai baht (US$121,000) raised by various K-pop fan clubs within days in October 2020. The funds were in turn used to finance the provision of safety helmets, gloves, and other materials for the protesters.[41] Parallel to the fundraising efforts were campaigns by the Thai K-pop fandom, calling for boycotts of pro-establishment services. These included calls to cease buying billboard spaces on the stations of the Bangkok Mass Transit System (BTS) to publicly commemorate K-pop idols' birthdays after the network was shut down in attempts by the authorities to deny the movements of protesters.[42] This momentum also extended to calls for K-pop groups and individual artists to voice their support for the protesters as part of the larger moral responsibilities to their fans.[43] Although these artists remained largely silent to these appeals, resulting in angry responses within fan communities,[44]

39. Paritta Wangkiat, "What K-Pop Can Teach Us about Politics," *Bangkok Post*, December 7, 2020, https://www.bangkokpost.com/opinion/opinion/2031059/what-k-pop-can-teach-us-about-politics.
40. Penchan Phoborisut, "The 2020 Student Uprising in Thailand: A Dynamic Network of Dissent," *ISEAS*. Issue 2020, no. 29 (2020), https://www.iseas.edu.sg/wp-content/uploads/2020/11/ISEAS_Perspective_2020_129.pdf.
41. Supalak Ganjanakhundee, "Youthquake Evokes the 1932 Revolution and Shakes Thailand's Establishment," *ISEAS*, Issue 2020, no. 27 (2020).
42. Hannah Beech and Muktita Suhartono, "'We Have to Speak Out': Thai Students Defy Protest Ban," *New York Times*, October 18, 2020, https://www.nytimes.com/2020/10/18/world/asia/thai-students-protest-democracy.html.
43. Erich Parpart and Cod Satrusayang, "Thai Netizens Target Thai Members of K-Pop Bands for Not Speaking on Pro-Democracy Protests," *Thai Enquirer*, August 31, 2020, https://www.thaienquirer.com/17777/thai-netizens-target-thai-members-of-k-pop-bands-for-not-speaking-on-pro-democracy-protests/.
44. "แฮชแท็ก #แบนดาราสลิ่ม #แบนแทกุกไลน์ ขึ้นเทรนทวิตเตอร์ ชาวเน็ตเรียกร้องให้แสดงจุดยืนทางการเมือง" [Authors' translation: "Hashtag #BanProgovernmentActors #BanTaekukLineIdols became hot

Table 8.1: Fundraising efforts for protest movements based on K-pop groups; donations from Thai K-pop fan clubs to the pro-democracy activities in 2020

K-pop band	Amount (100TBH = US$3.2)
Girls' Generation	779,562
Super Junior E.L.F.	700,000
EXO	350,000
BTS	480,000
GOT7	340,000
TVXQ!+JYJ	206,000
BLACKPINK	204,000
NCT	67,367
Wanna One	55,000
NU'EST	55,000
X1	41,000
DAY6	35,000
Red Velvet	30,000
Monsta X	27,000
WOODZ	27,000
Shinee	22,000
R1SE	8,000

Source: PPTVOnline and Khaosod English. PPTVOnline: แฟนคลับเกาหลี บริจาคเงินหนุน ม็อบกว่า 4 ล้านบาท.

the situation highlighted the shifting fan expectations of K-pop idols, from that of affective to political expression, in the changing relationship between femininities and desires.

Along with the fundraising initiatives, K-pop-inspired public performances have been staged by demonstrators at the protest grounds. Thai protesters have also appropriated K-pop cover dances during the demonstrations. The political-cultural references to the Korean democratization movement from K-pop is evident in an English-language press interview with one of the protesters:

> "I once went to the protest and there was a dance floor," said Monprariya L., a young Thai activist and K-pop fan who volunteered with Amnesty International

Twitter trends, Thai Twitter users calls celebrities to express their political stands"], *Matichon Online*, September 20, 2020, https://www.matichon.co.th/news-monitor/news_2357498. As developments are still ongoing, we are not revealing details of the published conversations and their authors in the Taekuk Line platform.

during the protests in 2020. "And a K-pop fan club started to dance to the song 'Into the New World.' Part of us wants the new world, too, wants democracy . . . In the past, young people in Korea fought for democracy. It's the same for us. We have to speak up."[45]

These cover dances are also part of the highly decentralized, sporadic, and mobile flash mob gatherings and public spaces whereby participants bring their own equipment and protest materials. Like the public fundraising initiatives, these gatherings are organized online through the codes established in the vocabularies and grammar of K-pop fan clubs. Largely evading security agencies, these codes have become powerful tools as hashtags in projecting the presence of the pro-democracy movement in cyberspace.

In 2020, K-pop as a trending topic online hit a new record of 6.7 billion tweets globally. Thailand was the top market after Indonesia and seventh in terms of unique voices.[46] The volume surged with the heightened activities of Thai K-pop fans as digital activists during the protests in 2019 and 2020. Thai K-pop fans have mobilized their vast social media presence to collectively raise political awareness, spam pro-establishment hashtags, and donate money in support of the protests, often in the names of their favorite stars. A Twitter thread by user @phabetdahouse compiled a list of Korean idol celebrities who have supported the Thai pro-democracy movement. Twitter hashtags connect users to tweets and thus to the loosely connected network of people who share common interests. The student networks in Thailand have expanded exponentially via hashtags for each student-led flash mob and rally. The fluidity that came from these protest tactics reveals in turn the kinds of feminist mobilities engendered by the K-pop fan practices of what were supposedly the once apolitical female juvenile tings.

From the negative portrayals of tings as juvenile K-pop fans to frontliners in public protests, the political participation of the mainly female-dominated Thai K-pop fan communities in public protests exemplified the coming of a new generation of political activism in Southeast Asia. Like their counterparts around the world, the critical digital literacies, expansive networks, and resource and community mobilization skills acquired by Thai K-pop fandom have been creatively applied in turn to the political realms. It is in these things that we find the transformative potential of K-pop in Southeast Asia, from a trans-pop individual consumer endeavor to a forum for public activism for youths in Southeast Asia.

45. Jessica Rawnsley, "How K-Pop Fans Are Helping Thai Protesters Stay out of Jail," *New Statesman*, March 4, 2021, https://www.newstatesman.com/world/asia/2021/03/how-k-pop-fans-are-helping-thai-protesters-stay-out-jail.
46. Kim YeonJeong, "#KpopTwitter Achieves New Record of 6.7 Billion Tweets Globally in 2020," BlogTwitter, February 4, 2021, https://blog.twitter.com/en_us/topics/insights/2021/kpoptwitter-achieves-new-record-of-6-billion-tweets-globally-in-2020.html.

Conclusion: Tourists to Activists in Southeast Asia's K-Pop Pivots

While K-pop's BTS and the Korean film *Parasite* (dir. Bong Joon-ho, 2019) may form its canopy, the lush understory of a more vibrant multitude of narratives from Southeast Asia is also deserving of recognition within Hallyu's globalizing trajectories. Emerging from cosmopolitan trans-pop tourists to community-oriented fan clubs and politically conscious frontline protesters, this chapter has sought to frame the evolution of Hallyu fandom in Southeast Asia for the past two decades.

Such activities reflect the types of feminist mobilities gained from women in the region by assuming greater visibility in the international and local public spaces as K-pop performers, promoters, and protesters. As K-pop idols, women artists from Southeast Asia personify the cosmopolitan world stage of the globalizing K-pop industry prominently as performing artists within and beyond their national boundaries. As fan communities, they have transformed private commemoration of the suicide of K-pop artist Jonghyun from the group SHINee into public memorials, in turn raising greater public consciousness of social issues such as mental health. Finally, from cultural to political frontliners, in the case of Thailand, the juvenile K-pop tings, once disregarded as obsessive, are now at the forefront of the kingdom's youth-based protest movement. For the digitally mobile and networked youths and women in the region, the Korean Wave also serves to leverage and pivot platforms for local community formations, creative performances, and political activism.

Bibliography

Adobo Magazine. "Digital: Kpop Continues to Rise on Twitter with 6.1 Billion Tweets Globally in 2019, Philippines Makes Top 5 Tweeting Countries." January 14, 2020. https://www.adobomagazine.com/digital-news/digital-kpop-continues-to-rise-on-twitter-with-6-1-billion-tweets-globally-in-2019-philippines-makes-top-5-tweeting-countries/.

Ainslie, Mary. "Korean Soft Masculinity vs. Malay Hegemony: Malaysian Masculinity and Hallyu Fandom." *Korea Observer* 48, no. 3 (2017): 609–38.

Allkpop. "Yuqi & Minnie Touch MC Eunhyuk by Proving They're Real E.L.Fs + (G)I-DLE Try to Make Up Their Own 'Random Play Dance' Rules on 'Weekly Idol.'" May 6, 2020. https://www.allkpop.com/video/2020/05/yuqi-minnie-touch-mc-eunhyuk-by-proving-theyre-real-elfs-gi-dle-try-to-make-up-their-own-random-play-dance-rules-on-weekly-idol.

Andaya, Barbara. "Studying Women and Gender in Southeast Asia." *International Journal of Asian Studies* 4, no. 1 (2007): 113–36. https://doi.org/10.1017/S147959140700054X.

Arbi, Ivany Atina. "K-Pop Promotes LGBT Lifestyles, Free Sex, Famous Preacher Tells Muslim Fans." *Jakarta Post*, February 27, 2019. https://www.thejakartapost.com/

news/2019/02/27/k-pop-promotes-lgbt-lifestyles-free-sex-famous-preacher-tells-muslim-fans.html.

ASEAN Secretariat. *ASEAN Statistical Yearbook 2019*. Jakarta: ASEAN Secretariat, 2019. https://www.aseanstats.org/wp-content/uploads/2020/10/ASYB_2019-rev2020 1031.pdf.

ASEAN Secretariat. *First ASEAN Youth Development Index*. Jakarta: ASEAN Secretariat, 2017.https://asean.org/wp-content/uploads/2017/10/ASEAN-UNFPA_report_web-final-05sep.pdf.

Basbas, Franchesca Judine. "New Research Says Southeast Asian K-Pop Fans Spend over $1,400 for Their Favourite Groups." *Bandwagon Asia*, November 26, 2020. https://www.bandwagon.asia/articles/new-research-says-k-pop-bts-army-twice-blackpink-blinks-fans-spend-over-us-1400-for-their-favourite-groups-iprice-november-2020.

Beech, Hannah, and Muktita Suhartono. "'We Have to Speak Out': Thai Students Defy Protest Ban." *New York Times*, October 18, 2020. https://www.nytimes.com/2020/10/18/world/asia/thai-students-protest-democracy.html.

Chan, Kwok-bun, and Yung Sai-shing. "Chinese Entertainment, Ethnicity, and Pleasure." *Visual Anthropology* 18 no. 2–3 (2005): 103–42. https://doi.org/10.1080/08949460590914813.

Chee, Lilian. "The Domestic Residue: Feminist Mobility and Space in Simryn Gill's Art." *Gender, Place and Culture* 19, no. 6 (2012): 750–70. https://doi.org/10.1080/09663 69X.2012.674924.

Chua, Beng Huat. "Pop Culture China." *Singapore Journal of Tropical Geography* 22, no. 2 (2001): 113–21.

DOLLA. "@DOLLA – Dolla Make You Wanna (Official Music Video)." Produced by Universal Music Malaysia. March 20, 2020. Video, 2:58. https://www.youtube.com/watch?v=OvTqxSuN9go&ab_channel=UniversalMusicMalaysia.

DOLLA. "DOLLA – Impikan (Official Music Video)." Produced by Universal Music Malaysia. October 30, 2020. Video, 4:04. https://www.youtube.com/watch?v=RwV M0jo_0JI&lc=Ugyqoo4BkbMulhEKk_V4AaABAg.

Dong, Sun-hwa. "BLACKPINK's Lisa Victim of Online Racial Remark." *Korea Times*, January 16, 2019. http://www.koreatimes.co.kr/www/news/nation/2019/01/682_262177.html.

Dong, Sun-hwa. "My Shame at Having Filipino Accent – K-Pop Star Sandara Park of 2NE1, Former Girl Group." *South China Morning Post*, August 2, 2019. https://www.scmp.com/lifestyle/entertainment/article/3020884/my-shame-having-filipino-accent-k-pop-star-sandara-park.

Ferrarese, Marco. "Blackpink's Ice Cream without the Sexual Overtones? Malaysian Bands Release Islamic-Friendly K-Pop Covers Less Likely to Upset Muslims." *South China Morning Post*, January 10, 2021. https://www.scmp.com/lifestyle/entertainment/article/3116962/blackpinks-ice-cream-without-sexual-overtones-malaysian.

Fredrickson, Terry. "Like K-Pop? Then You're a "Ting."" *Bangkok Post*, May 12, 2013.

Ganjanakhundee, Supalak. "Youthquake Evokes the 1932 Revolution and Shakes Thailand's Establishment." *ISEAS* 2020, no. 27 (2020). https://www.iseas.edu.sg/wp-content/uploads/2020/10/ISEAS_Perspective_2020_127.pdf.

Google, Temasek, and Bain and Company. *e.Conomy SEA 2019: Swipe up and to the Right: Southeast Asia's $100 Billion Internet Economy*. January 5, 2020. https://www.bain.com/globalassets/noindex/2019/google_temasek_bain_e_conomy_sea_2019_report.pdf.

Herman, Tamar. "10 Years On, Twitter Is Shaping the Spread of K-Pop." *Forbes*, September 21, 2020. https://www.forbes.com/sites/tamarherman/2020/09/21/10-years-on-twitter-is-shaping-the-spread-of-k-pop/?sh=2da00d5399a7.

IMDb. "Blackpink: Light Up the Sky." Accessed January 26, 2021. https://www.imdb.com/title/tt13058290/.

Jung, Joo-ri, and Lee Jihae. "Map Showing K-Pop's Popularity by Global Region Released." Korea.net, August 27, 2019. https://www.korea.net/NewsFocus/Culture/view?articleId=174587.

Kim, Hyelin, and Kim Hwaya. "SE Asian Interest in Visiting Korea Rises for Five Straight Years." Korea.net, March 20, 2019. https://www.korea.net/NewsFocus/Society/view?articleId=169385.

Kim, YeonJeong. "#KpopTwitter Achieves New Record of 6.7 Billion Tweets Globally in 2020." BlogTwitter, February 4, 2021. https://blog.twitter.com/en_us/topics/insights/2021/kpoptwitter-achieves-new-record-of-6-billion-tweets-globally-in-2020.html.

Kongkirati, Prajak. "Thailand: The Cultural Politics of Student Resistance." In *Student Activism in Asia: Between Protest and Powerlessness*, edited by Meredith Weiss and Edward Aspinall, 229–58. Minneapolis: University of Minnesota Press, 2012.

KProfiles. "DOLLA Members Profile and Facts." Updated November 5, 2020. https://kprofiles.com/dolla-members-profile-facts/.

KProfiles. "SKarf Members Profile." Updated April 11, 2019. https://kprofiles.com/skarf-members-profile/.

Lee, Hye Jin. "Rethinking the K-Pop Industry's Silence during the Black Lives Matter Movement." *The Conversation*, June 26, 2020. https://theconversation.com/rethinking-the-k-pop-industrys-silence-during-the-black-lives-matter-movement-141025.

Lee, Jin-kyung. "Visualizing and Invisibilizing the Subempire: Labor, Humanitarianism, and Popular Culture across South Korea and Southeast and South Asia." *Journal of Korean Studies* 23, no. 1 (2018): 95–109.

Lertchoosakul, Kanokrat. "The White Ribbon Movement: High School Students in the 2020 Thai Youth Protests." *Critical Asian Studies* 53, no. 2 (2021): 206–18.

Liew, Kai Khiun. "Symbolic Migrant Workers: Southeast Asian Artists in the East Asian Entertainment Industry." In *Pop Culture Formations across East Asia*, edited by Shim Doobo, Ariel Heryanto, and Ubonrat Siriyuvasak, 181–208. Seoul: Jimoodang, 2010.

Liew, Kai Khiun. *Transnational Memory and Popular Culture in East and Southeast Asia*. London: Rowman & Littlefield, 2016.

Lim, Bryan. "Once a K-Pop Idol, Ex-SKarf Member Tasha Low became a Sales Manager and Is Now Making Her Comeback." *Asiaone*, October 26, 2019. https://www.asiaone.com/entertainment/once-k-pop-idol-ex-SKarf-member-tasha-low-became-sales-manager-and-now-making-her.

Liow, Joseph Chinyong. "Political Islam in Malaysia: Problematising Discourse and Practice in the UMNO-PAS 'Islamisation Race.'" *Commonwealth and Comparative Politics* 42, no. 2 (2004): 184–205.

Matichon Online. "Hashtag #BanProgovernmentActors #BanTaekukLineIdols Became Hot Twitter Trends, Thai Twitter Users Calls Celebrities to Express Their Political Stands"]. Matichon Online, September 20, 2020. https://www.matichon.co.th/news-monitor/news_2357498.

McCurry, Justin. "K-Pop Singer Jonghyun's Death Turns Spotlight on Pressures of Stardom." *Guardian*, December 19, 2017. https://www.theguardian.com/world/2017/dec/19/k-pop-singer-jonghyun-death-shinee-pressures-of-stardom.

Okwodu, Janelle. "With 'Lalisa,' Blackpink's Brightest Star Steps into the Spotlight." *Vogue*, October 22, 2021. https://www.vogue.com/article/lisa-blackpink-lalisa-pop-breakthrough.

Ong, Jasmine. "The Dark Side of the K-Pop Phenomenon: When Fans Turn Obsessive." *Nylon*, January 6, 2020. https://www.nylon.com.sg/2020/01/the-dark-side-of-the-k-pop-phenomenon-when-fans-turn-obsessive/.

Otmazgin, Nissim, and Eyal Ben-Ari, eds. *Popular Culture Co-productions and Collaborations in East and Southeast Asia.* Singapore: NUS Press, 2013.

Parpart, Erich, and Cod Satrusayang. "Thai Netizens Target Thai Members of K-Pop Bands for Not Speaking on Pro-Democracy Protests." *Thai Enquirer*, August 31, 2020. https://www.thaienquirer.com/17777/thai-netizens-target-thai-members-of-k-pop-bands-for-not-speaking-on-pro-democracy-protests/.

Peletz, Michael. "Neoliberalism and the Punitive Turn in Southeast Asia and Beyond: Implications for Gender, Sexuality, and Graduated Pluralism." *Journal of the Royal Anthropological Institute* 26, no. 3 (2020): 612-32. https://doi.org/10.1111/1467-9655.13317.

Phoborisut, Penchan. "The 2020 Student Uprising in Thailand: A Dynamic Network of Dissent." *ISEAS* 2020, no. 29 (2020). https://www.iseas.edu.sg/wp-content/uploads/2020/11/ISEAS_Perspective_2020_129.pdf.

Qi, Wu. "Lack of Opportunities Drove Ferlyn G out of SKarf." *8days*, December 27, 2019. https://epopstation.blogspot.com/2015/01/lack-of-opportunities-drove-ferlyn-g.html?m=0.

Rabithah (feat. Fitri Haris). "Rabithah Ft. Fitri Haris – HATIKU (ICE CREAM BLACKPINK VERSI DAKWAH)." Produced by Tarbiah Sentap. October 16, 2020. Video, 5:19. https://www.youtube.com/watch?v=dZaV2TnyQtA.

Rawnsley, Jessica. "How K-Pop Fans Are Helping Thai Protesters Stay out of Jail." *New Statesman*, March 4, 2021. https://www.newstatesman.com/world/asia/2021/03/how-k-pop-fans-are-helping-thai-protesters-stay-out-jail.

Rodzi, Nadirah H., Tan Hui Yee, and Raul Dancel. "Streaming Battle: Who's Watching What in Southeast Asia." *Straits Times*, September 20, 2020. https://www.straits-times.com/asia/se-asia/whos-watching-what-in-south-east-asia-0.

Sarkissian, Margaret. "'Religion Never Had It So Good': Contemporary Nasyid and the Growth of Islamic Popular Music in Malaysia." *Yearbook for Traditional Music* 37 (2005): 124-52.

Sarmento, Clara. "Culture, Politics and Identity: Critical Readings on Gender in Southeast Asia." *Indian Journal of Gender Studies* 19, no. 3 (2012): 437–67. https://doi.org/10.1177/097152151201900305.

Siriyuvasak, Ubonrat, and Shin Hyunjoon. "Asianizing K-Pop: Production, Consumption and Identification Patterns among Thai Youth." *Inter-Asia Cultural Studies* 8, no. 1 (2007), 109–36. https://doi.org/10.1080/14649370601119113.

Straits Times. "K-Pop Boy Band at Centre of Controversy over Hugging Three Muslim Girls." January 18, 2015. https://www.straitstimes.com/asia/se-asia/k-pop-boy-band-at-centre-of-controversy-over-hugging-three-muslim-girls.

Suacillo, Angela Patricia. "BLACKPINK's Lisa Breaks Taylor Swift's YouTube Record with 'Lalisa.'" *NME*, September 14, 2021. https://www.nme.com/en_asia/news/music/blackpink-lisa-lalisa-break-youtube-record-most-viewed-24-hours-taylor-swift-3045185.

Tanakasempipat, Patpicha. "K-Pop's Social Media Power Spurs Thailand's Youth Protests." Reuters, November 2, 2020. https://www.reuters.com/article/us-thailand-protests-k-pop-idUSKBN27I23K.

Wangkiat, Paritta. "What K-Pop Can Teach Us about Politics." *Bangkok Post*, December 7, 2020. https://www.bangkokpost.com/opinion/opinion/2031059/what-k-pop-can-teach-us-about-politics.

Yahoo! News. "Malaysian Girl Group Dolla Says Similarities with K-Pop's Blackpink Just a 'Coincidence.'" October 23, 2020. https://malaysia.news.yahoo.com/malaysian-girl-group-dolla-says-045422536.html?guccounter=1.

Yip, Wai Yee. "A Black and White Memorial for SHINee's Jonghyun by Singaporean Fans at Hong Lim Park." *Straits Times*, December 21, 2017. https://www.straitstimes.com/lifestyle/entertainment/a-black-and-white-memorial-for-shinees-jonghyun-by-singaporean-fans-at-hong.

Yosephine, Liza. "K-Pop Fans Unite in Viral Charity Campaign after Jonghyun's Death." *Jakarta Post*, December 21, 2017. https://www.thejakartapost.com/life/2017/12/21/k-pop-fans-unite-in-viral-charity-campaign-after-jonghyuns-death.html.

Zainal, Humairah. "The Irony of Islamization: Sexuality, Piety and Power on Malaysian Screens." *Continuum* 33, no. 1 (2019): 16–36.

Zhang, Weiyu. *The Internet and New Social Formation in China: Fandom Publics in the Making.* London: Routledge, 2016.

9

Riding the Korean Wave in Iran

Cyberfeminism and Pop Culture among Young Iranian Women

Gi Yeon Koo

Iranian new media are producing an alternative public sphere in the Islamic Republic of Iran. The year 2009 was particularly significant for this sphere, receiving much attention for the "cyberfeminist" and civil society movements of the younger generations and progressive forces. Within Iran, the internet and social media have become spaces of newfound freedom for younger generations. This is especially true for young women, who have the opportunity for greater freedom of expression amid the oppressive reality of Iranian society. For this reason, the online activity of Iranian women may at times put them at risk in the real world. For example, in 2014, a young couple filmed a music video using Pharrell Williams's song "Happy" and were consequently sentenced to a year in prison; the woman in the video suffered a harsher punishment than her male counterpart. Furthermore, in July 2018, an eighteen-year-old girl, Maedeh Hojabri, was arrested by the Iranian government for uploading a video of herself dancing to Instagram. As a mark of solidarity and resistance to her arrest, many people also uploaded videos of themselves dancing. These two cases show how singing or dancing to Western music has been perceived by Iranian authorities as anti-Islamic activity that upsets public morality and warrants punishment.

Iranian women began their socially conscious activities and demonstrated resistance through online media in earnest from 2005 to 2009, with notable examples including networks of women's campaigns such as One Million Signatures, Meydan-e Zanan, the Feminist School, and Focus on Iranian Women.[1] A recent

---

1. Mahboubeh Abbasgholizadeh, "'To Do Something We Are Unable to Do in Iran': Cyberspace, the Public Sphere, and the Iranian Women's Movement," *Signs: Journal of Women in Culture and Society* 39, no. 4 (June 2014): 831–40, https://doi.org/10.1086/675722.

example that clearly shows the relationship between the resistance of Iranian women and new media is My Stealthy Freedom, founded by Masih Alinejad in 2014. The website began as the manifestation of Iranian women's opposition to compulsory hijab wearing, but as of 2019 its initiatives had expanded to demands for other rights. For example, the site has supported strikes by female teachers or factory workers and has called for the expansion of women's rights involving their entry into stadiums. This online space represents how Iranian citizens, and especially women, both at home and abroad, can unite in transnational solidarity to exercise their right to freedom of choice.[2]

Karin Van Nieuwkerk, Mark LeVine, and Martin Stokes, studying the various forms of popular culture in Muslim society, emphasize its significance in the Middle East as follows: "Popular culture helps us understand major processes of transformation in the Muslim world. Second, popular culture in the Muslim world does not equal 'westernization' or 'secularization,' or a 'cultural grey-out.' Third, popular culture in the Muslim world can no longer simply be viewed and dismissed as 'real politics.'" As they point out, popular culture in Muslim society must be understood as a wider, "flexible rubric of globalization" as opposed to the traditional view associated with Westernization and secularism.[3] John Fiske defines fandom as a cultural and economic function with the following characteristics: "discrimination and distinction" between the individual or collective vis-à-vis the outer world, social "enunciation" based on the significance attached to cultural products, "productivity and participation" of fans who make their own texts and slogans, and "capital accumulation" through the collection of knowledge and goods.[4] Henry Jenkins describes online fan communities as preparing the way for a meaningful public culture.[5]

2. Sedigheh Karimi, "Iranian Women's Identity and Cyberspace: Case Study of Stealthy Freedom," *Journal of Social Science Studies* 2, no. 1 (2015): 221, https://doi.org/10.5296/jsss.v2i1.6284; Gi Yeon Koo, "To Be Myself and Have My Stealthy Freedom: The Iranian Women's Engagement with Social Media," *Revista de Estudios Internacionales Mediterráneos* 21 (2016): 141–57, https://doi.org/10.15366/reim2016.21.011; Gi Yeon Koo, "Constructing an Alternative Public Sphere: The Cultural Significance of Social Media in Iran," in *Media in the Middle East: Activism, Politics, and Culture*, ed. Nele Lenze, Charlotte Schriwer, and Zubaidah Abdul Jalil (Cham: Palgrave Macmillan, 2017), 21–43, https://doi.org/10.1007/978-3-319-65771-4_2; Alison N. Novak and Emad Khazraee, "The Stealthy Protester: Risk and the Female Body in Online Social Movements," *Feminist Media Studies* 14, no. 6 (2014): 1094–95, https://doi.org/10.1080/14680777.2014.975438; Annabelle Sreberny, "Women's Digital Activism in a Changing Middle East," *International Journal of Middle East Studies* 47, no. 2 (2015): 357–61, https://doi.org/10.1017/S0020743815000112.
3. Karin Van Nieuwkerk, Mark LeVine, and Martin Stokes, eds., *Islam and Popular Culture* (Austin: University of Texas Press, 2016), 14.
4. John Fiske, "The Cultural Economy of Fandom," in *The Adoring Audience: Fan Culture and Popular Media*, ed. L. A. Lewis (London: Routledge, 1992), 34–37.
5. Henry Jenkins, *Convergence Culture: Where Old and New Media Collide* (New York: New York University Press, 2006), 239.

Ultimately, fandom is shaped by the different social, cultural, and economic environments of the society that produces it.[6] In other words, fandom has been accepted and reproduced in various ways, depending on the region and cultural background of those who endorse it. The value of this research lies in the fact that the fandom phenomenon of Iranian Muslim women moving toward Korean popular culture, and not American Western culture, has rarely been discussed so far. Therefore, this study explores the fandom of Korean culture in the Islamic Republic of Iran and follows the process by which Iranian women consume Korean popular culture in line with their own cultural particularities. This is considered in the context of their general pop culture consumption and how they create a fan culture through social media. Through this study, I also demonstrate how fandom activities on social media and the internet provide a channel for Iranian women to engage in autonomous social activities. Simultaneously, I show how global popular culture, a highly controversial subject in Iran, has significantly influenced postrevolutionary Iranian society.

Young Iranian women stand at the heart of the enjoyment and promotion of Korean culture in the Middle East. Consumption of Korean popular culture by these women as active fans or leaders of fan clubs carries important social implications in terms of gender perspectives, as they have become the active agents in shaping a new subculture. Therefore, that young women, who are in many ways socially repressed and controlled, have the capacity to independently form a subculture is crucial when we examine the role of women in Iranian society. Although they are highly educated, urban, young generation, they still experience significant unemployment and glass ceilings in Iranian society.

This study is based on data collected from one year of field research in 2009 and several short-term anthropological field studies between 2015 and 2017. Based on the results from these field studies, I conducted a literature review as well as follow-up studies regarding Iranians' reactions to Korean dramas, with data collected from the official websites and Facebook pages of Persian-language broadcasting channels and the official website of the Farsi1 channel.[7] Moreover, I used various social media platforms, such as Telegram,[8] Instagram,[9] and other

---

6.   Sohn Seunghye, "Local Context and Global Fandom of Hallyu Consumption: The Case of Korean Connection in France," *Journal of Media Economics & Culture* 10, no. 1 (February 2012): 45–85, http://www.dbpia.co.kr/journal/articleDetail?nodeId=NODE01965296.

7.   The channel closed on December 31, 2016.

8.   Telegram is a cloud-based instant messaging and VoIP (voice over Internet protocol) service.

9.   The following are the main media resources used in my anthropological research: https://www. instagram.com/btsfunclub.iran/, https://www.instagram.com/_bts.iran_/, https://www.instagram. com/hamechi_koreyi/, https://www.instagram.com/irankorea/, https://www.instagram.com/ gemkoreatv/, https://www.instagram.com/korea_mydream/, https://www.instagram.com/army-world/, https://www.instagram.com/exoiran/, https://www.instagram.com/_irankorea_/, https:// www.instagram.com/koreannews.ir/, https://www.instagram.com/koreanculture_iran/. Channel

forms of user-generated content to examine how Iranian fans of the Korean Wave engage with and share Korean popular cultural content and accept Korean popular culture as part of their own subcultures.

Cyberfeminism and Fandom on Social Media

Critical discussions on postfeminism have examined the relationships between feminism in the cultural sphere, gender mainstreaming in the institutional sphere, and postmodern, neoliberal economic systems. Since the first decade of this century, the internet and social-networking services have become increasingly gendered by a stronghold of postfeminist women.[10] The cultural and technological characteristics of social networking—such as activity, freedom, and autonomy—align well with postfeminist attributes such as consumerism and individualism. Social networking, in comparison with other cultural media, has provided individuals with a platform to more freely display themselves and to enjoy their own autonomous and unique spaces. Victoria Newsom and Lara Lengel argue that "online activism provides the potential for empowerment to marginalized voices, provides the opportunity for cross-cultural dialogue, and provides an impetus for social changes."[11] This can be applied to women in Iran who are also building their own social connections and actively constructing their own narratives via individualist means, free from the constraints of a heavily tradition-oriented society.

New media are also widely used in the Middle East as an important means of solidarity and empowerment of women and other minorities. In Iran, the government has largely monopolized the media and kept TV and newspapers under tight control. Global media have provided viewers in the Middle East with an opportunity to participate in public discourse that evades the restrictions of state

links to which I was invited that were closed to Telegram channels are excluded from this list. Also, five fan club leaders in Iran whom I interviewed offline and followed online are omitted for their protection.

10. Anita Harris, *Future Girl: Young Women in the Twenty-First Century* (New York: Routledge, 2003); David Machin and Joanna Thornborrow, "Branding and Discourse: The Case of Cosmopolitan," *Discourse and Society* 14, no. 4 (July 2003): 453–71, https://doi.org/10.1177/0957926503014004003; Angela McRobbie, *Aftermath of Feminism* (London: Sage, 2008); Jessica Ringrose and Katarina Eriksson Barajas, "Gendered Risks and Opportunities? Exploring Teen Girls' Digitized Sexual Identities in Postfeminist Media Contexts," *International Journal of Media and Cultural Politics* 7, no. 2 (2011): 121–38, https://discovery.ucl.ac.uk/id/eprint/10018427.
11. Victoria A. Newsom and Lara Lengel, "Arab Women, Social Media, and the Arab Spring: Applying the Framework of Digital Reflexivity to Analyze Gender and Online Activism," *Journal of International Women's Studies* 13, no. 5 (October 2012): 33, https://vc.bridgew.edu/jiws/vol13/iss5/5.

censorship.[12] Deborah L. Wheeler points out that online media in the Middle East are also dominated by men.[13] However, in 2009 and 2011, on the emergence of the Green Movement of Iran and the Arab Spring, respectively, online space, represented by social media, shifted to become a platform for social and women's movements. These women's movements have rewritten the history of feminism in the Arab region and Iran.[14]

In fact, the internet has allowed the voices of women in the Middle East to reach a global audience. Moreover, women have been able to access information previously unavailable due to cultural, political, and regional barriers.[15] Hala Guta and Magdalena Karolak emphasize that "the Internet creates a space where women have an equal access and they are able to contribute to the public sphere in ways that are not possible outside the virtual world where they are always regarded as women, being subordinate to men."[16] Rita Stephan, focusing on the solidarity of Arab women in cyberspace, says that "cyberspace has given women an additional outlet to the public sphere and the opportunity to advocate for women's rights."[17] New media have played an important role, hitherto limited by conservative regulations, in shaping civil society. This was conveyed during the Green Movement (June 12, 2009), when new and old media worked together to expand the outreach of anti-government protests and to influence public opinion. Currently, social media are promoting Iranian civil society movements and rallying global support. For women especially, social media are

12. Hala Guta and Magdalena Karolak, "Veiling and Blogging: Social Media as Sites of Identity Negotiation and Expression among Saudi Women," *Journal of International Women's Studies* 16, no. 2 (January 2015): 115–27, https://vc.bridgew.edu/jiws/vol16/iss2/7; Naomi Sakr, "Women-Media Interaction in the Middle East: An Introductory Overview," in *Women and Media in the Middle East: Power through Self-Expression*, ed. Naomi Sakr (London: Bloomsbury, 2004), 1–14; Loubna H. Skalli, "Communicating Gender in the Public Sphere: Women and Information Technologies in the MENA Region," *Journal of Middle East Women's Studies* 2, no. 2 (Spring 2006): 35–59, https://doi.org/10.2979/MEW.2006.2.2.35; Shahper Vodanovich, Cathy Urquhart, and Maha Shakir, "Same but Different: Understanding Women's Experience of ICT in the UAE," *Electronic Journal of Information Systems in Developing Countries* 40, no. 1 (January 2010): 1–21, https://doi.org/10.1002/j.1681-4835.2010.tb00286.x.
13. Deborah L. Wheeler, "Blessings and Curses: Women and the Internet Revolution in the Arab World," in *Women and Media in the Middle East: Power through Self-Expression*, ed. Naomi Sakr (London: Bloomsbury, 2004), 138–61.
14. Sahar Khamis, "Islamic Feminism in New Arab Media Platforms for Self-Expression and Sites for Multiple Resistances," *Journal of Arab and Muslim Media Research* 3, no. 3 (2010): 237–55, https://doi.org/10.1386/jammr.3.3.237_1; Newsom and Lengel, "Arab Women, Social Media, and the Arab Spring," 31–45.
15. Wheeler, "Blessings and Curses," 138–60.
16. Guta and Karolak, "Veiling and Blogging," 117.
17. Rita Stephan, "Creating Solidarity in Cyberspace: The Case of Arab Women's Solidarity Association United," *Journal of Middle East Women's Studies* 9, no. 1 (Winter 2013): 84, https://doi.org/10.2979/jmiddeastwomstud.9.1.81.

a site of transformative politics,[18] a feminist tool kit for thwarting state ideology,[19] an alternative public sphere,[20] and an online field on which motherhood and political activism create and cocreate digital identities.[21]

Since the development of social media in Iran, women have been very active online. Through blogging and social media, they have brought issues of gender roles, gender conventions, and cultural practices to the forefront of discussion.[22] Social media and cyberfeminism allow Iranian women not only to partake in the national and transnational debates on political gender issues, but also to share their perspectives on more personal and taboo subjects such as sexuality, divorce, and hijab-wearing.[23] Women in Iran are using social media as a platform to raise gender awareness and to gain opportunities to engage with political and cultural activities.[24] Despite the Iranian government's strict cultural censorship and arrests of online activists and bloggers, Iranian women are persisting in their online activities relating to social, political, cultural, and economic inequality and environmental issues.[25]

Iranian fandoms on social media also reveal gender characteristics and provide a sense of solidarity among women. Female fans, having similar characteristics to the aforementioned female users of social media, are socially empowered through the experience of reciprocal relationships in fandom communities. In this respect, the recognition of fandoms as communities based on women's cultures can be regarded as a positive achievement from a feminist perspective. Henry Jenkins and Sangita Shresthova argue that fandoms can go beyond individual hobbies and become platforms for civic activism and alternative

18. Victoria Tahmasebi-Birgani, "Social Media as a Site of Transformative Politics: Iranian Women's Online Contestations," in *Iran's Struggles for Social Justice: Economics, Agency, Justice, Activism*, ed. Peyman Vahabzadeh (Cham: Palgrave Macmillan, 2017), 181–98.

19. K. Soraya Batmanghelichi and Leila Mouri, "Cyberfeminism, Iranian Style: Online Feminism in Post-2009 Iran," *Feminist Media Histories* 3, no. 1 (January 2017): 50–80, https://doi.org/10.1525/fmh.2017.3.1.50.

20. Koo, "Constructing an Alternative Public Sphere," 21–43.

21. Elham Gheytanchi, "Gender Roles in the Social Media World of Iranian Women," in *Social Media in Iran: Politics and Society after 2009*, ed. David M. Faris and Babak Rahimi (Albany: State University of New York Press, 2015), 41–56.

22. Niki Akhavan, *Electronic Iran: The Cultural Politics of an Online Evolution* (New Brunswick, NJ: Rutgers University Press, 2013); Nasrin Alavi, *We Are Iran: The Persian Blogs* (London: Portobello, 2005); Masserat Amir-Ebrahimi, "Transgression in Narration: The Lives of Iranian Women in Cyber-space," *Journal of Middle East Women's Studies* 4, no. 3 (Fall 2008): 89–118, https://doi.org/10.2979/MEW.2008.4.3.89; Batmanghelichi and Mouri, "Cyberfeminism, Iranian Style," 50–80; Koo, "To Be Myself and Have My Stealthy Freedom," 141–57; Koo, "Constructing an Alternative Public Sphere," 21–43; Annabelle Sreberny and Gholam Khiabany, *Blogistan: The Internet and Politics in Iran* (London: Tauris, 2010); Tahmasebi-Birgani, "Social Media as a Site of Transformative Politics," 181–98.

23. Batmanghelichi and Mouri, "Cyberfeminism, Iranian Style," 50–80.

24. Sreberny, "Women's Digital Activism in a Changing Middle East," 357.

25. Tahmasebi-Birgani, "Social Media as a Site of Transformative Politics," 181–98.

communities.[26] Analogous to the example of how fans can raise their voices through various collective activities, Iranian women immersed in the Korean Wave embody a fandom consciousness as an alternative community.

The fandom phenomenon of Iranian women has also extended into a rights movement. For instance, #LetWomenGoToStadium, led by female volleyball fans for the past few years, became a campaign for female soccer fans asserting their right to watch the 2018 FIFA World Cup in Russia. In Saint Petersburg's stadium, where the first match for Group B between Iran and Morocco was played, there were numerous banners around the stadium with "#NoBan4Women," "We support the entrance of Iranian women into the stadiums," and the like. In 2018, the Azadi Stadium in Tehran opened its doors to women for the first time since the Islamic Revolution forty years earlier. Kim Toffoletti's research explores the fandom phenomenon of Iranian female soccer fans through the movie *Offside* (dir. Jafar Panahi, 2006). She finds that "in the movie, female football fandom is understood as a vehicle to subvert regulatory mechanisms that determine gender articulations in contemporary Iran." Furthermore, "Iranian women's football fandom is less a consequence of rejecting religious protocols than it is a negotiation between the cultural intersections of the local and global spheres in which the female sports fans live."[27] Essentially, the common outlook of Iranian society toward popular culture as either an obsession with the West or a rejection of tradition is reductionist; Iranian women are only confronting the realities of their changing sociopolitical environment while trying to negotiate with their local culture. Understanding the fandom of Muslim women as a cultural phenomenon arising from constant encounters between the global and local more accurately reflects the complex interaction between these two.

Korean Media Content in Iran: Korean TV Dramas

Recent studies have shown how Korean popular culture is appropriated differently according to the cultural particularities of the recipient region.[28] It is

---

26. Henry Jenkins and Sangita Shresthova, "Up, Up, and Away! The Power and Potential of Fan Activism," *Transformative Works and Cultures*, no. 10 (June 2012): 1–5, https://doi.org/10.3983/twc.2012.0435.

27. Kim Toffoletti, "Iranian Women's Sports Fandom: Gender, Resistance, and Identity in the Football Movie *Offside*," *Journal of Sport and Social Issues* 38, no. 1 (December 2012): 89, https://doi.org/10.1177/0193723512468758.

28. Koichi Iwabuchi, "Globalization, East Asian Media Cultures and Their Publics," *Asian Journal of Communication* 20, no. 2 (May 2010): 197–212, https://doi.org/10.1080/01292981003693385; Jin Dal Yong, *New Korean Wave: Transnational Cultural Power in the Age of Social Media* (Champaign: University of Illinois Press, 2016); Shim Doobo, "Whither the Korean Media?," in *Pop Culture Formation across East Asia*, ed. Shim Doobo, Ariel Heryanto, and Ubonrat Siriyuvasak (Seoul: Jipmoondang, 2010), 115–35.

correct to interpret the Korean Wave as a cultural flow of exchange and communication across time and spatial barriers. To accurately analyze the Korean Wave phenomenon, we must identify its regional features as well as understand the regional consumers of Korean Wave–related content. Studies on the Korean Wave are being conducted through multifaceted approaches, yet there is still a lack of scholarly research on the Middle East, not to mention the paucity of research examining the Korean Wave in Iran. Compared to studies on the Korean Wave in East Asia or Southeast Asia, it is no exaggeration to say that studies on the Korean Wave in the Middle East, especially those with a consumer-centered approach, are only now commencing, despite the significant cultural influence of the Korean Wave in the region. Korean dramas ("K-dramas") are broadcast on various channels in Iran, including Islamic Republic of Iran Broadcasting (IRIB), a state-run television and radio channel, as well as on illegal satellite channels, illegal digital content sold in black markets, illegal file-sharing websites, and YouTube (Table 9.1).

The advent of the Korean Wave in Iran can be traced back to 2007, when the Korean drama series *Dae Jang Geum* (also known as *Jewel in the Palace*) was first broadcast there. This series kindled public interest in K-dramas for the first time in Iran. It was followed by another MBC drama series, *Jumong*, aired on IRIB in 2009. The drama became a sensational hit, drawing more attention to K-dramas in Iran. In 2009, when the popularity of K-dramas peaked, Iranian dramas that aired on national broadcasting channels failed to grab the public's attention and were superseded by K-dramas. With more exposure to Hollywood movies and K-dramas via satellite media and pirated media, the public's expectations became harder to meet.

Instead of watching state-run television programs regulated by strict censorship and conservative cultural and social mores, Iranians turned to imported media that better satisfied their tastes. To combat declining viewership, Iran's state-run media gave in to popular demand and began to broadcast K-dramas on its networks. They recaptured the public's attention. With *Dae Jang Geum* setting the stage for the Korean Wave, interest in K-dramas escalated remarkably as other K-drama series, such as *Thank You* (2007), *Hae-sin* (2004–2005), *Jumong* (2006–2007), and *Behind the White Tower* (2007), aired in Iran. *Jumong* was popular with people of all ages and genders. In fact, the K-dramas that aired on state-run channels captivated conservative and middle-aged audiences.

Until 2009, the open-minded young generation living in the urban areas of Iran preferred to watch American series on illegal DVDs or satellite television programs to watching K-dramas on state-run television channels. As illustrated in the cases below, the appeal of K-dramas to the Iranian audience included the theme of love and the close resemblance in cultural and emotional sentiments between Koreans and Iranians. The popularity of K-dramas in Iran

Table 9.1: List of Korean TV dramas aired on IRIB

Date	Title	TV channel number	Number of reruns
2006–2007	*Dae Jang Geum*	Channel 2	54
2007–2008	*Emperor of the Sea*	Channel 3	51
2008	*Thank You*	Channel 5	16
2008–2009	*Jumong*	Channel 3	81
2009	*Behind the White Tower*	Channel 5	20
2010	*Yi San*	Eshragh TV	77
2010–2011	*The Kingdom of the Winds*	Channel 3	36
2011	*The Return of Iljimae*	Channel 3	24
2012	*Dong Yi*	Channel 3	60
2014	*Hong Gil-dong*	Namayesh TV	24
	Kim Su-ro, the Iron King	Channel 3	32
	Brain	Channel 5	20
2015	*Faith*	Namayesh TV	24
	Moon Embracing the Sun	Channel 3	22
	Fermentation Family	Namayesh TV	24
	Gyebaek	Namayesh TV	36
	Good Doctor	Channel 2	20
2016	*Pasta*	Namayesh TV	20
	The King's Daughter, Soo Baek-Hyang	Channel Tehran	20
2017	*The Fugitive of Joseon*	IRIB TV3	
	Jeongdojeon	Channel 5	
2018	*New-Heart*	Channel 2	
	Moon Embracing the Sun		
	The Iron Empress		

can be explained by cultural ideas such as tradition, moderation, and justice, which underpin their narratives. Such cultural values are in line with Islamic ideals, making K-dramas more relatable to an Iranian audience. Moreover, Jafar Morvarid states that the high level of K-drama consumption in Iran can be attributed to the Korean Confucian values found especially in some of the period dramas.[29] These values closely resemble those of the Islamic faith in that they prioritize the common good above individual interests.

Case No. 1: interview with a twenty-six-year-old Iranian woman in 2009. I asked her why Korean dramas are popular in Iran. This was her response:

> The reason why K-dramas are so popular in Iran is because most K-dramas are about "love." Since Iran is a society where most contents released to the public are controlled by the government, there are strict regulations imposed on dramas and movies. Against this backdrop, K-dramas, which are so open about the topic of love, are definitely appealing to many young Iranians who are interested in dating and love. Dramas or other forms of popular culture in Iran rarely deal with freedom or love. In a much-controlled society like the Iranian society, young Iranians who are never allowed to openly talk about love are enthralled by K-dramas. The women in K-dramas are cute and fashionable in an adorable way. I do not know if it would be appropriate to put it this way, but I feel that K-dramas are a bit closer to Islamic sentiments compared to dramas from South America or the other countries in the West.

Modern and trendy K-dramas broadcast through satellite media offer the Iranian audience vicarious psychological gratification. Period dramas like *Dae Jang Geum* and *Jumong*, aired on state-run channels, provide emotional intimacy and garner interest from audiences of all ages. Modern Korean dramas, which emphasize the importance of "family love," identify with the part of Iranian culture that values family above all.[30] Similarly, in a conservative and male-dominated society like Iran's, K-dramas that focus on female submission to men and articulate the need for single women to get married strike a chord with the Iranian audience. This particular feature of K-dramas can be seen in *My Lovely Sam Soon* (2005), which captured the attention of Iranian women by providing a modern female perspective on love (Table 9.2).

Most K-dramas aired on satellite-media channels are based on the theme of love, which cannot be expressed publicly or discussed openly in Iran. Nonetheless,

29. Jafar Morvarid, "Analysis of Korean Drama Series with an Emphasis on the Notions of Tradition and Modesty, as Their Main Themes, from a Religious Point of View," presentation at the First KIEP-IMEA Forum on "Economic and Cultural Cooperation between Korea and Iran," Institute of Middle Eastern Affairs, Myongji University (IMEA), Korea, May 2013.
30. Shima Hemati, "Against All Odds: South Korea's Nation Branding Campaign in Iran," paper presented at the International Conference, "The 'Miracle' Narrative of the Korean Cultural Industries: Perspectives from the Middle East," Hebrew University of Jerusalem, May 7–9, 2013.

Table 9.2: List of K-dramas aired on Iran's most popular satellite channel, Farsi1

Broadcast year	Title of drama
2009	*Couple or Trouble, My Lovely Sam Soon, When It's at Night, Phoenix, My Beloved Sister*
2010	*Queen of Housewives, Miss Mermaid, White Lie, Assorted Gems*
2011	*Marry Me, Stay by My Side, Still Marry Me, Temptation of Wife, Temptation of an Angel*
2012	*Stay by My Side* (rerun), *Temptation of the Wife, Forty-Nine Days, Golden Fish, Queen of Housewives, The Greatest Love, Que Sera Sera*
2013	*Temptation of an Angel, A Hundred-Year Legacy, Queen Seondeok, Missing You*
2014	*Queen Seondeok* (rerun), *A Hundred-Year Legacy* (rerun), *Twinkle Twinkle, A Thousand Kisses, Yellow Boots*
2015	*Flames of Desire, You Are So Pretty, Lady of the Storm*
2016	*Flames of Desire* (rerun), *Lady of the Storm, You Are So Pretty* (rerun)
2017	*You Are So Pretty* (rerun), *Love of Eve, Queen Seondeok* (rerun)

Iranian viewers stress that K-dramas exhibit cultural and traditional values that are closer to Iranian and Islamic sentiments. Therefore, the immense popularity of K-dramas in Iran is rooted in the perceived cultural proximity and emotional affinity between the two cultures.

Case No. 2: interview with a twenty-one-year-old female K-pop fan in Tehran in 2017.

> I was just watching one or two episodes of K-dramas for fun, but by the time I got into my third and fourth episode, I found myself completely absorbed in the drama, to the point where I couldn't stop watching them. K-dramas are like dreams come true. All the men are rich, talented, successful, and nice to women. Ever since the Iranians' interest in K-dramas grew, Iranians have a more positive image of Korea. Most Iranians used to be completely ignorant about Korea and had absolutely no interest in Korean culture. However, as K-dramas became a nationwide sensation, the interest in Korea soared as well. Most people watch K-dramas on Farsi1 channel or on shared video files. This is possible because Iran does not have strict regulations on intellectual property. For instance, I got the entire series of *You're Beautiful* from a friend and watched the entire series in just a week. K-drama files are passed around among friends in school dormitories. YouTube is another channel we use to watch K-dramas when files with English subtitles are uploaded.

As demonstrated in Case No. 2, K-dramas may emerge as an alternative form of popular culture in Iran. This is largely due to the strict cultural censorship of popular culture and the consequent lack of diverse cultural content in Iran. The rise of satellite-media channels in the Iranian media landscape poses a challenge to state-run broadcasting channels.[31] Satellite channels occupy a unique position in Iran's media landscape because they allow for more "modern" and engaging content than state-run channels, which strictly regulate news, drama, and music videos. Therefore, the K-dramas broadcast on satellite channels are more varied than the ones broadcast on state-run channels, which mostly air Korean historical dramas. Moreover, the tastes of the primary viewers of satellite channels differ from those of the primary viewers of state-run channels.

In many ways, K-dramas are leading a change in the types of programs aired on Iranian satellite channels, which are shifting from entertainment programs to dramas. Before satellite channels started airing dramas, they mainly featured music videos of Iranian or foreign singers, as well as foreign movies. However, the launch of a channel called Farsi1 in 2009 added a new dimension to the satellite-media landscape in Iran. Drama series and sitcoms imported from Colombia, Korea, and the United States were aired on Farsi1, appealing to a wider audience. The satellite-media channel GEM TV, launched in the fall of 2018, introduced K-pop and Korean drama (Figure 9.1). The channel's opening confirms once again the immense interest in Korean pop culture in Iran. In this way, K-dramas have become a part of Iran's subcultures through two media—national broadcast channels and satellite channels—that dealt with very difference audiences and contents.

How Did the Korean Wave Become an Alternative Culture among Young Iranian Women?

With the new millennium and the development of online communication, fandom activities around the world began to use online platforms. Nancy Baym argues that such methods of communication and networking have overcome the limitations of time and space.[32] Online fandom activities not only increase accessibility for such activities within a single country but also contribute greatly to the formation of transnational fan communities. The recent expansion of online social networks has allowed online fandoms to strengthen and

---

31. Gi Yeon Koo, *Making Their Own Public: Emotion and Self among the Urban Iranian Youth* (Seoul: Seoul National University Press, 2017).

32. Nancy Baym, "Why, Despite Myself, I Am Not Leaving Facebook. Yet," *Online Fandom*, no. 13 (May 13, 2010), https://www.onlinefandom.com/archives/why-despite-myself-i-am-not-leaving-facebook-yet/index.html.

 **gemkoreatv**   •••

Figure 9.1: Screen grab of GEM KOREA TV Instagram page (www.instagram.com/gemkoreatv)

diversify. Significantly, this has given rise to transnational communities as internet communities.[33]

Research on fandom in Iranian society is limited. However, the fandom of Iranian youth existed long before that. Using videos, cassettes, and CD albums and MP3 files, Iranian youth have been consumers of Western music ranging from Michael Jackson, Madonna, Beyoncé, Bruno Mars, and Usher to Justin Bieber. Furthermore, for the soccer-loving Iranian society, players within the European league like Cristiano Ronaldo and Lionel Messi have always been respected figures. Every year, just after Nowruz (the Iranian New Year) or during the Christmas season, advertisements of Iranian diaspora singers holding concerts in the United States and Europe are repeatedly distributed through

33. C. Lee Harrington and Denise D. Bielby, "Global Fandom/Global Fan Studies," in *Fandom: Identities and Communities in a Mediated World*, ed. Jonathan Gray, Cornel Sandvoss, and C. Lee Harrington (New York: New York University Press, 2007), 179–97.

diaspora broadcasting channels. Concerts held for the Iranian diaspora in the United States, Canada, Germany, and France and concerts of artists from the Iranian diaspora in nearby Dubai, Istanbul, or Azerbaijan attract large audiences. Artists even debuted in North America and Europe during the Revolution. But the artists who have attracted the most attention are the old stars who were active before the Revolution. The most notable example is Googoosh, who is so popular that whenever she holds a concert in Dubai, all flight tickets are sold out, and there have even been instances of ticket fraud.[34] Yet the fandom phenomenon has been largely prohibited by Iranian authorities. In Iran, the Iranian diaspora singers active in Western regions are considered a part of "Westoxification." Listening to their music or watching their music videos on satellite channels is also officially prohibited. One of the most notable cases is that of Sasy Mankan, an Iranian singer who was exiled and whose song "Gentleman" became a hit in the United States in 2019. When a video of students dancing to it was circulated in an Iranian girls' school, it shocked many conservative Iranians. They argued that there was "an enemy plot" behind such videos.[35] Due to strict censorship, it is hard to see such forms of Iranian diaspora popular culture and popular culture of the Pahlavi period on official channels.

What is particularly noteworthy here is the formation of two separate layers in Iranian popular culture. On the one hand, popular culture—namely, music and dance—is heavily censored and hidden in Iranian society and presented in the public sphere only once it has been subjected to the strict regulations of the post-Revolution state. On the other hand, different forms of popular culture have long existed in the hidden corners of Iranian private spheres as underground music, spanning Western musical genres from rock, heavy metal, techno, and rap to reggae.[36] Furthermore, the difference between music listened to in public and in private spheres has given rise to different cultural and social discourses in Iranian society and has provided an "alternative history of the Islamic Republic."[37]

In 2018–2019, the Korean Wave in Iran developed quite differently than in 2009–2010. This change can be attributed to the evolving media environment in Iran, centered on the accessibility of social media via smartphones. Effectively, the space occupied by the Korean Wave has shifted from television to online spaces. Smartphone activity is extremely high in Iran, especially among the younger

---

34. Gi Yeon Koo, *Making Their Own Public.*
35. Center for Human Rights in Iran, "Iran's Minister of Education Sees 'Plot' behind Videos of Dancing Schoolchildren," May 9, 2019, https://www.iranhumanrights.org/2019/05/irans-ministry-of-education-sees-plot-behind-youtube-videos-of-dancing-schoolchildren/.
36. Laudan Nooshin, "Underground, Overground: Rock Music and Youth Discourses in Iran," *Iranian Studies* 38, no. 3 (September 2005): 463–94, https://doi.org/10.1080/00210860500300820.
37. Nahid Siamdoust, *Soundtrack of the Revolution: The Politics of Music in Iran* (Stanford, CA: Stanford University Press, 2017).

generation. Some 70 to 80 percent of young people living in urban areas are smartphone users. Even though Twitter and Facebook are still officially blocked, almost everyone has access to these social media platforms through unofficial means. Until 2014, Facebook was the main social media network channel. Since then, Instagram and Telegram have taken hold of social media. Instant messaging services such as Viber, a free messaging and calling application, are the most popular smartphone apps in Iran. With the increase of smartphone users in 2017–2018, Telegram has become a key medium for both Iranian women's online fandom and other online social movements.[38]

The Korean Wave has hit Iran in two forms of popular culture: first, through K-dramas aired on state-run television channels and satellite channels; and second, through the rise of K-pop. K-dramas opened the floodgates for the Korean Wave to enter Iran. However, K-pop now takes center stage in Iranian popular culture. K-pop has been the growth engine behind the new Korean Wave, which has extended its reach to encompass the younger generation, following the older generation's love for K-dramas. As Jin Dal Yong states, since the 2010s, K-pop has reinvigorated the Korean Wave across the globe, and its popularity has been especially noticeable in Asian countries. The rapid growth of K-pop and its worldwide popularity correlates to the worldwide growth of social media. Social networking services such as Facebook, Twitter, and YouTube have facilitated the introduction and popularization of Korean music to a much broader international audience.[39] Personal interviews with Korean Wave fans in Iran show that the widespread use of social networking services provided their initial exposure to Korean culture and K-pop.

Case No. 3: interview with N., a twenty-three-year-old female university student, in January 2017. I asked her how she became a Korean Wave fan.

> I started off as a member of Cassiopeia, Dongbangsinki's fan club, in 2009. My aunt is Japanese, and she liked Dongbangsinki, so she introduced me to them. I think I gradually developed an interest for Japanese animation and other East Asian cultures because she was Japanese. As a Dongbangsinki fan, I would have birthday parties and order birthday cakes for the members' birthdays. The fan club members also exchanged gifts with each other. After Dongbangsinki disbanded, I became a SHINee fan, and I became the leader of the SHINee fan club. I even bought their albums and Onew's photocard, which are extremely hard to buy in Iran.

Case No. 4: interview with M., a nineteen-year-old woman, in January 2017. I asked her how she became a Korean Wave fan.

---

38. Batmanghelichi and Mouri, "Cyberfeminism, Iranian Style," 50–80.
39. Jin Dal Yong, *New Korean Wave*, 118–21.

> I was initiated into K-pop when I became a member of the SS501 fan club in 2010. At first I liked SS501 after I saw Kim Hyun-joong acting *in Boys over Flowers*. Before that, I used to like Western pop music. After watching the K-drama *Dream High*, where I was introduced to actors/singers like IU, Suzy, 2PM, and 2AM, I began watching Korean music videos. While I like K-pop, I still watch a lot of K-dramas and movies. For example, I am watching the drama *Goblin* by downloading it from the internet, but because Persian subtitles are uploaded late, I started watching them in Korean first. In that way, my Korean has improved a lot.

Furthermore, the introduction of social media in Iranian society has changed the consumption patterns of Korean cultural content. These changes are marked by real-time viewings of and immediate access to K-dramas and news related to Korean celebrities. This has transformed how Iranian fans consume Korean popular culture.

Table 9.3 shows how fandom between 2015 and 2019 changed to comprise mostly women in their teens and twenties. These Korean Wave fans share information related to Korean cultural content by posting photographs and videos online and on mobile apps. They are chiefly university students who celebrate their interest in Korean popular culture by creating Instagram pages dedicated to specific singers or movie stars. Members of online-based fan communities also participate in offline activities, celebrating the birthdays of singers or movie stars, organizing regular meetings for fan club members to interact with each other, and collecting membership fees to fund the design and production of goods such as small souvenirs related to celebrities (see Figures 9.2 and 9.3).

In recent years, with the spread of new media and social media, the phenomenon of star management within the fan community has strengthened. It is possible to witness the cultural practice of fandom's multifaceted intervention in the production, management, and consumption of their star's image. For instance, on one Korean singer's Iranian Telegram fan page in July 2018, an announcement calling for fans to participate in the "Petition to Close Down Dispatch" was posted. *Dispatch* is a Korean online entertainment newspaper that has received

Table 9.3: Difference between K-drama and K-pop in the dominant medium and the age group and gender of the primary audience

	K-drama	K-pop
Dominant medium	State-run broadcasting channels and media	Social media platforms such as Instagram and Telegram
Age group and gender of primary audience	Teenagers and women of all ages	Teenagers and single women in their twenties

Figure 9.2: EXO fan club meeting
in Tehran

Figure 9.3: The souvenirs from an offline
BTS Fanclub (Persian Army) meeting

Figure 9.4: Celebratory announcement posted by Iranian fans in the subway in Seoul,
South Korea

much attention in Korean society for its exclusive reports on Korean celebrities' private lives. Participation in such a petition demonstrates how fans actively engage with the personal lives of these stars. The fans' organization points to the diverse global fandom culture that social media facilitate. Moreover, although Iranian society is commonly thought to be isolated from the rest of the world, social media have enabled Iranian women's fandom, like other countries' fan clubs, to cross geographic boundaries (see Tables 9.4 and 9.5).

Iranian fans actively participate in global networking. Although they are unable to go to Korea themselves, they can send gifts to their stars with the help of global fandom. For instance, when a new album comes out, Iranian fans send flowers or rice wreaths or post celebratory announcements on the Korean subway under the name Iranian Fans (Figure 9.4).

Table 9.4: Major Korean celebrity fan pages on Instagram

Instagram fan page	Celebrity	Number of followers	Number of postings
Bts_army.ir	BTS	20,000	311
btsirarmy	BTS	9,189	319
Army_World	BTS	5,877	841
Bangtan_stan7	BTS	5,763	204
got7.bts.iran	GOT7/BTS	6,417	1,369
iranian_exo.l	EXO	5,955	494
shiva_exol	EXO	23,000	455
Exo.bts_iran	EXO/BTS	13,000	1,111
exoiran	EXO	31,371	2,200
chanyeol.iran	EXO chanyeol	14,000	900
Leeminho_korean.drama	Lee Min-ho	93,000	39

Table 9.5: Most-visited fan pages devoted to Korean Wave content on Instagram

Fan page	Contents	Number of followers	Number of postings	Telegram account
kdramapersian	Introduction to latest K-dramas	29,000	6,346	tlgrm.me/ kpop_persia
hamechi_koreyi	Korean entertainment and celebrity news/ Korean culture	27,000	2,221	@hamechi_ koreyi
News_korea	Korean entertainment and celebrity news	24,000	4,734	
Koreannews.ir	Korean entertainment and celebrity news	23,000	13,000	tlgrm.me/ koreannews
koreandrama shop	K-drama online store	21,000	432	
irankorea	Korean entertainment and celebrity news	18,000	2,178	

Case No. 5: meeting with the female leaders of Iranian fan clubs for the South Korean boy bands EXO[40] and BTS[41] on December 28, 2016.

> EXO Iranian fan club leader: "Most of our activity is online. First, people visit my Instagram, and then they enter the Telegram chat group, where we share news about EXO. When a new album comes out, we share the related news and information or buy related 'goods.'"
>
> BTS fan club leader: "We have offline meetings when it is a member's birthday or when a new album is launched."
>
> Researcher: "Are any parents against the young female students holding fan meetings?"
>
> EXO Iranian fan club leader: "There are barely any parents that are against it. As most of the members are female, there is no real danger. All we're doing is getting together to share information about the artists that we like and chat. Sometimes, we meet in women-only parks to have our regular meetings in a freer environment."

Fan clubs in Iran are not restricted to women, and anyone can join and be an active member, regardless of gender. However, the leaders of boy band fan clubs are customarily women. While the fan club members of Case No. 5 could not attend K-pop concerts in Korea or hold one in Iran, they actively participated in the YG Family[42] fan event, represented by the Iranian fan clubs. Furthermore, when their idol groups held concerts in Korea, they collected money to send rice wreaths to the concert. In addition, on the anniversary of BTS' debut, they posted celebratory announcements in the Korean subway and, in the name of the Iranian fan club, gave donations to facilities for disabled people in Iran (Figure 9.5). They partake in these activities in the same way the Korean fan clubs do, volunteering to raise the profile of their favorite star. In particular, BTS fans not only participate in fan club activities but also make donations or volunteer by, for instance, producing a notebook with a famous BTS quote—"Love

---

40. EXO, formed by SM Entertainment, debuted in 2012. Their music spans genres like pop, hip-hop, and R & B, alongside electronic dance genres like house, trap, and synth-pop. From 2014 to 2018, the band was ranked among the top five most influential celebrities on the *Forbes Korea* Power Celebrity list, while other media outlets hailed it as "the biggest boy band in the world" and "the kings of K-pop" (https://en.wikipedia.org/wiki/Exo).

41. BTS (Bangtan Sonyeondan, which translates as "the Bangtan Boys") is a seven-member South Korean boy band that debuted in 2013. BTS has led the Korean Wave worldwide and broken numerous sales records in the United States. It became the first Korean group to receive Recording Industry Association of America (RIAA) certification with the single "MIC Drop." In 2019, BTS topped the *Billboard* 200 with its studio album *Love Yourself: Answer*. They were the first Korean artists to achieve this feat (https://en.wikipedia.org/wiki/BTS).

42. YG Family, a project group created by YG Entertainment, consists of current artists under the YG Entertainment label. It officially debuted in 1999 with its first album, *Famillenium* (https://en.wikipedia.org/wiki/YG_Entertainment_discography).

Figure 9.5: Iranian BTS fans' financial support of people with mental health issues

yourself"—to donate to orphanages. There are accounts of fans who coordinate trips to Korea on the dates of their favorite artists' concerts and even participate in signing events. In this way, Iranian fans have the opportunity to meet both Korean fans and other fans from around the world. This establishes solidarity in the online community.

Before the Korean Wave hit Iran, little attention had been paid to Korea in Iranian society. However, the popularity of K-dramas and K-pop fundamentally changed the national image of Korea in a favorable way. Interest in and love of Korean popular culture by Iranian female fans has precipitated a general fascination for Korean language and culture, exemplified by the growing competition on entrance exams to study Korean at the King Sejong Institute in Tehran. Cultural interaction between Korea and Iran has also spurred educational exchanges between the two countries. Indeed, most of these exchanges were born of the initial interest in Korean culture. In fact, curiosity about Korean culture is prompting more and more fans to travel to Korea both to attend K-pop concerts and to study there.

The online world enables fans to take the lead in constructing their own autonomous spaces. In other words, while women do not hold a solid position in the "real world," in the world of online fandom they are free to express themselves and occupy positions of authority. Furthermore, because most of their activities take place online, these women have a safe public space clearly distinct from the offline world, where they are constantly given signs of disapproval.

These women do not simply engage in fandom activities; rather, they attempt to connect fandom with their careers. For example, one girl who led a fan club used her experience to learn Korean at the King Sejong Institute and then, through global networking, started to communicate with international fans of the artist she liked. More recently, she has begun to work as a teacher in a Korean institute in Iran.

By providing Korean Wave-related content to others through their personal social-networking system or by creating fan pages, young Iranian women voluntarily assume the role of promoting Korean culture in Iran in private spheres. Even the South Korean government has become aware that the younger generation in Iran, especially women, is voluntarily promoting Korean culture. As a result, the government actively disseminates Korean cultural content through the Korean Embassy in Iran's Cultural Section's official page and the Sejong Institute page on Instagram. Such cases of cultural exchange were invoked as examples of good intercultural practice in high-level diplomatic talks between Iran and Korea in May 2016.

Conclusion

New media in Iran, enabled by smartphones and the internet, have allowed Iranian women to do more than access global culture. In addition to spreading the global cultural phenomenon of the Korean Wave, new media have created a channel for Iranian women to become active consumers of popular culture as well as leaders of a new subculture. Discourse regarding democratization through global communication channels and advocacy for women's and human rights has permeated Iranian society. Despite the global expansion of the media landscape, regulations imposed on the media remain heavily politicized in Iran. The massive anti-government protest in 2009 was a wake-up call for the Iranian regime. Alarmed by the power of social-networking services and the internet, the Iranian government declared a "soft war" and has attempted to fortify the state against the infiltration of Western culture. The Iranian government is exercising particularly strict vigilance over the internet and illegal copies of Western popular cultural content. New media have created not only a private sphere in which individuals can unmask their ideological orientations and truly express themselves, but also a public sphere that serves as a space of solidarity for pursuing the common purpose of resistance. At this critical juncture, investigation and analysis of Iran's new media can function as a window through which to observe the political issues of modern Iranian society.

Young Iranian women constitute a close fandom community, like the young generation of any society. Recently, they have carried out a diverse range of activities through Instagram and Telegram. They engage in fan activities within an alternative space of their own, which is especially significant against the backdrop of the generally conservative Iranian society. These online communities are forging a sense of global solidarity through their communications with other fans. The young urban women of Iran have the space to create online and offline fan clubs and thus carry out social activities. These women are enjoying the Korean Wave not only as popular culture but also as an opportunity to learn the Korean language and develop their careers, either by finding jobs in Iran that are related to Korea or by moving to Korea to study.

Analysis of the Korean Wave, which is yielding an alternative popular culture for Iran's young generation of women, will provide meaningful insights regarding the interests of young Iranian women and the growing demand for popular culture in Iranian society. These women are filling this cultural void by developing and embracing their own domains of subculture through online and offline interactions. The fandom of global popular culture led by Iranian women inside Iran is unimaginably diverse. Furthermore, some fan clubs led by young Iranian women are helping orphanages and centers for disabled people in Iran in solidarity with Korean or other global fan clubs. Nevertheless, as one young Iranian woman said, smiling bitterly, "Iranian women have no limits! Except everything is undercover!" The tug-of-war between young Iranian women's passion and the government's regulations is ongoing.

The Iranian popular culture that might appeal to younger generations is limited by strict cultural censorship. Amid this drought of domestic popular culture, Korean culture is considered more neutral than Western culture and is thus gradually growing a solid fan base in Iran. In such a social environment, Iranian women are leading the fandom through autonomous fan activities in their daily lives. In doing so, they foster solidarity with other women and global fans and pave the way for cultural changes in Iranian society.

Acknowledgments

This work was supported by the Ministry of Education of the Republic of Korea and the National Research Foundation of Korea (NRF-2020S1A6A3A02065553).

Bibliography

Abbasgholizadeh, Mahboubeh. "'To Do Something We Are Unable to Do in Iran': Cyberspace, the Public Sphere, and the Iranian Women's Movement." *Signs: Journal of Women in Culture and Society* 39, no. 4 (June 2014): 831–40. https://doi.org/10.1086/675722.

Akhavan, Niki. *Electronic Iran: The Cultural Politics of an Online Evolution.* New Brunswick, NJ: Rutgers University Press, 2013.

Alavi, Nasrin. *We Are Iran: The Persian Blogs*. London: Portobello, 2005.

Amir-Ebrahimi, Masserat. "Transgression in Narration: The Lives of Iranian Women in Cyberspace." *Journal of Middle East Women's Studies* 4, no. 3 (Fall 2008): 89–118. https://doi.org/10.2979/MEW.2008.4.3.89.

Batmanghelichi, K. Soraya, and Leila Mouri. "Cyberfeminism, Iranian Style: Online Feminism in Post-2009 Iran." *Feminist Media Histories* 3, no. 1 (Winter 2017): 50–80. https://doi.org/10.1525/fmh.2017.3.1.50.

Baym, Nancy. "Why, Despite Myself, I Am Not Leaving Facebook. Yet." *Online Fandom*, no. 13 (May 13, 2010). www.onlinefandom.com/archives/why-despite-myself-i-am-not-leaving-facebook-yet/index.html.

Center for Human Rights in Iran. "Iran's Minister of Education Sees 'Plot' behind Videos of Dancing Schoolchildren." May 9, 2019. https://www.iranhumanrights.org/2019/05/irans-ministry-of-education-sees-plot-behind-youtube-videos-of-dancing-schoolchildren/.

Fiske, John. "The Cultural Economy of Fandom." In *The Adoring Audience: Fan Culture and Popular Media*, edited by L. A. Lewis, 30–49. London: Routledge, 1992.

Gheytanchi, Elham. "Gender Roles in the Social Media World of Iranian Women." In *Social Media in Iran: Politics and Society after 2009*, edited by David M. Faris and Babak Rahimi, 41–56. Albany: State University of New York Press, 2015.

Guta, Hala, and Magdalena Karolak. "Veiling and Blogging: Social Media as Sites of Identity Negotiation and Expression among Saudi Women." *Journal of International Women's Studies* 16, no. 2 (January 2015): 115–27. https://vc.bridgew.edu/jiws/vol16/iss2/7.

Harrington, C. Lee, and Denise D. Bielby. "The Lives of Fandoms." In *Fandom: Identities and Communities in a Mediated World*, edited by Jonathan Gray, Cornel Sandvoss, and C. Lee Harrington, 205–21. New York: New York University Press, 2007.

Harris, Anita. *Future Girl: Young Women in the Twenty-First Century*. New York: Routledge, 2003.

Hemati, Shima. "Against All Odds: South Korea's Nation Branding Campaign in Iran." Paper presented at the International Conference "The 'Miracle' Narrative of the Korean Cultural Industries: Perspectives from the Middle East," Hebrew University of Jerusalem, May 7–9, 2013.

Iwabuchi, Koichi. "Globalization, East Asian Media Cultures and Their Publics." *Asian Journal of Communication* 20, no. 2 (June 2010): 197–212. https://doi.org/10.1080/01292981003693385.

Jenkins, Henry. *Convergence Culture: Where Old and New Media Collide*. New York: New York University Press, 2006.

Jenkins, Henry, and Sangita Shresthova. 2012. "Up, Up, and Away! The Power and Potential of Fan Activism." *Transformative Works and Cultures*, no. 10 (June 15, 2012): 1–5. https://doi.org/10.3983/twc.2012.0435.

Jin, Dal Yong. *New Korean Wave: Transnational Cultural Power in the Age of Social Media*. Champaign: University of Illinois Press, 2016.

Karimi, Sedigheh. "Iranian Women's Identity and Cyberspace: Case Study of Stealthy Freedom." *Journal of Social Science Studies* 2, no. 1 (2015): 221–33. https://doi.org/10.5296/jsss.v2i1.6284.

Khamis, Sahar. "Islamic Feminism in New Arab Media Platforms for Self-Expression and Sites for Multiple Resistances." *Journal of Arab & Muslim Media Research* 3, no. 3 (December 2010): 237–55. https://doi.org/10.1386/jammr.3.3.237_1.

Koo, Gi Yeon. "Constructing an Alternative Public Sphere: The Cultural Significance of Social Media in Iran." In *Media in the Middle East: Activism, Politics, and Culture*, edited by Nele Lenze, Charlotte Schriwer, and Zubaidah Abdul Jalil, 21–43. Cham: Palgrave Macmillan, 2017. https://doi.org/10.1007/978-3-319-65771-4_2.

Koo, Gi Yeon. *Making Their Own Public: Emotion and Self among the Urban Iranian Youth.* Seoul: Seoul National University Press, 2017.

Koo, Gi Yeon. "To Be Myself and Have My Stealthy Freedom: The Iranian Women's Engagement with Social Media." *Revista de Estudios Internacionales Mediterráneos* 21 (2016): 141–57. https://doi.org/10.15366/reim2016.21.011.

Machin, David, and Joanna Thornborrow. "Branding and Discourse: The Case of Cosmopolitan." *Discourse and Society* 14, no. 4 (July 2003): 453–71. https://doi.org/10.1177/0957926503014004003.

McRobbie, Angela. *The Aftermath of Feminism: Gender, Culture and Social Change.* London: Sage, 2008.

Morvarid, Jafar. "Analysis of Korean Drama Series with an Emphasis on the Notions of Tradition and Modesty, as Their Main Themes, from a Religious Point of View." Presentation at the First KIEP-IMEA Forum on "Economic and Cultural Cooperation between Korea and Iran," Institute of Middle Eastern Affairs, Myongji University (IMEA), Korea, May 2013.

Newsom, Victoria A., and Lara Lengel. "Arab Women, Social Media, and the Arab Spring: Applying the Framework of Digital Reflexivity to Analyze Gender and Online Activism." *Journal of International Women's Studies* 13, no. 5 (October 2012): 31–45. https://vc.bridgew.edu/jiws/vol13/iss5/5.

Nooshin, Laudan. "Underground, Overground: Rock Music and Youth Discourses in Iran." *Iranian Studies* 38, no. 3 (September 2005): 463–94. https://doi.org/10.1080/00210860500300820.

Novak, Alison N., and Emad Khazraee. "The Stealthy Protester: Risk and the Female Body in Online Social Movements." *Feminist Media Studies* 14, no. 6 (2014): 1094–95. https://doi.org/10.1080/14680777.2014.975438.

Ringrose, Jessica, and Katarina Eriksson Barajas. "Gendered Risks and Opportunities? Exploring Teen Girls' Digitized Sexual Identities in Postfeminist Media Contexts." *International Journal of Media and Cultural Politics* 7, no. 2 (2011): 121–38. https://discovery.ucl.ac.uk/id/eprint/10018427.

Sakr, Naomi. "Women-Media Interaction in the Middle East: An Introductory Overview." In *Women and Media in the Middle East: Power through Self-Expression*, edited by Naomi Sakr, 1–14. London: Bloomsbury, 2004.

Siamdoust, Nahid. *Soundtrack of the Revolution: The Politics of Music in Iran.* Stanford, CA: Stanford University Press, 2017.

Shim, Doobo. "Whither the Korean Media?" In *Pop Culture Formation across East Asia*, edited by Shim Doobo, Ariel Heryanto, and Ubonrat Siriyuvasak, 115–35. Seoul: Jipmoondang, 2010.

Skalli, Loubna H. "Communicating Gender in the Public Sphere: Women and Information Technologies in the MENA Region." *Journal of Middle East Women's Studies* 2, no. 2 (Spring 2006): 35–59. https://doi.org/10.2979/MEW.2006.2.2.35.

Sohn, Seunghye. "Local Context and Global Fandom of Hallyu Consumption: The Case of Korean Connection in France." *Journal of Media Economics & Culture* 10, no. 1 (February 2012): 45–85. http://www.dbpia.co.kr/journal/articleDetail?nodeId=NODE01965296.

Sreberny, Annabelle. "Women's Digital Activism in a Changing Middle East." *International Journal of Middle East Studies* 47, no. 2 (2015): 357–61. https://doi.org/10.1017/S0020743815000112.

Sreberny, Annabelle, and Gholam Khiabany. *Blogistan: The Internet and Politics in Iran.* London: Tauris, 2010.

Stephan, Rita. "Creating Solidarity in Cyberspace: The Case of Arab Women's Solidarity Association United." *Journal of Middle East Women's Studies* 9, no. 1 (Winter 2013): 81–109. https://doi.org/10.2979/jmiddeastwomstud.9.1.81.

Tahmasebi-Birgani, Victoria. "Social Media as a Site of Transformative Politics: Iranian Women's Online Contestations." In *Iran's Struggles for Social Justice: Economics, Agency, Justice, Activism*, edited by Peyman Vahabzadeh, 181–98. Cham: Palgrave Macmillan, 2017.

Toffoletti, Kim. "Iranian Women's Sports Fandom: Gender, Resistance, and Identity in the Football Movie *Offside.*" *Journal of Sport and Social Issues* 38, no. 1 (December 2012): 75–92. https://doi.org/10.1177/0193723512468758.

Van Nieuwkerk, Karin, Mark LeVine, and Martin Stokes, eds. *Islam and Popular Culture.* Austin: University of Texas Press, 2016.

Vodanovich, Shahper, Cathy Urquhart, and Maha Shakir. "Same but Different: Understanding Women's Experience of ICT in the UAE." *Electronic Journal of Information Systems in Developing Countries* 40, no. 1 (January 2010): 1–21. https://doi.org/10.1002/j.1681-4835.2010.tb00286.x.

Wheeler, Deborah L. "Blessings and Curses: Women and the Internet Revolution in the Arab World." In *Women and Media in the Middle East: Power through Self Expression*, edited by Naomi Sakr, 138–61. London: Bloomsbury, 2004.

10

Into the New World

From the Objectification to the Empowerment of Girls' Generation

Erik Paolo Capistrano and Kathlyn Ramirez

Introduction

> I love you, just like this
> The longed end of wandering
> I leave behind this world's unending sadness
> Walking the many unknowable paths
> I follow a dim light
> It's something we'll do together to the end
> Into the new world.
>
> —Girls' Generation, *Dasi Mannan Segye* [Into the New World]

Girls' Generation, or So Nyeo Si Dae (SNSD) in Korean,[1] officially debuted in 2007 with their song "Into the New World." Starting out as nine members, the group consisted of Taeyeon, Jessica, Sunny, Tiffany, Hyoyeon, Yuri, Sooyoung, Yoona, and Seohyun. Making their way to the top for the next fifteen years with group hits such as "Gee," "Oh!," "I Got a Boy," "The Boys," "Lion Heart" and "Holiday," and solo hits such as SNSD's leader Taeyeon's "I," "Four Seasons," and "INVU," they have been recognized domestically and internationally. In 2020, *Billboard* named SNSD one of the top 100 best music video artists of all time, listing them in 37th place, the highest achieved by a K-pop act.[2] More recently,

---

1. The Korean name of Girls' Generation is "So Nyeo Si Dae," which actually literally translates to "Era of Maidens." For the rest of this chapter, the group will be referred to by its stylized abbreviation SNSD.
2. *Billboard*, "The 100 Greatest Music Video Artists of All Time: Staff List," August 27, 2020, https://www.billboard.com/articles/news/list/9440075/100-best-music-video-artists.

Figure 10.1: SNSD at the FOREVER 1 15th Anniversary Press Conference (courtesy of Tibiten [티비텐] under Wikicommons)

The *Korea Herald* documented how "Into the New World" became an anthem of solidarity that was adopted in both South Korea and around the region.[3]

These events add to the long list of accolades[4] spanning fifteen years and counting for the archetype of K-pop girl groups—nicknamed the "Nation's Girl Group" of South Korea.[5] As an enduring second-generation group,[6] they have been compared to South Korea's chaebol business model as well as the embodiment of neoliberal politics and economics, which is also deeply rooted in sexual commodification and objectification.[7] Contradicting this impression

3. Yim Hyun-su, "'Into the New World': Girls' Generation's Debut Song Lives on as Millennials' Anthem of Solidarity," *Korea Herald*, April 14, 2022, http://www.koreaherald.com/view. php?ud=20220414000732.
4. SNSD has won multiple awards across several categories, including multiple Best Female Artist, Best Artist, Best Song, and Best Album awards at the Mnet Asian Music Awards, the Melon Music Awards, the Seoul Music Awards, and the Golden Disc Awards. Outside South Korea, SNSD also won at the MTV Video Music Awards Japan, Japan Gold Disc Awards, and, most notably, the YouTube Music Awards. To date, the group has earned 119 awards from more than 226 nominations.
5. Kim Arin, "What the Return of Girls' Generation Means," *Jakarta Post*, August 31, 2018, https:// www.thejakartapost.com/life/2018/08/30/what-the-return-of-girls-generation-means.html.
6. Depending on their year of debut, K-pop groups have been generally classified. These are estimated as follows: first generation (debuted 1994–2002), second generation (2003–2011), third generation (2012–2017), and fourth generation (2018–present). To date, most of the second-generation girl groups have officially disbanded: Wonder Girls (2007–2017); KARA (2007–2016); 2NE1 (2009–2016); 4minute (2009–2016); Secret (2009–2018); miss A (2010–2017); SISTAR (2010–2017).
7. Kim Gooyong, "K-Pop Female Idols: Culture Industry, Neoliberal Social Policy, and Governmentality in Korea," in *The Routledge Handbook of Global Cultural Policy*, ed. Victoria Durrer, Toby Miller and Dave O'Brien (Abingdon: Routledge, 2017), 520-37; Kim Gooyong, "Neoliberal Feminism in Contemporary South Korean Popular Music: Discourse of Resilience, Politics of Positive Psychology, and Female Subjectivity," *Journal of Language and Politics* 18, no. 4 (2019): 560-78, https://doi.org/10.1075/jlp.18058.kim; Oh Ingyu and Jang Wonho, "From Globalization to Glocalization: Configuring Korean Pop Culture to Meet Glocal Demands,"

is the depiction of the group of embodying strength and independence.[8] This perceived transition within a spectrum of female empowerment has significantly challenged the negative representation of K-pop girl groups within the industry.[9]

In this respect, this chapter seeks to position SNSD's popularity as a case study discussing the possibilities of a more dynamic and subjective agency of K-pop female groups beyond the rigid labels of manufactured sexual objectifications placed on them. Based on this premise, this chapter has two objectives: to chart the trajectory of SNSD's evolution; and to contextualize the otherwise differing perceptions of the group between and among industry, academia, and fandom.

The first objective illustrates how a K-pop girl group can actually grow and prove that they are more than what the industry originally projected them to be—and what society initially expected and perceived them to be. These identities are not static.[10] Rather, it should be perceived as a journey that has an origin, allowing for growth and development, and even discovering ways to break away from disempowering values and norms.[11] Observers of the Korean Wave have named SNSD as one of the most significant contributors in building the international interest in this phenomenon,[12] paving the way for more contemporary female K-pop groups.

The second is to echo calls on the importance of breaking down barriers between and among fandoms, industry practitioners, and academic researchers.[13]

Culture and Empathy: International Journal of Sociology, Psychology, and Cultural Studies 3, no. 1–2 (2020): 23–43.

8. Oh Chuyun, "The Politics of the Dancing Body"; Park T. K. and Kim Youngdae, "How BLACKPINK, Red Velvet, and More Are Redefining Womanhood in K-Pop," MTV News, June 6, 2019, https:// www.mtv.com/news/3126395/k-pop-girl-groups-womanhood-agency/amp/; Oh Ingyu, "From Localization to Glocalization: Contriving Korean Pop Culture to Meet Glocal Demands," *Kritika Kultura* 29 (August 2017): 157–67.

9. Liz Jonas, "Crafted for the Male Gaze: Gender Discrimination in the K-Pop Industry," *Journal of International Women's Studies* 22, no. 7 (2021): 3–18, https://vc.bridgew.edu/jiws/vol22/iss7/2; Oh Chuyun, "The Politics of the Dancing Body."

10. Mark Duffet, *Understanding Fandom: An Introduction to the Study of Media Fan Culture* (New York: Bloomsbury, 2013); Michael A. Unger, "The Aporia of Presentation: Deconstructing the Genre of K-Pop Girl Group Music Videos in South Korea," *Journal of Popular Music Studies*, 27, no. 1 (2015): 25–47.

11. Oh Ingyu, "From Localization to Glocalization."

12. Ahn Shin-Hyun, "Girls' Generation and the New Korean Wave," *SERI Quarterly* 4, no. 4 (2011): 80–86; *Billboard*, "100 Greatest Girl Group Songs of All Time: Critics' Picks," July 10, 2017, https:// www.billboard.com/articles/columns/pop/7857816/100-greatest-girl-group-songs; Jung Eun-young, "Hallyu and the K-Pop Boom in Japan," in *K-Pop – The International Rise of the Korean Music Industry*, ed. Choi JungBong and Roald Maliangkay (Abingdon: Routledge, 2014), 116–32.

13. Duffet, *Understanding Fandom*; Matthew Hills, *Fan Cultures* (London: Routledge, 2002); Stephen Epstein and James Turnbull, "Girls' Generation? Gender (Dis)Empowerment, and K-Pop," in *The Korean Popular Culture Reader*, ed. Kim Kyung Hyun and Choe Youngmin (Durham, NC: Duke University Press, 2013), 314–36.

Therefore, in recognizing the importance of SNSD's place within the discourse of women and female empowerment in K-pop, sentiments from academics, industry figures, and fans must be considered together. This chapter angulates existing academic narratives with those from fan communities through more specific interviews with individual dedicated fans, who are considered to be authoritative and prominent members within the SNSD fandom.[14] Their responses add some more on-the-ground real-life perspectives to the arguments for and against SNSD's place in this discussion. This chapter also documents some highlights of the group's impact, built on both the individual and collective efforts of its members in establishing themselves as the standard bearers for subsequent generations of K-pop girl groups to follow, thereby disrupting many of predetermined social and cultural labels that have trapped the agency of K-pop female idols.[15]

The Background Story

Hello! We are Girls' Generation!

> Girls Generation's legacy is about hard work. We worked our asses off for what we believed in, what we wanted to create, and who we wanted to be. It's about being positive and being the best that you can be, given your circumstances. It's about supporting your girls, between us members, the team, the creatives behind it, and the fans. Our friendship and work ethic inspires so many other females around the world to have a group of friends to grow with.
>
> —Tiffany Young, *HYPEBAE* interview, 2018

After the initial success of SM Entertainment's male idol group Super Junior in 2005, many speculated that the company was already forming a female equivalent. In a move considered to be bold at that time, Super Junior debuted with

---

14. This chapter also presents insights from four well-known and longtime SNSD fans, known as SONE (pronounced "so-won"), gathered from interviews conducted by the authors. Twitter user @yulneck (https://twitter.com/yulneck) is a Filipino fan in her mid-twenties and a feminist, who has one of the largest Twitter followings in Southeast Asia. Twitter user @SonexStella (https://twitter.com/sonexstella) is a South Korean fan in her early thirties, a feminist, based in Canada, and one of the most well-known and recognized translators for SONE. She also holds the distinction of being acknowledged by Tiffany for her translation work. Twitter user @itnw0628 (https://twitter.com/itnw0628) is a South Korean fan in his early forties who is one of the longest tenured and most respected SONE, as well as one of the most well-known SNSD live events fan account writers. Twitter user @sonexjinro (https://twitter.com/sonexjinro; the Twitter account has since been suspended) is another longtime fan, also based in Canada, who has been instrumental in doing translations for SONE since 2009, a time when translated works distributed online were hard to come by.

15. Stephen Epstein, "'Into the New World': Girls' Generation from the Local to the Global," in *K-Pop – The International Rise of the Korean Music Industry*, ed. Choi JungBong and Roald Maliangkay (Abingdon: Routledge, 2015), 47–62.

13 members. SM Entertainment took significant risks by introducing a male idol group with numerous members, and the company was about to do it again with a female version, spending an estimated US$2.6 million per member to scout, train, and debut the group.[16] Rumors were already giving the female group the pet name "Super Girls"[17] in direct homage to Super Junior. SNSD formally debuted on August 5, 2007, on Seoul Broadcasting System (SBS)'s live music show, *Inkigayo*.[18] It was initially composed of nine members, which was uncommon in the mid-2000s.

"Into the New World" debuted at no. 5 in the South Korean music charts.[19] But despite establishing an omnipresence to appeal to both the industry and the market over the next two years, it was not until 2009, with the release of their

Table 10.1: Girls' Generation's members' stage names, real names, and positions in the group

Stage name	Real name	Position	Date of birth
Taeyeon	Kim Taeyeon	main vocalist	March 9, 1989
Jessica	Jeong Suyeon	main vocalist (former member, left in 2014)	April 18, 1989
Sunny	Lee Sungyu	lead vocalist, sub rapper	May 15, 1989
Tiffany	Hwang Miyeong	lead vocalist, rapper	August 1, 1989
Hyoyeon	Kim Hyoyeon	main dancer, main rapper, vocalist	September 22, 1989
Yuri	Kwon Yuri	lead dancer, lead rapper, vocalist	December 5, 1989
Sooyoung	Choe Suyeong	lead dancer, lead rapper, vocalist	February 10, 1990
Yoona	Im Yuna	lead dancer, lead rapper, vocalist	May 30, 1990
Seohyun	Seo Juhyeon	lead vocalist	June 28, 1991

16. Kim Gooyong, *From Factory Girls to K-Pop Idol Girls*.
17. Ahn, "Girls' Generation and the New Korean Wave."
18. In South Korea, there are four major weekly live music shows where artists promote their songs and albums: Mnet's *M Countdown*, Korean Broadcasting System (KBS)'s *Music Bank*, Munhwa Broadcasting Corporation (MBC)'s *Show! Music Core*, and SBS's *Inkigayo*. In recent years, SBS MTV added *The Show* and MBC M added *Show Champion*. Each of these shows currently has its own weekly music chart with different scoring systems.
19. Music Industry Association of Korea, "2007.8wol—Gayoeumban Panmaeryang," accessed February 6, 2022, https://web.archive.org/web/20090228163343/http://miak.or.kr/stat/kpop_200708.htm.

monumental hit "Gee," that the group finally earned superstar status. When asked about their early debut days, some longtime fans recalled:

> SM patiently waited and gave enough time for them to be successful before debut. Hard to see such a method will be duplicated anymore, even for SM.
> —@itnw0628

> Seeing SNSD grow up during 2007–2008 and then blow up with "Gee" was unbelievable. They were LITERALLY everywhere. Music, CF, variety, drama, and the whole entertainment industry were flooded with content of SNSD. You probably couldn't go a day without seeing SNSD somewhere.
> —@sonexjinro

> Their growing popularity led to various variety shows of their own; endorsements of various products: From a popular South Korean online search engine to a chicken delivery brand and a pizza chain; and having different sidelines for each member: K-drama OSTs (Taeyeon, Jessica, Sunny, Tiffany), music show hostings (Tiffany and Yuri), radio DJing (Taeyeon), K-drama (Yoona, Sooyoung, Yuri) and musical (Taeyeon, Tiffany, Jessica) acting, and guesting in variety shows (Sunny, Hyoyeon, Yuri, Seohyun).
> —@yulneck and @SonexStella

Furthermore, "Gee," eventually became widely recognized as a K-pop standard and a frontier in modern Korean bubblegum pop music,[20] setting a significant precedent for later K-pop acts to follow.[21] With a then-record nine consecutive weeks at No. 1 in the KBS *Music Bank K-Chart* (broken in 2012 by the current record holder to date, PSY and "Gangnam Style") and the group's first Triple Crown in SBS *Inkigayo*, its success has been compared to the likes of Lady Gaga's 2008 hit "Poker Face." Before PSY and "Gangnam Style" took the world by storm in 2012, "Gee" was the most viewed K-pop music video on YouTube.[22] It was also one of the first music videos to spawn multiple official and fan-made YouTube videos, boosting its popularity even more.

---

20. Bubblegum pop music is a subgenre of pop music that is characterized by upbeat music marketed toward preteens, teenagers, and young adolescents. According to Michael Fuhr in his 2016 book *Globalization and Popular Music in South Korea*, K-pop bubblegum pop music is characterized by the heavy use of dance-pop to complement the upbeat music, and by lyrics that touch on themes appealing to younger audiences, such as having crushes, puppy love encounters, and one's first love.

21. Korea.net, *K-Pop: A New Force in Pop Music*, Ministry of Culture, Sports and Tourism and Korean Culture and Information Service, 2011; Shim Doobo and Noh Kwang Woo, "YouTube and Girls' Generation Fandom," *The Journal of the Korea Contents Association* 12, no. 1 (2012): 125-37.

22. Epstein and Turnbull, "Girls' Generation? Gender (Dis)Empowerment, and K-Pop."

Onward to Japan, and then the world

The success of their second full-length album, *Oh!*, and its repackaged version, *Run Devil Run*, both released in 2010, solidified the group's hold on the K-pop industry,[23] setting the stage for them to significantly expand their international presence. In addition, *Oh!* earned the group a spot in history for being the first album to include photocards of the band members, setting a precedent for the development of K-pop merchandising.[24] When they started promoting in Japan during the same year (where the group was rebranded as "Shoujo Jidai," the Japanese translation of the group's Korean name), SNSD became the third South Korean artists (after SM Entertainment labelmates BoA and TVXQ!) to be certified double-platinum album-sellers by the Recording Industry Association of Japan (RIAJ), citing the Oricon Albums Chart, a first for a K-pop girl group.[25] This fueled several successful runs of Japanese promotions.[26] These included performing at the 2011 Summer Sonic Festival—an annual music festival show-casing predominantly Japanese rock artists, which also featured the Red Hot Chili Peppers, Avril Lavigne, and Panic! At the Disco[27]—and winning the 2011 Best Group Video and 2012 Album of the Year and Artist of the Year at the MTV Video Music Awards Japan.[28] Cementing their position as the representa-tive K-pop girl group, SNSD has also been featured in a slew of tourism cam-paigns, culminating in becoming the ideal national representatives and physical embodiment of South Korea's self-image,[29] earning them distinctive recognition from the South Korean government.[30] It also led to a slew of endorsement runs

---

23. Jonas, "Crafted for the Male Gaze"; Lee Ji-hun, Im Hi-yun, and Jeong Yang-hwan, "Banjjak Banjjak Nun-i Busyeo . . . BigBaeng-Sonyeosidae Yeokdae Choego Aidol," *dongA*, September 1, 2016, https://www.donga.com/news/NewsStand/article/all/20160901/80071885/1.
24. Kim Hyo-jin, "'2010nyeonbuteo Sijakdoen Munhwa'... Sonyeosidae, Hanguk Aidol Choecho Aelbeom Potokadeu Doip" *topstarnews*, March 29, 2021, http://www.topstarnews.net/news/arti-cleView.html?idxno=868424.
25. Ahn, "Girls' Generation and the New Korean Wave"; Korean Culture and Information Service, *K-Pop: A New Force in Pop Music*.
26. Korean Culture and Information Service, *K-Pop: A New Force in Pop Music*; Michael Fuhr, *Globalization and Popular Music in South Korea: Sounding Out K-Pop* (New York: Routledge, 2016); Jung Sun and Hirata Yukie, "Conflicting Desires: K-Pop Idol Girl Group Flows in Japan in the Era of Web 2.0," *Electronic Journal of Contemporary Japanese Studies*, 12, no. 2 (2012), http://japanesestudies.org.uk/ejcjs/vol12/iss2/jung.html.
27. Ahn, "Girls' Generation and the New Korean Wave."
28. Epstein, "'Into the New World.'"
29. Epstein, "'Into the New World'"; Kim Gooyong, "K-Pop Female Idols"; Kim Gooyong, *From Factory Girls to K-Pop Idol Girls*.
30. SNSD was named members of the G20 Star Supporters and Talking to the G20 Leaders campaign for the 2010 G20 Seoul Summit; Honorary Ambassadors for the 2010–2012 Visit Korea campaign; and Ambassadors for Incheon Airport Customs in 2010. In recognition of these efforts, they became the first K-pop group to receive the Prime Minister's Award at the 2011 Korean Popular Culture and Arts Awards, organized by the Korea Creative Content Agency. In addition, Korea Post officially published and circulated SNSD postage stamps in 2012.

with global brands such as Intel, LG, and Casio. These are noteworthy because, for one, Intel's decision to make SNSD their brand ambassadors sparked a resurgence of international interest in the Korean Wave, bringing K-pop out from a regional East Asian phenomenon to the global stage.[31]

SNSD was also heavily involved in K-pop's initial forays into Europe and the United States. Aside from the notable events of 2011 SM Town Live in Paris, which included a massive flash mob organized by fans calling for a second night of the concert,[32] and SM Town Live 2011 at Madison Square Garden in New York City, they also appeared on numerous high-profile Western television shows, such as Canal+'s *Le Grand Journal*, NBC's *Late Night with David Letterman*, WABC-TV's *Live! With Kelly Ripa*, and NBC's *Extra*—a first for any K-pop group.[33]

In 2013, "I Got a Boy," the lead single of the group's third full-length album *I Got a Boy*, was named Video of the Year at the inaugural YouTube Music Awards (YTMA). This opened many doors for the K-pop industry, especially in using social media activity as a success metric, and significantly increased usage of YouTube to distribute K-pop content.[34] Along with "Gee" and "The Boys," "I Got a Boy" enabled SNSD to be an integral part of K-pop's first significant stride toward the global mainstream exposure that the group enjoys at present.[35] When asked about their thoughts about SNSD's international ventures, fans have this to say:

> In the last twenty years, K-pop took off and became a worldwide phenomenon in the music industry, which was unimaginable before. And SNSD certainly played a big part in that. Their huge success in Korea and other countries made people respect K-pop artists as musicians, not just good-looking boys and girls. Current generations of successful K-pop groups should thank SNSD (and other older generation groups) for paving the way.
> —@itnw0628

> Along with other second-generation groups, they helped expand and solidify K-pop's presence all over Asia. They also knocked on the doors of the American market but the breakthrough only happened later with BTS and BLACKPINK.

31. Oh Ingyu and Park Gil-Sung, "From B2C to B2B: Selling Korean Pop Music in the Age of New Social Media," *Korea Observer* 43, no. 3 (2012): 365–97.
32. Ahn, "Girls' Generation and the New Korean Wave"; Korean Culture and Information Service, *K-Pop: A New Force in Pop Music*.
33. Kim Gooyong, "Between Hybridity and Hegemony in K-Pop's Global Popularity: A Case Of Girls' Generation's American Debut," *International Journal of Communication* 11 (2017): 2367–86.
34. Oh Ingyu, "From Localization to Glocalization"; Seoulbeats, "A Reflection on SNSD's YouTube Music Awards Win," November 9, 2013, https://seoulbeats.com/2013/11/reflection-snsds-youtube-music-awards-win/; Jeff Yang, "Why Girls' Generation and K-Pop Won Big at the YouTube Music Awards," *Wall Street Journal*, November 4, 2013, https://www.wsj.com/articles/BL-SEB-78043.
35. Fuhr, *Globalization and Popular Music in South Korea*.

But the one that I remember the most, not particularly for its significance but more for its consequences, is the YouTube Music Award for "I Got a Boy." I feel like beating out well-established big named American artists to take this award really put K-pop on the map. At the same time, it cranked up this YouTube views race that I personally really dislike.

—@sonexjinro

SNSD debuted at a time when the internet wasn't as accessible as it is now. Music shows didn't have their own YouTube channels for performances. When the "Gee" MV went viral and held the record for being the most viewed K-pop MV with 80 million views, it took years to actually achieve those numbers.

Remember when "I Got a Boy" achieved 20 million views in a span of days and became the fastest K-pop music video to achieve such a feat? Nowadays groups like BTS and BLACKPINK could achieve those numbers in hours!

—yulneck@Twitter

However, Jessica's controversial removal from the group in 2014, months after another successful run with their fourth mini-album *Mr. Mr.*, followed by her leaving SM Entertainment the following year,[36] rocked the industry, with lingering speculations on the reasons behind the move. Nevertheless, in 2015, the prerelease mini-album *Party* and the fifth full album *Lion Heart* went on to top domestic and international charts, signaling a fresh start for the now-eight-member group. In 2017, the group's sixth full album, *Holiday Night*, which commemorates their tenth anniversary, went on to top the *Billboard* World Albums chart.[37] Months later, following Jessica's dramatic departure, Tiffany, Sooyoung, and Seohyun amicably left SM Entertainment.[38] The three are still listed on the group's active roster, and are still very much widely supported by fans. In 2022, all eight active members came back to commemorate their 15th anniversary with their seventh full album *FOREVER 1*, eclipsing their own record of first week album sales along the way and joining the likes of the current generation of girl group sensations Le Sserafim, New Jeans, IVE, and BLACKPINK in topping the physical and digital charts. As further proof of their ability to keep up with this current generation, the lead single, "FOREVER 1" was praised as one of the best K-pop releases for 2022[39] by South Korean music webzine *Idology*, and by Western media outlets such as *Cosmopolitan*, *Dazed*, *Nylon*, and *Teen Vogue*.

36. As of this writing, Jessica is signed with Coridel Entertainment while managing her own fashion brand, Blanc & Eclare.
37. Kim, "What the Return of Girls' Generation Means."
38. As of this writing, Tiffany was signed with Sublime Artist Agency, while Sooyoung was with Saram Entertainment, and Seohyun was managed by Namoo Actors.
39. Crystal Bell, "The 20 Best K-Pop Releases of 2022," *Nylon*, December 8, 2022, https://www.nylon.com/entertainment/best-kpop-albums-songs-2022; Taylor Glasby, "The Best K-Pop Tracks of 2022," *Dazed*, December 14, 2022, https://www.dazeddigital.com/music/article/57774/1/

Considering their popularity, SNSD has an interesting place in K-pop's globalization. The group is one of the leading personalities in that critical period of the Korean Wave's international market expansion.[40] They were one of the first K-pop acts who attempted to break into the European and American markets during this period when K-pop international presence in the Western markets was still insignificant.[41] Nonetheless, they opened doors for future generations of K-pop acts to follow.[42] These achievements also took place at a time when the K-pop industry was visibly dominated by male idol groups such as TVXQ!, Super Junior, Big Bang, and EXO.[43]

Girl Factory or Role Model: What Critics Have to Say

Disempowering a generation of females?

However, a closer look at SNSD reveals that their rise is riddled with challenges, with substantial public commentaries casting doubt on its potential. SNSD's early years became in some ways reduced to being a typical K-pop girl group deliberately designed to appeal to older male audiences.[44] Nonetheless, such labeling became history as the group's career progressed. When fans were asked to reflect on this particular stage, one interesting insight came out:

the-best-k-pop-tracks-of-2022-billlie-ive-ateez; *Idology*, "Gyeolsan 2022: 3Olhaeui Aelbeom 20seon," January 1, 2023, https://idology.kr/17276; Aedan Juvet, "Wanna Know Which K-Pop Song Is the Best of 2022? Here's Our Definitive Ranking," *Cosmopolitan*, December 16, 2022, https://www.cosmopolitan.com/entertainment/music/a42258288/best-k-pop-songs-2022/; *Teen Vogue*, "The 79 Best K-Pop Songs of 2022", December 15, 2022, https://www.teenvogue.com/story/best-k-pop-songs-2022.

40. Oh Chuyun, "The Politics of the Dancing Body"; John Seabrook, "Factory Girls: Cultural Technology and the Making of K-Pop," *New Yorker*, October 1, 2012, https://www.newyorker.com/magazine/2012/10/08/factory-girls-2.

41. Kim Gooyong, "Between Hybridity and Hegemony"; Park Jun-hee, "Girls' Generation to Make Full-Group Comeback in August after Five Years." *Korea Herald*, May 17, 2022. http://www.korea-herald.com/view.php?ud=20220517000703.

42. Jung Eun-young, "K-Pop Female Idols in the West: Racial Imaginations and Erotic Fantasies," in *The Korean Wave: Korean Media Go Global*, ed. Youna Kim (New York: Routledge, 2013), 106–19.

43. To illustrate the dominance of male groups, there are four major award-giving bodies in the South Korean music industry. These are the Mnet Asian Music Awards, the Melon Music Awards, the Seoul Music Awards, and the Golden Disc Awards. SNSD is the first—and to date the only—girl group to win the Golden Disc Awards Disc Daesang, doing it in 2010. They are also only one of two girl groups to have won Artist of the Year at the Mnet Asian Music Awards, winning it in 2011. The group is also one of only two female artists to win Artist of the Year, doing so in 2009 and 2010, and Song of the Year, winning it in 2009 at the Melon Music Awards. The following years were dominated by the likes of Super Junior, EXO, and BTS.

44. Epstein and Turnbull, "Girls' Generation? Gender (Dis)Empowerment, and K-Pop"; Jonas, "Crafted for the Male Gaze."

If survival shows were a thing back then, then SNSD's would be just like that. The fact that they had to go through that rigorous process and be met with very harsh criticisms once their debut was announced still baffles me to this day.

—@yulneck

For one, SNSD faced a slew of misogynistic, racist, and sexually suggestive comments and feedback from a variety of public audiences through the years. Even early in their careers, an incident, dubbed as the "Black Ocean," occurred during the 2008 Dream Concert in Seoul.[45] Through their 10-minute performance, almost the entire crowd in attendance, except for their own fans, switched off their light sticks and stayed silent. Some even called for Wonder Girls, another then-popular K-pop group, instead. Fans still recall how painful the experience was back then, as accounted by the following:

It's kind of bittersweet thinking back at it. Wonder Girls, SNSD, and KARA debuted in an era where boy groups were all the rage and girl groups were a scarcity. It was already a difficult situation to be in, but the disgusting "black ocean" incident was such a hateful thing to have to face. Nowadays, non-fans and even some SONE seem to glorify that incident as some kind of rag-to-riches story, but it's such a painful memory that I personally, and I think the girls themselves don't really wish to recall.

—@sonexjinro

SNSD's popularity was like a double-edged sword. It was so disappointing to see them get harassed for the simplest things just because they were women. But the reasons why people didn't like them were reasons they wouldn't even say if SNSD was a boy group. They get called nasty and sexist things like "plastic," "sluts," "boring," "too annoying," "attention seekers," "fake," etc.

—@yulneck

One of the more telling issues against the group is the discourse around "Gee." Despite noting its phenomenal commercial success, the adverse scholarly regard for SNSD remains as examples of infantilization and objectification. Both Liz Jonas's and Brad Osborn's respective studies noted that by their portrayals of being cute, but helpless and clueless about how to deal with one's "first love story," as the song opened, SNSD practically disempowered women and merely pandered to the male superiority complex.[46] Stephen Epstein and James Turnbull made more detailed discussions of "Gee," "Tell Me Your Wish (Genie)," and "Oh!," concluding that these releases painted SNSD as doll-like fantasy figures

45. Soy, "Shin Haechul's Radio Broadcast about Dream Concert & Suju's Manager's Cyworld Entry," Soompi, June 10, 2008, https://forums.soompi.com/topic/149610-shin-haechuls-radio-broadcast-about-dream-concert-sujus-managers-cyworld-entry/.
46. Jonas, "Crafted for the Male Gaze"; Brad Osborn, "Resistance Gazes in Recent Music Videos," *Music and the Moving Image* 14, no. 2 (2021): 51-67, https://doi.org/10.5406/musimoviimag.14.2.0051.

exhibiting submissiveness, fragility, and cuteness that greatly appealed to patri-archal expectations of South Korean womanhood. They also critiqued the focus, as a major selling point, on the members' physical attributes, particularly the objectification and fetishization of the members' "leggy" performances.[47] Jung Sun and Hirata Yukie highlighted how SNSD's Genie earned the group the nick-name "beautiful legs group" by some Japanese media outlets, and[48] Kim Gooyong described SNSD as providing some shallow manufactured neoliberal notions of female imagery and empowerment.[49] Michael Unger even warned that one very telling conclusion out of all of this is that, because of this lack of authenticity among K-pop girl groups, the tendency is that individual members cannot rise beyond the group itself.[50]

These perspectives have been significantly exacerbated in their overseas activities. Their lukewarm 2012 American debut with the English-language version of their 2011 hit "The Boys" was described as falling into the trap of sexualized objectification to appease audiences, especially Western ones.[51] Jung Eun-young echoes these sentiments, pointing out that being preposterously objectified by the American audiences was a clear indication that SNSD were not taken seriously as musicians.[52] Oh Chuyun categorized this performance as another example of how, because of its aesthetics, choreographies, and even lyrics, SNSD was designed and packaged for the male audience, romanticizing the supposed submissive nature of conventional femininity.[53] Kim Gooyong even went so far as to say that "The Boys" is a case study of the sexualized representa-tion of Korean-ness on the world stage.[54] However, all of these pales in compari-son to their YTMA Video of the Year win for "I Got a Boy." The win was met with a muted reaction from the live crowd and strongly worded, hateful, and racist social media posts, labeling the group as a joke and irrelevant, mistaking them for Chinese or Japanese nationals, and complaining about how a non-English-language song won on American soil.[55]

47. Epstein, "'Into the New World'"; Epstein and Turnbull, "Girls' Generation? Gender (Dis) Empowerment, and K-Pop."
48. Jung Sun and Hirata Yukie, "Conflicting Desires: K-Pop Idol Girl Group Flows in Japan in the Era of Web 2.0," *Electronic Journal of Contemporary Japanese Studies*, 12, no. 2 (2012), http://japaneses-tudies.org.uk/ejcjs/vol12/iss2/jung.html.
49. Kim Gooyong, "Neoliberal Feminism."
50. Unger, "The Aporia of Presentation."
51. Seabrook, "Factory Girls"; Unger, "The Aporia of Presentation."
52. Jung Eun-yong, "K-Pop Female Idols in the West."
53. Oh Chuyun, "The Politics of the Dancing Body."
54. Kim Gooyong, *From Factory Girls to K-Pop Idol Girls*; Kim Gooyong, "Between Hybridity and Hegemony."
55. Park Si-soo, "Girls' Generation Faces Racial Attack over 'US Dream,'" *Korea Times*, November 7, 2013, http://www.koreatimes.co.kr/www/art/2020/02/688_145820.html.

Individual incidents of racial and gender attacks included Taeyeon disclosing in SBS *Strong Heart*, which aired in December 2009, that she was being harassed by an older male celebrity, highlighting one incident where he would call her in the middle of the night when he was drunk and moody. In another incident, there was tremendous backlash against Tiffany for a Snapchat and Instagram post with a Japanese "rising sun" flag and filter while in Japan for an SM Town Live concert in 2016 (the backlash continued despite her taking down or editing the posts and issuing a handwritten public apology for it).[56]

However, most of these seemingly unfavorable critiques that have hounded SNSD are either from their early careers or are based on a few snapshots of certain events. Because the group has been active for longer than expected, new sources of information and new developments in their careers inevitably challenge these perspectives.

Rewriting the playbook on K-pop girl groups

> The music video ("Sober") is about liberating girls who feel trapped, and tired of the norm. I wanted to express that they can get out there, rebel against social norms and show everyone who they're really meant to be.
>
> —Kim Hyoyeon, *Paper* interview, 2018

On the other hand, their music releases also created equally interesting waves that significantly contribute to how the world now defines and appreciates K-pop. For instance, through the years, "Into the New World" evolved from a K-pop debut song to a protest anthem.[57] This prompted a review of SNSD, where emerging commentaries—noting the message of "Into the New World"—are praising the group's efforts to empower females and further the cause of gender equality, pointing out that it was very difficult for them to do so at a time when priorities and mindsets were different because the Korean Wave was just starting to spread around the world.[58]

---

56. From 1910 to 1945, the Korean peninsula was under the rule of the Empire of Japan. This part of their history has on occasion caused some tension between the South Korean and Japanese governments, and even some resentment of the Japanese government by South Koreans. The "rising sun" flag, a symbol of Japanese imperialism, is considered an offensive image by many South Koreans.
57. Yim, "'Into the New World'"; Yim Hyun-su, "LGBT Support Growing in K-Pop," *Korea Herald*, June 10, 2019, http://kpopherald.koreaherald.com/view.php?ud=201906101452119456437_2.
58. Tamar Herman, "9 K-Pop Songs that Recently Became Part of South Korean Politics," *Billboard*, May 2, 2018, https://www.billboard.com/articles/columns/k-town/8436957/k-pop-songs-politicized-south-korea; Oh Chuyun, "The Politics of the Dancing Body"; Park and Kim, "Redefining Womanhood in K-Pop."

"Gee" still holds a significant degree of recognition as a "must-listen" song in the history of K-pop.[59] With catchy melodies and easy-to-follow choreographies, "Gee" appealed not just to fans, but to the general South Korean public and eventually to many international audiences.[60] In 2016, a widely cited survey[61] in South Korea showed that people consider "Gee" the best female pop song and SNSD the best female artist of the last 20 years.[62] Fans have been equally aware of the impact of the song's success on SNSD's career trajectories from that point on:

> They became the most popular girl group in 2009 with "Gee," and it was a perfect blend of well written music, catchy choreography, and styles. After "Gee," they released "Genie," which is completely different yet almost equally breathtaking. They didn't look back after that.
>
> —@itnw0628

> It's a very well-known fact that "Gee" put SNSD on the map in South Korea, as it went viral. After "Gee," they released hit after hit, all with very different concepts and sound. At the same time, they were also active on TV shows, as radio DJs, and were able to let their personalities shine in front of the public.
>
> —@SonexStella

SNSD's Japanese-language productions and activities have changed the overall demographics of their fanbase, reportedly gaining significantly more female fans who are in their teens and twenties. Both Stephen Epstein and James Turnbull, and Jung Sun and Hirata Yukie have acknowledged that some of the very same elements that were used as a basis to criticize the group's pandering to male audiences were actually found to be appealing to young Japanese women—especially the confidence of the artists, which many Japanese fans felt were not present in J-pop idols.[63] In their respective works, Jung Eun-yung and Oh Chuyun have observed that a significant reason for this is that the group was able to demonstrate a complex identity projecting a smooth crossover between J-pop and K-pop characteristics, achieving a degree of cosmopolitan flexibility while preserving its South Korean origins.[64] Oh Ingyu further noted that their Japanese-language releases "Mr. Taxi," "The Great Escape," "Paparazzi," and "Flower Power" have distinct, highly synchronized executions associated with

---

59. Adesh Thapliyal, "How Girls' Generation's 'Gee' Paved the Way for K-Pop in the US," *Daily Californian*, January 11, 2019, https://www.dailycal.org/2019/01/11/girls-generation-gee/.

60. Shim and Noh, "YouTube and Girls' Generation Fandom."

61. The survey was a collaboration of media outlet *Dong-A Ilbo*, web magazine *Idology*, and research company M-Brain. The survey covered 2,000 people and 30 pop music experts.

62. Lee Ji-hun, Im Hi-yun, and Jeong Yang-hwan, "Banjjak Banjjak Nun-I Busyeo . . ."

63. Epstein and Turnbull, "Girls' Generation? Gender (Dis)Empowerment, and K-Pop"; Jung and Hirata, "Conflicting Desires."

64. Jung Eun-yong, "Hallyu and the K-Pop Boom in Japan"; Oh Chuyun, "The Politics of the Dancing Body."

K-pop dance choreographies.[65] As a result, there were significant changes in their image to be more cool, mature, and tough, rather than cute, allowing them to appeal to more female fans and gradually breaking the sexual stereotype that the group had been associated with. Michael Unger additionally emphasized that K-pop girl groups do and can change, noting SNSD's evolution from "Gee" to "The Boys" to "Paparazzi."[66] Han Ae-Jin echoed these sentiments, noting SNSD's transformation through their releases, as to how the concepts of each comeback showed the group growing into maturity.[67]

Moreover, "I Got a Boy" was praised for being musically ahead of its time.[68] It secured the No. 21 spot on *Billboard*'s list of the 100 greatest girl group songs of all time,[69] and even earned recognition as K-pop's version of Queen's "Bohemian Rhapsody."[70] These recognitions changed many of the perceptions regarding K-pop's success, especially in the global market. It also changed the perception regarding SNSD's strategy of appealing to audiences, with many fans paying significantly more attention to the technical aspects of their songs, such as the choreography and vocal qualities, over the usual critiques of sexualization.

All in all, this enabled SNSD to appeal to a broader and more inclusive fanbase over time, catering both to girly, bubbly teenagers and to modern, unruly, opinionated, feisty, powerful, and professional young women.[71] In the respective studies of Oh Ingyu and Jang Wonho and that of Han Ae-Jin, they all pointed out SNSD's contributions to the elevation of self-empowering female imagery and a female universality that defies traditional social stereotypes in South Korea.[72] Kim Gooyong further commented that SNSD communicates a message of self-resilience.[73] For instance, many female fans have perceived SNSD as an embodiment of how to achieve a certain degree of physical attractiveness that represents South Korean female universality, and employ it as an effective means of challenging and overcoming socially imposed gender limitations.

65. Oh Ingyu, "From Localization to Glocalization."
66. Unger, "The Aporia of Presentation."
67. Han Ae-Jin, "A Study on the Virtuosity of K-Pop through Culture and Arts Education," *Korean Journal of Culture and Arts Education Studies* 13, no. 3 (2018): 1-19, https://doi.org/10.15815/kjcaes.2018.13.3.1.
68. Tamar Herman, "Songs that Defined the Decade: Girls' Generation's 'I Got a Boy,'" *Billboard*, November 21, 2019, https://www.billboard.com/articles/columns/k-town/8543901/girls-genera-tion-i-got-a-boy-songs-that-defined-the-decade; Yang, "Why Girls' Generation and K-Pop Won Big."
69. *Billboard*, "100 Greatest Girl Group Songs of All Time."
70. Herman, "Songs that Defined the Decade."
71. Tamar Herman, "Every Girls' Generation Single Ranked from Worst to Best: Critic's Take," *Billboard*, August 11, 2017, https://www.billboard.com/articles/columns/k-town/7898154/girls-generation-singles-ranked-worst-to-best-stream/; Park and Kim, "Redefining Womanhood in K-Pop."
72. Han, "A Study on the Virtuosity of K-Pop"; Oh and Jang, "From Globalization to Glocalization."
73. Kim Gooyong, "Neoliberal Feminism."

Also, this level of physical attractiveness has been instrumental to the personal growths of each individual member, allowing them to develop and progress at different directions, paces, and intensities.[74] As a result, they have broken the boundaries that originally dictated that they should mostly cater to older male markets, and are now appealing to a broader audience across different races, genders, and classes.[75] Fans are very much echoing these sentiments as well:

> I believe that the members are great role models as people and particularly as women. Their thoughts are mature and deep and they express them well. Whether it's about their experience in the industry or just as individuals and life, I believe you can learn a lot from them.
>
> —@sonexjinro

> Female empowerment is being able to embrace all that you are as a woman. And I think SNSD has embodied it in their journey as a group, breaking free from what people have reduced them to in terms of the songs they sing or the clothes they wear.
>
> —@yulneck

Figure 10.2: SNSD performing "Mr. Mr." at Mnet's *M Countdown* in 2014 (courtesy of Korean Culture and Information Service [KOCIS] under Wikicommons)

---

74. Chen, "Tiffany Young: Artist"; Epstein, "'Into the New World'"; Han, "A Study on the Virtuosity of K-Pop."
75. Oh Ingyu, "From Localization to Glocalization"; Unger, "The Aporia of Presentation."

A balancing act, toeing the line

Hence, these mixed observations have resulted in a tug-of-war involving the portrayals of SNSD. On the one hand, the group represents the most desired qualities of contemporary femininity and traditional womanhood.[76] But on the other, they are a product of female commodification,[77] and embody neoliberal concepts of resilience and conformity to existing norms and standards rather than question or break them.[78] However, many fans have also witnessed first-hand the effects of these opposing forces on the group through the years, and how they managed to address these challenges through the years. SNSD's fan community seems generally indifferent to these gender- and sexuality-themed criticisms against the group, and instead shows genuine concern for their welfare to fuel the group's popularity.[79] This implies that fans are more cognizant of a number of things that critics either miss or perceive in a significantly different light. Some of these reasons that fans have shared are as follows:

> SNSD became a cultural icon in Korea because they are talented, funny, beautiful, and well educated. The Korean public is harsh on girl groups, sometimes very unfair, but whether the public standard is right or wrong, they passed the test in every regard. Also, I believe people love the chemistry when they are together. The synergy is off the chart.
> —@itnw0628

In for the Long Run: Rising beyond the Group

Hence, despite these negative remarks that attempt to portray SNSD in an unfavorable light, the group remains popular. More recent revelations and events regarding SNSD's activities have provided more insight about the legacy of the group. One attribute could be SM Entertainment's more holistic idol training system, which focused not just on singing and dancing but also on a variety of other performative skill sets such as acting, modeling, MCing, and DJing.[80] Such training has enabled individual members to grow outside of the group

---

76. Epstein, "'Into the New World'"; Jonas, "Crafted for the Male Gaze."
77. Han, "A Study on the Virtuosity of K-Pop"; Kim Gooyong, "K-Pop Female Idols"; Seabrook, "Factory Girls."
78. Kim Gooyong, "Neoliberal Feminism"; Oh Chuyun, "The Politics of the Dancing Body."
79. Epstein and Turnbull, "Girls' Generation? Gender (Dis)Empowerment, and K-Pop."
80. Ahn, "Girls' Generation and the New Korean Wave"; Epstein, "'Into the New World'"; Jung Eun-yong, "Hallyu and the K-Pop Boom in Japan: Patterns of Consumption and Reactionary Responses"; Han, "A Study on the Virtuosity of K-Pop"; Korean Culture and Information Service, "K-Pop: A New Force in Pop Music"; Oh and Park, "From B2C to B2B"; Seabrook, "Factory Girls."

dynamics.[81] As such, even with the initial concerns, Oh Chuyun acknowledged that SNSD was able to steadily grow out of their initial image, which was burdened by racialized, gendered, and classed statuses imposed on K-pop female idols, and on Asian women in general.[82] SNSD have built individual identities founded on their particular personal and unique qualities.[83] A number of them even experienced initial success.[84] And the fans have been very cognizant of this as well, noting that the members were starting to redefine what female K-pop idols can and should do with their careers:

> SNSD has been successful in breaking down the stereotype of an "idol" and has had a lot of success in other areas. Sunny has been a successful radio host and as a variety show host, alongside industry pros like Kang Hodong. Yoona is an actress in her own right, after a series of successful TV shows and has now transitioned to movies. Seohyun, Sooyoung and Yuri are consistently cast in dramas. Tiffany is a solo artist outside of Korea. Hyoyeon is known in the DJ circuit and showcases at EDM festivals around the world. Taeyeon is one of the most popular solo artists and is the voice behind many OST hits. I don't think there are many idol groups where every single member can claim this much success independent of their activities as an idol.
>
> —@SonexStella

These observations are more pronounced in the individual career trajectories of each member in recent years in the areas of television dramas, musicals, and endorsements, which was also pertinently shown in the music video of "FOREVER 1." Musically, Taeyeon and Hyoyeon have developed to become more assertive and significantly edgier. Tiffany recently took on the lead role of the murderous and egomaniac Roxie Hart in the South Korean adaptation of the stage musical *Chicago*, and then followed it up with a supporting role as a financial analyst in JTBC *Reborn Rich*. On the other hand, Seohyun has progressively taken on acting roles that are perceived as controversial, such as an office worker interested in BDSM (bondage and discipline, dominance and submission, and

---

81. Christy Chua, "9 Ways Girls' Generation Re-defined K-Pop Since 'Into the New World,'" *bandwagon*, August 5, 2020, https://www.bandwagon.asia/articles/9-ways-girls-generation-re-defined-k-pop-since-into-the-new-world-13-years-with-snsd-sm-entertainment; Kim Gooyong, *From Factory Girls to K-Pop Idol Girls*.

82. Oh Chuyun, "The Politics of the Dancing Body."

83. Lily Chen, "Tiffany Young: Artist," *Hypebae*, December 3, 2018, https://hypebae.com/2018/12/tiffany-young-editorial-interview-girls-generation-solo-kpop.

84. For example, Yoona, in her first lead role in KBS's drama *You Are My Destiny*, won Best New Actress at the 2008 KBS Drama Awards and at the 2009 Baeksang Arts Awards. Sunny won the Rookie Radio DJ Award at the 2014 MBC Entertainment Awards for her first solo radio show, MBC FM4U's *Sunny's FM Date*. For her first solo music release, "I," Taeyeon won the 2015 Mnet Asian Music Best Female Artist awards. Seohyun also won Best New Actress at the 2017 MBC Drama Awards for her first lead role in MBC's *Good Thief, Bad Thief*.

sadomasochism) in the 2022 Netflix movie *Love and Leashes*. Sooyoung took on acting roles where she played a feisty female CEO fighting against her inability to inherit her father's conglomerate because of her bisexual orientation in the JTBC drama *Run On* and a celebrity struggling to manage her image with the public in the MBC mini-series *Fan Letter, Please*. Yoona has further progressed in her acting career, taking on the role of an idealistic intern reporter in the office politics-themed JTBC drama *Hush*. Furthermore, Sunny has been dabbling in various variety and reality TV show appearances to demonstrate her versatility, while Yuri has showcased her developing cooking skills on her own YouTube channel. These significant departures from their group image further intensify how SNSD developed into maturity.[85] Furthermore, because they now represent different aspects of being a female idol, their appeal toward broader audiences across different backgrounds has also intensified.

Because of this, despite a hiatus of group activities, they have consistently ranked in the top 20 of the Korean Business Research Institute (KBRI) brand reputation rankings, even reaching fifth in October 2020 and eleventh in January 2021. More recently, after an appearance on the tvN cable television show *You Quiz on the Block* in September 2021, SNSD landed in second place for the month of September and third for October. Furthermore, in May 2022, SM Entertainment's stock price closed 12% higher on the Korean Stock Exchange following news that SNSD was scheduled for a comeback in August later in the year. Even the successes of current K-pop powerhouses like BTS and BLACKPINK are still being compared and contrasted to theirs,[86] making the group a standard to which many of today's K-pop acts are measured against. One interesting implication of this is articulated as follows:

> Let's say, there have been no girl groups who stayed on top for this long. SNSD became the most popular girl group in Korea in 2009, and they maintained such status until 2015, and I'm being really conservative on this take. It's unheard of.
>
> —@intw0628

---

85. Park and Kim, "Redefining Womanhood in K-Pop."
86. *Billboard*, "The 100 Greatest Music Video Artists of All Time"; Taylor Glasby, "How Blackpink Became the Biggest K-Pop Girl Band on the Planet," *British Vogue*, May 14, 2020, https://www.vogue.co.uk/miss-vogue/article/blackpink-biggest-k-pop-girl-band; Park and Kim, "Redefining Womanhood in K-Pop"; Thapliyal, "Girls' Generation's 'Gee.'"

From Girls to Women: Changing Perspectives

Encouraging social changes: "Into the New World," a decade later

SNSD's debut song "Into the New World" is one of the most significant illustrations to date of how the group exuded some significant form of influence.[87] It is considered a textbook performance for many girl groups and reality shows that should be done, including Mnet's idol-making survival shows *Produce 101* and *Produce 48*, and girl groups Cherry Bullet, WJSN, fromis_9, GFRIEND, TWICE, I.O.I, Red Velvet, and Dreamcatcher, to name a few. Interestingly, "Into the New World" is not the typical bubblegum pop song. Instead, the lyrics and the music video touch on themes of achieving dreams and aspirations, on leaving past heartaches and disappointments behind, emphasizing one's individual strengths, recognizing that the road ahead can be tough and uncertain, and hoping that they can do it all together.[88] These messages significantly resonate with young people, male and female alike, representing their many of their hopes and dreams.[89]

"Into the New World" also became an anthem of protest,[90] such as the 2016 student protest at Ewha Womans University against certain cronyism-like charges, which were eventually linked to the corruption scandal that brought down South Korean President Park Geun-hye. In addition, the song was also used during the protests against President Park in 2017; the 2018 Seoul Queer Culture Festival; the 2018 #MeToo movement; and in the lifting of the abortion ban by South Korea's Constitutional Court in 2019. More recently, it was used at a 2022 feminist rally by the Korea Cyber Sexual Violence Relief Center and the Korean Women Workers Association. Outside of South Korea, the latest use of the song is during the pro-democracy gathering in Bangkok to demand government reforms in 2020.[91]

Other than this, SNSD encouraged the next generation of Korean Wave celebrities to pursue their careers.[92] For instance, during Mnet's *Good Girl* in 2020, rappers Sleeq, Lee Young-ji, and Yeeun (of CLC) have mentioned on numerous occasions that they consider Hyoyeon a mentor and a role model. In an episode of *Yuri's Winning Recipe*, host and producer Jaejae revealed that Yuri

87. Chua, "9 Ways Girls' Generation Re-defined K-Pop"; Herman, "9 K-Pop Songs"; Park and Kim, "Redefining Womanhood in K-Pop"; Yim, "'Into the New World'"; Yim, "LGBT Support Growing in K-Pop."
88. Kim Gooyong, "Neoliberal Feminism"; Park and Kim, "Redefining Womanhood in K-Pop."
89. Yim, "'Into the New World.'"
90. Yim, "'Into the New World'"; Yim, "LGBT Support Growing in K-Pop."
91. Patpicha Tanakasempipat, "K-Pop's Social Media Power Spurs Thailand's Youth Protests," *Reuters*, November 2, 2020, https://www.reuters.com/article/us-thailand-protests-k-pop/k-pops-social-media-power-spurs-thailands-youth-protests-idUSKBN27I23K.
92. Chen, "Tiffany Young: Artist"; Oh and Jang, "From Globalization to Glocalization"; Park Si-soo, "Girls' Generation Faces Racial Attack."

is one of her inspirations in the entertainment business. Also, Tiffany (for Mnet's *Girls Planet 999*) and Yuri (for MBC's *My Teenage Girl*) have recently served as mentors for girl group survival shows, resulting in the rookie girl groups Kep1er and CLASS:y, respectively. Additionally, in season two of Mnet's *Queedom*, various members of girl groups VIVIZ, WJSN, LOONA, and Kep1er all publicly expressed their admiration for Taeyeon, citing her as an inspiration and role model. Similarly, in 2018, Sooyoung received much public attention for openly saying she has read Cho Nam-Joo's book *Kim Ji-Young, Born 1982*, which has been hailed as an important feminist novel for its depiction of everyday sexism experienced by the title character.[93] Also, SNSD's group and individual career developments have been seen as a blueprint for Red Velvet. The five-member girl group debuted in 2014 under SM Entertainment and has also diversified its members' activities after a successive string of group promotions. A longtime fan had this to say regarding how much SNSD has made its mark:

> Korea was, and still is, full of misogyny, especially in the entertainment business. That SNSD being successful for so long is itself a monumental achievement considering such circumstances. They showed that women can be as successful as men, and still on top of their profession even in their 30s. To me, that is one of their biggest legacies.
>
> —@intw0628

Outside the industry, inspired fans shared the following regarding their own personal takes of what SNSD is to them:

> To me, SNSD is the following:
>
> Open-Mindedness: I used to belittle K-pop groups for making inferior music, taking care of their looks only. They changed such prejudice, making me much more open-minded towards not just K-pop, but everything in my life.
>
> Passion: Never thought I'd love celebrities this passionately before, but here we are.
>
> Friends: I always say the best gift I receive from them is friends all over the world. I would've never met that many friends around the world if not for them. Not to mention that it's the reason why I'm doing this interview.
>
> —@intw0628

---

93. As reported by Soompi (https://www.soompi.com/article/1355836wpp/jung-yu-mi-and-gong-yoo-explain-why-they-chose-to-star-in-upcoming-film-despite-backlash). Other celebrities affected by their public acknowledgement of having read the book include Red Velvet's Irene and actress Seo Ji-Hye. Actress Jeong Yu-mi, who played the title character in the movie adaptation alongside actor Gong Yoo, also received a flurry of negative and hateful comments following the announcement that she would be taking on the film project. The book itself has stirred up some anti-feminist backlash, and has been criticized for being biased and overgeneralizing men as oppressors, which was further amplified when celebrities started sharing that they had read the book, and more so when the movie version was announced and released.

SNSD has brought me an infinite amount of joy and happiness, but what struck me the most is really their perseverance in improving in their craft and as people and also seeking out potential paths for themselves. They do it all but never accept mediocrity. They pour themselves into what they do.

—@sonejinro

SNSD embodies the following:

Positive example of female friendship—In a world where women are often pitted against one another, SNSD embodies "women supporting women." The members support and encourage one another in their paths to pursue their dreams and goals.

Hard work—They are always shown giving 110%. They never rested on their laurels. They work extra hard to prove that they deserve to be at the top. Sunny, as the niece of SM's founder, worked extra hard to fight against the idea that she's only in the group because of family connections. Tiffany took the risk of pursuing a solo career outside of South Korea, a country where she has super-star status, to North America, where she basically had to start from the ground up.

Source of happiness—For myself and for millions of fans around the world, SNSD is our joie de vivre. They enhance and enrich our lives by being who they are, through their music and through their work and contributions to the world.

—@SonexStella

The things I think about involving SNSD:

On friendships and teamwork: It really opened my eyes back then that you can always love a person and spend half of your life with them but still get mad or upset with them. But just because we started the journey with the same people doesn't mean we'll end the journey with them.

On confidence and hard work: I just love seeing their enthusiasm and drive to make sure that they deliver only the best through their work. I love how passionate they are with the work they do and how confident they become when they do it.

On self-love and growth: One word—Tiffany. She is the embodiment of self-love and growth. She really went through a lot and she faced it with hard work, a humble heart and a kind soul. When she started promoting in the US, she became more open in her own personal struggles and how she overcame them.

—@yulneck

These commentaries are probably a small sample of the affirmation of SNSD's fandom that often goes unnoticed, as fan subjectivities are often not trusted as credibly objective. However, being continually mentioned increasingly in more detached retrospection close to two decades after SNSD's debut, these voices should lend considerable weight as witnesses of the group's maturation and influence on the K-pop industry and its followers.

Concluding Remarks: Right Now, in the Future, Forever

> Hey girls let's speak out
> Hands up and stand up
> The world is in our hands
> Like we want it to be
> Hey girls brave it out
> Wake up and look up
> Make your wish come true in your own voice
>
> —Kim Taeyeon, "GirlsSpkOut" (feat. Chanmina)

To reiterate, this chapter discusses SNSD as a case study illustrating that a K-pop girl group can grow and transcend the racialized, gendered, and classed categories applied to female celebrities in the pop culture industry. Rather, repeated examinations must be made, especially for artifacts that are proving to have longer than expected lifespans.

Second, this chapter highlights the importance of recognizing otherwise often infantilized fan insights that are the forefront of witnessing the evolution of celebrities within the entertainment industry, which may occur often as afterthoughts for less invested media and academic observers. In short, what fans say should not be discounted.[94] As discussed in this chapter, there has been some notable contrary views from numerous fans regarding various preconceived perceptions of what SNSD is and what the group stands for, especially in the context of female empowerment, prompting a second look at the group and the individual members.

Because of this, a defining thing about SNSD's identity as a K-pop girl group is its slogan, "Jigeumeun So Nyeo Si Dae! Apeurodo So Nyeo Si Dae! Yeongwonhi So Nyeo Si Dae!" which translates to "Right now it's SNSD, in the future it's SNSD, forever it's SNSD!" At present, this slogan has taken on a whole new meaning. Because of their experiences and achievements, SNSD may have started as embodiments of manufactured femininity and sexual objectification in the hypercompetitive K-pop industry. But after close to two decades, the group

---

94. Hills, *Fan Cultures*.

and their individual members have matured into inspiring pop icons whose performances and experiences are relatable to women.

Bibliography

Ahn, Shin-Hyun. "Girls' Generation and the New Korean Wave." *SERI Quarterly* 4, no. 4 (2011): 80–86.
Bell, Crystal. "The 20 Best K-Pop Releases of 2022," *Nylon*, December 8, 2022. https://www.nylon.com/entertainment/best-kpop-albums-songs-2022.
Billboard. "100 Greatest Girl Group Songs of All Time: Critics' Picks." July 10, 2017. https://www.billboard.com/articles/columns/pop/7857816/100-greatest-girl-group-songs.
Billboard. "The 100 Greatest Music Video Artists of All Time: Staff List." August 27, 2020. https://www.billboard.com/articles/news/list/9440075/100-best-music-video-artists.
Chen, Lily. "Tiffany Young: Artist." *Hypebae*, December 3, 2018. https://hypebae.com/2018/12/tiffany-young-editorial-interview-girls-generation-solo-kpop.
Chua, Christy. "9 Ways Girls' Generation Redefined K-Pop Since 'Into the New World.'" *bandwagon*, August 5, 2020. https://www.bandwagon.asia/articles/9-ways-girls-generation-re-defined-k-pop-since-into-the-new-world-13-years-with-snsd-sm-entertainment.
Duffett, Mark. *Understanding Fandom: An Introduction to the Study of Media Fan Culture.* New York: Bloomsbury, 2013.
Epstein, Stephen. "'Into the New World': Girls' Generation from the Local to the Global." In *K-Pop – The International Rise of the Korean Music Industry*, edited by JungBong Choi and Roald Maliangkay, 47–62. Abingdon: Routledge, 2015.
Epstein, Stephen, and James Turnbull. "Girls' Generation? Gender (Dis)Empowerment, and K-Pop." In *The Korean Popular Culture Reader*, edited by Kyung Hyun Kim and Youngmin Choe, 314–36. Durham, NC: Duke University Press, 2013.
Fuhr, Michael. *Globalization and Popular Music in South Korea: Sounding Out K-Pop.* New York: Routledge, 2016.
Glasby, Taylor. "How Blackpink Became the Biggest K-Pop Girl Band on the Planet." *British Vogue*, May 14, 2020. https://www.vogue.co.uk/miss-vogue/article/blackpink-biggest-k-pop-girl-band.
Glasby, Taylor, "The Best K-Pop Tracks of 2022," *Dazed*, December 14, 2022. https://www.dazeddigital.com/music/article/57774/1/the-best-k-pop-tracks-of-2022-billlie-ive-ateez.
Han, Ae-Jin. "A Study on the Virtuosity of K-Pop through Culture and Arts Education." *Korean Journal of Culture and Arts Education Studies* 13, no. 3 (2018): 1–19. https://doi.org/10.15815/kjcaes.2018.13.3.1.
Herman, Tamar. "Every Girls' Generation Single Ranked from Worst to Best: Critic's Take." *Billboard*, August 11, 2017. https://www.billboard.com/articles/columns/k-town/7898154/girls-generation-singles-ranked-worst-to-best-stream/.
Herman, Tamar. "9 K-Pop Songs that Recently Became Part of South Korean Politics." *Billboard*, May 2, 2018. https://www.billboard.com/articles/columns/k-town/8436957/k-pop-songs-politicized-south-korea.

Herman, Tamar. "Songs that Defined the Decade: Girls' Generation's 'I Got a Boy.'" *Billboard*, November 21, 2019. https://www.billboard.com/articles/columns/k-town/8543901/girls-generation-i-got-a-boy-songs-that-defined-the-decade.

Hills, Matthew. *Fan Cultures*. London: Routledge, 2002.

Idology. "Gyeolsan 2022: Olhae-ui Aelbeom 20seon" [End-of-year 2022: Top 20 albums]. January 1, 2023. https://idology.kr/17276.

Jonas, Liz. "Crafted for the Male Gaze: Gender Discrimination in the K-Pop Industry." *Journal of International Women's Studies* 22, no. 7 (2021): 3-18. https://vc.bridgew.edu/jiws/vol22/iss7/2.

Jung, Eun-young. "Hallyu and the K-Pop Boom in Japan: Patterns of Consumption and Reactionary Responses." In *K-Pop – The International Rise of the Korean Music Industry*, edited by JungBong Choi and Roald Maliangkay, 116-32. Abingdon: Routledge, 2014.

Jung, Eun-young. "K-Pop Female Idols in the West: Racial Imaginations and Erotic Fantasies." In *The Korean Wave: Korean Media Go Global*, edited by Youna Kim. New York: Routledge, 2013.

Jung, Sun, and Hirata Yukie. "Conflicting Desires: K-Pop Idol Girl Group Flows in Japan in the Era of Web 2.0." *Electronic Journal of Contemporary Japanese Studies* 12, no. 2 (2012). http://japanesestudies.org.uk/ejcjs/vol12/iss2/jung.html.

Juvet, Aedan, "Wanna Know Which K-Pop Song Is the Best of 2022? Here's Our Definitive Ranking." *Cosmopolitan*, December 16, 2022. https://www.cosmopolitan.com/entertainment/music/a42258288/best-k-pop-songs-2022/.

Kim, Arin. "What the Return of Girls' Generation Means." *Jakarta Post*, August 31, 2018. https://www.thejakartapost.com/life/2018/08/30/what-the-return-of-girls-generation-means.html.

Kim, Gooyong. "Between Hybridity and Hegemony in K-Pop's Global Popularity: A Case of Girls' Generation's American Debut." *International Journal of Communication* 11 (2017): 2367-86.

Kim, Gooyong. *From Factory Girls to K-Pop Idol Girls: Cultural Politics of Developmentalism, Patriarchy, and Neoliberalism in South Korea's Popular Music Industry*. Lanham, MD: Lexington Books, 2019.

Kim, Gooyong. "K-Pop Female Idols: Culture Industry, Neoliberal Social Policy, and Governmentality in Korea." In *The Routledge Handbook of Global Cultural Policy*, edited by Victoria Durrer, Toby Miller, and Dave O'Brien, 520-37. Abingdon: Routledge, 2017.

Kim, Gooyong. "Neoliberal Feminism in Contemporary South Korean Popular Music: Discourse of Resilience, Politics of Positive Psychology, and Female Subjectivity." *Journal of Language and Politics* 18, no. 4 (2019): 560-78. https://doi.org/10.1075/jlp.18058.kim.

Kim, Hyo-jin. "'2010nyeonbuteo Sijakdoen Munhwa' . . . Sonyeosidae, Hanguk Aidol Choecho Aelbeom Potokadeu Doip" ["Culture that started in 2010" . . . Girls' Generation introduces the first Korean idol album photo card]. *topstarnews*, March 29, 2021. http://www.topstarnews.net/news/articleView.html?idxno=868424.

Korea.net. *K-Pop: A New Force in Pop Music*. Ministry of Culture, Sports and Tourism and Korean Culture and Information Service, 2011.

Lee, Ji-hun, Lim Hi-yun, and Jeong Yang-hwan. "Banjjak Banjjak Nun-i Busyeo . . . BigBaeng-Sonyeosidae Yeokdae Choego Aidol" [Twinkle twinkle dazzling . . . big bang-Girls' Generation best idols ever]. *Donga Ilbo*, September 1, 2016. https://www.donga.com/news/NewsStand/article/all/20160901/80071885/1.

Music Industry Association of Korea. "2007.8wol—Gayo-eumban Panmaeryang" [August 2007—Sales of Korean pop albums]. Accessed February 6, 2022. https://web.archive.org/web/20090228163343/http:/miak.or.kr/stat/kpop_200708.htm.

Oh, Chuyun. "The Politics of the Dancing Body: Racialized and Gendered Femininity in Korean Pop." In *The Korean Wave*, edited by Yasue Kuwahara, 53–81. New York: Palgrave Macmillan, 2014.

Oh, Ingyu. "From Localization to Glocalization: Contriving Korean Pop Culture to Meet Glocal Demands." *Kritika Kultura* 29 (August 2017): 157–67.

Oh, Ingyu, and Jang Wonho. "From Globalization to Glocalization: Configuring Korean Pop Culture to Meet Glocal Demands." *Culture and Empathy: International Journal of Sociology, Psychology, and Cultural Studies* 3, no. 1-2 (2020): 23–43.

Oh, Ingyu, and Park Gil-Sung. "From B2C to B2B: Selling Korean Pop Music in the Age of New Social Media." *Korea Observer* 43, no. 3 (2012): 365–97.

Osborn, Brad. "Resistance Gazes in Recent Music Videos." *Music and the Moving Image* 14, no. 2 (2021): 51–67. https://doi.org/10.5406/musimoviimag.14.2.0051.

Park, Jun-hee. "Girls' Generation to Make Full-Group Comeback in August after Five Years." *Korea Herald*, May 17, 2022. http://www.koreaherald.com/view.php?ud=20220517000703.

Park, Si-soo. "Girls' Generation Faces Racial Attack over 'US Dream.'" *Korea Times*, November 7, 2013. http://www.koreatimes.co.kr/www/art/2020/02/688_145820.html.

Park, T. K., and Kim Youngdae. "How BLACKPINK, Red Velvet, and More Are Redefining Womanhood in K-Pop." MTV News, June 6, 2019. https://www.mtv.com/news/3126395/k-pop-girl-groups-womanhood-agency/amp/.

Seabrook, John. "Factory Girls: Cultural Technology and the Making of K-Pop." *The New Yorker*, October 1, 2012. https://www.newyorker.com/magazine/2012/10/08/factory-girls-2.

Seoulbeats. "A Reflection on SNSD's YouTube Music Awards Win." November 9, 2013. https://seoulbeats.com/2013/11/reflection-snsds-youtube-music-awards-win/.

Shim, Doobo, and Noh Kwang Woo. "YouTube and Girls' Generation Fandom." *The Journal of the Korea Contents Association* 12, no. 1 (2012): 125–37.

Soy. "Shin Haechul's Radio Broadcast about Dream Concert & Suju's Manager's Cyworld Entry." *Soompi*, June 10, 2008. https://forums.soompi.com/topic/149610-shin-haechuls-radio-broadcast-about-dream-concert-sujus-managers-cyworld-entry/.

Tanakasempipat, Patpicha. "K-Pop's Social Media Power Spurs Thailand's Youth Protests." *Reuters*, November 2, 2020. https://www.reuters.com/article/us-thailand-protests-k-pop/k-pops-social-media-power-spurs-thailands-youth-protests-idUSKBN27I23K.

Teen Vogue. "The 79 Best K-Pop Songs of 2022." December 15, 2022. https://www.teen-vogue.com/story/best-k-pop-songs-2022.

Thapliyal, Adesh. "How Girls' Generation's 'Gee' Paved the Way for K-Pop in the US." *Daily Californian*, January 11, 2019. https://www.dailycal.org/2019/01/11/girls-generation-gee/.

Unger, Michael A. "The Aporia of Presentation: Deconstructing the Genre of K-Pop Girl Group Music Videos in South Korea." *Journal of Popular Music Studies* 27, no. 1 (2015): 25–47. https://doi.org/10.1111/jpms.12109.

Yang, Jeff. "Why Girls' Generation and K-Pop Won Big at the YouTube Music Awards." *Wall Street Journal*, November 4, 2013. https://www.wsj.com/articles/BL-SEB-78043.

Yim, Hyun-su. "'Into the New World': Girls' Generation's Debut Song Lives on as Millennials' Anthem of Solidarity." *Korea Herald*, April 14, 2022. http://www.korea-herald.com/view.php?ud=20220414000732.

Yim, Hyun-su. "LGBT Support Growing in K-Pop." *Korea Herald*, June 10, 2019. http://kpopherald.koreaherald.com/view.php?ud=201906101452119456437_2.

Notes on the Contributors

Crystal Abidin is a professor of internet studies, principal research fellow, and ARC DECRA Fellow at Curtin University. She is the founder of the TikTok Cultures Research Network. She is a digital anthropologist and ethnographer of vernacular internet cultures, and researches internet celebrity, influencer cultures, and social media pop cultures. She has published five books and more than sixty articles and chapters on various aspects of internet cultures. For her public scholarship and continual engagements with industry, Crystal Abidin was listed on the ABC Top 5: Humanities (2020), *Forbes* 30 Under 30 Asia (2018), and *Pacific Standard* 30 Top Thinkers Under 30 (2016).

Erik Paolo Capistrano is the Antenor S. Virata Professor of Business Administration in the Cesar E. A. Virata School of Business, University of the Philippines. He is also a principal investigator for the University of the Philippines Korea Research Center. He earned his PhD in international management from National Cheng Kung University. His teaching, research, and industry experience are in the areas of operations management, management of information technology, management of innovation, and the Korean Wave (Hallyu). He is also a moderator for Soshified, the largest international fan forum site for the K-pop girl group Girls' Generation, and an administrator for its Philippine chapter.

Stephanie Jiyun Choi is a postdoctoral associate in Korean studies at the State University of New York at Buffalo. Her research focuses on cultural globalization, gender and labor politics, and the affective economy of Korean popular culture. She is currently working on her first book project that interrogates how global K-pop fans proclaim cultural diversity, postcolonial feminism, and antiracism through digital surveillance, media tribalism, and gendered fetishization of K-pop idol bodies.

Douglas Gabriel is a lecturer in the College of Liberal Studies at Seoul National University. Previously he was a 2021–2022 Getty/ACLS postdoctoral fellow in the history of art and held postdoctoral positions at Harvard University and the George Washington University. His research has appeared in *Art History*, *Oxford Art Journal*, *Art Journal*, *Situations: Cultural Studies in the Asian Context*, and the *Journal of Korean Studies*.

Malinee Khumsupa is an assistant professor in the School of Politics and Government, the Faculty of Political Science and Public Administration at Chiang Mai University in Thailand. She is a political scientist (PhD) and the winner of the Amarin Publishing Prize as the author of *The Underneath Meaning of Democracy Monument of Thailand* (2006). Her research interests include postcolonialism, cultural studies, media studies, and K-pop fan and youth politics. Her coauthored articles include "Counter-Memory: Replaying Political Violence in Thai Digital Cinema" in *Kyoto Review* (2016), "Notes on Camp Films in Authoritarian Thailand" in *South East Asia Research* (2019), and "Film Is Dangerous: Ten Years of Censorship in Thailand's Cinema, 2010–2020" in *South East Asia Research* (2022).

Gi Yeon Koo is a HK research professor at the Seoul National University Asia Center. She was a visiting senior research fellow of the Middle East Institute at the National University of Singapore. Her current interest focuses on ethos, emotion, globalization, media and social movements in Iran, the younger generation's popular culture, and Iranian women. Among her publications, she has contributed book chapters to *Participation Culture in the Gulf: Networks, Politics and Identity* (2018) and *Media in the Middle East: Activism, Politics, and Culture* (2017). She holds a bachelor's degree in Iranian studies from the Hankuk University of Foreign Studies and master's degrees and a PhD in cultural anthropology from Seoul National University.

Kate Korroch is a coeditor of *Visual Studies* and PhD candidate in visual studies at the University of California, Santa Cruz. Her research interests focus on gender, sexuality, and the body in visual culture. Korroch was the founding managing editor of *Refract: An Open Access Visual Studies Journal*. In 2022 Korroch curated *What Is an image?*, a multi-media digital exhibition for the International Visual Sociology Association's annual conference. Korroch's publications include "Cover Guys: Trans Male Portraits from *Original Plumbing*" in *Art Journal* (2021) and "The Isolated Queer Body: Harisu's Dodo Cosmetics Advertisement" in *Queer Asia: Decolonising and Reimagining Sexuality and Gender* (2019).

Maud Lavin has published recently in *JAKE*, *Roi Faineant*, *Heimat Review*, *Afterimage*, and *Red Ogre Review*, and earlier in the *Nation*, *Harper's Bazaar*, *Artforum*, and elsewhere. One of her books, *Cut with the Kitchen Knife*, on the Berlin Dada artist Hannah Höch, was named a New York Times Notable Book.

Another, *Boys' Love, Cosplay, and Androgynous Idols: Queer Fan Cultures in Mainland China, Hong Kong, and Taiwan*, co-edited with Ling Yang and Jing Jamie Zhao, was nominated for a Lambda. She is a Guggenheim Fellow and lives in Chicago.

Jieun Lee is an assistant professor in the Women's, Gender, and Sexuality Studies Department at Wake Forest University. She holds a PhD in theater and performance studies as well as a graduate certificate in women's studies from the University of Georgia. Lee is currently working on her book project on Korean transnational adoption and adoptees represented in theater and performance in South Korea, the United States, and Europe. She also serves as a volunteer translator for the South Korean feminist journal *ILDA*.

Jin Lee studies media intimacies in social media cultures, particularly focusing on media practices and visibility of social minorities across the "old" and "new" media. Her recent work appears in peer-reviewed journals, including *Communication, Culture and Critique, Convergence, Media International Australia*, and *Social Media and Society*. She is a postdoctoral research fellow in internet studies at Curtin University, Australia.

SooJin Lee is an art historian and writer, teaching as an assistant professor at Hongik University in South Korea. With a PhD in art history, she previously taught at the University of Chicago, the University of Illinois, and the School of the Art Institute of Chicago. Her recent articles include "Public Appearance as Art as Protest as Event: Yoko Ono's Events with John Lennon" (2020), "Yours: Performing (in) Nikki S. Lee's 'Fan Club' with Nikki S. Lee" (2019), and "Emoji at MoMA: Considering the 'Original Emoji' as Art" (2018). Her curatorial contributions include the 2018 Gwangju Biennale and Lee Bul's solo exhibition *Utopia Saved* at Manege, St. Petersburg (2020).

Liew Kai Khiun has been conducting research and teaching on topics relating to the Korean Wave in Asia since the first publication in 2005 on the Korean Wave in Singapore, part of his broader scholarly trajectories on transnational popular culture in Asia. His subsequent publications are related not only to individual localities of Korean pop influences like Hong Kong, China, and Thailand, but also to television dramas and K-pop dance cultures. Kai Khiun is currently an assistant professor at the Hong Kong Metropolitan University.

Kathlyn Ramirez is a filmmaker, photographer, and editor with a bachelor's degree in film from the University of the Philippines Diliman. She has extensive industry experience as a content producer for ShowBT Philippines, a Philippine-based Korean entertainment company that handles the P-pop boy group SB19 and KAIA, and a celebrity social media manager at ABS-CBN, one of the largest

Philippine multimedia companies. She also volunteers as an event photographer for KStreetManila, a Manila-based site focusing on Korean pop culture, and an administrator for the Philippine chapter of Soshified, the largest international forum site for Girls' Generation.

Atchareeya Saisin holds a BA in journalism and mass communication (broadcasting) from Thammasat University and an MA in regional (Southeast Asian) studies from Chiang Mai University. Currently, she is teaching in the Faculty of Political Science and Public Administration of the School of International Affairs, Chiang Mai University. She is interested in media and mass audience culture, an interest derived from her background as a journalist. She also has experience in conducting research on media, including the roles of exile media and the democratic movement in Myanmar and Thai drama series consumption in East and Southeast Asian countries.

Hyangsoon Yi is a professor of comparative literature at the University of Georgia. Her research interests include Korean literature and film, Buddhist aesthetics, and Buddhist nuns. Her book *Piguni wa Han'guk Munhak* [Buddhist nuns and Korean literature] was selected as one of the "Outstanding Scholarly Books of the Year" (2009) by the National Academy of Sciences of the Republic of Korea. She coedited special issues of *Journal of Global Initiatives* (2010), *International Journal of Korean Studies* (2019), and *Korea Journal* (2020). In addition to two forthcoming books, she is currently working on a book manuscript on Korean Buddhist films.

Index

Wangjaesan Light Music Band
(*Wangjaesan Gyeongeumakdan*),
95, 106

patriarchal (patriarchy), 3, 98, 117–21,
125, 127–28, 131, 145–46, 150, 212
Philippines (Republic of the Philippines),
158, 160, 231–32
polymorphous, 34, 37, 46–52. *See also*
erotic; sexuality
postindustrial, 7, 54. *See also* neoliberal
PSY, 2, 206

queer, 2–7, 16, 22, 30–31, 49, 124, 130,
140, 145–47, 151, 220
Seoul Queer Culture Festival, 130, 220

race, 30, 72, 76, 80–82, 89–90, 211–18,
223. *See also* ethnicity
mixed-race, 71–76, 79–80, 84–85,
89–90
Reddit (reddit.com), 59, 78, 84–86, 88

Secret Garden, 7, 15–31, 35, 38, 40, 143
Seoul Broadcasting System (SBS), 20,
205–6, 213
sexism (sexist), 117, 120, 128–30, 211, 221
sexuality (sex; sexual), 1, 3–7, 17, 25,
29–31, 34–50, 52, 63, 72, 74, 81–83,
86–90, 118–19, 121, 123–24, 129–30,
138–53, 162, 181, 202–3, 211, 212,
215, 217, 220, 223
SHINee, 157, 165–66, 169 table 8.1, 171,
190
Jonghyun, 165–66, 171
Singapore (Singaporean), 161–63, 165
SM Entertainment, 73, 74, 85, 143, 160,
165, 204–9, 213, 217, 219, 221–22.
See also K-pop
social media, 8, 62, 71, 72–74, 76–84,
86–90, 110, 130, 140, 143–44,
148, 158, 165, 170, 176, 178–81,
189–92, 208, 212. *See also* Facebook;
Instagram; Telegram; TikTok;
Twitter; YouTube

Soompi (soompi.com), 78
South Korea (Republic of Korea; Korean),
1–5, 7–8, 15–18, 22, 25–26, 30, 34,
36–37, 39–40, 42–46, 49, 51, 54–66,
71, 73–77, 79–85, 87, 105–7, 116–17,
119–20, 122–24, 127, 129–31,
137–47, 150–53, 158, 161, 165,
191–92, 194–97, 202, 205–7, 209,
212, 214–15, 217–19, 220, 222
ssen-unni (*ssen-eonni*), 8, 116–21, 123–25,
127–31
Super Junior, 143, 146, 150, 160, 169 table
8.1, 204–5, 210

Taiwan (Taiwanese), 4, 37, 76 160–61
Telegram, 178, 190–91, 191 table 9.3, 193
table 9.5, 194, 196. *See also* social
media
Thailand (Thai), 156–57, 160, 166–71
theqoo (theqoo.net), 77–79, 84–85
TikTok, 86, 162. *See also* social media
tomboy, 7, 27, 29, 34–43, 45–47, 50, 52
transcultural, 2, 3, 18
transnational, 5, 42, 52, 157, 159–60, 164,
177, 181, 187–88
TVXQ, 143, 146, 169 table 8.1, 207, 210
Twitter, 77–79, 86–88, 107–9, 158, 170,
190, 209. *See also* social media

Uhm, Jung-hwa, 117, 123

Viki (viki.com), 39

West (Western), 2, 18, 51, 65, 76, 80, 90,
99, 105, 107–18, 139, 176–78, 182,
185, 188–91, 196–97, 208–12. *See
also* America; Europe
Winter Sonata, 2, 18, 26–27. *See also* Bae,
Yong-joon
"women", 1–5, 7–8, 17, 21–23, 34–35,
37, 40–42, 44, 46–49, 51–52, 54,
61–66, 77, 86–89, 101, 107, 110,
116–21, 123–31, 139, 144, 146–47,
150, 157–59, 162–64, 171, 176–82,